Research in Recreation, Parks, Sport, and Tourism

Second Edition

Carol Cutler Riddick
Ruth V. Russell

Publishers: Joseph J. Bannon/Peter Bannon
Production Manager: Laura Podeschi
Layout/Interior Design: Dustin Hubbart/Kenneth J. O'Brien
Cover Design: Angela Patton/Laura Podeschi
Cover Photo: Image copyright tm-media, 2007
                Used under license from Shutterstock, Inc.

Library of Congress Catalog Card Number: 2007940363
ISBN print edition: 978-1-57167-566-8
ISBN ebook: 978-1-57167-600-9
Printed in the United States.

10 9 8 7 6 5

Sagamore Publishing, LLC
1807 N Federal Dr.
Urbana, IL 61801
www.sagamorepub.com

To Dr. Betty van der Smissen—our first research methods teacher. Betty's commitment and enthusiastic teaching style inspired us to believe objective inquiry is fascinating to study and critically important for our profession. Thank you, Dr. van der Smissen, for this as well as all the years of support and interest you have shown in our careers.

CONTENTS

Preface

This is a second edition of the text originally entitled *Evaluative Research in Recreation, Park, and Sport Settings: Searching for Useful Information.* Feedback received from students, instructors, and practitioners guided us during the revision process.

Target Audience

The target audience for this book is upper-level undergraduates and graduate students, as well as professionals working in the field of recreation, parks, tourism, or sports. This text was written for individuals who have had little or no prior involvement in research undertakings.

There are two purposes for the book. The first objective is to acquaint and teach you to use the basic practices and techniques required to carry out or monitor a small-scale research investigation. The second aim is to teach you the questions to ask when critiquing a proposed or reported research investigation.

Content Changes Introduced in the Second Edition

In this edition, coverage was expanded to include not only how to plan for an evaluative research investigation, but also how to complete basic research projects. In an effort to make the subject matter clearer, the content was reorganized and a step-by-step format was adopted.

This revision contains the following *new* chapters entitled:

- Overview.
- Decide on a Topic.
- Identify Theoretical Underpinnings.
- Explain Study's Significance.
- Consider Measurement.
- Seek Proposal Approval.
- Conduct a Pilot Test.
- Prepare for Data Collection.
- Present Results Using Visual Aids.

Other topics that have been *added or expanded* include:

- Measuring program effectiveness (Step 1).
- Writing a literature review (Step 2).
- Quantitative, qualitative, and mixed-methods designs (Step 7).
- Funding sources for research (Step 11).

- Preparing a written report (Step 16).
- Delivering an oral report (Step 17).

Organization of the Book

The book is divided into five major units. The first part, *Overview*, reviews: definitions, rationale, and categories of research and introduces the stages and steps involved in the research process. The second section, *Getting Started*, covers: deciding on a topic, reviewing the literature, identifying theoretical underpinnings, developing a scope of study, and explaining a study's significance. The third segment, *Developing a Plan*, contains: selecting a sample, choosing a design, considering measurement, specifying data-collection instruments, addressing ethical responsibilities, and seeking proposal approval. The fourth unit, *Implementing the Plan*, reviews: conducting the pilot study, preparing for data collection, and analyzing quantitative and qualitative data. Finally, the fifth section, *Reporting the Research*, includes information on: presenting results using visual aids, preparing a written report, and delivering an oral report on the research.

New Learning Features Introduced in the Second Edition

The writing and presentation styles have been dramatically altered in the new edition. Each chapter now leads off with an orientation outline and relevant quote. Furthermore, as a trigger device, important words and concepts are bolded and italicized.

Six new "features" have also been added:

- *Case* illustrates a point by citing research or a real-world example.
- *Something to Remember* underscores an important point.
- *Idea* provides straightforward, practical, "how to" advice.
- *Your Research* presents an opportunity for applying chapter materials to planning your own research project.
- *Review and Discussion Questions* assist in determining mastery of chapter content.
- *Exercises* contain activities (including Web-based assignments) that complement and expand upon chapter material. (NOTE: Every effort was made to cite Web sites that were operational when this edition went to publication. Nevertheless, it may be that one or more of the cited URLs will change or cease to operate.)

Supplemental Resource

The *Instructor's Manual*, accompanying this text, has also been revised. The *Manual* contains, for each chapter, a PowerPoint® presentation and exam questions. For information on how to acquire this supplement, contact Sagamore Publishing Inc. at www.sagamore.com or phone toll free 800.327.5557.

Feedback

As with the first edition of this book, we'd be interested in receiving comments and suggestions from students and instructors. We're already on the lookout for new material and changes to incorporate into the next edition! Our contact information is:

Carol Cutler Riddick
Gallaudet University
Department of Physical Education and Recreation
800 Florida Ave N.E.
Washington, D.C. 20002
carol.riddick@gallaudet.edu

Ruth V. Russell
Indiana University
Department of Recreation, Park, and Tourism Studies
133 HPER Building, 1025 East Seventh Street
Bloomington, IN 47405
russellr@indiana.edu

Acknowledgments

Joint thanks are extended to three people who stuck by us as we wrote this second edition. First, the patience that our publisher Dr. Joe Bannon demonstrated as we chiseled away on the revision, is greatly appreciated. Dr. Anne Simonsen was gracious enough to review and provide extensive comments on many of the chapters drafted for the book. Finally, Jodie Ackerman was absolutely invaluable in making the revision a reality. Jodie spent many, many hours—always with a smile on her face (even as we worked very late into the night)—creating graphics and tables, entering corrections, finding and checking references, etc. We are indebted to you, Jodie.

We also want to let the world know how much we value each other and our friendship. We met in 1972 during our first semester in the recreation and park graduate program at the Pennsylvania State University. Among our many gifts to each other then and still today is the ability to participate in engaging conversations when we don't see eye to eye. We began with an ongoing conversation across the desk partition in the graduate student "bullpen" about the meaning of leisure, and are still at it.

Carol acknowledges the love and support of her family and friends. My sons, Blake and Ryan, are the joys of my life. To all of you, now I finally can come out to play more often than I have during the past three years! Carol also extends appreciation to Dr. Ron Dreher, Chair of the Department of Physical Education and Recreation at Gallaudet University. Brother Ron, on more than one occasion told me to go home, take a break, and enjoy my family. Finally, the undergraduate and graduate student recreation majors at Gallaudet have made me a better teacher. They have taught me a lot about the importance of expressing oneself clearly and the value of visual aids. Long live Gallaudet University and the beautiful and unique Deaf cultures found around the world.

Ruth also extends appreciation to those who have both directly and indirectly supported her enterprise on this book. I owe special thanks to Patricia D. Setser, who has been supportive beyond what is reasonable and fair, and to Dad, whose constant refrain of "Haven't you finished that book yet?" kept me going. And, to other family and friends whose confidence in me I appreciate so very much. I also owe a debt to my faculty colleagues and undergraduate and graduate students in the Department of Recreation, Park, and Tourism Studies at Indiana University, Bloomington for challenging and trusting me. In particular, I thank the five semesters of undergraduate students who enrolled in my research methods course and with the directness of curious learners set me straight many times on what worked and what didn't work in our first edition of the book.

Carol Cutler Riddick
Ruth V. Russell
April 2007

Part I: Overview

What is Research?

Characteristics of Research Investigations

Why Conduct Research?

Categorizing Research
Applicability
  Basic Research
  Evaluative Research
Goal
  Descriptive Research
  Explanatory Research
  Predictive Research
Data Source
  Primary Source
  Secondary Source

The Research Process

*I now want to know all things under the sun, and the moon, too. For all things
are beautiful in themselves, and become more beautiful
when known to man. Knowledge is life with wings.*
Kahil Gibran

We're bombarded with research on a daily basis. The back of a cereal box proclaims that if, in place of regular meals, you eat two bowls of this cereal a day you will lose six pounds in two weeks. The manufacturer claims it is "proven" because the company's nutrition team has " . . . worked closely with researchers at a leading university to thoroughly test the . . . diet" (Kellogg, 2003). Yet, even after two cups of coffee, you can't find the details of how the research was conducted! What, for example, were the daily physical energy expenditures of the individuals involved in the study?

And how about all the studies conducted at universities, hospitals, and other "think tank" settings? The Rand Corporation, for instance, released a report stating that urban sprawl is statistically related to harming physical health (Stein, 2004). After analyzing data on more than 8,600 Americans in 38 metropolitan areas, it was reported that rates of asthma, headaches, and other physical complaints increased with urban sprawl. The researchers noted, "This study provides some initial support to the hotly debated claim that suburban sprawl is bad for health" (Milloy, 2004). Is sprawl, per se, the cause of these physical ailments, or could it be that the pollution found in these communities contributed to ill health?

The bottom line is that we encounter, in both our personal and professional lives, all sorts of claims and assertions arising from research. The fundamental challenge is being able to discern "good" science from "junk science." Hopefully, by the time you conclude reading this text, you'll be able to read about and conduct your own research with a discerning eye and mind.

What is Research?

Research has been defined two ways.

- One perspective is that research is a " . . . process of collecting, analyzing, and interpreting information" (Leedy & Ormrod, 2005, p. 2).
- A second viewpoint is that research is to " . . . advance human knowledge . . . The aim is discovery" (Elias & Dunning, 1986, p. 20).

We embrace both viewpoints. Research encompasses *how* we know *what* we know. Simply put, research involves following a process or processes to gain more knowledge about a specific topic.

Characteristics of Research Investigations

Misconceptions abound about research. It is, for instance, more than going to the library and looking up references, although this action is an element in the research process. Likewise, research goes beyond simply asking people to answer questions, even though we often survey people as part of a study.

Research is conducted following the ways of thinking to which scientific inquiry adheres. *Scientific inquiry* has the following characteristics (Lastrucci, 1963). It is:

- *Logical.* One component of being logical is that the study idea as well as the way the study is executed, makes sense. Logic should also prevail when making conclusions based on study findings.
- *Objective.* Empirical *data* or information are collected by using formal observation or measurement. Not being objective is being subjective or using divine or spiritual revelation, intuition or personal opinion as the basis for "knowledge."
- *Systematic.* One aspect of being systematic is that the study is executed in an orderly, non-prejudiced fashion, so that *valid* or accurate information is recorded. Another side to being systematic is that extensive documentation is provided so that others can replicate or repeat the study.

When one or more of these characteristics have been violated, the resulting product is *pseudoscience* or *junk science* (Case 1). The by-products of these sorts of ill-conceived endeavors are findings and conclusions that lack integrity and are therefore meaningless.

Case 1. An Ill-Conceived Thesis Idea Illustrating Violations of Scientific Inquiry.

Denise, a master's candidate, initially proposed developing a "leisure education" program for adults who were developmentally disabled and mentally ill and who were living in a group home. Proposed session topics included: setting up a personal fish aquarium, planting a potted plant, sewing a teddy bear, walking with two-pound weights, participating in floor aerobics instruction, and learning how to hip-hop dance. Each topic would be the focus of three, one-hour meetings held over the course of one week.

Denise "just knew" that such a program would make a difference in the lives of participants! Her thesis advisor wanted Denise to come up with a game plan that would enable her to be more objective in reaching conclusions about the merits of the program. Specifically, Denise was asked to identify a way to document some benefits that she anticipated would accrue from program participation.

After thinking about it, Denise anticipated that the leisure education program would enhance participants' social skills. So she proposed that each participant would be asked to recall, a day or two after participating in a session or whenever they could be "caught" awake and not busy, the number and kinds of social interactions they had with other participants during the activity session.

Denise's thesis Chair had several other concerns with the proposal. First, she questioned if it was logical to reason that the selected non-cooperative activities would promote social interaction. For instance, would adults participating in the walking program, swinging two-pound weights, really feel like chatting with each other?

Another issue was the unsystematic way data would be collected. Realistically, would participants be able to accurately recall, a day or two later, the frequency of certain social behaviors during a session?

In contrast, when research has been logically, objectively, and systematically planned and implemented, it is referred to as *scientific research*. For word economy reasons, in this book "research" is used interchangeably with "scientific research."

Something to Remember!

When designing or reading a research study, ask yourself if the study:

• Is logically conceived?
• Provides detailed and precise information on what was studied and how?
• Is based on objective and systematically collected data?
• Contains conclusions that are reasonable considering what was examined and how the study was executed?

Why Conduct Research?

What is the catalyst for research? While any number of reasons can precipitate research, there are three major forces behind research:

• **Organization motivation**. Recreation, park, tourism, and sport organizations continually seek to assess program effectiveness, as well as determine ways to improve service delivery, operations, procedures, or policy (Case 2). Agencies also conduct research in order to justify expenditures.
• **Academic motivation**. Students are called upon to complete a research paper as part of an undergraduate or graduate degree requirement. Professors are driven to engage in research because of the need to: "publish or perish," attain grant support, and/or understand or improve the social world in which they live.
• **Personal motivation**. Sometimes individuals get involved in a research topic because of their personal experiences or "personal troubles" (Mills, 1959). For example, being a kayaking enthusiast could inspire one to conduct research on the impacts of flood control projects on the sport.

Case 2. A Recreation Organization's Need for Research.

Andereck, K., Vogt, C., Larkin, K., & Freye, K. (2001). Differences between motorized and nonmotorized trail users. *Journal of Park and Recreation Administration, 19*, 62-77.

The purpose of this study, commissioned by the Arizona State Parks Department, was to determine and consider the attitudes of three types of trail users for better planning and managing of state trails. Phone and mail surveys were used to identify 1,216 motorized, mixed, and non-motorized trail users.

The findings showed that there was support for multiple-use trails but only when motorized and non-motorized activities were separated. Each group differed in the issues they deemed most important. Over one-half of the motorized and mixed groups identified the two pressing issues as being, "Lack of trail ethics practiced by other trail users," and "Too much litter and trash along the trail." In contrast, the top issues for a majority of the non-motorized group were, "Lack of funding for trails," "Lack of trails close to home," and "Lack of directional signs along trails." Regarding management actions, all three groups felt efforts should be directed at maintaining existing trails and keeping trail areas clean of litter and trash. It was concluded that the results of the study supported a maintenance policy rather than a purchase or growth policy.

Research helps leisure service agencies improve services. Frequent evaluations at Colonial Williamsburg in Virginia, for example, continually support the planning and operation of visitor interpretive programs. *Copyright © 2008 Ruth V. Russell*

Categorizing Research

Research investigations can be characterized or classified any number of ways. Hearing people talk about research or when reading research reports, you inevitably encounter terminology that can be quite confusing. For simplicity sake, research studies can be classified three ways or by applicability, goal, and data sources (Figure 1).

Figure 1. Categories of Research.

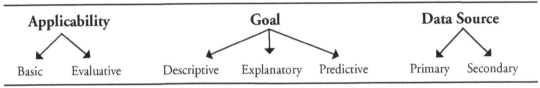

Applicability

One way to categorize research is to think of its application usefulness. Are you intrigued, just for the sake of learning, about some aspect of the world around you? Or, are you interested in trying to find answers to practical sorts of things? These two orientations to scientific inquiry are respectively labeled as basic research and evaluative research.

Some ways basic and evaluative research can be distinguished, in terms of contexts and research methodology, are found in Figure 2. Student and university faculty research, for example, runs the gambit between evaluative research and basic research. Practitioners, by and large, are interested in evaluative research endeavors.

Figure 2. Typical Characteristics of Basic versus Evaluative Research.

Characteristic	Basic Research	Evaluative Research
Unit of Analysis	Group, usually college students (in a course or on an athletic team)	Group or individuals in community or clinical settings
Research Design	Quantitative designs (especially experimental designs, quasi-experimental designs, or non-experimental designs), qualitative designs (or case study, critical theory, ethnography, grounded theory, narrative, and phenonmenology), or mixed-methods design	Quantitative designs (especially pre-experimental designs, single-subject designs, and survey research), qualitative designs (or case study, critical theory, ethnography, grounded theory, narrative, and phenonmenology), or mixed-methods design

Characteristic	Basic Research	Evaluative Research
Data Collection	Interview, questionnaire, observation, and/or projective methods	Interview, questionnaire, observation, focus groups, and/or record review

[1]Adapted from Hedrick, Bickman, and Rog (1993).

Basic research. **Basic research** seeks to understand phenomena or behavior at an abstract or theoretical level, "acquiring knowledge for knowledge sake." Basic research arises from intellectual curiosity and is more esoteric; meaning it typically has little or no immediate practical application. Nevertheless, this does not mean basic research is less worthwhile than evaluative research.

Basic research can expand our knowledge base by providing some fundamental understanding about a topic of interest. "Quality basic research is the lifeblood of any scientific discipline. Without it, disciplines would stagnate, failing to advance past their current limits of understanding" (Wann, 1997, p. 17).

Sometimes basic research findings ultimately do have practical usefulness (Case 3). An example of how a basic research discovery led to numerous everyday applications was a discovery made by Dr. Roy Plunkett, when he was experimenting with chemical reactions to refrigerant gases. A stuck cylinder valve produced a waxy solid mass with a very high melting point. Eventually, this glob was named Teflon™. Through the years many applications for Teflon™ have been found, including its use in cookware coating, soil and stain repellant for fabrics and textile products, wire coating, and pharmaceutical production (Inventor of the Week, 2000).

Case 3. Using Basic Research to Guide Practical Applications.

Petrick, J., Backman, S., Bixler, R., & Norman, W. (2001). Analysis of golfer motivations and constraints by experience use history. *Journal of Leisure Research, 33,* 56-70.

Using past golfing experiences and behaviors, distinct segments of golfers were identified from 1,397 golfers randomly selected from six golf courses. Golfers differed on their motivations and constraints to play golf.

The authors speculated how findings from this basic research inquiry could be extended or applied to golf course operations. For instance, it was noted that:

1. "Loyal infrequents" considered lack of time to play to be a large barrier. Thus, marketing strategies could be directed at promoting weekend and after-work play.
2. "Locals" were motivated to play for leisure reasons. Consequently, advertising to this group might be directed at stress relaxation and "get away" messages.
3. "Visitors" were less constrained by lack of time to play. It was speculated that one way to attract this group to a course would be to offer special rates for tee times that generally go unfilled.

Evaluative research. **Evaluative research**, sometimes referred to as program evaluation, focuses on assessing or appraising a program or **social intervention**. Any number of angles may be explored in evaluative research including: determining if there is a need for the program; examining program design; monitoring program operations; assessing program impacts; and assessing program economics (Step 1 and see Figure 3). For instance, one evaluative research study has examined how levels of participation in an after-school academic and recreation program (i.e., non-participant or participant) affected school absences, tardiness, and grades (Baker & Witt, 1996b).

Figure 3. Additional Articles Illustrating Different Kinds of Applicability.

Applicability	Published Examples
Basic Research	More, T., & Averill, J. (2003). The structure of recreation behavior. *Journal of Leisure Research, 35,* 372-395. Stodolska, M., & Yi, J. (2003). Impacts of immigration on ethnic identity and leisure behavior of adolescent immigrants from Korea, Mexico, and Poland. *Journal of Leisure Research, 35,* 49-79. Zarnowski, C. (2004). Working at play: The phenomenon of 19th century worker competitions. *Journal of Leisure Research, 36,* 256-281.
Evaluative Research	Byers, T., & Slack, T. (2001). Strategic decision-making in small businesses within the leisure industry. *Journal of Leisure Research, 33,* 121-136. Caldwell, L., Baldwin, C., Walls, T., & Smith, E. (2005). Preliminary effects of a leisure education program to promote health use of free time among middle school adolescents. *Journal of Leisure Research, 36,* 310-335. McKean, J., Johnson, D., Taylor, R., & Johson, R. (2005). Willingness to pay for non angler recreation at the Lower Snake River Reservoirs. *Journal of Leisure Research, 37,* 178-194.

Basic research and evaluative research "inform each other" (Lewin as cited in Stangor, 2006, p. 12). Evaluative research can trigger topic ideas for basic research, and basic research can disclose ways to solve specific problems.

Idea . . . Getting Started.

Whether you're embarking on research as a practitioner or student, consider identifying a faculty member at a local college or university who is interested in assisting you. Such a partnership can be a "win-win" situation. You want to identify someone to serve as your *mentor* or teacher, someone whose personality and work habits are compatible with your own style. Some of the factors to consider when identifying a mentor are:

1. **Availability.** Does he or she maintain weekly office hours and routinely check email messages? Will he or she be taking a *sabbatical* (a paid leave of absence to conduct an approved research project) during the time of your study? In general, do you anticipate having reasonable access to your mentor?
2. **Enthusiasm.** Is he or she open to working with research apprentices in general and with you in particular?
3. **Constructive criticism manner.** Is his or her feedback understandable? Is his or her delivery style agreeable with you?
4. **Comfort level.** Do you feel you can confide in the person regarding your concerns about your research project?

Goal

A second way to categorize research is according to its goal. There are three goals of scientific research. Research can be undertaken in order to attain: a description, an explanation, or a prediction. There are advantages and disadvantages associated with each of these kinds of research (Figure 4).

Figure 4. Comparison of Three Research Goals.

Research Goal	Advantages	Disadvantages
Descriptive	Provides a snapshot of "what, where, and when" something is occurring.	Does not examine relationships or linkages between or among phenomena.
Explanatory	Helps understand "why," by examining relationships between or among phenomena.	Should not be used to infer a causal relationship.
Predictive	Estimates future events or behaviors or provides estimates of population values.	Cannot consider all the important phenomena that affect events or behaviors.

Descriptive research. **Descriptive research** focuses on the "what, where, and when." In other words, phenomena about a sample or population are described (Case 4).

Case 4. Descriptive Research.

Loeffler, T. (2004). A photo elicitation study of the meanings of outdoor adventure experiences. *Journal of Leisure Research, 36,* 536-556.

The study explored participation in a college-based outdoor program. Fourteen program participants were asked to photograph their outdoor trips and were also interviewed. Inductive thematic analysis was conducted on the photographs as well as interview transcripts. Participants' experiences with the outdoors broke down into one of three themes: spiritual connection, connection with others, and self-discovery.

Explanatory research. **Explanatory research** examines why something happens. Relationships or linkages between or among social phenomena are examined. These linkages are determined by correlating how phenomena relate to each other or are derived from results stemming from experimentation (Case 5).

Case 5. Explanatory Research.

Wakefield, K., & Sloan, H. (1995). The effects of team loyalty and selected stadium factors on spectator attendance. *Journal of Sport Management, 9,* 153-172.

The study investigated how various stadium factors affected spectators' desire to stay at the stadium and their intentions to return to the stadium. A systematic random sampling method was used to distribute questionnaires before the end of the first quarter of college football games played at five different Southeastern Conference stadiums. Of 3,400 surveys distributed, 1,491 (43.9%) were returned.

Statistical analyses revealed that spectators desiring to stay at a game were more likely to: hold strong team loyalty feelings, have positive experiences surrounding the stadium (parking, cleanliness, and food), perceive crowding not to be a problem at the stadium, and feel fan behavior to be acceptable. Intention to return to the stadium was found to be linked to team loyalty as well as desire to stay at the stadium.

It was concluded that stadium administrators should make every effort to ensure spectators' experiences are positive ones so the spectators will return. In particular, the researchers maintain that special attention should be paid to enhancing stadium design and stadium services.

Predictive research. **Predictive research** deals with two perspectives. First, it can focus on how specific factors affect future behavior or events (Case 6). Second, predictive research is undertaken to provide estimates of population values. Figure 5 provides additional references for articles illustrating varying research goals.

Case 6. Predictive Research Focused on a Future Behavior.

Lyons, K. (2000). Personal investment as a predictor of camp counselor job performance. *Journal of Park and Recreation Administration, 18,* 21-36.

The purpose of the study was to examine the relationship between motivational factors that led people to apply for a camp counselor position and their ensuing job performance. The theory of personal investment guided the investigation.

Ninety-eight camp counselors working at two residential summer camps serving children from low-income families were surveyed. The Reasons for Working at Camp Inventory was used to identify six motivational factors. Staff assessed job performance, in six areas, by using the Job Performance Evaluation instrument.

Ethical interest motives, practical skills and experience motives, as well as gender, emerged as predicting camp counselor job performance. Recommendations were made regarding ways to structure selection interviews so the motives of interviewees could be determined by camp administrators.

Figure 5. Additional Articles Illustrating Different Research Goals.

Goal	Published Examples
Descriptive Research	Caldwell, L., Finkelstein, J., & Demers, B. (2001). Exploring the leisure behavior patterns and experiences of youth with endocrinological disorders: Implications for therapeutic recreation. *Therapeutic Recreation Journal, 35,* 236-249. Hutchinson, S., & Kleiber, D. (2000). Heroic masculinity following spinal cord injury: Implications for therapeutic recreation practice and research. *Therapeutic Recreation Journal, 34,* 42-54. Stodolska, M., & Alexandris, K. (2004). The role of recreational sport in the adaptation of first generation immigrants in the United States. *Journal of Leisure Research, 36,* 379-413.

Goal	Published Examples
Explanatory Research	Alexandris, K., Tsorbatzoudis, C., Grouios, G. (2002). Perceived constraints on recreational sport participation: Investigating their relationship with intrinsic motivation, extrinsic motivation, and amotivation, *Journal of Leisure Research, 34,* 233-252. Iwasaki, Y., Mannell, R., Smale, B., & Butcher, J. (2002). A short-term longitudinal analysis of leisure coping used by police and emergency response workers. *Journal of Leisure Research, 34,* 311-339. Sibthorp, J. (2003). An empirical look at Walsh and Golins' adventure education model: Relationships between antecedent factors, perceptions of characteristics of an adventure experience, and changes in self-efficacy. *Journal of Leisure Research, 35,* 80-106.
Predictive Research	Chen, R., Bloomfield, P., & Fu, J. (2003). An evaluation of alternative forecasting methods to recreation visitation. *Journal of Leisure Research, 35,* 441-454. Herbert, J. (2000). Therapeutic adventure staff attitude preferences for working with persons with disabilities. *Therapeutic Recreation Journal, 34,* 211-236. McCormick, B., Funderbunk, J., Lee, Y., & Hale-Fought, M. (2005). Activity characteristics and emotional experience: Predicting boredom and anxiety in the daily life of community mental health clients. *Journal of Leisure Research, 37,* 236-253.

Data Source

A third way of categorizing research is to identify the source of **data** or information used to conduct the study. Data come from either a primary source or from a secondary source.

Primary source. If you collect your own data, then you have generated your own ***primary data source***. An example of a study that used primary data was one reported by Glancy (1987). Dr. Glancy joined a women's recreational softball team as a participant observer. Through the season, she recorded personal observations of how softball performance affected social relations and cooperation.

Secondary source. Data that have been collected by one person and are used by another person is known as a ***secondary data source***. In other words, some other entity (individual, organization, agency, etc.) collected the information. When these data are used by another researcher, it is thought of as being passed along to a "second set of hands." For instance, one study reported using data originally collected and archived by the state of West Virginia in order to examine if increased recreation opportunities led to increased rates of physical activity and decreased health care expenditures and rates of obesity (Rosenberg, Sneh, Phipps, & Gurvitch, 2005).

Idea . . . *Existing Secondary Data Sources.*

A number of secondary data sources exist. While the purposes of these surveys vary along with content, some may contain data related to leisure time, recreation behaviors, and similar topics.

At least one excellent reference exists in online resources for social surveys conducted in Europe and other countries. For more information, consult *Social Research Updates* published by the Department of Sociology at the University of Surrey (www.soc.surrey.ac.uk).

Additionally, the University of Michigan's Inter-University Consortium for Political and Social Research has become a repository for over 9,000 secondary data sources from over 325 colleges in North American and 130 institutions worldwide. Researchers and students can purchase these computerized data sets. For more information go to http://www.icpsr.umich.edu or phone 734.998.9799.

The Research Process

How you go about planning and executing a research study is vitally important to its success. The ***research process*** is a structured and planned approach to discovering knowledge. If there is a dramatic deviation from this process, the integrity of the study will be questioned.

Idea . . . *Online Writing Resources.*

A critical ingredient to "good" research is that its proposal and final report are well written. Prior to submitting a proposal or distributing a final report, you will go though many drafts. Content is obviously important, but so is "good" writing.

To help you assess and improve your writing skills, consider using the "Online Writing Lab" or OWL (its acronym) at Purdue University, http://owl.english.purdue.edu. Click on "The Original OWL Can Be Found Here," and under "Purdue's OWL" click on: "English as a Second Language (ESL) Resources, Handouts, and Exercises" and "Grammar, Punctuation and Spelling (you might want to see how well you do in the "Practice Exercises" section).

Basically, the research process has four stages:

1. *Getting Started.* The initial stage of research consists of deciding on a topic. After that, a literature review is conducted, a theoretical approach is identified, and a scope of study is developed. The last step, in this stage, is making a case for the study's significance.
2. *Developing a Plan.* The second phase entails spelling out the methods or how you plan to conduct the study. This is the juncture where you identify a sampling plan, the design, instrumentation, and data-collection approaches that will be used. You also need to address ethical responsibilities and seek approval of your proposal during this stage.
3. *Implementing the Study.* The implementation phase includes conducting a pilot test and making the necessary adjustments before initiating the full-fledged study. At this stage, attention is also given to logistical concerns related to data collection and data analysis.
4. *Reporting the Research.* The final stage includes presenting visually attractive results and sharing information about the study, in written and oral formats, with diverse audiences.

The four stages of research, in turn, can be broken down into 17 steps (Figure 6). Each of these steps is featured as a separate chapter in this book.

Figure 6. Stages and Steps to Scientific Research.

Getting Started	Developing a Plan	Implementing the Study	Reporting the Research
Step1: Decide on a topic	Step 6: Select a sample	Step 12: Conduct a pilot test	Step 15: Present results using visual aids
Step 2: Review the literature	Step 7: Choose a design	Step 13: Prepare for data collection	Step 16: Prepare a written report
Step 3: Identify theoretical underpinnings	Step 8: Consider measurement	Step 14: Analyze data	Step 17: Deliver an oral report
Step 4: Develop a scope of study	Step 9: Specify data-collection methods		
Step 5: Explain study's significance	Step 10: Address ethical responsibilities		
	Step 11: Seek proposal approval		

Your Research

1. **Are you drawn to undertaking a basic or evaluative research project? Why?**
2. **Do you envision getting involved with a descriptive, explanatory, or a predictive research investigation? Why?**
3. **Do you anticipate using a primary data source or a secondary data source? Why?**
4. **If you plan on using a secondary data source, what ideas do you have for locating it?**

Review and Discussion Questions . . . What have you learned in this introductory chapter?

1. What are the two ways research can be defined?
2. What are three characteristics of scientific inquiry?
3. What is the difference between *basic research* and *evaluative research*?
4. Any one of three goals can be behind a research investigation. Name and define these goals.
5. What does it mean when you read that someone has used a *primary data source*? A *secondary data source*?
6. What are the four stages in the research process? Describe the multiple steps within each stage.

Exercises

1. Read three **abstracts** (initial summary) of articles in a recent issue (assigned by your instructor or chosen by you) of one of the major professional journals in recreation, parks, tourism or sport. Using only the information provided in the abstract, how would you classify the research?
    A. Is it basic research or evaluative research?
    B. Is it descriptive research, explanatory research, or predictive research?
    C. Does it rely on a primary data source or secondary data source?

2. Are you drawn to basic or evaluative research? And what intrigues you most, descriptive, explanatory, or predictive research? Try to determine your research orientations by visiting Intute, a web resource put together by a consortium of seven universities in England, at http://www.intute.ac.uk. Choose "Social Sciences" and browse by headings. Once you've chosen a heading, go to the "Filter Box" and choose "Papers/Reports/Articles (Individual)." Review the entries and identify reference titles that spark your interest. What do you lean toward regarding applicability and research goals?

3. Connect to the University of Michigan's Inter-University Consortium for Political and Social Research web site at http://www.icpsr.umich.edu.
    A. Identify two secondary data sets that contain leisure, recreation, park or sport information. Search term hints: "Leisure," "Recreation," "Sports," "Physical Activity," "Social Activities," "Backpacking," "Outdoors Activities," "Tourists" or other terms related to recreation.
    B. Print out a description of the selected data sets.
    C. For each data set, identify (write in the margin of the printout) if it is an example of:
        i. Basic or evaluative research;
        ii. Descriptive, explanatory, or predictive research.

4. Go to Robert T. Carroll's the Skeptic's Dictionary webpage at www.skepdic.com.
    A. If your instructor doesn't assign you a topic, choose one from "Topical Indexes."

        i. Briefly state the "strange belief, amusing deception, or dangerous delusion" that is reviewed.

        ii. Using bulleted points, summarize the arguments.

        iii. Which of these arguments is most convincing? Least convincing?

    B. Describe your overall reaction to this website.

5. Which of the following additional resources, for this chapter and book, do you find most useful as a novice researcher?

    A. Professor Saint-Germain's (at University of California-Long Beach) Research Methods (PPA 696) web page, www.csulb.edu/~msaintg/ppa696/696menu.htm. For this chapter, see "Session One."

    B. W.K. Kellogg's Foundation Evaluation Handbook at www.wkkf.org/Pubs/ Tools/Evaluation/Pub770.pdf. For this unit, see Chapters 2 and 3.

    C. The peer-reviewed electronic journal, *Practical Assessment, Research, and Evaluation* at http://pareonline.net/. Click on "Articles" and under "Articles of Special Interest To," click on "Research Students" and "Evaluation Students."

Research entails adopting a scientific inquiry process in order to discover knowledge and gain useful information and wisdom. General Electric Building, New York City. *Copyright © 2008 Carol Cutler Riddick*

16

Part II: Getting Started

STEP 1: Decide on a Topic

Sources for Research Ideas
Real Life
Reflection
University Faculty
Literature on the Subject

Measuring Program Effectiveness: The Five Ps
Program Need
Program Design
Program Process
  Standards Compliance
  Competency Assessment and Performance Appraisal
  People Involvement
  Marketing and Promotion
  Perceptions
Program Impact
  Knowledge
  Attitudes
  Skills or Functional Abilities
  Practice
Program Economics
  Cost Effectiveness
  Economic Impact

Sort Through Ideas
Interesting
Plausible
Ethical
Manageable
Valuable

**It is our choices . . . that show what we truly are,
far more than our abilities.**
J.K. Rowling, *Harry Potter and the Chamber of Secrets*

So, here you are at the beginning of the research process. For many of us, the "getting going" step of research is a challenge. This is because you need to think of some general subject matter or topic that YOU are interested in researching.

In order to come up with a "good" idea, a lot of thinking and creativity is needed. Insights typically unfold after spending many hours on this step. Plainly put, there is no easy way to identify a research idea.

Conducting research can be thought of as a process like that of an hourglass (Figure 1). You start broadly, narrow your focus, and then broaden again. The initial stage of determining a topic is a wide-open enterprise. After the topic is determined and you begin making decisions about how and when to collect the information needed for the study, the scope of the project narrows. Finally, once the collected data have been analyzed and you have the information you sought for your topic, it's time to open up your perspective again so that your conclusions and recommendations can be used by others.

Figure 1. Hour Glass Shape of Research.[1]

- Identify broad subject area

- Collect data

- Discuss and interpret results, state conclusions, and make recommendations

- Narrow topic and focus on concepts, instruments, and design

- Analyze data and present results

[1]Adapted from Trochim (2005).

So, where do ideas for research come from? If you're interested in conducting a program evaluation, what can be examined? What should you consider when sorting through ideas in order to narrow them down to a manageable topic? Read on to find some answers to these questions.

Sources for Research Ideas

Research reports seldom describe how the investigator came up with the original idea. Ideas for research can come from almost anywhere. The inspiration and perspiration that goes into finding a topic can stem from any number of sources, however, the bulk of research ideas come from practical problems, personal reflection, interests of university faculty or staff, or previous research.

Real Life

There are any number of practical problems and issues facing the recreation, parks, sport and tourism professions as well as society. Real life provides at least three ways for discovering a possible research topic:

- Confer with staff working within a recreation organization or program.
- Gain insights from professionals working outside an organization.
- Consult popular press, newspapers, magazines, and television news.

Ideas for research studies can be solicited from individuals who have worked in recreation, park, tourism and sport settings. If you are not already a staff member, make an appointment with the director of a recreation organization or program that interests you. At the meeting, explain that you would like to perform some service by doing research that will aid the organization in some way, such as exploring challenges that face program operations or evaluating a particular program's effectiveness.

Idea . . . Ask Professionals.

For research topic ideas, consider contacting individuals in charge of leisure-related services on campus. For instance, seek ideas from:

- **Coaches.** Ask them if they are open to exploring ways to determine factors that affect playing ability and/or ways to help the team reduce competitive anxiety.
- **Campus intramural (IM) sports program directors.** Inquire about interest in having a survey conducted to identify constraints encountered by users and non-users of the IM program.
- **Fitness room directors.** Do they have a need to solicit ideas from fitness room users regarding how to improve facility operations?
- **Campus health educators.** Ask them if they see any merit in soliciting student opinions regarding topics for wellness programs or workshops?

Another way to discover research ideas that deal with the problems and issues confronting practitioners is to attend a state, regional, or national professional conference. There are many professional organizations that support people working in recreation, park, tourism or sport settings (Figure 2). A number of national and international organizations have also emerged for program evaluators, many of which hold professional meetings [a listing of these organizations can be found at the American Evaluation Association's website (www.eval.org/EvaluationLinks/links.htm)].

Figure 2. Organizations that Support Recreation, Park, Tourism and Sport Service Professionals.

- Academy of Leisure Sciences (www.academyofleisuresciences.org)
- American Alliance for Health, Physical Education, Recreation and Dance (www.aahperd.org)

- American Association for Physical Activity and Recreation (www.aahperd.org/ aapar/)
- American Camp Association (www.acacamps.org)
- American College of Sports Medicine (www.acsm.org)
- American Psychological Association (www.apa.org) [NOTE: One section of the organization (Division 47) is devoted to exercise and sport psychology.]
- American Recreation Coalition (www.funoutdoors.com/arc)
- American Therapeutic Recreation Association (www.atra-tr.org)
- Aquatic Fitness Professional Association International (www.aquacert.org)
- Association for the Advancement of Applied Sport Psychology (www.aaasponline.org)
- Association for Experiential Education (www.aee.org)
- Association of National Park Rangers (www.anpr.org)
- Association of Outdoor Recreation and Education (www.aore.org)
- Australia and New Zealand Association for Leisure Studies (www.staff.vu.edu.au/anzals)
- British Association of Sport and Exercise Sciences (www.bases.org.uk/newsite/home.asp)
- Canadian Association for Leisure Studies (www.eas.ualberta.ca/elj/cals/home.htm)
- Canadian Parks and Recreation Association (www.cpra.ca)
- Canadian Society for Psychomotor Learning and Sport Psychology (www.scapps.org)
- European Federation of Sport Psychology (www.fepsac.org)
- IDEA Health and Fitness Association (www.ideafit.com/)
- International Festivals & Events Association (www.ifea.com)
- International Fitness Association (www.ifafitness.com)
- International Society of Sport Psychology (www.issponline.org)
- International Society of Travel and Tourism Educators (www.istte.org)
- National Association of Recreation Resource Planners (ww.narrp.org)
- National Association of State Park Directors (http://naspd.indstate.edu/index.html)
- National Dance Association (www.aahperd.org/nda)
- National Forest Recreation Association (www.nfra.org)
- National Intramural-Recreational Sports Association (www.nirsa.org)
- National Parks Conservation Association (www.npca.com)
- National Recreation and Park Association (www.nrpa.org)
- North American Society for the Psychology of Sport and Physical Activity (www.naspspa.org)
- North American Society for the Sociology of Sport (www.nasss.org)
- Park Law Enforcement Association (www.parkranger.com)
- Resort and Commercial Recreation Association (www.r-c-r-a.org)
- The Roundtable Associates, Inc. (www.therounddtableassociates.org) (NOTE: Organization dedicated to assure the park, recreation, and conservation profession and its practitioners serve the best interests of African American and other minority groups.)
- Travel and Tourism Research Association (www.ttra.com)
- World Leisure (www.worldleisure.org)
- World Tourism Organization (www.world-tourism.org)

Idea . . . Attend a Professional Conference.

If you're a student pursuing a thesis or dissertation topic, consider attending a professional conference the first year you're in graduate school. Some pointers:

- Three major professional conferences in North America, which report research in leisure studies, are: (1) the Leisure Research Symposium (held during the annual meeting of National Park and Recreation Association); (2) the annual meeting of the American Alliance for Health, Physical Education, Recreation and Dance; and (3) the Canadian Congress on Leisure Research held every other year.
- Conferences that include research reports are also held by many of the professional organizations listed in Figure 2. All typically offer a discounted student registration. Some will let students volunteer to help in exchange for a reduced registration fee.
- If you're a master's student in leisure studies and are planning on continuing for your doctorate within the next three years, think about applying for financial assistance from the Lucille and Derby Dustin Future Scholars Program (www.academyofleisuresciences.org) to attend the annual meeting of the National Recreation and Park Association.
- The point of your attendance at a conference is to network. As you are waiting for a session to begin, introduce yourself to the people around you. Mingle at the breaks. Attend scheduled social activities. You will find most researchers are friendly and eager to talk about their projects and give feedback about your research ideas.
- Most conferences publish a book of *abstracts,* or a summary of research presentations made at the conference. Leafing through this resource can provide topic ideas and the names of researchers interested in your topic. Correspond with these individuals.

Finally, the popular press might provide a tip for a real-life topic. News coverage may trigger your interest in something you hadn't thought much about before, such as park site graffiti, fan violence at sporting events, or rave parties. Or, you may read about a problem or issue that propels you to want to make a difference. For example, the existence of gang violence or children-at-risk may get you involved in evaluating the impact of innovative recreation programs for these population groups.

Reflection

We often use personal experiences to come up with a research idea (Case 1). Review and reflect upon your personal hobbies as well as job, volunteer, practicum, and internship experiences. Try to recall something you observed that interested you or that you found perplexing.

Case 1. Searching for a Thesis Topic: Interfacing Observations with Published Research.

A student was struggling to find a thesis topic related to college students. He was bothered that organized campus recreational opportunities, especially on weekends, were lacking something and that a lot of students became bored and got "into drinking."

After reading more on the subject, he discovered that a number of studies had documented the prevalence of alcohol use and abuse on other college campuses. He also noticed some literature existed on how constraints can affect recreational activity participation.

Putting these pieces of research together, he came up with a proposal. The gist of the study was to examine the extent leisure constraints and boredom affected the use and abuse of alcohol by students at his university.

Ideally, you'll want to spend some time living or observing the phenomenon you're thinking about studying. For example, if you're considering designing a new program for children, visit after-school programs to see what goes on. Or, before conducting research on factors affecting exercise adoption by older persons, engage some elders in a discussion of the topic. After going through these sensitivity-raising experiences, you should approach the getting-started phase with an enlightened perspective.

University Faculty

When struggling for a research idea, consider setting up appointments with faculty and/or university staff members. Start within your own major. Most faculty members have been or are involved in research, and many welcome an opportunity to talk about their research interests. Sometimes the faculty person is actually looking for someone to assist with his/her research.

One thing you need to realize is that a faculty member's discipline influences how he or she sees the world. In technical terms, this is known as ***reductionism,*** " . . . seeing and explaining complex phenomena in terms of a single, narrow concept or set of concepts" (Babbie, 2004, p. 101). For example, sociologists tend to study the world using sociological factors (such as group behavior); whereas, psychologists lean towards examining psychological explanations (e.g., personality); and economists normally focus on economic determinants (such as supply and demand).

Idea . . . Tips for Working with a Research Advisor.

If you're working with a faculty member to guide you in your research, consider the following tips:

1. **Schedule weekly meetings at a fixed time with the faculty member.** These meetings, though time consuming, can be used to keep you on track and progressing.
2. **Take a diary notebook to all meetings.** Invest in a spiral-bound notebook. Date each written entry. Write out questions or concerns you want to discuss at your upcoming meeting. Dedicating one notebook to record your progress will be invaluable to you.
3. **Take notes during your meeting.** Write down any brainstorming that went on in the meeting, issues that popped up, ideas on how to handle problems, and what you need to do or follow up on.
4. **Submit your study proposal several days in advance of your weekly meeting.** Ask the faculty advisor how much lead-in time she or he needs to review your proposal revisions. Once you know this deadline, stick to it.
5. **Clarify how feedback and revisions will be submitted and handled (comments on printed paper, email attachments, etc.).** Make sure your revisions are dated; you'll be amazed at how many drafts/revisions you'll go through!

Literature on the Subject

Another good source of study topic ideas is the professional and research literature. When we speak of completing a literature review or searching through the literature we mean consulting published works found in professional outlets, such as journals, master's theses, doctoral dissertations, and similar documents. If you consider these previously published works, the amount of information available is staggering.

It has been said that very few original ideas exist. It is quite likely that your idea has been refined and explored in the research literature a number of times. This is a good thing! Old research informs new research. Find out what has already been learned about the topic you're thinking about.

Idea . . . Tips for Reading a Research Article.

Some tips when starting out reading research:

1. **Begin browsing through journals within your field.** It is more likely you'll understand the content and language used in your major discipline. If you don't know which journal to begin with, ask an instructor for advice.
2. **Ignore articles with titles that don't match your idea.** If you don't understand the title or it doesn't grab your attention, move on. Don't make the mistake of trying to read every article.
3. **Read the abstract first.** If the title has captured your attention, then find the article and read the abstract. The *abstract* is found at the beginning of the article (usually boxed in or in a type set different from the article) and is about 100-200 words long. It will identify the purpose of the research, methods used, and summarize important findings and main conclusions.
4. **Skip the statistical analyses section.** Initially, as you start out reading research, don't pay much attention to what statistical tests were used. Instead, flip to the end and read the Discussion and Conclusion sections. Typically, this is where the writers admit to the limitations of their study and suggest how to overcome these limitations in future research. Pay particular attention to these ideas.

If you dig around, you'll come across at least one "gold" reference. A *gold reference* is the one that triggers an idea or shows you the way.

Idea . . . Still Searching for a Topic?

If you're still searching for a topic, here is an idea. Review the following studies. Maybe one or more of the topics addressed in these studies will interest you?

Auster, C. (2001). Transcending potential antecedent leisure constraints: The case of women motorcycle operators. *Journal of Leisure Research, 33,* 272-298.

Birenbaum, A., & Sagarin, E. (Eds.). (1973). *People and places: The sociology of the familiar.* London: Nelson. (NOTE: Details observational studies of leisure activities, including pinball, bars, card games and restaurants.)

Blau, J. (2001). Alley art: Can we see . . . at last, the end of ontology. In J. Turner (Ed.), *Handbook of sociological theory* (pp. 187-210). NY: Kluwer Academic/Plenum Publishers.

Cavan, S. (1966). *Liquor license: An ethnography of bar behavior.* Chicago: Aldine Publishing Co.

Drew, R. (2001). *Karaoke nights: An ethnographic rhapsody.* Walnut Creek, CA: Altamira Press.

Duncan, M. (1990). Sports photographs and sexual difference: Images of women and men in the 1984 and 1988 Olympics. *Sociology of Sport Journal, 7,* 22-43.

Eccles, J., & Barber, B. (1999). Student council, volunteering, basketball, and marching band: What kind of extracurricular involvement matters. *Journal of Adolescent Research, 14,* 10-43.

Firth, R. (1930). A dart match in Tipia: A study in the sociology of primitive sport. *Oceania, 1,* 361-368.

Geertz,C. (1972). Deep play: Notes on Balinese cockfight In C. Ceertz (ed.), *Interpretation of cultures* (pp. 412-453). NY: Basic Books.

Goffman, I. (1959). *The presentation of self in everyday life.* Garden City, NJ: Double-day/Anchor. (NOTE: Includes observtions of everyday events found in pubs and on promenades in England.)

Henderson, K., & Bedini, L. (1995). "I have a soul that dances like Tina Turner, but my body can't." *Research Quarterly for Exercise and Sport, 66,* 151-161.

Humphries, D. (1997). Shredheads go mainstream?: Snowboarding and alternative youth. *International Review for the Sociology of Sport, 32,* 147-160.

Klein, A. (1993). *Little big men: Bodybuilding subculture and gender construction.* Albany, NY: SUNY Press.

Lyng, S., & Snow, D. (1986). Vocabularies of motive and high-risk behavior: The case of skydiving. *Advances in Group Processes, 3,* 157-179.

Muir, D. (1991). Club tennis: A case study of taking leisure very seriously. *Sociology of Sport Journal, 8,* 70-78.

Nixon, H. (1986). Social order in a leisure setting: The case of recreational swimmers in a pool. *Sociology of Sport Journal, 3,* 320-332.

Pearson, K. (1979). *The surfing subcultures of Australia and New Zealand.* St. Lucia: University of Queensland Press.

Ryan, V. (1999). *Motivation to participate in risk sports among young adults.* Unpublished dissertation, University of Guelph, Guelph, Canada. (NOTE: Study examines factors that motivate young adults to participate in snowboarding and alpine skiing.)

Sugden, J. (1996). *Boxing and society An international analysis.* Manchester: Manchester University Press.

Thompson, H. (1999). *Hell's angels: A strange and terrible saga.* NY: Random House.

Thompson, H. (1972). *Fear and loathing in Las Vegas: A savage journey to the heart of the American Dream.* London: Picador.

Weinberg, S., & Around, H. (1952). The occupational culture of the boxer. *American Journal of Sociology, 57,* 460-469.

Both the novice and experienced researcher should try to build on the work of others. You might decide to explore contradictory or unexpected findings. Reading the literature may provide you with ideas for a replication study or an extension study.

The intent of a ***replication study*** is to find out if results from a previous study can be confirmed. The original research is repeated again, using subjects whose characteristics more or less match those involved in the first study. No one, two, or three studies are definitive by themselves. You shouldn't place too much confidence in a study's findings until it has been replicated multiple times.

On the other hand, one purpose of an ***extension study*** is to embellish earlier research. For instance, it might be argued that examining an additional factor may be the key to understanding the phenomena under study.

Sometimes it becomes apparent that an earlier study can be both replicated and extended. For example, a number of investigations have examined how an outdoor program affects the self-esteem of hearing participants (for a summary of these studies see Hattie, Marsh, Neill, & Richards, 1997). A student, as part of her thesis, wound up replicating (in terms of theory and research design) as well as extending (using the Rosenberg Self-Esteem Scale that had been translated into American Sign Language) earlier research in a study that monitored how an outdoor-based program affected the self-esteem of college students who were deaf (Fisher, 2005).

When reading, remember science provides us with a tentative way of knowing. The bulk of research findings are evolutionary, producing gradual, piece-meal changes in our understanding. Every once in a great while, a study's results contribute to a major upheaval in our scientific understanding of how the world works. Radical changes that overturn prevailing wisdom in a scientific field have been referred to as a ***scientific revolution*** (Kuhn, 1996).

Learn to question what you read. Being skeptical, questioning and reexamining what others have reported in their research can lead to new knowledge, the so-called ***paradox behind science.*** What is believed to be true at one point in time may later be dispelled or updated. For instance, for many years it was believed that older people preferred to engage in sedentary activities. This conventional wisdom later became revised when studies revealed that people of all ages enjoy participating in robust activities.

New research findings can replace old explanations. "Science demands that evaluators never be satisfied, always find flaws, criticize, and never permanently accept anything" (Walizer & Wienir, 2000, pp. 7-8).

Measuring Program Effectiveness: The Five Ps

Sponsored leisure events, activities, or interventions can be thought of as ***programs.*** The authors' bias is that evaluating programs, or ***evaluative research,*** should be viewed as an integral part of recreation, park, sport, and tourism service provision.

Many different angles can be used when undertaking evaluative research. Scriven (1967) proposed two types of evaluation, formative evaluation and summative evaluation. ***Formative evaluation*** deals with clarifying target population needs and improving program delivery, implementation, or operations. One way to think of formative evaluation is that it encompasses three functions, or the three Ps of Program Needs, Program Design, and Program Process.

Contrastingly, *summative evaluation* focuses on program performance, accomplishments, effects, or outcomes. Summative evaluation can be thought of as measuring two functions or the two Ps: Program Impact and Program Economics. Figure 3 provides details on the types of questions asked in research studies focused on formative and summative evaluations.

Figure 3. Blueprints for Evaluating the Effectiveness of a Recreation, Park, Sport or Tourism Program.[2]

Type of Evaluation/Function	Examples of Questions That Can Be Asked
Formative Evaluation/ *Program Need*	• What is the magnitude of the problem? • What are the needs of the population, clients, citizens, or staff? • What programs should be provided?
Formative Evaluation/ *Program Design*	• What programs could be used to produce the desired changes? • Which of the program approaches is best? • What educational and leadership techniques should be used? • How should the program be organized? • How can the program foster attendance? • What is the total program cost?
Formative Evaluation/ *Program Process*	• Is the program operating according to standards or stated policies? • Does the program follow safety/risk management standards? • Are administrative and program objectives being met? • How are personnel performing? • Are persons in need of or desiring the program receiving it? • What marketing or promotion changes are warranted? • What are the perceptions of program and non-program users? • How can program operations be improved?
Summative Evaluation/ *Program Impact*	• Are outcome goals and objectives being met (changes in knowledge, attitudes, skills, functional abilities, or practice)? • Does the program have beneficial effects on the participants? • Are some participants affected more by the program than others?
Summative Evaluation/ *Program Economics*	• Is the program cost reasonable relative to the magnitude of the benefits? • Would alternative programs produce equivalent benefits at less cost? • What is the economic impact of the park and recreation program/activity/event?

[2]Adapted from Rossi, Lipsey, and Freeman (2004).

Case 2 provides ideas for how each evaluation function has been examined in research studies. Let's now consider each in more detail as possible sources of research topics.

Case 2. Research Conducted on the Five Ps to Evaluation.

Evaluation Function	Literature Examples
Program Need	**Target Audience Needs** • Statewide assessment of recreation needs of persons with disabilities in community settings (Anderson & Heyne, 2000). • Self-reported leisure needs of adult males with HIV and AIDS (Kibler & Smith, 2000). • Identifying the content of a regional leisure wellness program for care givers of older adults (Bedini & Phoenix, 1999). **Needs of Professionals** • Self-reported multicultural competencies of the Certified Therapeutic Recreation Specialist® (Stone, 2003). • Therapeutic adventure staff's views regarding their competency in meeting the needs of persons with disabilities (Herbert, 2000).
Program Design	**Program Models** • Academic cultural enrichment program for African American youth (Shinew, Hibbler, & Anderson, 2000). • After-school programs (Danish, 2000). • Exercise prescription (American College of Sports Medicine, 2005). • Relationship-based programming (or building a healthy relationship between a worker and participants using the program as a medium) when working with youth (Bocarro & Witt, 2003). • Outdoor programs for youth with disabilities (Brannon, Fullerton, Arick, Robb, & Bender, 2003). • Community physical activity interventions (Marcus, Banspach, Lefebvre, Rossi, Carleton, & Abrams, 1992). • Physical activity interventions in workplace settings (Marcus et al., 1998). • Management practices in natural recreation settings (Manning, Ballinger, Marion, & Roggenbuck, 1996). • Playgrounds (Hudson, Thompson, & Olsen, 2004). • Sport imagery training (Van Raalte & Brewer, 2002). • Leadership variations found in coaching, community recreation, fitness, and outdoor recreation (Little & Watkins, 2004). • Recreational activity leadership (Long, Ellis, Trunnell, Tatsugawa, & Freeman, 2001). • Therapeutic recreation practice (Baldwin, Hutchinson, & Magnuson, 2004; Hutchinson & Dattilo, 2001; Pedlar, Hornibrook, & Hassen, 2001; Shank & Coyle, 2002; Sylvester, Voelkl, & Ellis, 2001) and service delivery (Dieser, 2002).

Evaluation Function	Literature Examples
Program Process	**Standards Compliance** • How well American playgrounds conformed to the National Program for Playground Safety standards (Hudson, Thompson, & Olsen, 2004). • Extent that Florida's municipal recreation and park agencies followed lighting policies/standards set forth by three different organizations (Spengler, Connaughton, Zhang, & Gibson, 2002). • Quality indicators representing resource, social and managerial conditions of park visitor experiences (Newman, Manning, Dennis, & McKonly, 2001). **Competency Assessment** • Entry-level public park and recreation professionals (Hurd, 2005). • Board members of public park and recreation agencies (Hurd, 2004). • Sport administrators in campus, public and military recreation settings (Barcelona & Ross, 2004). • Sport facility managers (Case & Branch, 2003). • Park and recreation professionals' cultural competencies (Anderson & Stone, 2005). **Performance Appraisal** • Staff's perceptions of executives and middle managers (Kent & Chelladurai, 2003). • Ratings by state park visitors of features that come under the control of park managers that are deemed important to a positive or satisfying visit (Fletcher & Fletcher, 2003). **People Involvement** • Outdoor recreation behaviors among four Asian American cultural groups (Chinese, Japanese, Korean, and Filipino) residing in the San Francisco Bay area (Winter, Jeong, & Godbey, 2004). • Sociodemographic differences between older adult park users versus non-park users and differences in perceived health between park users and non-users (Payne, Orsega-Smith, Roy, & Godbey, 2005). • Outdoor recreation participation of people with mobility disabilities (Williams, Vogelsong, Green, & Cordell, 2004).

Evaluation Function	Literature Examples
Program Process (continued)	• Leisure-time physical activity patterns of urban women with mobility problems (Santiago & Coyle, 2004). • Recreation activity patterns of rural residents (Warnick, 2002). • Recreation activities of families that include children with developmental disabilities (Mactavish & Schleien, 2000). • How greenway use was influenced by attributes (natural and management features), reasons/benefits sought, and underlying personal values (Frauman & Cunningham, 2001). **Marketing and Promotion** • Segmenting forest recreationists via their commitment profiles (Kyle, Absher, & Chancellor, 2005). • A comparison of four ways (personal appeal, Web site, and two different brochures) to promote homecoming at a university (Tew & Havitz, 2002). • Perceptions different public groups have of a public recreation agency (Borrie, Christensen, Watson, Miller, & McCollum, 2002). • Information sources used by urban park users (Lee, Floyd, & Shinew, 2002). • The influence of alternate information messages on perceptions of price and stated willingness to pay (Kim & Crompton, 2001). • A comparison of two sorts of marketing messages (prescriptive message urging individuals toward a behavior versus a proscriptive message urging individuals against a behavior) for use in wild land urban areas (Winter, Sagarin, Rhoads, Barrett, & Cialdini, 2000). **Perceptions: Service Satisfaction** • Park users' feedback on the quality of services experienced at state parks (Vaske, Donnelly, & Williamson, 1991). • Importance-performance analysis (Hendricks, Schnedier, & Budruk, 2004). • Recreation conflict and tolerance among skiers and snowboarders (Thapa & Graefe, 2004). • Assessment of the relative importance of factors affecting the decision to visit a South African national park (Leberman & Holland, 2005). • Perceived constraints to state park visitation by former users and non-users (Kerstetter, Zinn, Graefe, & Chen, 2002).

Evaluation Function	Literature Examples
Program Process (continued)	**Perceptions: Organizational Performance** • Performance ratings, by the public, of park and recreation agencies on nine dimensions of importance to a community's economic prosperity (Crompton & Kaczynski, 2003). • Perceptions of Boys and Girls Club members, parents, and staff regarding how well the organization's activities supported the agency's mission statement (Carruthers & Busser, 2000). **Perceptions: User Fees and Price Changes** • The public's perceptions of funding recreation services on public lands (Bowker, Cordell, & Johnson, 1999; Vogt & Williams, 1999), increased admission fee to parks (Crompton & Kim, 2001; Ostergren, Solop, & Hagen, 2005) and public outdoor areas (More & Stevens, 2000). • How the presence or absence of fees affect site location (Schneider & Budruk, 1999). • Opinions regarding contemplated price changes for 10K road race (Kyle, Kersteltter, & Guadagnolo, 1999). • A content analysis of news media stories on increased fees at recreation sites (Bengston & Fan, 2001). **User Preference Perceptions** • Citizen preferences for corporate sponsorship of urban park agency activities (Mowen & Graefe, 2002). • Attitudes of municipal recreation practitioners concerning preferences for implementing various marketing strategies for a municipal golf course (McClean, Havitz, & Adkins, 2002). • Watercraft park users' perceptions regarding the maximum number of watercraft that should be encountered on a river experience (Warzecha & Lime, 2001). • Users' evaluation of environmental and landscape aspects of rock climbing (Jones, Hollenhorst, & Hammitt, 2004) and wilderness campsites (Farrell, Hall, & White, 2001). • Landscape preferences for parks and nature areas by individuals with mobility limitations as well as their companions/caregivers (Brown, Kaplan, & Quaderer, 1999).

Evaluation Function	Literature Examples
Program Impact	**Knowledge** • How a computerized leisure education program affected the social skills knowledge of youth with intellectual disabilities (Dattillo, Williams, & Cory, 2003). • How a horseback riding program affected knowledge about basic horsemanship by adults with long standing histories of psychiatric disabilities (Bizub, Joy, & Davidson, 2003). • How participation in an after-school program (that had a recreation activities component) affected the math, science, reading, and language grades of the participants (Baker & Witt, 1996a). **Attitudes** • How program design and delivery attributes of two different rope courses affected group efficacy and excitement (Hara, Bunting, & Witt, 2005). • Evaluation of a program to promote sportsmanship in youth sports (Wells, Ellis, Paisley, & Arthur-Banning, 2005). • How a therapeutic recreation program, for community-based consumers of a mental health service, affected feelings of empowerment (Pegg & Patterson, 2002). • How a late night basketball program for gang members affected participants, staff, families, and the community (Derezotes, 1995). **Skill or Functional Abilities** • How participation in an outdoor program affected problem solving and self-discipline skills (Bruyere, 2002). • An instructional hip-hop dance program had positive consequences on children's rhythm skills and bilateral coordination (Gaines, 2004). • How staff training affected skill self-perceptions of seasonal camp staff (Powell, Bixler, & Switzer, 2003). • The effect of watching highlight peak performances, prior to a game, on playing performance of intercollegiate basketball players (Templin & Vernacchia, 1995). **Practice** • Ability to decrease such depreciative visitor behaviors as: deer feeding, amount of noise visitors make in grizzly bear country, petrified wood theft at national parks, and visitor removal of pumice at a national volcanic monument (Wirsching, Leung, & Attarian, 2003). • How two types of appeal messages (fear or moral appeal) as well as how three kinds of volunteer messenger sources (biker, hiker or uniformed) affected mountain bicyclists' compliance with trail etiquette (Hendricks, Ramthun, & Chavez, 2001). • How a therapeutic recreation program affected coping skill behaviors of individuals with alcoholism (Carruthers & Hood, 2002). • Effect of the introduction of a token economy system, within the context of cooperative games, on the social behaviors of adolescents with emotional and behavior disorders (Wolfe, Dattilo, & Gast, 2003).

Evaluation Function	Literature Examples
Program Economics	**Economic Impact** • Impacts of regional parks on property values (Nicholls & Crompton, 2005). • Impact of urban greenways on property values and recreation benefits (Lindsey, Man, Payton, & Dickson, 2004). • Revenue generated from snowmobiling (Coupal, Bastian, May, & Taylor, 2001). • Costs and economic benefits to a community of a proposed athletic complex (Kanters, Carter, & Pearson, 2001). • Economic impact of 30 sports tournaments, festivals, and spectator events held in seven American cities (Crompton & Lee, 2000).

Program Need

Program need examines the gap between the real and the ideal and can be assessed by identifying a problem or service need. Program need, sometimes referred to as *needs assessment,* essentially involves determining the needs or preferences of clients or service providers. For example, a multi-faceted study was undertaken on three groups of stakeholders (teachers, parents and students) involved with an after-school enrichment program. They were queried about their needs in order to help develop the goals and content of the program (Baker & Witt, 2000).

Program Design

Program design examines program logic and organization. Many practitioners are interested in paying attention to *how* outcomes occur. "Practitioners working in real life situations may design programs based . . . on best practices or conventions that have evolved over time through experience" (Baldwin, Hutchinson, & Magnuson, 2004, p. 17).

Program design evaluations include questions about components, content, elements, activities, and educational methods and techniques (see Borich, 2006 and Slavin, 2002). Case 3 presents an example of evaluating program design by way of assessing its components.

Case 3. Benchmarking State Park Performance.

Jordon, D., & Caneday, L. (2005). *Assessing state parks: The state of the art*. Presentation at the Annual Meeting of the National Recreation and Park Association's Leisure Research Symposium, San Antonio, Texas.

One way program design can be evaluated is by benchmarking. *Benchmarking* consists of comparing the performance of one organization to other comparable organizations. Forty measures of operations (such as operating budget, funding sources, types of properties, acreage, educational background of

32

staff) were used to identify park systems that were similar and dissimilar to each other. The state park systems clustered into seven groups or: Cluster A (AK, AZ, AR, CT, DE, HI, KS, LA, ME, MA, MN, MS, NE, NV, NJ, NM, NC, PA, RI, SC, UT, VT, VA, WI, WY), Cluster B (AL, GA, IN, KY, OH, OK, SD, TN, WV), Cluster C (FL, IL, MI, MO, OR, TX, WA), Cluster D (CO, ID, MT, NH, ND), Cluster E (IA, MD), Cluster F (CA), and Cluster G (NY). Ultimately, researchers found two state park systems that were similar and four state parks that were dissimilar to the Oklahoma Tourism and Recreation Department (OTRD). Eight performance measures were then used to compare components in the OTRD to those of their benchmarking partners.

Also, study topics about total program cost are useful. This is calculated by itemizing expenditures related to a program, also known as ***performance-based program budgeting*** [for one of the few studies that can be found on this topic see Crompton & Kaczynski (2003)].

An important part of program design is examining adherence to what some have labeled a program model. A ***program model*** can be thought of as a prescription for how to set up a program (Bickman, 1990). Program model has been referred to under various names, including program organizational plan, program theory and action theory (Rossi, Lipsey, & Freeman, 2004). The assumption behind using a program model to evaluate program design is that if certain program elements, resources, and activities are in place, it is assumed that specific program outcomes will be attained (Wooley as cited by Bickman, 1990).

Program Process

Program process monitors program operations. This can entail examining any number of elements including: compliance with standards, competency assessment and performance appraisal, people involvement, marketing and promotion, and perceptions.

Standards compliance. **Standards compliance** means comparing how a program, facility, or organization operates against the standards. Standards emerge from a concern to manage risks, address safety concerns, and generally to reassure the public that the services are of high quality. Standards can be established by professional organizations or regulatory entities and therefore may be either elective or required by law (Figure 4).

Figure 4. Standards for Recreation, Park, Sport, and Tourism Settings.

Entity	Standards Regarding	For More Information Contact
American Academy for Park and Recreation Administration and National Recreation and Park Association	Public park and recreation agencies	www.rpts.tamu.edu/ AAPRA www.nrpa.org

Entity	Standards Regarding	For More Information Contact
American Camp Association	Camp operations (including site and food services, transportation, health and wellness, operational management, human resources, and program design and activities).	www.ACAcamps.org
American College of Sports Medicine (1997)	Health/fitness facilities (exercise rooms, fitness floor, gym, sports court areas, pool areas, locker rooms)	www.acsm.org
Americans with Disabilities Act	Buildings, facilities and programs	www.usdoj.gov/crt/ada/adahml.htm
International Association of Amusement Parks and Attractions	Safety, general management, guest relations	www.iaapa.org
Joint Commission on Accreditation of Health Care Organizations	Provision of recreation services within health care institutions	www.jcaho.org
National Program for Playground Safety	Four areas of playground safety: supervision, age appropriate design, fall surfacing, and equipment and surfacing maintenance	www.uni.edu/playground/home.htm
National Aquatic Management School	Management of aquatic facilities and programs	www.nrpa.org/content/default.aspx?documentId=1642
National Playground Safety Institute	Certification as Playground Safety Inspector (hazard identification and risk management)	www.nrpa.org/content/default.aspx?documentId=778
Park Maintenance and Resource Management School	Maintenance management of parks and public facilities	www.nrpa.org/content/default.aspx?documentId=1767
Professional Convention Management Association	Professional performance	http://www.pcma.org
Travel Industry Association of America	Pricing, forecasting, research	www.tia.org

Entity	Standards Regarding	For More Information Contact
United States Access Board	Compliance with the Americans with Disabilities Act or removal of architectural barriers in facilities and parks. Standards now address: amusement rides; boating facilities; fishing piers and platforms; golf courses; miniature golf courses; play areas; playground surfaces; exercise equipment and machines, bowling lanes and shooting facilities; swimming pools; wading pools; and spas.	www.access-board.gov

Competency assessment and performance appraisal. An alternative way to examine program process is to assess how staff or personnel are performing. Personnel performance can be examined by competency assessment or performance appraisal.

Competency assessment focuses on the knowledge, skills, and characteristics needed to successfully perform a job (Hurd, 2004). Competency models have been developed and used for assessing a variety of roles.

A related idea to competency assessment is ***performance appraisal.*** These appraisals examine a person's (full-time, part-time, seasonal employees, and volunteers) work performance in terms of skills/abilities/traits, behaviors and/or results (Milkovich & Boudreau, 1996).

People involvement. Another way to evaluate program process is to determine ***people involvement***—the numbers of people participating in a program or activity. Typically, the percentage of program participants or users is reported. An embellishment is to break down users by their socioeconomic characteristics and/or some other classifier.

Marketing and promotion. ***Marketing and promotion*** encompasses determining what does and does not motivate a person to participate in or use a service. Evaluating the marketing of a program typically consists of measuring how well advertising, public relations strategies, brochures and/or web sites accomplish what is intended.

Perceptions. A final popular approach to examining program process is to assess people's perceptions or beliefs regarding aspects surrounding service delivery. This involves asking individuals to provide feedback on service satisfaction, public's perceptions about organizational performance, user fees, price changes, user preferences, etc.

Some recreation, park, sport, and tourism organizations establish their own standards against which to evaluate services. For example, the commercial campground company KOA uses retirees as field services representatives who travel around regions of North America inspecting campgrounds for compliance with such company standards as site cleanliness, customer relations, recreation programming, etc. *Copyright © 2008 Ruth V. Russell*

Program Impact

Program impact focuses on program outcomes. One way to think of measuring program impact is to think of it as *benefits-based programming* or: articulating outcome-oriented goals, developing programs that specifically address those goals, and evaluating the ability of programs to meet the goals (Allen, Stevens, & Harwell, 1996).[3]

Program impact can be multifaceted. For example, one approach for examining program impact is to determine how a program affects: knowledge, attitudes, skills, functional abilities, and practice outcomes across one or more of the three domains of health (Bennett, 1979).[3]

Something to Remember!

One way to assess program impact is to examine how program participation contributes to the health of an individual or group. The World Health Organization provides an expansive way to approach and define health, "*Health* is a state of complete physical, mental and social well-being and not merely the absence of disease and infirmity" (World Health Organization, 1947).

---

[3] A good resource on writing program goals and objectives is Melcher (1999).

The essence of health, therefore, might be portrayed by the following figure:

Thus, an impact study can examine how the program affects one or more of these three aspects of health, particularly from the vantage points of influencing knowledge, attitude, skills or functional abilities, and/or practices outcomes related to physical, mental, and social health domains.

Knowledge. **Knowledge** outcomes for program participants can examine any number of things including comprehension of subject matter, awareness of specific services available within a community, and knowing how to access services or programs.

Attitudes. **Attitude** outcomes refer to participants' feelings, opinions, or views. The literature is replete with examples of research undertaken in this program impact area (see Cases 2 and 4).

Case 4. Promoting the Mental Health of College Students.

Szabo, A. (2003). The acute effects of humor and exercise on mood and anxiety. *Journal of Leisure Research, 35,* 152-162.

The purpose of this study was to gather preliminary evidence regarding which of two programs yield better results in promoting mental health feelings of college students. At three one-week intervals, 39 British college students participated in 20 minutes of aerobic exercise, watched 20 minutes of a stand-up comedy videotape, and viewed a neutral, documentary videotape. Both exercise and humor emerged as having equally positive effects on mood and anxiety (as measured by self-reported attitudes on these two measures).

Skill or functional abilities. **Skill or functional ability outcomes** focus on performing a task. Case 2 contains examples of studies that have examined skills or functional abilities.

Practice. **Practice outcomes** examine the new behaviors that have been adopted by program participants. For examples of studies that have looked at practice outcomes refer to Case 2.

Program Economics

Program economics determines the economic value or the economic impact of the program. Program economics can either examine cost effectiveness or calculate cost impact (Yates, 1996).

Cost effectiveness. **Cost effectiveness** analysis examines the costs of two or more alternatives relative to their effects. One of the few cost effectiveness studies available in the recreation literature reported on how communities can determine if it is more cost effective to purchase open space or have the space used for residential development (Crompton, 2001).

To underscore what information a cost effectiveness study can provide, a hypothetical comparison of three employee weight loss programs is presented in Case 5. In this example, as in the real world, costs and outcomes differ by program.

Case 5. Hypothetical Example of Cost Effectiveness of Three Employee Recreation Services for Loosing 12 Pounds or More During a One-Year Period.

Suppose three different approaches—a cooking class, aerobics class and a combination cooking and aerobics class—are being analyzed. Cost effectiveness data are presented in the figure below.

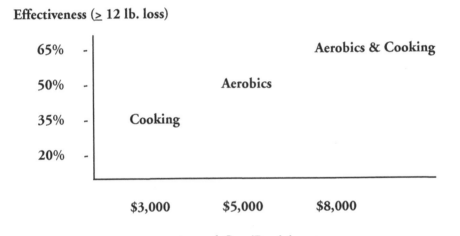

Effectiveness (≥ 12 lb. loss)

Data in this figure reveal that cooking classes were calculated as having an annual cost of $3,000/participant and were determined to be 35% effective (since 35% of enrollees lost 12 pounds or more during the year). Aerobic classes cost $5,000/participant and yielded a 50% success rate. And, the most expensive ($8,000/participant), yet most effective program approach to weight reduction, was participating in both cooking and aerobic classes. Almost two-thirds of the individuals participating in a joint aerobics-cooking class experienced a significant weight loss over a year's time.

Economic impact. Another way to determine a program's economics is to conduct an economic impact study of a specific activity or site. **Economic impact** can be determined by calculating travel costs or dollars spent on an activity or site relative to how much revenue will be generated directly and indirectly by the activity or site. Case 2 cites some economic impact studies.

Sort Through Ideas

After you have come up with possibilities for your research topic, you need to narrow down the possibilities. This is more difficult to do than it might sound. To help you we recommend that you take stock of each idea according to whether it is: interesting, plausible, ethical, manageable, and valuable.

Interesting

Is the topic interesting to you? If not, there's little point in pursuing it. This topic will be with you for a while, so if you don't like it initially, you'll hate it by the end of the study. You need an idea that will motivate and sustain you, especially if you're embarking on a thesis or dissertation.

Plausible

Is the idea plausible or feasible (Case 6)? Are data already available or can data be collected easily on the topic? Is it too sensitive a topic? Will you have access to study participants and will they be cooperative? Gambling habits of professional baseball players may be intriguing to you, but do you really think players will divulge this sort of information?

Case 6. An Idea that Was Not Plausible.

A graduate student wanted to conduct research on social interactions among amateur racing cyclists. His idea was to mount surveillance cameras on the rooftops along a bike route in Washington, D.C. Not obvious to the student were the multiple problems in being able to conduct such a study:

- Would permission be easily attained from building owners, many of which are owned by the federal government?
- Was it realistic to think that a lot of talking would occur between cyclists intent on winning a race?
- Could video cameras actually capture dialogue and interactions between and among cyclists as they rode?

By conferring with his thesis advisor, the student soon realized the impracticality of his initial idea!

Ethical

In the course of carrying out your research project, you shouldn't expect other people or yourself to do anything that is morally wrong. Step 10 goes into greater detail about ethical responsibilities and the mechanisms that are in place to remind and insure that you act ethically.

Many would argue the most compelling ethical issue at the proposal stage is **protection of human subjects.** This means there should be minimal risk of any form of physical harm or social psychological discomfort to those involved in the research.

Manageable

When pondering a topic to pursue, you should give thought to the resources that will be required to carry out the study. In most research situations, it takes time and money to plan, implement, and complete a study.

Regarding time, you must try to forecast how long each idea will take to study and then balance this length of time with the reality of your situation. If you are a student, think in terms of when you want or need to graduate. If you're a practitioner, think about how much time you will realistically have to devote to the research project. If you're involved in evaluating a program, then a certain amount of time needs to elapse as the program is conducted. Measuring program impact over an extended period of time undoubtedly can provide some useful insights. Nevertheless, the reality is that monitoring a program's impact over an extended period of time (six months or longer) is probably unrealistic.

Idea . . . Time Line for a Student Research Project.

Creating a time line for a student research project can be very useful. It helps you and those you are working with to know your aspirations. Using a time line also enables you to accomplish a number of things including: assessing your progress, planning personal time, and knowing when you will wrap things up (e.g., planning your graduation). Naturally, the list of activities, as well as time estimates, can be adapted to suit your specific situation.

Activity	Anticipated Completion Date	Actual Completion Date
1. Select an advisor/mentor/research supervisor.		
2. Submit potential topic(s) ideas to advisor/mentor/research supervisor.		
3. Narrow down and select a research topic you're interested in and is approved by your advisor/mentor/research supervisor.		
4. Select thesis/dissertation/research advisory committee members, if applicable.		
5. Draft and revise proposal per research supervisor's suggestions.		
6. Proposal draft approved by research supervisor.		
7. Meet with individual committee members, or others, to receive comments on distributed proposal.		
8. Review individual proposal comments with research supervisor.		

Activity	Anticipated Completion Date	Actual Completion Date
9. Revise proposal.		
10. Obtain research supervisor's approval of proposal changes.		
11. Proposal distributed to committee, if applicable.		
12. Proposal committee meeting, if applicable.		
13. Revise proposal, if needed.		
14. Seek and obtain approval from institutional human subjects review board.		
15. Final approval of proposal.		
16. Begin data collection.		
17. Analyze data and draft report.		
18. Draft and revise final report per research supervisor's suggestions.		
19. Final report draft approved by research supervisor.		
20. Meet with individual committee members, or others, to receive comments on final report, if applicable.		
21. Review final report comments with research supervisor.		
22. Revise final report.		
23. Obtain research supervisor's approval of final report changes.		
24. Copy of final report to committee members, if applicable.		
25. Defense committee meeting, if needed.		
26. Corrections as specified by committee members, if applicable.		
27. Final approval.		
28. Disseminate study results.		
29. Celebration!		

Another thing to consider is the financial resources necessary to carry out the study. What costs will be incurred? And, who will be able to pay these costs? Will the costs be covered by the organization that serves as the setting for the research project? If not, and you are a student, does your university have a small grants program? If so, what is the maximum amount of money you can request to cover non-personnel costs? If other entities are not able to support you, are you prepared to pick up the tab yourself?

Valuable

When selecting a research topic, it is important to consider its ultimate value (Thomas, 2004). Basically, you need to make a case for the study's relevance or significance (discussed more in Step 5) to a discipline's knowledge base, society, and/or professional practice.

> "Evaluation use is not something to be concerned about at the end of an evaluation; how the evaluation is to be used is a primary matter of concern from the very beginning of the evaluation and throughout every step of the evaluative process" (Patton, 1987, p. 73).

A prime consideration is stakeholders. Research projects happen within a social and political environment. A study's value is defined by the "players" or stakeholders present in these environments (Cronbach, 1982). Viewpoints held by stakeholder groups are diverse, sometimes resulting in disagreement or even friction. For example, the United States Department of Agriculture's Forest Service has had to balance various groups' views toward wolf control in the national parks.

Stakeholders are individuals who have different perspectives about a research undertaking. There are six categories of stakeholders that can be associated with any study:

- *Policy Makers & Decision Makers:* people who decide whether a program is to be initiated, (dis)continued, expanded, or curtailed.
- *Program Sponsors:* the organization that funds the program. The funding organization may be the same entity in which the policy and decision makers are found.
- *Program Participants:* persons or households that receive the service or intervention.
- *Program Managers:* those responsible for overseeing and administering the program.
- *Front Line Staff:* people responsible for delivering the program or service.
- *Contextual Stakeholders:* individuals, organizations, groups, and others interested or affected by the program under study (e.g., other agencies or programs, public officials, and/or citizens groups found in the community where the study is conducted).

Stakeholders' interests and priorities are important considerations when selecting a research topic. To help, we offer this advice:

1. **Actively** solicit information from the primary stakeholders about their questions of real interest.
2. **React** to these information needs by drafting a responsive proposal.
3. Based on stakeholders' feedback, **adapt** the proposal before implementing it.

It is important to remember that a student who undertakes a program evaluation has to balance stakeholders in two arenas—the community setting and university (Figure 5).

Figure 5. Example of Stakeholders in a Thesis that Examines the Effectiveness of a Municipal Recreation Department's Master's Swim Program.

Stakeholder Group Type	Examples From the Community	Examples From the University
Policy Makers & Decision-Makers	• Mayor or county executive • Recreation board • Municipal park & recreation director	• Thesis committee members • Institutional review board
Program Sponsors	• County council	• University's small grants program
Program Participants	• Swim participants	• Not Applicable
Program Managers	• Aquatics program director • Swim team coach	• Thesis chair
Front Line Staff	• Lifeguards • Pool operator • Front desk staff • Maintenance staff	• Student investigator • Interviewer(s)
Contextual Stakeholders	• Other master's swim teams • Local newspapers	• Student's academic department • University • Student's parents

Your Research

1. Identify topic(s) you are interested in researching that emerge from:
    A. Real life.
    B. Reflection.
    C. Discussions with university faculty.
    D. Literature.
2. Is your idea:
    A. Interesting?
    B. Plausible?
    C. Ethical?
    D. Manageable?
    E. Valuable?
3. Is your idea about program: need, design, process, impact, or economics?

Review and Discussion Questions . . . What have you learned about deciding on a topic to study?

1. What sources can be used to find a research topic?
2. How can the paradox behind science guide you in identifying a topic?
3. What are the five ways (or *Ps*) a program's effectiveness can be assessed?
4. What is the one overarching ethical concern that should always be considered when selecting a research topic?
5. Name four other considerations for choosing a research topic.
6. What does it mean when you design a research project that is responsive to your stakeholders?

Exercises

1. Make an appointment to interview two practitioners and/or university faculty or staff (coaches, intramural sports director, etc.) about research.
   A. What are their research interests?
   B. What are some ideas they think need to be researched?

2. Discover the kinds of research topics being investigated by doing one or both (if directed by your instructor) of the following activities. Identify one research topic or idea that caught your interest or attention.
   A. Examine three "Research Update" columns appearing in the past year in *Parks & Recreation*.
   B. Visit the Social Sciences Resources section of the Internet Public Library (www.ipl.org/ref?RR/static/soc00.00.00.html/).

3. Learn about the national and international organizations that exist to promote evaluation by going to the American Evaluation Association's web site at www.eval.org/Resources/ProfessionalGroups.asp and linking to "Professional Groups." Choose three of these organizations that interest you most. For each, briefly describe what activities/services they offer for someone wanting to learn more about research.

4. Review some real world efforts of recreation organizations and communities to measure program effectiveness by going to the California Park and Recreation Society Web site at www.cprs.org, clicking on "Training and Educational Resources," then "Information & Referral." Browse through the numerous listings under "Information & Referral," and find examples of how the following have been defined and measured:
   A. Program Need
   B. Program Design
   C. Program Process
   D. Program Impact
   E. Program Economics

HINT: Go to "Needs Assessment . . . ," choose "Leisure Interest Survey," "Needs Assessment Survey," "Youth Program Evaluation Example," "Programming Survey," and "Event, Park, and Sport Comment Cards." Then visit "Outcome Tools and Evaluation." Next log on to Creating Community: VIP Planning Tools," choose "Performance Evaluation," and "Performance Appraisal Evaluation for Management Employees."

5. Find out more about standards compliance. If your teacher doesn't assign you one of the entities identified in Figure 4, choose one to investigate. Go to their Web site.
   A. What, if stated, is the purpose of having these standards in place?
   B. Briefly summarize the areas of operation that are covered.
   C. What do you think of the standards? Do they seem reasonable?

6. Locate one or more (as directed by your instructor) of the following resources that exist to assist novice researchers with conducting impact studies. Then, answer the posed question.
   A. A report sponsored by the American Association for the Advancement of Science that was written by S. Bond, S. Boyd, & K. Rapp (1997) entitled *Taking Stock: A Practical Guide to Evaluating Your Own Programs* and is available at http://www.horizon-research.com/reports/1997/taking_stock.php. What one thing did you glean from Chapter 2, 3, or 4 that you think will help you most as you learn how to do research?
   B. Project STAR Corporation's *A User's Guide for National Service Programs* available at http://nationalserviceresources.org/resources/online-pubs/perf-meas/index.php. Go to "General Resources," then "User's Guide to Evaluation for National Service Programs" and look at the Chapter 1 section on "Desired Result." Do you think the advice holds true for evaluative research in recreation, parks, or sport settings? Explain your answer.
   C. United Way of America's, "Outcome Measurement Resource Network" available at http://national.unitedway.org/outcomes. Identify one thing you learned about outcome measurement?

7. Read *The Value of the Sports Economy in England: Final Report* by going to Sport England's Web site at www.sportengland.org/pring/sporteng_eng_june03.pdf. Identify one major point you learned about the economic impact of sports.

8. Find out about grants, funding resources, and programs available to prevent and reduce juvenile delinquency by visiting the United States Office of Juvenile Justice and Delinquency Prevention's Web site at www.ojjdp.ncjrs.org.

Deciding on a useful and important topic for a research study is not that mysterious. Sources for ideas are logically found in personal and professional experiences. Covent Garden, England. *Copyright © 2008 Carol Cutler Riddick*

STEP 2: Review the Literature

How Literature Reviews Can Help You
Find a Suitable Topic
Identify a Conceptual Approach
Provide Rationale for Study's Significance
Pinpoint Methods
Understand and Interpret Results

Conduct the Search
Think of Keywords
Review Secondary Sources
Review General References
Obtain Primary Sources

Review and Analyze Primary Sources

Write Up the Literature Review
Integrative Literature Review
Theoretical Literature Review

To be conscious that you are ignorant is a great step to knowledge.
Benjamin Disraeli

A *review of literature* is the glue that holds the research endeavor together. In conducting a literature review, we find and study relevant information and work previously done by others. In this way, we can create a synthesis of the research already carried out on related topics (Pan, 2004).

Admittedly, this is a time-consuming process but, if done thoroughly, yields huge dividends. Our collective experience is that all too often researchers (from the novice to the veteran) spend insufficient time discovering the findings and thoughts of those who have gone before them.

Something to Remember!

A literature review is not a simple string of summaries of the works of others. A literature review is a *synthesis*. This means interpreting and evaluating individual pieces of literature, and then integrating and restating these earlier studies in order to create a new, coherent, and original work.

How Literature Reviews Can Help You

What are the dividends for identifying and reviewing earlier writings? Overall, a literature review can assist you with the whats and hows of your study, that is finding a suitable topic, identifying a conceptual approach, providing rationale for your study's significance, identifying data-collection methods, and thinking in advance about how to interpret findings.

Find a Suitable Topic

Sometimes authors point out something you had not previously thought about. A literature review can reveal gaps in knowledge, thus helping you frame a problem, research question, or hypothesis (see Step 4). A review of literature may also suggest the usefulness of doing a replication or extension study (see Step 1).

Identify a Conceptual Approach

Sociologists, psychologists, and anthropologists have studied individual or group behavior to produce formal theories or conceptual approaches that can be used to guide your research. A literature review can help identify a theoretical approach to test, as well as relevant concepts to examine (Creswell, 2003). Also, hypotheses and research questions can emerge from a literature analysis. Make sure you record where you find these leads so later on you can properly cite these sources.

Provide Rationale for Study's Significance

A review of literature can help you develop a justification for your study by showing how your work will address an important need or unanswered question. These references might cite statistics regarding the magnitude of the problem you are studying or point out the need for the kind of research you are proposing.

Earlier works can also inform your decisions about methods. Criticism of methods used in earlier studies can underscore the merit and significance of the methods you have adopted.

In short, being able to state the significance of your research is important. Step 5 will go into this point in greater detail.

Pinpoint Methods

One of the biggest bonuses that can come from reading through previous studies is getting ideas on measurement tools. Pay particular attention to the "Instrumentation" section found in research reports. This is where the author identifies the various measurement tests used to conduct the study and/or offers a rationale for the items contained in an instrument. For example, one study reported on the rationale for items used in a questionnaire designed to measure attitudes about park impact fees (Fletcher, Kaiser, & Groger, 1992).

Reviewing what others have done may also help steer you towards or away from a particular data-collection approach. Someone else's insights on what did or didn't work regarding how to conduct a study can minimize your errors and lead to success.

Understand and Interpret Results

Additionally, earlier works provide you with a backdrop to interpret and understand your own findings. A literature review not only helps you plan a study, it also serves two purposes after your data have been collected. First, in discussing your results (Step 16) you need to compare your findings to what others have reported. Is there an accumulation of knowledge? Or, has an inconsistency been found? If your results are different, then you have an obligation to speculate why they are different. Were the differences due to design, instrumentation, and/or data collection methods?

A second dividend from a literature review is to help you to interpret your findings. Specifically, when you're preparing your report, you need to refer back to the theoretical foundation(s) used for the study and make inductive and/or deductive conclusions. Additionally, you need to interject ideas for future research. Other researchers may have suggested ideas that in retrospect, you now have a greater appreciation for and support wholeheartedly.

Conduct the Search

A literature review is best handled by beginning with a computerized database search. A *database* collects and organizes information. Online databases permit quick identification of journal articles, books, and a multitude of other references on a particular topic of interest. You can limit your search many different ways, using keywords, full-text, author, journal name, language, and so on. Accessing computerized databases provides a fast and efficient way to conduct a literature search. Once you have completed the search, you can save the results by printing, downloading, or emailing them to yourself.

Idea . . . Reviewing Literature Tips.

When beginning your review of literature, here are some pointers:

1. **Use a university library rather than a public library.** Public libraries do not have professional journals among their holdings. Even when using a university library, there will be times when materials you need are not readily available.
2. **Most university libraries provide interlibrary loan services.** This service obtains copies of journal articles and books from other libraries. It can take up to a week or two to fill a request.
3. **An alternative to interlibrary loan services is online document delivery services.** For journal articles, there is IngentaConnect (www.ingentaconnect.com). For dissertations, turn to ProQuest Digital Dissertations at wwwlib.umi.com/Dissertations/. For ERIC documents, there's ERIC Document Reproduction Service (http://searcheric.org). Additionally, the Center for Research Libraries (www.crl.edu/) makes available scholarly research resources of the major research libraries of America. The University of Michigan's School of Information's Internet Public Library (www.ipl.org/) service provides online texts and references. And for British library system holdings, consult InsideWeb (www.bl.uk/services/current/inside.html).
4. **Another service that can be offered by a university library is a table-of-contents service.** This service accesses the tables of contents to thousands of periodicals, also identifying an article's title and author. Two on-line table-of-contents services are Infotrieve (www.infotrieve.com) and IngentaConnect (covers 28,000 journals in a variety of academic fields including social science, science, and humanities; go to www.ingentaconnect.com).

Libraries pay subscription fees for databases, therefore specifics on how to conduct a database search vary by library and database. You are encouraged to contact a *reference librarian,* or an individual who has received specialized training on how to identify and locate materials on a specific topic. Many colleges, at the beginning of each semester, offer library research workshops.

At this time, we think it is important to stress and advise you to not rely solely on the Internet to conduct a literature search. Even today, research on the Internet is not a substitute for library work. Information found on Web sites does not undergo rigorous quality control prior to posting, thus what is posted may not be valid or objective information. At best, you may find some leads or background information from an Internet search. In these instances, you still should cross-check information obtained from the Internet with authoritative resources or references found at a library, such as from an electronic data base.

There are basically four phases involved in a database literature search (adapted from Fraenkel & Wallen, 2005):
1. Think of keywords.
2. Review secondary sources.
3. Review general references.
4. Obtain primary sources.

Think of Keywords

You need to think about the topic you have in mind and then come up with *keywords* or words or phrases summarizing your topic. Use terms that identify the relevant references for your project. You don't want to be too narrow or limited, nor do you want to wind up with many useless citations.

Sometimes journal articles themselves contain keywords. Other times, a word will appear in a title of a retrieved reference and you realize it is more encompassing. Pay attention to these leads, making sure you're not missing a good search or descriptor term. Sometimes you'll have to back up and use a new keyword.

Most online databases have two kinds of searches, "Quick" and "Advanced." You can connect keywords together (using what is known as a *Boolean* operator) to narrow or broaden a search.

The bad news is that each database has a unique operating system, so again you're encouraged to contact a librarian to find out nuances of each database you plan to use. If too many leads emerge from a database search, you may want to limit your search by specifying: a particular language; journal articles and dissertations but not conference papers (which can be difficult to acquire); and/or materials published during a certain time frame.

Idea… Keywords to Use. Speak the language of the Scholars!!

---

1. **Consider these as keywords in your database search:**
   History – learning the history of a topic can help you develop a broad understanding of how scholars' thoughts on an issue developed over time.
   Definition – while not always fruitful, sometimes an especially useful reference that discusses definitions will be discovered.
   Review – if you locate a previous literature review on your topic, your own review can build on it, bringing it up to date (see discussion on secondary sources below).

2. **Try the IOP strategy:**
   I = an Intervention. If you're dealing with an intervention, identify the program/activity/intervention, such as "aquatic therapy."
   O = the outcomes. Specify the kinds of outcomes of interest, such as "behavior change," "attitude change," "leisure satisfaction." Try also using the words, "impact," "effect" and "evaluation."
   P = the "people or population of interest." The demographic characteristics, such as "elderly women," "college students," "youth-at-risk," "hospital patients") should be identified.

For example, searching on the PsychINFO database, using the IOP strategy and the keywords, "Aerobic Exercise AND Body Image AND Females," 11 hits or leads emerged. In other words, with less than a minute of typing and searching time, 11 articles relevant to the topic at hand were identified. Sweet!

Review Secondary Sources

Typically, when reading about a subject you're not very familiar with, it is a good idea to consult secondary sources. A ***secondary source*** is a publication that provides introductory background information about a topic. The emphasis taken in a secondary source is to organize and distill what others have thought and written about a topic.

Common secondary sources are textbooks, encyclopedias (Figure 1), and research reviews. While these resources can provide a general overview, they usually suffer from a lack of depth, breadth, and timeliness (or being outdated).

Figure 1. Encyclopedia Reference Examples.

Borgatta, E., & Montgomery, R. (2000). *Encyclopedia of sociology* (2nd ed.). NY: Macmillan Reference USA.

Ekerdt, D. (Ed.). (2002). *Encyclopedia of aging.* NY: Macmillan Reference USA.

Research reviews are specialized and detailed literature summaries published either as monographs or by an existing professional journal (Figure 2). The reviews synthesize what is known about a topic by providing an integrated summary (Case 1). Oftentimes, the research review identifies further research needs on the topic.

Figure 2. Research Reviews Containing Topics Related to Recreation, Park, and Sport/Fitness.

American Sociological Review
Annals of Leisure Research
Annual Review of Anthropology
Annual Review of Medicine
Annual Review of Physiology
Annual Review of Psychology
Annual Review of Public Health
Annual Review of Sociology (www.jstor.org/journals/03600572.html)
Annual in Therapeutic Recreation
Annals of Tourism Research
Clinical Sociology Review
Exercise and Sport Science Reviews
International Review of Sociology of Sport
Physiological Reviews
Psychological Review
Psychological Bulletin
Review of Educational Research
Review of General Psychology
Review of Research in Education

Case 1. Research Reviews Appearing in Parks and Recreation.

Parks and Recreation is a monthly **periodical** or magazine. Research reviews appear in a featured column entitled "Research Update." Some topics that have been covered in this column are:

Berg, S., & Puymbroeck, M. (2005). Under-represented groups need physical activity. *Parks & Recreation, 40,* 24-29.

Cooper, N., Estes, C., & Allen, L. (2004). Bouncing back. *Parks & Recreation, 39,* 28-33. NOTE: A synthesis of literature on the impacts of recreation programs, designed to foster resiliency in children at-risk.

Diaz, S. (2005). Can sports promote competence? *Parks & Recreation, 40,* 26-33.

Dorwart, C., Leung, Y., & Moore, R. (2004). Managing visitors' perceptions. *Parks & Recreation, 39,* 24-31.

Malkin, M., & Rabinowitz, E. (1998). Sensation seeking and high-risk recreation. *Parks Recreation, 33,* 34-35, 43-45.

Munson, W. (2002). Recreation and juvenile delinquency prevention: How recreation professionals can design programs that really work. *Parks & Recreation, 37,* 31-37.

Place, G. (2004). Youth recreation leads to adult conservation. *Parks & Recreation, 39,* 29-38.

Rosol, M. (2000). Wilderness therapy for youth-at-risk. *Parks & Recreation, 35,* 42-53.

Wirsching, A., Leung, Y., & Attarian, A. (2003). Swatting litter bugs. *Parks & Recreation, 38,* 16-22.

A variation to traditional research reviews is the meta-analysis. A **meta-analysis** provides an integrated literature review on a topic by summarizing the quantitative results from multiple studies (Case 2). Multiple databases are searched systematically to identify the scope of relevant studies (research published in journals, dissertations, etc.) to the topic. Meta-analysis reveals how findings are influenced by variations in the methods used.

Case 2. Published Meta-Analyses.

A number of meta-analyses have been completed on a range of topics. If you're interested, please see below.

Bunting, C., & Donley, J. (2002). *Ten years of challenge course research: A review of affective outcome studies.* Poster presented at the 6th Coalition for the Education in the Outdoors Research Symposium, January 11-13, Bradford Woods, IN.

Fox, K. (2000). The effects of exercise on self-perceptions and self-esteem. In S. Biddle, K. Fox, and S. Boutcher (Eds.), *Physical activity and psychological well-being* (pp. 88-117). London: Routledge.

Hans, T. (2000). A meta-analysis of the effects of adventure programming on locus of control. *Journal of Contemporary Psychotherapy, 30,* 33-60.

Kennet, J., Burgio, L., & Schulz, R. (2000). Interventions for in-home caregivers: A review of research 1990 to present. In R. Schulz (Ed.), *Handbook of dementia caregiving* (pp. 61-126). NY: Springer.

Lyddon, W., & Jones, J. (Eds.). (2001). *Empirically supported cognitive therapies: Current and future applications.* NY: Springer Publishing.

Manfredo, M. (1996). Measuring leisure motivation: A meta-analysis of the recreation experience preference scales. *Journal of Leisure Research, 28,* 188-213.

Marshall, S., Biddle, S., Gorley, T., Cameron, N., & Murdey, I. (2004). Relationships between media use, body fatness and physical activity in children and youth: A meta-analysis. *International Journal of Obesity and Related Metabolic Disorders, 28,* 1238-1246.

Neil, J. (2003). Reviewing and benchmarking adventure therapy outcomes: Applications of meta-analysis. *Journal of Experiential Education, 25,* 316-322.

O'Farell, T., & Fals-Stewart, W. (2003). Alcohol abuse. *Journal of Marital and Family Therapy, 29,* 121-146.

Pierskalla, C., Lee, M., Stien, T., Anderson, D., & Nickerson, R. (2004). Understanding the relationship among recreation opportunities: A meta-analysis of nine studies. *Leisure Science, 26,* 163-180.

Staunton, N. (2003). *Meta analyses of adventure therapy outcomes.* Unpublished master's thesis, University of New Hampshire, Durham, NH.

Tuffrey-Wijne, I. (2003). The palliative care needs of people with intellectual disabilities: A literature review. *Palliative Medicine, 17,* 55-62.

West, S., & Crompton, J. (2001). A review of the impact of adventure programs on at-risk youth. *Journal of Park and Recreation Administration, 19,* 113-140.

Wilson, S., & Lipsey, W. (2000). Wilderness challenge programs for delinquent youth: A meta-analysis of outcome evaluations. *Evaluation and Program Planning, 23,* 1-12.

Software exists (e.g., Johnson, 1989) to help with the steps involved in conducting a meta-analysis. These steps include abstracting study characteristics and then quantifying, coding, and assembling these characteristics into a database that is statistically analyzed and presented. Several excellent print references (Cooper & Hedges, 1994; Cooper & Lindsay, 1997; Lipsey & Wilson, 2001) and online references (www.uky.edu/ComputingCenter/SSTARS/MetaAnalysis.htm) exist on how to understand and/or conduct meta-analyses.

Before moving on, we must alert you to a special caution. Never depend entirely on what you read in a secondary source. It has been noted, "Authors who write about the research or theories of others usually have different interests or backgrounds that lead them to overemphasize certain aspects and de-emphasize or leave out other aspects of the work" (Eichelberger, 1989, p.86). In short, if you are relying heavily on information presented in a secondary source, find the original article and confirm that the secondary source has reported it accurately.

Review General References

Once you have checked out secondary sources, you then need to turn your attention to locating and reviewing general references. ***General references*** identify primary sources, or publications that contain the reports of actual studies. ***Primary sources*** include research appearing in refereed journals, theses, dissertations, and reports published by governments or private organizations. Three popular general references are indices, abstracts, and bibliographies.

Indices list, by subject categories, the author, title, and place of publication. Many indices have been set up as online databases (Figure 3).

Figure 3. Indices with Holdings Related to Recreation, Park, Sport/Fitness and Tourism Topics.

ABI/Inform: Indexes articles from over 1,000 business journals, covering a variety of topics including personnel issues, consumer behavior, organizational behavior, and human resource management.

British Education Index: Provides contents of over 300 education and training journals published in The British Isles, dealing with evaluation and assessment, education policy and administration, and special education needs.

Cumulative Index to Nursing and Allied Health: Index to English-language and selected foreign-language journals covering nursing and specialized health care areas.

Current Contents Connect®: Bibliographic information from over 8,000 journals and 2,000 books and meeting abstracts related to the social and behavioral sciences.

Chicano Index: Contains citations of books, articles, reports and other documents written by and about Chicanos and other Latinos in the United States.

Current Index to Journals in Education: Published monthly, cites citations and brief abstracts on thousands of articles on educational topics published each year.

E-Psyche: The database journal source includes over 3,600 multidiscipline titles produced by approximately 1,000 publishers as well as dissertations, books, technical reports, Web sites, and conference proceedings.

Education Resources Information Center: Online bibliographic database with full-text non-journal documents that are available for free (go to www.eric.ed.gov).

Exceptional Child Education Resources: Contains 120,000 citations and abstracts related to exceptional children (both disabled and gifted). Cites related service references.

Expanded Academic Index: Abstracts articles (some available in full text) in more than 500 scholarly journals related to social science, health sciences, and humanities.

FastDoc: Contains citations from more than 1,000 journals that relate to science, social science, and arts and humanities.

GENMED: Collection of full text databases covering the contents of hundreds of journals (including health, social work, psychology, and biomedical).

Hispanic American Periodicals Index: Reference annual that indexes, by subject and author, over 400 social sciences and humanities journals.

Hospitality & Tourism Index: A bibliographic database indexing scholarly research relating to all areas of hospitality and tourism.

Index Medicus: Accesses, by subject field, approximately 4,100 biomedical national and international journals.

Index to Theses: Abstracts theses completed at universities in Great Britain and Ireland (go to www.theses.com).

INFOTRAC®: An online database that covers over 20 million full-text articles from over 6,000 scholarly periodicals (go to http://infotrac.thomsonlearning.com).

International Index to Black Periodicals: Cites articles, on an array of topics (education, health, sociology, etc.), appearing in 150 periodicals.

Leisure Tourism Database: An index to over 400 publications in the field of travel and tourism, recreation, leisure studies, and the hospitality and culture industries.

Physical Education Index: Subject index to literature (in coaching, dance, health, physical education, physical fitness, recreation, physical therapy, sports, and sports medicine) appearing in 303 national and international journals.

Proquest Dissertations and Theses: Contains dissertations and theses in over 3,000 subject areas from over 1,000 universities. Students, as institutional subscribers to this database, can download free titles published from 1997 onwards.

PsychARTICLES: Online data base containing full text articles from over 40 journals.

PsychINFO: Computer search database providing citations and abstracts to nearly 2,000 journals as well as dissertations and books dealing with psychology and behavioral sciences.

Science Citation Index: Citations and abstracts to more than 6,000 international social science and scientific journals.

Search ERIC: Online data base of education related journal articles and federally funded reports appearing in over 1,000 plus journals. Can download, for free, more than 100,000 documents in ERIC® (go to http://searcheric.org).

Social Sciences Citation Index®: Lists cited authors in over 1,700 social sciences journals (covering 50 disciplines) as well as authors who have discussed the cited works in articles. Using this index you can quickly build a collection of references that are likely to be very specific to your topic.

Social Science Index: Indexes and abstracts articles in hundreds of periodicals as well as provides full-text for some of the journal articles in the social sciences (such as sociology, psychology, anthropology, and environmental science).

SPORT DISCUS: Online data base that contains 500,000 references, 20,000 theses and dissertations, and 10,000 website addresses related to sports medicine, fitness, sport science, coaching, recreation, physical education, training, kinesiology, administration, sport law, and physical therapy.

TourCD: Contains 32,000 references from leisure, recreation and tourism abstracts.

University of Oregon's International Institute for Sport and Human Performance: Archives and distributes, in microfiche and in electronic formats, dissertations and theses related to exercise and sport sciences, health, physical education, and dance (go to http:// kinpubs.uoregon.edu/KinAbs.html).

Wilson Education Index: Covers a wide range of topics (e.g., athletics, instructional media, multicultural/ethnic education) in 79 journals (37 with full text) not covered by *Current Index to Journals in Education.*

In contrast to indices that only list citation information, **abstracts** additionally provide a short summary. Figure 4 identifies abstracts (most of these are available as online databases) containing holdings related to recreation, park, sport, and tourism topics.

Figure 4. Abstracts Containing Holdings Related to Recreation, Park, Sport and Tourism, Topics.

I. Abstracts of Research Published in Journals

Biological Abstracts: References biomedical and biological reports, reviews, and meeting literature; covers articles from nearly 7,000 periodicals.

*E*Subscribe:* Online electronic subscription service providing full-text access to Educational Resources Information Center (ERIC) documents.

MEDLINE: The National Library of Medicine's database of published medical citations and abstracts appearing in more than 4,800 international journals covering the fields of medicine, nursing, the health care system, and the preclinical sciences.

Psychological Abstracts: Covers over 1,300 journals, plus reports, monographs, and other documents (including books and other secondary sources); abstracts are presented in addition to bibliographical data.

PsycLit: Contains references and abstracts for articles from approximately 1,300 psychological and behavioral journals as well as book chapters and books.

Social Work Abstracts: Online data base containing more than 35,000 citations, with abstracts to journal articles, doctoral dissertations, and other materials on social work and related areas.

Sociofile: Contains abstracts to approximately 1,700 sociology and related journals as well as citations to dissertations, books, book chapters, and association papers.

Sociological Abstracts: Online data base providing abstracts of journal articles and citations to book reviews drawn from over 1,800 serials publications as well as abstracts of books, book chapters, dissertations and conference papers.

Women's Studies Abstracts: Provides citations with abstracts on women's studies that appear in 35 American and international journals.

II. Abstracts of Research Presented at Professional Meetings

Abstracts from the Annual Meeting of the American College of Sports Medicine: Published annually as a supplement to *Medicine and Science in Sports and Exercise.*

Abstracts from Research Consortium Program at the Annual Meeting of the American Alliance of Health, Physical Education, Recreation, and Dance: Published annually as a supplement to the *Research Quarterly for Exercise and Sport.*

Abstracts from the Annual Meeting of the Gerontological Society of America: Published in October as a supplement to the *Gerontologist.*

Abstracts from the Annual Meeting of the Leisure Research Symposium: Published annually by the National *Recreation & Park Association.*

A bibliography is also considered a general reference. A ***bibliography*** lists books and articles relevant to a specific topic.

Bibliographies can appear in three formats. First, a bibliography may appear as a feature or special article in a journal. Second, a bibliography may emerge as a freestanding publication. One such example of a freestanding bibliography is *The Literature and Research on Challenge Courses: An Annotated Bibliography* (Attarian & Holden, 2001). Third, a bibliography may emerge as a product of a bibliographic service. For example, *Focus on: Sports Science & Medicine* is a monthly bibliographic service (produced by the Institute for Scientific Information®, the same organization that publishes *Current Contents*) that reviews 900 source items related to biomechanics, conditioning, exercise, physiology, orthopedics, rehabilitation, sport psychology, and training.

Obtain Primary Sources

All literature searches should ultimately lead to primary sources. Most scientific research is published in refereed journals (see Appendix 1 for a listing of journals that publish articles on topics related to parks, recreation, sports, and fitness). ***Refereed journals*** are primary sources that print original research after the manuscript has been read and approved by peer researchers. An increasing number of journals are being distributed on the Internet (see the University of Houston's Libraries online bibliography at http://info.lib.uh.edu/wj/webjour.html).

All literature searches ultimately lead to primary sources. This often means you'll need to locate and read the journals subscribed to by a university library. *Copyright © 2008 Ruth V. Russell*

Something to Remember!

Do you know how people get their research published in refereed professional journals?

1. **Refereed journals use peer reviews.** *Peer review* means a manuscript submitted for publication consideration is reviewed and assessed by independent experts. The purpose of peer review is to assure the published manuscript meets the appropriate quality standards set by the journal.
2. **A majority of the editors of refereed journals are members of a university faculty and serve a three-year term.** An editor does not receive financial compensation to assume this responsibility.
3. **The editor typically convenes an editorial board, selecting educators and practitioners, based on their research expertise, interest, and availability.** Members of this editorial board are known as Associate Editors. Associate Editors serve three-year appointments.
4. **The process begins when a researcher sends a manuscript to the journal's editor.** Guidelines on manuscript requirements, as well as to whom and where to send the manuscript, appear in each edition of a journal.
5. **The editor then directs the submitted manuscript to an Associate Editor, who in turn is responsible for identifying two external experts (outside the Editorial Board) who agree to review it.** The submitted manuscript undergoes a *blind review*, meaning the author(s) of the manuscript are not revealed to the three reviewers.

6. **The editor combines the three reviews and makes the final decision about the manuscript.** Rejection rates vary, by year and by journal. The *Journal of Leisure Research,* for instance, reports that about: 20% of the submitted articles are rejected outright, 25% are rejected after full review, 20% of the papers not rejected are never revised and resubmitted by the researchers, and the remaining 35% are eventually published in the journal (D. Scott, personal communication, May 31, 2005). The rejection rate of the *Therapeutic Recreation Journal,* during 2002-2004, ranged between 27% - 79% (C. Hood, personal communication, June 3, 2005).

Idea . . . For Managing References.

Although computer software exists to help keep track of references (e.g., go to www.endnote.com/enabout.asp to learn about *EndNote®, ProCite®, Reference Manager®*), we found using a card approach is an easy way to manage literature review references (Figure 5).

1. **Keep cards in a box in alphabetical order by author's last name.** As you search for literature, you won't spend time completing and ordering a reference you already know about!
2. **Record on the card the general reference source for the article.** That way, if you mistakenly copied something incorrectly, you can go back and double check your general reference.
3. **Record on the card the date you make a request and from whom.** Regularly review what you have and have not received. Inevitably, delays occur because a lending library cannot find the reference. In this event, you may have to request the reference from another library.
4. **Once you receive the requested reference, make some notation on the note card (for example, a check in the upper right hand corner).** Also as a safety precaution, double check and make sure the article's front page contains all the information (e.g., year, volume, page numbers) you need in the citation.
5. **If a copy of an article or dissertation has been received or downloaded, then we suggest filing the articles alphabetically by author's last name in a notebook.** Being organized this way will save you a lot of time when you're searching for a particular article.
6. **One question often asked is how far back in time to search.** Your advisor, teacher, or consultant may have definite ideas about this, so check, but the common standard is to go back five years or when you reach the *saturation point,* that is the time where you're unearthing the same references over and over again. Sometimes, the five-year time frame must be extended, such as when little or no recent work can be found on the topic or a "cutting-edge" reference has been found. Generally speaking, it is important that the literature you cite is up to date.
7. **When you have identified all pertinent primary sources, the full-fledged review can begin.** It is a good idea to begin with the most current or recent articles and references and work backward. The rationale for this advice is that most of the more recent writings will provide you with current perspectives on the topic and most likely will have noted and incorporated earlier works on the topic.
8. **Last, but not least, be thorough and legible.** Just about every student we've advised (plus ourselves) has been forced, at the last moment, to back up and retrieve or confirm information that is needed for a citation (such as a volume number or page numbers).

Figure 5. Set Up for a Coded Reference Index Card (5" X 8").

Date Interlibrary Loan Request: **Lending University:**

Author(s) Last Name, First Name, Middle Initial:
Year:
Title:

Journal or Book Name (if chapter):

Volume: **Page Numbers:**

Publisher:

Publisher Location:

Source Cited or Database Retrieved From:

Status: **Needs to be Reviewed**   **Reviewed & Used**   **Reviewed & Don't Use**

Idea . . . For Finding References.

Two ideas for finding references related to your topic.

- **If a primary source turns out to be a winner, pay particular attention to its cited references.** Study the reference section of the article, double-checking to see if you already know about the cited references. If not, make a new note card. This snooping around can discover some important leads.
- **If you find a gold article, find out who else has used it.** The easiest way to do this is to consult the *Social Sciences Citation Index®*. This is a multidisciplinary index to journals, published proceedings, and monographic series in the social, behavioral, and related sciences. By using this index, you can identify primary sources that have cited the same article. You may wind up finding other outstanding references by using this cross reference approach.

Review and Analyze Primary Sources

After identifying a reference, its relevance to your study must be determined. *Relevance* of a primary or secondary source is established by the degree of similarity between the earlier work and your study. There should be some connecting link—the same topic, a shared theoretical foundation, or similar data collection methods.

We're proponents of involved, active reading. This works particularly well when you're reading photocopies of articles, dissertations, or short chapters (rather than books you have checked out of the library). Highlight and make marginal notations and/or bracket (in red pen) the important information. For instance, if the passage deals with theory, write "Theory" in the margin or bracket the word. Likewise, if the paragraph addresses a point you might use in your introduction, write "Intro" in the margin.

Idea . . . Identifying Ways a Research Article Can Help You.

One good way to help you organize and track those references you possibly or definitely plan to use, is to rely on a literature coding system. Figure 6 provides an example of how this coding system can be set up.

Across the top of the card color code (use color pencils, so if later you need to change a code you can easily do so) how or where you might use the source. For instance, if you find the reference has made a point you think will prove the significance of your study, color in the third boxed area from the left side of the card. Likewise, if this same reference is a research article dealing with the same sort of intervention you're planning to study, then color in the fifth grid.

Clearly, a reference can be useful to you at several different junctures. When you sit down to draft your "Introduction" section, for instance, you then can simply pull all the references with the appropriate color code. This simple system helps you keep track of what you've read and will be invaluable when putting the information together.

Figure 6. Reference Card Used for a Study Examining the Effects of a Martial Arts Course on Physical and Psychological Health of Deaf Collegians (Jackson, 2003).[1]

1	2	3	4	5	6	7	8	9	10	11	12	13	14	15	16

Authors: Hong Y., Li, J., & Robinson, R.
Title: Balance control, flexibility, and cardio respiratory fitness among older Tai Chi practitioners

Source or
Database: MEDLINE (FirstSearch)
From: *British Journal of Sports Medicine*, 2000 Feb, *34*(1), 29-34
Abstract: BACKGROUND: There has apparently been no research into the effects of Tai Chi Chuan (TTC) on total body rotation flexibility and heart rate responses at rest and after a three minute step test. METHODS: In this cross sectional study, 28 male TCC practitioners were recruited to form the TCC group. Another 30 sedentary men aged 66.2 were selected to serve as the control group. Measurements included resting heart rate, left and right single leg stance with eyes closed, modified sit and reach test, total body rotation test (left and right), and a three-minute step test. RESULTS: Compared with the sedentary group, the TCC group had significantly better scores in resting heart rate, three-minute step test heart rate, modified sit and reach, total body rotation test on both right and left side, and both right and left leg standing with eyes closed.

[1]Suggested grid labeling: #1 = Introduction (green), #2 = Theory (brown), #3 = Significance (teal), #4 = Sample (yellow), #5 = Intervention (black), # 6 = Design (lime), # 7 = Name of first dependent variable (red), #8 = Name of

second dependent variable (blue), #9 = Name of third dependent variable (tan) , #10 = Name of fourth dependent variable (purple), #11 = Name of first independent variable (teal), #12 = Name of second independent variable (orange), #13 = Name of third independent variable (turquoise), #14 = open slot (choose a label and color), # 15 = Data collection (maroon), #16 = Data analyses (pea green).

NOTE: This card reflects that after the study was retrieved and reviewed it was deemed to contain information that would be helpful to Jackson when he was writing the following parts of his own study: "Introduction," "Theory," "Significance of Study," "Intervention," and the following dependent variables that were the foci of Jackson's research, "Flexibility," "Balance," and "Body Image."

Technical knowledge of research design, measurement and statistics will help you read the literature with a "skeptical yet sympathetic eye that is equipped with the ability to detect crap" (Joiner, 1972, p. 1). It is important not to take other people's conclusions at face value. Instead, determine for yourself whether the conclusions are justified, based on the research methods used. As you learn more about research methods, you should be able to develop skills to help you to determine if the conclusions are justified.

Write Up the Literature Review

Another difficult task confronting literature reviewers, especially novice ones, is how to synthesize and organize what they have read (Eichelberger, 1989). The challenge is to demonstrate how earlier works contribute to your study.

Something to Remember!

Concerning the literature review, on my honor, I pledge I've:

- √ Incorporated relevant information.
- √ Included subheadings to guide the reader.
- √ Used recent or up-to-date references. When older references are used it's because they are classics.
- √ Relied, whenever possible, on primary sources rather than secondary sources.
- √ Not given the impression that I read first-hand a study when I did not. In instances where I can't obtain a copy of the primary reference, I acknowledge in the text that my citing or quoting has come from a secondary source.
- √ Cited contrary findings.
- √ Raised methodological or problematic issues.

A review of literature is typically summarized using one of two themes. That is, there is an integrative literature review and a theoretical review.

Integrative Literature Review

An *integrative literature review* summarizes past research on a topic. It should consist of three parts (Case 3):

Reader should understand topic

- *Introduction.* State what online databases were used for the literature review. Also inform the reader how the "Literature Review" section is organized.
- *Body.* A summary of previous research studies is presented. It is a good idea to use subsections corresponding to the major factors or variables (discussed in Step 4) examined in the study.
- *Conclusion.* Identify possible reasons for the contradictory results. Highlight differences in: sample, including who was involved in the studies and how they were chosen (discussed in Step 6), and, instruments used (covered in Step 8).

Siding w/ theories

Case 3. Organizing the Body of a Literature Review.

Let's suppose you're going to conduct an evaluative research project on how participating in an outdoor adventure experiential program affects the emotional safety, trust, and intimacy of college students. A possible outline for the body of the literature review is:

Literature Review

Adventure Program's Effect on Participants' Emotional Safety
First paragraph summarizes studies reporting significant positive changes.
Second paragraph summarizes studies reporting no significant changes.
Third paragraph summarizes studies reporting significant negative affects or changes.

Adventure Program's Effect on Participants' Trust
First paragraph summarizes studies reporting significant positive changes.
Second paragraph summarizes studies reporting no significant changes.

Adventure Program's Effect on Participants' Intimacy
First paragraph summarizes studies reporting significant positive changes.
Second paragraph summarizes studies reporting no significant changes.

There are numerous examples of integrative literature reviews. Examples of some that have been published are:

- Benefits of inclusive volunteering (Miller, Schleien, Brooke, Fisoli, & Brooks, 2005).
- Women and leisure (Henderson, Hodges, & Kivel, 2002).
- Park marketing (Vogt & Andereck, 2002).
- Economic studies relating to sports tournaments (Crompton & Lee, 2000).
- Massage as a therapeutic recreation facilitation technique (Brownlee & Dattilo, 2002).
- Processing, a facilitation technique designed to promote learning, awareness, and change (Hutchinson & Dattilo, 2001).

If you find a lot of literature on the topic, a shorthand way to present the information found, is to use a summary figure (Case 4). This results in presenting a lot of information in a limited amount of space. Nevertheless, the "Introduction" and "Conclusion" sections should always be presented.

Case 4. Integrative Review: Effects of Selected Therapeutic Recreation Activities on the Elderly.

Investigator(s)	Subjects	TR Activity	Theoretical Foundations	Focus	Measure(s)	Outcome(s)
Cutler Riddick (1985)	Older residents in a public subsidized housing complex with a senior center N=22 (Randomly assigned to one of three groups: an aquarium group, a visitor group, or a control group)	Goldfish aquariums were placed in participants' homes; nine bi-weekly visits from the researcher (from 25-35 min./visit) for six months. Visitor group received 10 bi-weekly visits from the re-searcher (from 30-40 min./visit) for six months.	None	Blood pressure	Sphygmomanometer	Significant decrease in diastolic blood pressure in aquarium group (from the pre- to post-test)
DeSchriver & Cutler Riddick (1990)	Older residents in a public subsidized housing complex N=27 (Randomly assigned to one of three groups: viewed a fish aquarium, viewed a fish vid-eotape, or viewed a placebo videotape)	Viewing of the fish aquarium, fish videotape, or placebo videotape lasted eight minutes, once a week, over a three-week period	Relaxation Theory	Pulse rate Skin tempera-ture General skeletal muscle ten-sion	Lumiscope Digitronic I Model (beats per minute) Yellow Springs Temperature meter Bicep Electromyography (EMG)	No significant change No significant change No significant change
Gowing (1984)	Elderly home health care recipients N=33 (non-equivalent control group design)	Minimal care pets (goldfish) for a six-week period	None	Blood pressure	Sphygmomanometer (assumed, not stated)	No significant improve-ment when comparing pre- and posttest scores
Green (1989)	Elderly community residents enrolled in a community service program N=24 (one-group pretest-posttest design)	Water aerobic program (two times a week for 16 weeks)	None	Blood pressure Resting pulse	Sphygmomanometer Pulse rate	Significant reduction in diastolic blood pressure (when comparing pre- and posttest scores) No significant improvement

[1]From Riddick and Keller (1991). Reprinted with permission of the authors.

Theoretical Literature Review

A *theoretical literature review* can consist of one or more parts. First, the theoretical approach used to conduct the research should always be clearly identified. And, second, if the design and/or delivery of the intervention is directed by a theory, this theory also needs to be reviewed (Case 5).

Case 5. Example of a Theoretical Literature Review.

Jackson, F. (2003). *Effects of a martial arts course on physical and psychological health of deaf collegians.* Unpublished master's thesis, Gallaudet University, Washington, DC.

The intent of this study was to develop and then evaluate how a martial arts curriculum impacted on college students enrolled in the course. Theory guided the study in two ways. First, triangulation of methods was used as the approach to conduct the study. In particular, somatopsychic theory guided some of the hypotheses testing. And adoption of grounded theory resulted in asking study participants to identify, in their own words, any benefits they derived from participating in the martial arts course. Second, social learning theory influenced curriculum design. Using this theory, a martial arts curriculum was developed and implemented that used a five-step process: instruction, observation, modeling, imitation, and social reinforcement.

Your Research

1. Using the topic you've chosen (Step One), identify at least three keywords that can be used to conduct a literature search.
2. Using at least two general reference databases, locate three primary sources (such as research articles and dissertations) on your topic. If need be, use different keywords. Print the citation and abstract of these three primary sources.
3. Obtain a copy of each of these primary references.
4. Complete a reference index card for each of the three located primary sources.
5. Read one retrieved article adopting the involved active reader's posture described in this chapter. After you read the research article, color code (see Figure 6) the reference index card.

Review and Discussion Questions . . .
What have you learned about conducting a literature review?

1. What five purposes can be served by conducting a literature review?
2. What is a "keyword" and how is it used in online database searches?
3. What is the difference between a "secondary source," "general reference," and a "primary source?"
4. What does it mean to say a research manuscript appears in a "refereed" journal? Why are refereed journal articles considered primary sources?
5. Identify five pointers when writing up a literature review.

6. **What is the difference when writing an integrative literature review versus a theoretical literature review?**

Exercises

1. If your instructor does not assign you a research article appearing in a refereed journal, then choose an article on a topic of interest to you. Did the article:
   A. Cite literature to identify a conceptual approach used to conduct the research?
   B. Contain an integrative review of literature?
   C. Cite theoretical writings that were the foundation for hypotheses testing?
   D. Contain references to bolster the significance of the study?
   E. If a program or intervention was used, identify literature to support the program design?
   F. Identify literature to document instrumentation used to conduct the study?
   G. Rely on earlier writings or studies to explain and interpret results?

2. Familiarize yourself with some secondary sources available at Wilderdom's Outdoor Education Research and Evaluation Center (www.wilderdom.com). Complete the two tasks below and briefly summarize what you learned.
   A. Examine a research review by clicking on "Outdoor Education Research and Evaluation Center," under "Outdoor Education" click on "Research," and finally click on "Summary of the Effects of Outdoor Education."
   B. Now, examine a outdoor education meta-analyses by tracing the following three links at the Wilderdom site: click on "Outdoor Education Research and Evaluation Center," under "Outdoor Education" click on "Research," and finally click on "Meta-Analytic Research Reviews."

3. Examine some bibliographies that exist on the American Camp Association's Webpage at www.acacamps.org. Click on "Research," go to "Bibliography Search Box" and click on "Camp-Based Research Bibliographies."
   A. Conduct a search on two topics of your choice.
   B. What did you find?

4. Check out online general reference sources. Visit the following sites and indicate which you found most useful and why.
   A. American Psychological Association's, "PsycNet" at www.apa.org.
   B. "PsychWeb" at www.psywww.com.
   C. McMaster University's "WWW Virtual Library" at http://socserv2.mcmaster.ca/w3virtsoclib/.
   D. Wilderdom's "Outdoor Education Bibliographies, Reference Lists, Abstracts, Databases, and Indexes" at www.wilderdom.com/bibliographies.html.

5. Related to the kind of information provided by the *Social Sciences Citation Index*® (covered in the *Idea* box appearing earlier in this chapter) is a journal's impact factor. A ***journal's impact factor*** is purportedly a measure of a journal's importance and is calculated by determining the

average annual citation rate of a journal's articles over a defined period of time (usually the previous two years). In other words, how many times articles appearing in several issues of a particular journal are cited in the reference lists of articles appearing in other refereed journals is calculated.

    A. Read more about a journal's impact factor by going to www.sportsci.org.

    B. After studying information presented at this Web site, what journals in your major discipline are missing from the presented list?

    C. What issues or concerns might be raised about using a journal's impact factor?

Conducting a thorough review of the information available about your study topic helps point the way to the project's significance, as well as determines the best research approach, methods, and means of analyzing results. Theatre District, London, England. *Copyright © 2008 Carol Cutler Riddick*

STEP 3: Identify Theoretical Underpinnings

What is Theory?

Why Use Theory in Research?

Theory and the Leisure Research Gap

Theoretical Approaches for Conducting Research
Quantitative Approach
  Deductive Reasoning and Theory Testing
  Structured Inquiry
Qualitative Approach
  Inductive Reasoning and Theory Development
  Unstructured or Semistructured Inquiry
Mixed-Methods Approach

A theory is more impressive the greater the simplicity of its premises,
the more different the kinds of things it relates and
the more extended its range of applicability.
Albert Einstein

What is Theory?

Theory is used at every step of the research process. Theoretical frameworks influence the questions we ask, the design of the study, the collection of data, and the way we interpret findings. As researchers we have an obligation to account for our theoretical postures.

Yet, finding a theory to serve as the basis of a research project is a difficult task. Formally, *theory* has been defined as "a logically interrelated set of propositions about empirical reality" (Schutt, 2006, p. 69). Theories have been referred to as "tools of interpretation . . . as a form of scaffolding by which we build explanations about the social world we inhabit" (Maguire & Young, 2002, p. 3).

In simple terms, a theory is an explanation or assertion of why and how things happen. Other words used interchangeably with theory are *paradigms* or *models* or *epistemology.*

A *formal theory* comes about when someone, after observing the social world, tries to organize, explain, or understand how social phenomena are related or are connected (Jasso, 2001). All theories are tentative explanations of reality. Ideally, the formal theory is *parsimonious,* meaning it provides a short and concise explanation of reality.

Something to Remember!

No matter what anyone asserts, remember a theory can either be supported or not supported. A theory can never be proved; instead all theories are provisional. While empirical testing results may support a theory, there are always alternative explanations.

> " . . . corroboration gives only the comfort that the theory has been tested and survived the test, that even after the most impressive collaborations . . . it has only achieved the status of 'not yet disconfirmed.' This . . . is far from the status of 'being true'." (Cook & Campbell, 1979, p. 20)

Theories vary in their complexity, from simple to intricate, but they all do essentially the same thing. They build relationships between or among concepts (Figure 1). A *concept* (sometimes called a construct) is a label chosen to describe some phenomenon. A *phenomenon* can be concrete or abstract. A *concrete phenomenon* is an object, trait, or behavior that is found or can be observed in the physical environment. In contrast, an *abstract phenomenon* is something not visible to the naked eye; instead, it is an intrinsic trait or characteristic, such as a feeling or attitude. Ultimately, then, a theory links together concepts that describe either a concrete or abstract phenomenon.

Figure 1. Theory Construction: Bridging Conceptual Relationships.

Concepts need to be defined further. Breaking down or defining a concept entails identifying variables. A ***variable***, provides a "nominal definition" of the concept by addressing characteristics or qualities of a person or object. A variable must have a minimum of two attributes or values that are mutually exclusive (Babbie, 2004). Examples of variables are gender (two possible values exist for the attribute of gender: male or female) and social class (three values can be set for social class: lower class, middle class and upper class). Any number of variables can be identified for any given concept (Figure 2).

Figure 2. The Effects of Physical Fitness Training on Psychological Affect: Examples of Variables, or Nominal Definitions.

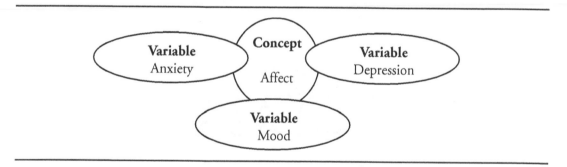

Let's apply this to recreation, parks, sports, and tourism. As we mentioned in Step One, one way to carve up the social world we live in is to think of our service profession affecting one (or more) of three aspects of our lives: our physical health, social health, and mental health. Each of these three concepts is very broad and could be nominally defined any number of ways.

For example, think of each of these three concepts—physical health, mental health, and social health—as being overarching umbrellas. The individual spokes of the umbrella represent a variable that is related to the concept under consideration (Figures 3-5).

concept = body

Figure 3. Physical Health as an Umbrella Concept and Related Spoke Variables.

Variables

Body Fat —

Activities of Daily Living

Blood Pressure —

Resting Pulse Rate

Figure 4. Mental Health as an Umbrella Concept and Related Spoke Variables.

Depression

Playfulness

Happiness

Anxiety

Figure 5. Social Health as an Umbrella Concept and Related Spoke Variables.

Trust —

Belonging

Cohesiveness —

Teamwork

Make literature fit the outline!!

Admittedly, this is a lot of information to remember. To recall what we have just learned, first you begin broadly. Then, you become more specific when you narrow down the concept by identifying a corresponding variable.

An analogy to this is hearing a friend exclaim, "Life is good." If you ask that person to clarify his/her statement and he/she replies, "I was just offered a great job when I graduate," then you're moving from a concept (the good life) to a specific variable (Employment status after graduation).

Something to Remember!

<table>
<tr><td colspan="2">It is vital that you master the following nomenclature. Please commit these definitions to memory.</td></tr>
<tr><td>**Word**</td><td>**Definition**</td></tr>
<tr><td>*Theory*</td><td>Identifies relationships between and among concepts in order to explain *why* or *how* things happen.</td></tr>
<tr><td>*Concept*</td><td>Label or name assigned to describe:
• ***Concrete phenomenon*** or an object, trait, or behavior that is found or observed in the physical environment.
• ***Abstract phenomenon*** or something not visible to the naked eye; instead, it is an intrinsic trait or characteristic.</td></tr>
<tr><td>*Variable*</td><td>• Elaboration or nominal definition of concept.
• Characteristic or trait that describes a person or object.
• At least two values or categories must exist.</td></tr>
</table>

Why Use Theory in Research?

There are two overriding reasons to use theory in research, as well as in professional practice. First, as already mentioned, theory directs research. If topics are selected and researched without any theoretical connections, shallowness and a lack of direction and focus may result (Ellis, 1993). It has been pointed out that " . . . theory gives shape to material that would otherwise appear shapeless" (Rojek, 1997, p. 383).

A theoretical foundation can influence how a study is conducted at a number of junctures. Theory can be used to:

- Establish a rationale for what is being examined (or identify the phenomena under study).
- Direct data-collection methods.
- Assist with interpreting the results.

- Make conclusions about how well the theory captures what is happening in the real world.

A second reason for grounding our research in theory is that it enables us to build a body of knowledge related to leisure (Burdge, 1985). Having a body of knowledge to refer to, informs professional practice, as well as the public, about what we know, what we do, and how we do it (Case 1). Research findings that have a theoretical connection, can ultimately lead to improved service delivery, effective leisure functioning, and a higher quality of life (Coyle, Kinney, Riley & Shank, 1991; Dunn, 1996).

Case 1. *Theory Based Study Directs Service Delivery Process and Guides an Impact Study.*

Ellis, J., Braff, E., & Hutchinson, S. (2001).Youth recreation and resiliency: Putting theory into practice in Fairfax County. *Therapeutic Recreation Journal, 35,* 301-317.

This publication focuses on Fairfax County, Virginia's Department of Community and Recreation Services efforts to incorporate theories of therapeutic recreation practice in revamping teen center programs. In particular, principles associated with the Leisure Ability Model, the Health Protection/ Health Promotion Model, and the Aristotelian Good Life Model served as the basis for operating teen center programs that fostered self-responsibility and self-directed leisure engagement. Ellis (as cited by Ellis, Braff, & Hutchinson) conducted a study of the teen centers that had implemented therapeutic recreation theories in their operations.

> "The results indicated that, when compared to a traditionally run community cen-ter teen program, the teen center participants developed a greater sense of self-ef-ficacy . . . and sense of voice . . . participants felt more confident they were respected by program leaders and other adults in the community." p. 314

Theory and the Leisure Research Gap

Even though we have attempted to emphasize why theory should be used in research, the re-ality is that many individuals choose not to articulate any theoretical foundation for their studies. This state of affairs is revealed by the results of reviews that rated the quality of research publica-tions appearing in our professional journals.

One such review examined articles published in four of our research journals (*Journal of Leisure Research, Leisure Sciences, Journal of Park and Recreation Administration,* and *Therapeutic Recreation Journal*), from 1981 to 1990 (Henderson, 1994). Of the almost 700 studies reviewed, about one-half did not address theory testing or theory development at all.

A follow-up study, involving articles published in the same four journals from 1992-2002, found the gap between theory and research had widened over time (Henderson, Presley, & Biale-schki, 2004). Three-fourths of the studies appearing in the aforementioned journals in this later time period made no attempt to test or develop a theory.

In sum, these published "report cards" on the quality of research in our profession underscore the divide between what should be and what is. Clearly, our track record reveals that theoretical foundations have not underpinned the bulk of published research.

Theoretical Approaches for Conducting Research

We nonetheless advocate that every research project should acknowledge the theoretical approach to inquiry adopted. Each of us has a mind set that helps us understand phenomena by advancing assumptions we have about the social world, defining what the problem is, and directing us on how the research inquiry shall proceed (Creswell, 2003). Mind sets help us break down the complexity of the real world; tell us what is important, legitimate and reasonable; and tell us what to do (Patton, 1987). Therefore, we should own up to our theoretical mindsets when preparing a research study project.

While asking you to identify a theoretical approach to inquiry may sound daunting, it really isn't. You essentially need to choose between a quantitative approach, a qualitative approach or a *mixed-methods* approach—a blend of quantitative and qualitative approaches. As Steps 7 and 9 will explain, the theoretical approach adopted for a study will have profound implications for the subsequent design and data-collection tools used for the study.

A quantitative approach is distinctly different from a qualitative approach (Figure 6), and to make things even more complicated, each goes by a variety of names. A *quantitative approach* to research has many labels, including postpostivist theory, empirical science, and normative theory. A *qualitative approach* to research is referred to as social constructivism theory, interpretative theory, and ideographic theory (Creswell, 2003).

Figure 6. Comparison of Quantitative and Qualitative Approaches to Research.

Quantitative Approach or Postpositivist Theory	Qualitative Approach or Social Constructivism Theory
Social reality is constant across different settings and times, thus universal facts exist.	Social reality is immediate and varies across settings and times.
Social reality is objective.	Social reality is subjective.
Goal is to conduct explanatory or predictive research.	Goal is to conduct descriptive research.
Questions relationships between and among phenomena.	Questions what and how.
Uses deductive logic.	Uses inductive logic.
Theory testing.	Theory development.
Samples a larger number of individuals than a qualitative study.	Samples smaller number of persons than a quantitative study.
Directed by structured inquiry that uses close-ended interviews, questionnaires, observations, or record reviews.	Directed by unstructured inquiry or semi-structured inquiry, meaning open-ended interviews, questionnaires, observations, or record reviews having no preset response categories.

Quantitative Approach or Postpositivist Theory	Qualitative Approach or Social Constructivism Theory
Data collection typically undertaken outside a program setting.	Data collection typically undertaken in a natural setting of a program.
Researcher is most likely to be "detached" from the study participants.	Researcher often develops a rapport and involvement with study participants.
Relies on numerical data.	Relies on non numerical data.

Quantitative Approach

A *quantitative approach* acquires knowledge by relying on " . . . cause and effect thinking, reduction to specific variables and hypotheses and questions, use of measurement . . . and collects data using predetermined instruments that yield statistical data" (Creswell, 2003, p.18). As you may have guessed, this approach originally was used in the natural sciences such as biology, chemistry and physics. Over time, individuals working in the social science disciplines, such as psychology and sociology, also adopted a quantitative approach to research. Two things that set a quantitative approach apart from a qualitative approach are its use of deductive reasoning and structured inquiry.

Deductive reasoning and theory testing. The crux of the difference between a quantitative approach versus a qualitative approach to research evolves around *logic* or reasoning (Figure 7). The quantitative approach relies on deductive reasoning. *Deductive reasoning* "moves from the general to the specific . . . from: (1) a pattern that might be logically or theoretically expected to (2) observations that test whether the expected pattern actually occurs . . . deduction begins with 'why' and moves to 'whether'" (Babbie, 2004, p. 25).

Figure 7. Linkages Among Logic, Theory and Observation.

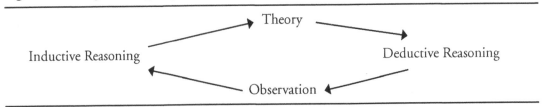

Deductive reasoning is why the quantitative approach to conducting a research project most often, but not always, is associated with theory testing. *Theory testing* consists of identifying a formal theory purporting to shed some light on how certain concepts are related and determining if they can be observed in reality. This is accomplished by way of *hypotheses,* which are discussed in depth in Step 4.

Finding a theory to test can come about in one of two ways. One approach is to examine a formal theory that has been proposed by someone else, known as *a priori theory testing.* Formal theories can be found by reading research articles or reports (Cases 2 and 3) or by consulting theory references (Appendix 2). Every once in a while you will find theoretical musings or applications dealing with a specific recreational activity. For instance, theories describing videogame play (Wolf & Perron, 2003) exist.

Case 2. Example of a Quantitative Approach to Research: Relying on Formal Theory to Guide the Study.

Nour, K., Desrosiers, J., Gauthie, P., & Carbonneau, H. (2002). Impact of a home leisure educational program for older adults who have had a stroke. *Therapeutic Recreation Journal, 36*, 48-64.

The objective of this study was to evaluate the impact of a leisure education program on the depression and quality of life of older adults who have had strokes and had been discharged from a rehabilitation program. Using several behavioral and social cognitive theories, a leisure education program was developed. A randomized clinical trial design was used to test the hypothesis that participation in the leisure education program would result in increased psychological adjustment. Participants were assigned to two groups, an experimental leisure education group (six persons) and a placebo "friendly visit" group (seven persons). Study participants received 10 individual sessions at home. Participants receiving the home leisure education program performed significantly better on psychological and physical quality of life measures than placebo participants. No significant improvement was found for depression. It was concluded that the findings supported the behavioral and social theories related to empowerment and self management.

Case 3. Studies Using a Quantitative Approach to Research.

Caldwell, L, Baldwin, C., Walls, T., & Smith, E. (2004). Preliminary effects of a leisure education program to promote healthy use of free time among middle school adolescents. *Journal of Leisure Research, 36*, 310-335.

Conatser, P., & Block, M. (2001). Aquatic instructors' beliefs toward inclusion. *Therapeutic Recreation Journal, 35*, 170-184.

Jones, D., Hollenhorst, S., Perna, F., & Selin, S. (2000). Validation of the flow theory in an on-site whitewater kayaking setting. *Journal of Leisure Research, 32*, 247-261.

Long, T., Ellis, G., Trunnell, E., Tatsugawa, K., & Freeman, P. (2001). Animating recreation experiences through face-to-face leadership: Efficacy of two models. *Journal of Park and Recreation Administration, 19*, 1-22.

A second way theory testing can unfold in the quantitative approach is by model development and testing. In **model development and testing** the ways in which various concepts relate to each other are outlined, based on integrating the works of others. More specifically, based on a review of literature, model development or **conceptual mapping** occurs by identifying a relationship or linkage (either graphically or in narrative form) between two or more concepts. Data are then collected to determine if there is support for the proposed model (Case 4). Model development and testing is also considered a priori theory testing.

Case 4. Theory Testing by Conceptual Mapping.

Barnes, M., & McCarville, R. (2005). Patron or philanthropist: Charitable giving to a performance-based leisure provider. *Journal of Park and Recreation Administration, 23*, 110-134.

What Assignment 4 should look like

The goal of the study was to identify a model that best explains charitable giving to a local not-for-profit symphony orchestra. The theoretical foundation for the study was the social exchange theory. It was anticipated that people who make charitable donations do so because of their expectation of receiving something in exchange for their donation.

Based on a review of literature, five factors were linked to charitable giving: incentives, opportunity assessment, involvement, empathy, and social norms. A schematic of the tested model is the following:

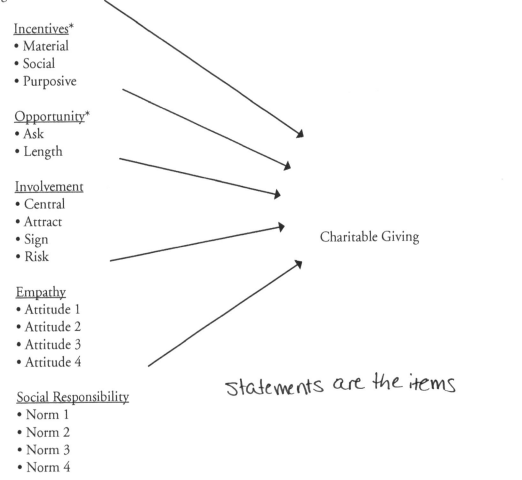

Incentives*
• Material
• Social
• Purposive

Opportunity*
• Ask
• Length

Involvement
• Central
• Attract
• Sign
• Risk

Empathy
• Attitude 1
• Attitude 2
• Attitude 3
• Attitude 4

Social Responsibility
• Norm 1
• Norm 2
• Norm 3
• Norm 4

Charitable Giving

Statements are the items

* Significant at the .05 level.

Data were collected at a local nonprofit symphony in Canada. Using random selection, 500 donors, from a list of approximately 1,500, were selected to receive a mail survey. The response rate was about 46%. Structural equation modeling was used to analyze data.

It was found that individuals were more likely to make charitable donations when they received incentives. Specifically, the following variables were significantly linked to charitable giving to the local symphony orchestra: (1) material incentive (such as a tax incentive), (2) social incentive (for instance, the intangible reward of the sense of group membership), (3) purposive incentive (for example, making a donation to help preserve the symphony), (4) request by a friend to make the charitable dona-tion, and (5) previous donor for an extended amount of time.

It was concluded that patrons of performance-based programs (such as symphony orchestras, sports teams, concert facilities, performing arts groups) are concerned with improving services they too can enjoy. Implications for fund-raising approaches were discussed, including the importance of appeal-ing to patron support in order to maintain high quality symphony performances. Findings were also discussed in terms of reinforcing the social exchange theory.

Structured inquiry. Deductive logic requires reasoning toward observations, meaning there must be systematic collection of data to evaluate how well a theoretical explanation holds up when scrutinized. Data are gathered by using structured interviews, questionnaires, observational checklists, projective methods, or record reviews (all of which are reviewed in greater depth in Step 9). **Structured inquiry** involves asking specific questions or observing specific behaviors and using **close-ended** or predetermined, preset categories to record the answers.

An example of structured inquiry is asking, "Indicate the extent you agree that our universi-ty's tennis courts are adequately maintained." Respondents are then asked to answer by selecting one of five multiple choice answers, "Strongly Agree," "Somewhat Agree," "Undecided/Don't Know," "Somewhat Disagree," and "Strongly Disagree."

Qualitative Approach

The **qualitative approach,** on the other hand, acquires knowledge by understanding the meaning study participants give to their lives and experiences, and the process by which events and actions take place (Maxwell, 1997). The qualitative approach is based on the notion that so-cial life varies across settings and times and is therefore "designed to capture social life as partici-pants experience it, rather than in categories predetermined by the researcher" (Schutt, 2006, p. 17). This approach has been embraced by many anthropologists, social workers, and sociologists.

Incidentally, Sherlock Holmes could be considered a follower of the qualitative theoretical approach. In Arthur Conan Doyle's *A Scandal in Bohemia,* Sherlock states, "It is a capital mistake to theorize before one has data. Insensibly one begins to twist facts to suit theories, instead of theories to suit facts."

Inductive reasoning and theory development. A qualitative approach uses **inductive reason-ing** that moves " . . . from the particular to the general, from a set of specific observations to the discovery of a pattern that represents some degree of order among all the given events" (Babbie, 2004, p. 25). In other words, interviews or observations are completed and then time is taken to reflect on the gathered information in order to articulate patterns or general principles that explain the relationship between the objects observed (Babbie, 2004). To help in understanding all this, take another look at Figure 7.

Thus, based on observations, theory emerges at the end of the study. Consequently, the qualitative approach is also referred to as an **ex post facto** explanation of phenomena.

Theories that can direct studies using a qualitative approach can also be found by reading research articles or reports (Cases 5 and 6). Additionally, a number of excellent qualitative theory references are available (see Appendix 3).

Case 5. Example of a Qualitative Approach to Research: Emerging Theory.

Klitzing, S. (2004). Women living in a homeless shelter: Stress, coping and leisure. *Journal of Leisure Research, 36,* 483-512.

The intent of the study was to learn more about stress, coping, and leisure experienced by women who were homeless. An interpretative paradigm steered the research project.

> "Feminist standpoint theory was used as the theoretical framework, and thus guided the process of designing and conducting the study, as well as the interpretation of the data . . . feminist standpoint theory . . . emphasizes that the everyday lives and experiences of women, especially women who have been oppressed or marginalized, should be the starting place for research." (p. 490)

A semistructured interview was conducted with 11 women. At the conclusion of this first interview the women were given a disposable camera and asked to snap pictures that captured their feelings on such things as: what they enjoy, what is fun for them, how they relax, and what helps them cope with stress. A second semistructured interview was set up to view the developed pictures and discuss the women's explanations of the photos. Interviews were analyzed and coded to identify themes that emerged from the women's insights. Likewise, the photos were examined, using microanalysis, to identify major categories of experiences. Data analyses from these sources revealed two themes.

The first theme that emerged from the interviews and photographs was about "experiencing stress." Most of the women had experienced stress almost all of their lives and had encountered long standing relationship problems. Frequently, the negative events in their lives that caused stress were finding jobs and housing, finding and keeping childcare, and the hassles of living in a shelter. The second theme that was evident dealt with coping with stress. Three subthemes for coping with stress were identified: diversionary activities, getting away, and social support. The use of feminist theory in this research revealed, contrary to previous research, women who are homeless: (a) face multiple types of stress in their lives, and (b) use leisure as a context for coping.

Case 6. Studies Using a Qualitative Approach.

Autry, C. (2001). Adventure therapy with girls at-risk: Responses to outdoor experiential activities. *Therapeutic Recreation Journal, 35,* 289-306.

Ford, N., & Brown, D. (2005). *Surfing and social theory: Experience, embodiment and narrative of the dream glide.* London: Routledge.

Shannon, C., & Shaw, S. (2005). "If the dishes don't get done today, they'll get done tomorrow": A breast cancer experience as a catalyst for changes to women's leisure. *Journal of Leisure Research, 37,* 195-215.

Sugden, J., & Tomlinson, A. (1999). Digging the dirt and staying clean: Retrieving the investigative tradition for a critical sociology of sport. *Internatioal Review for the Sociology of Sport, 34,* 385-397. (NOTE: Uses a critical interpretative framework to describe the world of football ticket scalpers.)

Uriely, N., Yonay, Y., & Dalit, S. (2002). Backpacking experiences: A type and form analysis. *Annals of Tourism Research, 29,* 520-538.

White, D., Hall, T., & Farrell, T. (2001). Influence of ecological impacts and other campsite characteristics on wilderness visitors' campsite choices. *Journal of Park and Recreation Administration, 19,* 83-107.

Unstructured or semistructured inquiry. Adoption of a qualitative framework requires using nonnumerical data that emerge from open-ended questions or observation (covered in greater detail in Step 9). An ***open-ended question*** or observation means the answers are not predetermined, thus the individual or observer is not forced to choose an answer from a list of given possibilities. Instead, the researcher "listens and learns" from participants (Morse & Richards, 2002).

Information is collected by using either unstructured inquiry or semistructured inquiry. ***Unstructured inquiry*** means posing one, or possibly a few open-ended question(s), or conducting open-ended observations. For instance, an unstructured interview could begin by asking Elder Hostel participants the following question: "Tell me about your impressions of your week-long Elder Hostel experience."

The purpose behind an unstructured interview is to " . . . let the participant tell his or her story . . . and if you have not learned about all aspects of whatever it is you want to know, you can ask questions" or probes when the participant finishes speaking (Morse & Richards, 2002, p.93). A ***probe*** is a follow-up question " . . . designed to elicit further information" (Morse & Richards, 2002, p. 93).

Semistructured inquiry entails developing, in advance, a series of open-ended questions or observations, along with prepared probes. Additionally, unplanned, unanticipated probes may be used. For example, Elder Hostel program participants may be asked to discuss, in a focus group, the following question, "Explain the reasons you decided to enroll in this Elder Hostel Program." After some discussion, the interviewer may probe the group regarding their thoughts about whether any of four possible motives—socialization, boredom, education, or challenge—factored into their decision to participate in the program.

Regardless of whether unstructured or semistructured inquiry is used, inductive logic dictates sorting through the resultant data to determine their significance. The ultimate goal is to develop a theoretical understanding of what has been learned or examined at the point in time the data were collected. Typically, the researcher interprets peoples' thoughts, feelings, or behaviors by identifying themes.

Idea . . . Finding a Theoretical Base for Your Research.

Searching for theoretical foundation options for your research? Consider completing a ***provenance grid*** (Jankowicz, 2004). The grid can be completed one of two ways. One strategy is to begin by identifying a topic and then searching through various disciplines to locate applicable theories. Another tactic is to first identify a specific theory used within a discipline, then figure out how to apply the theory to a topic. To illustrate the first strategy, suppose you want to conduct research on the topic of athletic performance. Sifting through various disciplines, you complete a provenance grid identifying theories that possibly lend themselves to your topic:

Discipline	Theory
Psychology	Social facilitation theory (Zajonc, 1965) focuses on the interplay of how task difficulty, skill level, and type of audience/crowd affect performance.
Sport Psychology	Sport competition anxiety theory (Martens, Vealey, & Burton, 1990) speculates how player anxiety affects performance.
Anthropology	Grounded theory (Glaser & Strauss, 1967) directs an examination of athletes' performance feelings and behaviors.
Sociology	Feminist theory (Swigonski, 1994) focuses on the feelings, attitudes, and perceptions of female athletes when participating in athletic competition.

In summary, it is important to remember that both deductive and inductive logic are means to the construction and/or refinement of theories (Babbie, 2004). "Deductive and inductive studies have the potential for informing theory depending on whether the theory is being tested or generated" (Henderson, 1994, p. 6).

Mixed-Methods Approach

Both quantitative and qualitative approaches to research have been criticized.

"Poorly conducted normative studies can produce findings that are so trivial as to contribute little to the body of research. On the other hand, interpretive studies can be so isolated, subjective, and idiosyncratic that there is no hope of any generalization or contribution to a greater body of knowledge." (Black, 1994, p. 3)

Yet, both quantitative and qualitative approaches have merit. To maximize their advantages, and minimize their disadvantages, increasingly both methods are being used together in research investigations. This practice is known as ***mixed-methods*** or ***triangulation***. A mixed-methods approach yields different views or slices of complementary data, which can guard against biases that may otherwise emerge when using a single approach (Case 7). Mixed-methods, or triangulation, allow researchers to transcend the disadvantages associated with any one approach (Sale, Lohfeld, & Brazil, 2002). Case 8 lists sample studies using a mixed-methods approach.

Case 7. Mixed-Methods Approach for Guiding Research on Littering.

Littering is a problem in park settings. Numerous theories exist that could be used to guide research on this topic. A few of these theories have been categorized below under either a *Quantitative Approach* or a *Qualitative Approach*. Refer to these summaries, and answer the following two questions. One of your answers should use a quantitative approach and the other answer should use a qualitative theory.

1. Suppose you were undertaking a research project designed to reduce littering. Which theoretical approach, from the list below, would you adopt to guide your work?
2. Then imagine you are interested in discovering the reasons behind littering behavior. Which theoretical approach would you choose to guide this basic research orientation?

Quantitative Approach:

Deterrence Theory speculates that people do not break the law when they perceive the costs outweigh benefits (Lempert & Sanders, 1986). The theory also proposes that people who are punished (e.g., fined for littering), because they broke the law, will not engage in the behavior again since they don't want to face punishment again.

According to the *Labeling Theory,* when a person is publicly tagged as being a deviant, the questionable behavior will continue (Hagan, 1994). Thus, an application of this theory is that being punished and labeled as a litterbug will promote more of the same behavior. The psychology behind this theory is that branding a person encourages him/her to "live up" to that label. In other words, labeling leads to a self-fulfilling prophecy.

The *Protection Motivation Theory* asserts that rule compliance is affected by exposure to awareness-of-consequences information (Gramann, Bonifeld, & Kim, 1995). Using this theory, hypothetically one would expect that individuals receiving sanction information upon park entry (such as a brochure outlining the fines imposed on people who litter) will be less likely to break littering rules compared to people who do not receive this information.

Qualitative Approach:

Grounded Theory directs discovery by asking people to explain their own behaviors (Creswell, 2003). In-depth unstructured interviews with people who litter could be conducted in order to determine the cause(s) of their behavior. Information learned from these interviews would be reviewed for themes or categories of reasons that explain littering behaviors. Then another round of interviews could be conducted to determine if the reasons for littering categories are affirmed or not.

The ***Ethnography Paradigm*** requires that, in order to understand them, the researcher visits or immerses him/herself in the world of people who litter (Creswell, 2003). Using observation, oral histories, interviewing, still photography, and/or video recording, the investigator gains a sense of the space, place, character and culture of people who litter.

Narrative could be used to judge the impacts of an anti-littering or environmental education program (Freeman, 1993). Applying this theory, study participants would be asked to write stories that describe their present experiences and insights surrounding their littering behaviors. Narratives would be examined from the perspective of whether self-change and self-understanding emerges over the course of time.

Case 8. Studies Using a Mixed-Methods Approach.

Henderson, K., Powell, G., & Scanlin, M. (2005). Observing outcomes in youth development: An analysis of mixed methods. *Journal of Park and Recreation Administration, 23,* 58-77.
Huff, C., Widmer, M., McCoy, K., & Hill, B. (2003). The influence of challenging outdoor recreation on parent-adolescent communication. *Therapeutic Recreation Journal, 37,* 18-37.
Leberman, S., & Holland, J. (2005). Visitor preferences in Kruger National Park, South Africa: The value of a mixed-method approach. *Journal of Park and Recreation Administration, 23,* 21-36.
Mobily, K., Mobily, P., Lessard, K., & Berkenpas, M. (2000). Case comparison of response to aquatic exercise: Acute versus chronic conditions. *Therapeutic Recreation Journal, 34,* 103-1119.

Our bias is that a mixed-methods approach is the preferable way to go. Research in recreation, park, sport, and tourism is interdisciplinary, meaning there isn't one single body of knowledge, academic discipline, or approach that directs us. Like medicine, we draw from a multitude of subjects including anatomy and physiology, sociology, anthropology, psychology, economics, marketing, geography, and physical education.

Your Research

1. **Are you planning on using a quantitative or a qualitative theoretical approach to conduct your research study? Explain the rationale for your choice.**
2. **If you're going to use a quantitative approach, will your study rely on theory testing or conceptual mapping? Briefly outline the theory you're planning on using.**
3. **Why are you or are you not using a mixed-methods theoretical approach?**

Review and Discussion Questions . . . What have you learned about theoretical foundations?

1. **What is a** *theory* **suppose to do?**
2. **How is a** *concrete phenomenon* **different from an** *abstract phenomenon?*
3. **Explain the interrelationships among a** *theory, concept,* **and a** *variable.*
4. **What are two reasons for using theory in research?**
5. **Identify and briefly explain the three theoretical approaches for conducting research?**

6. **Check whether the following characteristics are associated with a quantitative approach or a qualitative approach to research:**

Characteristic	Quantitative Approach	Qualitative Approach
Social reality is objective		
Social reality is subjective		
Inductive logic		
Deductive logic		
Theory testing (a priori or conceptual mapping)		
Theory building		
Structured inquiry		
Unstructured or semi-structured inquiry		

Exercises

1. Visit two or more of the following web sites that identify and discuss theories. Prepare a three-minute presentation and/or one-page typewritten paper on ONE theory. Explain: what the theory is about; if the theory can be used in a quantitative, qualitative, or mixed-methods approach to research; and, one idea of how the theory could be used to guide recreation, park, tourism sport or tourism research.
    A. McMaster University's "WWW Virtual Library: Sociology, Sociological Theory, and Theorists" web page at www.mcmaster.ca/socscidocs/w3virtsoclib/theories.htm.
    B. Wilderdom's web site at www.wilderdom.com. Choose "Experiential Learning," then "Experiential Learning Cycles," and finally "Experiential Learning Cycles."
    C. The University of Amsterdam's Sociosite web page at http://www2.fmg. uva.nl/sociosite/Topics. Click on "Sociologists."

2. Complete one of the following exercises:
    A. Locate (if not assigned by the instructor) three different articles appearing in research journals dealing with recreation, parks, sports, or tourism that illustrate each of the following: a quantitative, a qualitative, and a mixed-methods approach to research. For each article, identify the distinguishing characteristics (cite page number) of the approach being used in the study.
    B. Read about social research reported in the online journal, *Social Research Online,* at the web site www.socresonline.org.uk/home.html. Identify (using key terms such as "Leisure," "Sport") and read one article that interests you. Did the article illustrate a quantitative, qualitative, or mixed-methods approach to research?
    C. Learn more about qualitative research being conducted in sports by going to the online journal, *Forum: Qualitative Social Research* found at the Web site www.qualitative-re-

search.net/fqs-textte/1-03/1-03hrsg-e.htm. Look at the thematic issue on "Sport Sciences." What apparent clues (identify relevant page number) revealed that a qualitative approach to research was used?

4. Learn more about mixed-methods by consulting the National Science Foundation's publication, *User-Friendly Handbook for Mixed Method Evaluations,* found at the Web site www.ehr. nsf.gov/EHR/REC/pubs/NSF97-153/START.HTM. Identify three insights you learned from this reference.

Theoretical ideas support every decision we make in a research project – from determining the questions to ask, designing the study, collecting the data, and interpreting the findings. Covent Garden, England. *Copyright © 2008 Carol Cutler Riddick*

STEP 4: Develop a Scope of Study

Unit of Analysis

Variables
Dependent Variable
Independent Variable

Purpose Statement
Quantitative Study
Qualitative Study

Hypotheses Used in a Quantitative Study
Naive Hypotheses
Three Ways to Write a Hypothesis
  Null Hypothesis
  Non-Directional Hypothesis
  Alternative Hypothesis

Research Question
Quantitative Study
Qualitative Study

What's it all about . . .
Lyrics from the song "Alfie"

An idea for a study topic must be refined and defined. Based on a theoretical foundation (from the previous step), our idea now needs to be narrowed down into a manageable problem that can be studied. Essentially we must determine the study's scope.

Addressing a study's scope is analogous to the challenge confronting a painter. After thinking about it, the artist decides to paint a landscape. When the time comes to set up the easel, the painter must decide whether to paint a seaside or mountain landscape.

Likewise, as a researcher you need to define your study's *scope* by addressing two tasks (Figure 1). First, all studies should have a clearly identified purpose statement. Second, if the study is using a quantitative approach, then it is also necessary to formally specify the hypotheses or research question guiding the study. A research question must be formally designated if the study adopts a qualitative approach.

Figure 1. Defining the Scope of the Study: A Road Map.

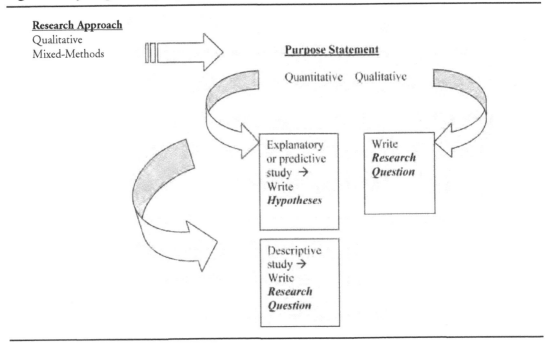

Before delving into the specifics of how to define the scope of a study, it is first necessary to introduce two new terms. These ideas, unit of analysis and variables, must be mastered in order to declare a study's scope.

Unit of Analysis

One important thing the evaluator needs to settle on, at this getting-started stage, is deciding on the entity that is to be examined, technically known as the unit of analysis. The *unit of analysis* is what or whom is studied.

The more common units of analysis are:

- **Individuals** (such as participants, members, guests).
- **Groups** (for instance, clubs, gangs, families).
- **Organizations** (such as recreation agencies, health clubs, colleges, hospitals, resorts).
- **Artifacts** (for example, newspapers, photos, songs, books, paintings).
- **Social interactions** (such as at playgrounds, bars, street corners, campgrounds).

In the past, the most popular units of analysis in leisure research have been individuals and groups (Riddick, DeSchriver, & Weissinger, 1991). Nevertheless, there are other units of analysis—such as communities, events, time periods, lifestyles, roles—that, to date, have received less research attention (Babbie, 2004).

Whether or not you've undertaken a quantitative, qualitative, or mixed-methods approach to your study, you must be clear about the unit of analysis. (Case 1). You must decide whether you are studying, for instance, gangs as a group or gang members as individuals, fitness clubs or fitness club members, municipal recreation directors or municipal recreation agencies, and so on.

Case 1. Group Versus Individual Unit of Analysis.

Researchers often get confused about their unit of analysis, particularly whether it is a group or individuals being examined. Perhaps an illustration will help you avoid confusion on this point. Suppose the purpose of your study was to examine if members of two groups differed regarding environmental attitudes. To this end, you sample members of the Sierra Club and the National Rifle Association. Even though the data are collected on the individual level, the data are treated in the *aggregate,* meaning an average environmental attitude score is calculated across individuals for each group and these two group averages are compared to each other. In this scenario, your unit of analysis is the group. Contrastingly, you may have a different study purpose, namely to monitor how environmental attitudes change before and after participation in a conservation program. You then record the environmental attitudes Sierra Club and National Rifle Association members have before and after completing a conservation program. You examine and report on how each individual changes in his/her environmental attitude over time (pre-program attitude score versus post-program attitude score). Your unit of analysis, in this situation, is the individual.

In summary, don't assume what you learn about a group says something about the individuals making up that group, nor should you assume what you learn about individuals says something about their group.

It is not acceptable science to study one unit of analysis and then deduce or conclude that findings hold true for a different unit of analysis. To commit this error is known as an ***ecological fallacy*** (Babbie, 2004). The bottom line is that you must be clear early on, when developing the study's scope, about the true unit of analysis (Case 2).

Case 2. Ecological Fallacy Regarding Society of Park and Recreation Educators' Election Results.

> Pretend you are interested in learning about the nature of support received by a female candidate for the presidency of the Society of Park and Recreation Educators (SPRE), a professional organization for recreation and leisure faculty working at colleges and universities. You have access to how SPRE members voted on a state-by-state basis and are able to determine which states gave the female candidate the greatest support and which gave her the least. You conduct a preliminary data analysis. Results indicate that states whose SPRE members were predominantly females gave the female candidate a greater proportion of votes than states whose SPRE voters were primarily males. If you concluded from these findings that female SPRE members were more likely to vote for the female candidate than male SPRE members (or that gender affected support for the female candidate), you committed an ecological fallacy. In other words, state SPRE voting patterns (a group) was the unit of analysis, yet you drew conclusions about individual SPRE members. It may have been that male SPRE members in states with predominantly female SPRE members also voted for the female candidate.

Variables

Recall from our Step 3 discussion that a variable is an elaboration of some concept. A ***variable*** identifies some characteristic or property that describes a person or object. A variable must be able to be observed or measured and have at least two mutually exclusive values or attributes. Examples of variables are such things as age, country of origin, and satisfaction with leisure.

Furthermore, there are two types of variables. That is, they can be distinguished as being either dependent variables or independent variables.

Dependent Variable

The ***dependent variable*** is the major variable of concern and is sometimes referred to as the outcome or consequence variable. Technically, the dependent variable deals with a concept we are trying to understand, explain, or predict. In a quantitative study, the dependent variable is examined in terms of how one or more independent variable(s) affects or influences it.

We encourage you to give a great deal of thought when you are designing a study, to what and how many dependent variables you will examine. The *Idea* box below provides some additional "food for thought" on this topic.

Idea . . . Consider Choosing at Least Three Dependent Variables for a Study.

When conducting a program evaluation, consider selecting multiple dependent variables. We suggest measuring at least three. After all, programs can affect people in different ways! For instance, a sport program can do a lot to bolster Sammy's goal-tending skills as well as his self-esteem. Patti, on the other hand, is in the same program, but experiences very little improvement in offensive skills but learns something about cooperation and team play. Goal-tending skills, self-esteem, cooperation, and team play are dependent variables. If a study had measured only one of these dependent variables, premature and incorrect conclusions about the program's actual value would have resulted. So how many dependent variables are enough in evaluative research? Again, we suggest you consider identifying at least three ways a program can impact an individual or group of participants. For example, consider choosing variables that fall into at least two of the following three domains: physical health, psychological health, and social health (see Step 1).

Independent Variable

The variable you introduce or manipulate, be it a treatment, program, intervention, or some other causal variable, is the ***independent variable.*** The independent variable is speculated to affect, influence, or have an impact upon another variable, that is, the dependent variable (Figure 2).

Figure 2. An Example of the Relationship Between an Independent Variable and a Dependent Variable.

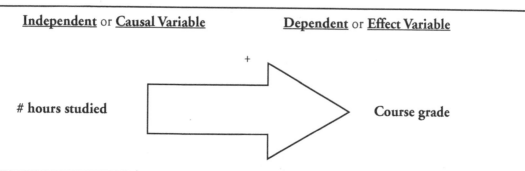

Independent variables influence dependent variables in different ways—sometimes directly and sometimes indirectly. For example, an independent variable can be an ***intervening*** or ***mediating variable.*** These variables intervene between an independent and a dependent variable and are statistically controlled in the analysis (Case 3).

Case 3. Intervening Variable.

Guillemin, F., Constant, F., Collin, J., & Boulange, M. (1994). Short and long-term effects of spa therapy on chronic low back pain. *British Journal of Rheumatolgy, 33,* 148-151.

The purpose of this study was to examine how spa therapy alleviated signs and symptoms associated with chronic low back pain. As things turned out, water temperature and mineral quality emerged as intervening variables in terms of tempering or facilitating the effects of spa therapy. In other words, a certain water temperature range and mineral content was needed for the spa therapy to be beneficial. Findings are represented in the diagram immediately following.

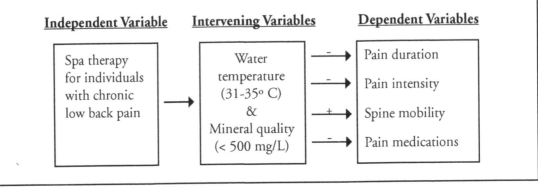

To illustrate the difference between independent and dependent variables, let's go to the track! Suppose horse number 7 wins the race. Winning is the dependent variable. Let's also suppose that horse number 7's jockey is the most skilled jockey this year. Jockey skill is the independent variable. That is, it's suggested that jockey skill had something to do with horse number 7 winning. *Copyright © 2008 Ruth V. Russell*

Something to Remember!

Initially, it may be problematic to remember the difference between an independent variable and a dependent variable. Perhaps the following analogy will help keep the distinction between these two kinds of variables straight in your mind. Suppose you've been outside playing for hours during a very hot and humid day and didn't stop to drink anything. You become physically ill and go to the emergency room. You're placed on a stretcher; the doctor asks you questions and then examines you. You're diagnosed as suffering from heat stroke and you're given intravenous fluid—"IV" in medical lingo. After a couple of hours you feel better and are discharged. Given this scenario, what is the independent variable (IV)? What is the dependent variable (DV)?

The IV is the medicine contained in the intravenous bottle . . . the doctor believes that pushing this fluid into your body will cause you to feel much better. The DV is your physical health . . . after all, the doctor is trying to understand, explain, or predict improved physical health for you! In evaluative research, many times we're trying to determine if our recreation, park, sport, or tourism program (the so called "IV") is having a beneficial effect on program participants' health (the "DV").

Purpose Statement — *guiding light*;
research questions should relate

A *purpose statement* should declare the overall intent of the study, clearly naming the unit of analysis and variables. The content and style of the purpose statement, also referred to as the *problem statement,* depends on whether a quantitative or qualitative approach to research has been adopted. Nevertheless, all studies, regardless of what is being examined, should contain an explicit purpose statement.

The theoretical approach adopted for a study (Step 3) has a profound influence on the purpose statement you prepare. In turn, the purpose statement impacts the methods you use to conduct the study. Case 4 illustrates the connection between a theoretical approach used to guide a study and the subsequent purpose statement.

Purpose
R1
R2
R3
— R1: research question
R2: research question
R3: etc.
} in depth

Case 4. Interface between a Research Theoretical Approach and a Purpose Statement.

Theoretical Approach to Research	Specific Theory Used	Purpose Statement	Citation
Quantitative	***Protection Motivation Theory:*** Rule compliance is affected by being exposed to fear tactics and awareness of consequences.	The purpose of the study is to examine how receipt of printed information, upon entering a park, subsequently affects littering behaviors.	Gramann, J., Bonifeld, R., & Kim, Y. (1995). Effect of personality and situational factors on intentions to obey rules in outdoor recreation areas. *Journal of Leisure Research, 27,* 321-343.
Qualitative	***Phenomenology Theory:*** Focus on people's subjective experiences and interpretations of the world.	The goal of the study is to understand, from the individuals' perspective, why people litter in parks.	Giorgi, A. (1997). The theory, practice, and evaluation of the phenomenological methods as a qualitative research procedure. *Journal of Phenomenological Psychology, 28,* 235-281.

Furthermore, a study may contain secondary purposes, usually referred to as subproblems. **Subproblems** can be thought of as "side bar" activities that are required in order to pursue the major purpose of a study (i.e., fulfill the problem statement). For instance, a master's student wanted to examine how an animal-assisted therapy program affected the social skills of deaf individuals who were patients in a psychiatric hospital. A literature review revealed that no social skills instrument, specifically for deaf individuals, had previously been developed. Thus, the student identified two subproblems for her study, namely to develop and then document the validity and reliability of a social skills instrument for use with deaf adults (Baron-Leonard, 2004).

Idea . . . Choosing Between the Present or Past Tense When Developing Your Scope of Study.

One issue many researchers struggle with is what verb tense to use at the proposal stage, the future or past tense. There are two schools of thought on this. First, there are those who believe the entire proposal, including the purpose statement, should be written in the future tense. The rationale behind this thinking is that a proposal denotes a study yet to be implemented. People of this mind-set advocate that once the study has been completed, then the future tense should be changed into the past tense. Contrastingly, some individuals think that it is a waste of time to use the future tense at the proposal stage. To do so necessitates the time-consuming task of backing up and changing tenses from the future to the past when writing the final report. Instead, it is argued that you go ahead and write the proposal in the past tense, maybe adding a disclaimer somewhere at the beginning as to why this is being done. Ultimately, it boils down to style preference. If you're working with a supervising faculty member or part of a research team, then you need to discuss this issue and come to terms regarding which verb tense to adopt in the getting-started stage, future or past.

Quantitative Study

A "good" purpose statement should be prepared according to specific principles (Creswell, 2003). Let's focus on these principles in terms of the theoretical approach adopted. For a quantitative study, the purpose statement begins with particular introductory wording (Case 5). Additionally, the theoretical foundation and the independent and dependent variables should be identified.

Purpose Statement: what are you measuring?

Case 5. Principles to Use When Writing a Purpose Statement for a Quantitative Study.

Principle[1]	Illustration	Citation
1. **Begin the purpose statement passage with the word *purpose, intent, focus,* or *objective.***	"The focus of this paper is an examination of the satisfaction of local park and recreation officials with park impact fees and alternative mechanisms for financing capital development" (p. 77). *I̅P̅ = statement* *U̅ β = description*	Fletcher, J., Kaiser, R., & Groger, S. (1992). An assessment of the importance and performance of park impact fees in funding park and recreation infrastructure. *Journal of Park and Recreation Administration, 10,* 75-97.
2. **Identify the theory or conceptual framework to be tested in the study.**	"The purpose of the study was to test Mehrabian's three-factor theory of emotions. The effects of video game play on the emotional states, affiliative behaviors, and pleasure state of nursing home residents were examined within the context of this theory" (p. 425).	Riddick, C., Spector, S., & Drogin, E. (1986). The effects of video game play on the emotional states and affiliative behavior of nursing home residents. *Activities, Adaptation & Aging, 8,* 95-108.
3. **Identify the proposed variables for the study, naming the independent variable(s) first followed by the dependent variable(s).**	"The purpose of the study was to test the relaxation theory by having elderly persons view an aquarium and determine whether engagement in this activity evoked a relaxation response or reduced physiological stress . . . or reduction in pulse rate, increase in skin temperature, and a reduction in muscle tension" (p. 44).	DeSchriver, M., & Riddick, C. (1991). Effects of watching aquariums on elders' stress. *Anthrozoos, 4,* 44-48.

[1]Adapted from Creswell (2003).

Qualitative Study

Likewise, a number of principles should be adhered to when writing a purpose statement for a qualitative study (Creswell, 2003). The ingredients for a good purpose statement in these situations are: certain introductory wording and the identification of the qualitative theoretical framework used to conduct the study (Case 6).

Case 6. Principles to Use When Writing a Purpose Statement for a Qualitative Study.

Principle[2]	Illustration	Citation
1. **Call attention to the purpose statement by using such words as *purpose, aim, intent, goal,* and *objective.***	The purpose of this interpretive study was to examine how nine residents in an outdoor residential psychiatric rehabilitation center for adolescent girls at-risk, perceived themselves after participating in adventure therapy programs offered by this facility.	Autry, C. (2001). Adventure therapy with girls at-risk: Responses to outdoor experiential activities. *Therapeutic Recreation Journal, 35,* 289-306.
2. **Identify the theoretical framework used to conduct the study.**	"Given the limited research on this topic, qualitative interviews were used to explore if, and in what ways, involvement in an adapted sports program influenced the self-perceptions of these youth, and if the experience of playing sports influenced the way in which these youth incorporated their disabilities into their identity" (p. 322).	Groff, D., & Kleiber, D. (2001). Exploring the identify formation of youth involved in an adapted sports program. *Therapeutic Recreation Journal, 35,* 318-332.

[2]Adapted from Creswell (2003).

Hypotheses Used in a Quantitative Study

While a purpose statement narrows the topic of interest down, you will still need to further refine your idea. This is the role of hypotheses and research questions.

Idea . . . Keeping Some Grammar Rules Straight.

Confusion seems to abound regarding a few rules of grammar. For example, let's quickly review the difference between *hypothesis* v. *hypotheses* and *affect* v. *effect*. First, what is the difference between **hypothesis** and **hypotheses?** The former is used in a singular context; the latter is used under plural conditions. That is, if you identify only one hypothesis, then you use the "*is*" ending. If you have two or more hypotheses, you use the "*es*" ending. Second, and related, is the distinction between ***affect*** and *effect*. The former is a verb and the latter is a noun. For instance, it may be hypothesized that, "Leisure attitude will affect leisure activity." As well, it may be hypothesized that, "Participation in a leisure education program will have profound effects on one's mental health."

If the goal of the quantitative approach is to explain or predict, then hypotheses must be identified. A *hypothesis* is basically a conjecture about the relationship between two or more variables (Kerlinger, 2000). You can think of a hypothesis as a tentative statement about empirical reality. A hypothesis contains an explanation or prediction about what is expected to happen.

Hypotheses generally emerge from theoretical musings. Case 7 summarizes several formal theories and then illustrates a study hypothesis that has been deduced from that theory.

Case 7. Examples of Hypotheses Deduced from Formal Theories.

Formal Theory	Hypothesis	Citation
Social Rank Theory: Social status of students with disabilities may be lower than the social status of students without disabilities. Improved social status positively influences peer relationships.	Training in a physically demanding dance video game will have a positive impact on friendship quality experienced between males with: high-functioning autism spectrum disorder and those without the disorder.	Chiang, I., Lee, Y., Frey, G., & McCormick, B. (2004). Testing the situationally modified social rank theory on friendship quality in male youth with high-functioning autism spectrum disorder. *Therapeutic Recreation Journal, 38*, 261-274.
Differential Association Theory: People learn from those with whom they are close, that participation in certain activities (e.g., drinking, illegal drug use) is acceptable. *Casual Leisure Theory:* Casual leisure is hedonistic; it offers a level of pleasure for those who participate.	Friends play a key role in influencing a student's decision to use substances (drinking and illegal drug use). Students who use drugs do so for social reasons and to have fun.	Shinew, K., & Parry, D. (2005). Examining college students' participation in the leisure pursuits of drinking and illegal drug use. *Journal of Leisure Research 37*, 364-386.

Formal Theory	Hypothesis	Citation

Social Learning Theory: Observational learning influences prosocial and antisocial behaviors.	Adolescents with disruptive behavior disorders, who undergo prosocial behavior training, will demonstrate during basketball games:
	
	A. An *increase* (when compared to baseline behavior) in the following prosocial behaviors:
	   i. Instances of encouragement made to other participants.
	   ii. Frequency of helping behaviors to other participants.
	   iii. Frequency of resolving conflicts with other participants.
	B. A *decrease* (when compared to baseline behavior) in the following antisocial behaviors:
	   i. Frequency of physically aggressive behaviors.
	   ii. Frequency of aggressive behaviors.
		McKinney, A., & Dattilo, J. (2001). Effects of an intervention within a sport context on the prosocial behavior and antisocial behavior of adolescents with disruptive behavior disorders. *Therapeutic Recreation Journal, 35,* 123-140.

As you can see from the above case, hypotheses differ from theory in two ways. First, you need to remember theory is like a large-scale map, with the different areas representing general ideas. Hypotheses, on the other hand, are blown-up small sectional maps, focusing on specific areas not designated by the larger theoretical map. Second, hypotheses are more focused than a theory. Consequently, hypotheses are more directly amenable to empirical examination (Rosenthal & Rosnow, 1991).

Naive Hypotheses

Truthfully, not all hypotheses emerge from formal theories. Sometimes, hypotheses emanate from educated guess-work. These kinds of hypotheses are known as *naive hypotheses* (Kidder & Judd, 1986).

Idea . . . Inspirational Sources for Naive Hypotheses.

Where can you get ideas for naive hypotheses? Unlike Chicken Little, these sorts of hypotheses do not fall from the sky! Instead, consider the following inspirational sources:

- **Authority.** Authorities or experts can provide insights on possible hypotheses to examine. This is only true, however, when the experts are indeed experts in the topic area, and can critically assess the situation creatively and appropriately.
- **Consensus.** Consensus-driven hypotheses emerge from the wisdom of peers or users of our services. For instance, suppose the issue is how to curb graffiti on recreational center properties. In order to identify ways to curb graffiti, ask center staff and participants for their ideas. These become "working" hypotheses.
- **Observation.** These hypotheses come from your own observations of a situation. For example, you may initially believe that prejudice toward individuals with physical disabilities is caused by a lack of personal contact with members of this group. To learn more, you might conduct some informal interviews with your friends, asking about their experiences with persons with physical disabilities as well as how they feel toward this group. If these preliminary results suggest there appears to be a relationship between these two variables, you could then proceed with adoption of the hypothesis for the study.

Three Ways to Write a Hypothesis

Regardless of the source for hypotheses, they can be written one of three ways. That is, a hypothesis can be written in the null, non-directional, or alternative format.

Null hypothesis. You may have already been trained to write in the **null hypothesis** format. A null hypothesis states there is no *relationship* between two or more variables (Case 8).

Case 8. Null Hypotheses.

Example	Citation
There will be no inter-group differences in the psychological response (emotions and stress) of the serious and hedonistic groups to participation in recreational tennis.	Kerr, J., Fujiyama, H., & Campano, J. (2002). Emotion and stress in serious and hedonistic leisure sport activities. *Journal of Leisure Research, 34,* 272-289.
In accordance with the segmentation model, there will be no difference between leisure-oriented and work oriented people regarding economic work orientations.	Snir, R., & Harpaz, I. (2002). Work-leisure relations: Leisure orientation and the meaning of work. *Journal of Leisure Research, 34,* 178-203.
Being a climber or non-climber does not significantly determine whether visual preference of scenes containing evidence of rock climbing is higher than visual preference of scenes containing no evidence of rock climbing.	Jones, C. (2004). Evaluating visual impacts of near-view rock climbing scenes. *Journal of Park and Recreation Administration, 22,* 39-49.

Non-directional hypothesis. In contrast to a null hypothesis, a **non-directional hypothesis** speculates there is a relationship among variables but does not provide any details about it. That is, it is speculated, a difference will exist, but the direction of this difference is not made clear (Case 9).

Case 9. Non-Directional Hypotheses.

Example	Citation
Women and men working in therapeutic recreation have different perceptions of gender equity.	Anderson, D., & Bedini, L. (2002). Perceptions of workplace equity of therapeutic recreation professionals. *Therapeutic Recreation Journal, 36,* 260-281.
There is a relationship between self-reported enduring involvement and flow experienced in leisure and non-leisure activities.	Havitz, M., & Mannell, R. (2004). Enduring involvement, situation involvement, and flow in leisure and non-leisure activities. *Journal of Leisure Research, 37,* 152-177.

Alternative hypothesis. Think of an **alternative hypothesis** as a non-directional hypothesis with the direction added. That is, it pinpoints the nature of the relationship among the variables. An alternate hypothesis can be set up one of three ways.

One strategy for identifying directionality is to identify and compare two or more groups in terms of the dependent variable. The first example in Case 10 demonstrates this approach.

Case 10. Alternative Hypotheses.

Example	Citation
Black-uniformed teams (in the National Football League and National Hockey League) will be penalized more than their non-black uniform rivals.	Frank, M., & Gilovich, T. (1988). The dark side of self and social perception: Black uniforms and aggression in professional sports. *Journal of Personality and Social Psychology, 54,* 74-85.
There is a negative relationship between perceived crowding and visitor satisfaction.	Budruk, M., Schneider, I., Andreck, K., & Virden, R. (2002). Crowing and satisfaction among visitors to a build desert attraction. *Journal of Park and Recreation Administration, 20,* 1-17.
Children participating in an after-school recreation program would differ from children who did not participate in the program in terms of better school attendance, grades, school and home behaviors, and self-esteem.	Baker, D., & Witt, P. (1996). Evaluation of the impact of two after-school programs. *Journal of Park and Recreation Administration, 14,* 60-81.

Something to Remember!

Trying to keep the three ways to write a hypothesis straight? If so, consider using the following shorthand system to distinguish among the three hypothesis formats. For a **null** hypothesis, use the **Ho** designation. **H** stands for hypothesis and the **o** subscript stands for the null form. A mnemonic is to remember o means the **o** part of **NO** relationship. For a **non-directional** hypothesis, use the **H** designation. Notice no subscript is used, indicating no directionality is stated in a non-directional hypothesis. Finally, for the **alternative** hypothesis, use the H_1 notation. The **1** subscript means a directionality has been specified.

Another strategy for indicating directionality is to identify the ***nature of the relationship*** between the variables under study. Specifically, a positive or negative relationship is declared to exist between the independent and dependent variable (see the second example cited in Case 10).

A ***positive relationship*** means the directionality of the two variables is the same. One way to understand a positive relationship is to think, "As the value of the independent variable goes up, the value of the dependent variable also increases." Using the same logic (i.e., the two variables move in the same direction), the converse also holds—as the value of the independent variables goes down, so too does the value of the dependent variable diminish.

A ***negative relationship***, sometimes called an ***inverse relationship***, means the directionality of the two variables are opposite. That is, as the value of the one variable changes (increases or decreases), the value of the second variable heads the opposite direction.

To demonstrate what we mean by a negatively stated relationship, take the alternative hypothesis (as illustrated in Figure 3), "There is a negative relationship between the hours spent per week watching television and final grade in a research course." This hypothesis also could be translated two ways. First, it is predicted that as television watching time increases, course grade declines. Second, the statement also could be interpreted as hypothesizing that as weekly television watching time decreases, points earned in the course increases.

Figure 3. Couch Potato Hypothesis: Example of a Negative Relationship Between Amount of Weekly Time Spent Watching Television and Research Course Grade (N = 12).

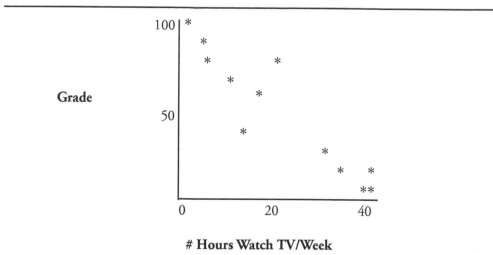

Something to Remember!

To help you tackle directional relationships among two variables, think about using the following thumb-pointing system. Use your LEFT thumb to represent the INDEPENDENT variable and reserve your RIGHT thumb for the DEPENDENT variable.

Practice Round One: Demonstrate, using your two thumbs, two ways to show a positive relationship between age and amount of time needed to learn new material. Again, use your left thumb to indicate the independent variable and the right thumb to indicate what happens to the dependent variable. (Answer: Your left and right thumbs should both be pointing to the sky thus indicating that as age increases more time is needed to learn new subject matter. Incidentally, the psychology of aging literature supports this statement. Older people are quite capable of learning new material, it just takes longer relative to how quickly they learned material in their younger years.)

As age goes up . . . amount of time needed to master new material increases.

A second way to illustrate this positive relationship is to have both your left and right thumbs pointing downwards. This translates into meaning as age decreases, the amount of time needed to master new material decreases.

Practice Round Two: Now, see if you can use this thumb-pointing technique successfully to portray the following:
1. Positive relationship between player's height and number of baskets made during a pick-up basketball game.
2. Positive relationship between weight and blood pressure.
3. Negative relationship between a lawn mower's use hours and lawn mower blade's sharpness.
4. Negative relationship between amount of litter found on a trail and hikers' satisfaction with the trail.
5. Negative relationship between physical condition and heart rate. (This is tricky, do you understand why a negative relationship was predicted?)

A third approach to drafting an alternative hypothesis is to use a combination of comparing and relating. While this is a more sophisticated approach, it can amount to, for instance, using a two-factor experiment where the evaluator has two or more groups, as well as a number of dependent variables (see Case 10, last example).

Idea . . . For Coming Up with a Study Title.

When choosing a title for your study, remember two things. First, the title should contain words that identify the concepts or variables examined in the investigation. And second, realize the title has organizational implications for how the study should be presented. For instance, if your study is entitled, "The Effects of Hip-Hop Dance Instruction on Rhythm, Bilateral Coordination, and Balance" then the organization of the hypotheses should be consistent with the order introduced in the title. That is, the first hypothesis should address how hip-hop instruction will affect rhythm. The second hypothesis should examine how hip-hop dance will impact bilateral coordination. And the third hypothesis should focus on how hip-hop instruction will influence balance.

Research Question

Not all studies have hypotheses. Qualitative studies, for example, do not use hypotheses. Likewise, sometimes a quantitative study is designed to be descriptive and thus doesn't need hypotheses. Regardless, for both quantitative and qualitative studies the research question should specify the unit of analysis that is of interest (Case 11).

Case 11. Linkage Between Unit of Analysis and Research Question.[3]

Unit of Analysis	Research Question
Individuals	• How does a college student spend his or her free time? • What teaching technique used by the cardio-boxing instructor is most effective? ⇒ *not specific enough*
Group	• What communication patterns are used by offensive versus defensive players? • What motivations and benefits are derived from being part of a tour group to Alaska?
Organization	• How are Recreation Department volunteers oriented? • What marketing strategies are used by the health club to recruit new members?
Artifacts	• What leisure roles for women are portrayed in Victorian novels? • Are editorials in the local newspapers supportive of the bond initiative for greenway expansion?
Social Interactions	• What will a content analysis of receptionists' check-in dialogues reveal? • What are the interaction patterns of the staff with each other and with the director during a staff meeting?

Test Stats
• sig relationship/ difference

Descriptive Stats
• evaluations
• describing answers
ex: # of people visit museum @ diff. times of year

Unit of Analysis	Research Question
Community	• How did the town maintain control over strip development decisions? • What actions does a neighborhood citizens group take to curb graffiti in its neighborhood parks?
Event	• How have Renaissance Fair participants' entertainment interests changed over the past two years? • What was the budget (revenue sources and expenses) for the *Race for the Cure* event just completed?
Time Period	• What are the points of destinations for Londoners vacationing in the summer months? • What's the difference in problem-solving strategies used by travel agency staff the week before Christmas break versus the week before the 4th of July?

[3]Adapted from Miles and Huberman (1994).

Quantitative Study

Some quantitative studies use one or more research questions. A ***research question*** in a quantitative study can take one of two forms: descriptive or normative (Hedrick, Bickman, & Rog, 1993). Case 12 distinguishes between these two forms and provides examples of each. As their labels suggest, descriptive research questions ask the "What," "How," "Do(es)" or "Is" about something. ***Normative questions*** ask how the phenomenon studied compares to a standard or norm.

Research Questions:
1 → descriptive
2 → normative

Case 12. Types of Research Questions Found in a Quantitative Study.

Type of Question[4]	Example	Citation
Descriptive questions typically begin with: • *What.* • *How.* • *Do(es).* • *Is.*	What are the expressed motives of sport participants?	Recours, R., Souville, M., & Griffet, J. (2004). Expressed motives for informal and club/association sports participation. *Journal of Leisure Research, 36,* 1-22.
	How do parents communicate and enforce rules concerning adolescents' patterns of free-time use?	Hutchinson, S., Baldwin, S., & Caldwell, L. (2003). Differentiating parent practices related to adolescent behavior in the free time context. *Journal of Leisure Research, 35,* 396-422.
	Do parks and open spaces contribute to increasing property values?	Crompton, J. (2001). The impact of parks on property values: A review of the empirical evidence. *Journal of Leisure Research, 33,* 1-31.
	Is there a difference in the number of hours of participation in leisure activities among adolescents with short stature, delayed puberty, and diabetes mellitus compared with adolescents with other endocrinological problems?	Caldwell, L., Finkelstein, J., & Demers, B. (2002). Exploring the leisure behavior patterns and experiences of youth with endocrinological disorders: Implications for therapeutic recreation. *Therapeutic Recreation Journal, 35,* 236-249.
Normative questions require comparing against a standard or expectation.	How do public recreation agencies, of various sizes, meet the structure, process, and outcome benchmarks for inclusive recreation services?	Klitzing, S., & Wachter, C. (2005). Benchmarks for the delivery of inclusive community recreation services for people with disabilities. *Therapeutic Recreation Journal, 39,* 63-77.
	To what extent are standards for inclusive recreation being met in special recreation associations in Illinois?	Wachter, C., & McGowan, A. (2002). Inclusion practices of special recreation agencies in Illinois. *Therapeutic Recreation Journal, 36,* 172-185.

[4]Adapted from Hedrick, Bickman and Rog (1993).

Qualitative Study

The research question for a qualitative study simply expands upon the study's purpose statement. Specifically, the research question for qualitative studies is customarily referred to as a grand-tour research question, which is often accompanied by supporting subquestions.

A *grand-tour research question* is a broad statement of what is being examined in the study. It is considered a "grand-tour" type of question because it is stated in very general terms so as not to prematurely limit inquiry. Typically, a study will have one or two grand-tour research questions, which become topics explored in interviews, observations, and/or archival material.

Branching off from a grand-tour research question are subquestions (Case 13). *Subquestions,* sometimes referred to as *subordinate questions,* tangentially relate to the grand-tour question examined. A grand-tour question example is "Why do campers annually return to participate in an agricultural fair (Kyle & Chick, 2002)?" Two subquestions identified in this same study were, "What is the focus of agricultural fair participants?" and "How is their involvement maintained?" (p. 426).

Case 13. Grand-Tour Question and Subquestions.

Yuen, F. (2004). "It was fun . . . I liked drawing my thoughts." Using drawing as a part of the focus group process with children. *Journal of Leisure Research, 36,* 461-482.

Purpose Statement: "Examine the extent to which participation in leisure activities directed toward effective communication and cooperation affect the development of social capital and community in children." (p. 465)

Grand-Tour Research Question: "How do you feel being at camp?" (p. 464)

Subquestions (NOTE: Children were asked to draw their responses to the following four questions):

1. How would you describe our camp community?
2. How did you communicate with others?
3. Think of the activities we did at camp and what you learned from them.
4. Think about what you did during free time, what you learned and why it was important to you.

Several principles should be followed when writing a research question for a qualitative study (Creswell, 2003). As illustrated in Case 14, a good grand-tour question should contain certain introductory wording, followed by the identification of the qualitative framework used for the study.

Case 14. Illustration of Principles Used To Write a Research Question for a Qualitative Study.

Hutchinson, S., LeBlanc, A., & Booth, R. (2002). "Perpetual problem solving": An ethnographic study of clinical reasoning in a therapeutic recreation setting. *Therapeutic Recreation Journal, 36,* 18-34.	

Principle[1]	**Illustration**
1. Begin the grand-tour question with the words "*Why*," "*What*," or "*How*."	How do recreation therapists think and interact with clients?
2. Tell the reader that the study will do one of the following: "*Discover*," "*Explain*," "*Seek to understand*," "*Explore a process*," "*Describe the experience*," or "*Examine the nature of the experience*." Remember **NOT** to use words that suggest or infer directional orientation (such as "*Affect*," "*Influence*," "*Impact*," "*Determine*," "*Cause*," and "*Relate*").	The study will examine the nature of clinical reasoning experiences associated with recreation therapy and the subjective meaning study participants attach to these experiences.
3. Identify the specific qualitative framework used for the study.	An ethnographic approach was used to present evidence of the problem-solving processes used by two therapeutic recreation therapists working in a Canadian inpatient rehabilitation service setting.

[1]Adapted from Creswell (2003).

Your Research

1. For the topic you've selected to study, write a:
   A. Problem statement.
   B. Subproblem statements.
   C. Three hypotheses (in either alternative or non-directional form, if appropriate).
   D. Research question (if appropriate).
2. What is/are the dependent variables for your study? Are there independent variables? If so, what are they?
3. What is the unit of analysis for your topic?

Review and Discussion Questions . . .
What have you learned about developing a study's scope?

1. What is meant by *unit of analysis?*
2. What are the two units of analysis most often used in leisure research?
3. Define the following terms and then give an example of each from your own interests: *Variable, Dependent Variable* and *Independent Variable.*

4. Distinguish between the content found in a purpose statement for a quantitative study versus a qualitative study.
5. What is a *hypothesis?* Using the same dependent and independent variables, write one null, one non-directional, and one alternative hypothesis.
6. Write one *descriptive* research question and one *normative* research question.
7. Identify a *grand-tour question* and one related *subordinate question.*

Exercises

1. If the leisure behaviors of students enrolled in your measurement and evaluation/research methods class were used to make generalizations about the leisure behaviors of students at your university, would an *ecological fallacy* be committed? Why or why not?

2. Pair up with another student and read one research article in a recent issue (assigned by your instructor or chosen by you) of one of the major research journals in your major. Together, discuss and complete the questions posed in Figures 4 and/or 5 worksheets. If the study used a positivist/quantitative approach, complete Figure 4. If the study used an interpretative/qualitative approach, complete Figure 5. If triangulation was used, complete Figures 4 and 5.

Figure 4. Worksheet: Establishing the Scope for a Quantitative Research Project.

1. The **unit of analysis** used for the study (circle answer and describe):

> Individuals
> Groups
> Organizations
> Artifacts
> Social interactions

2. The **purpose/intent/focus/objective** (circle one and elaborate about the concept under examination) was to:

> Describe

> Explain

> Predict

3. A subproblem(s) for the study was (if applicable, identify):

4.The study (choose one):

    A. Tested the (identify) _____ **theory** OR

    B. Studied a **conceptual model** [diagram the variables that were examined, ordering relationships from independent variable(s) to dependent variable(s)].

5.The **independent variable(s)** in the study were (specify):

6.The **dependent variable(s)** in the study were (specify):

    Answer Question 7 <u>OR</u> 8 and 9.

7. The research **hypothesis** was (specify and identify if a null, non-directional, or alternative format was used):

8.The **descriptive research question** was (if applicable, specify):

9. The **normative research question** was (if applicable, specify):

Figure 5. Establishing the Scope for a Qualitative Research Project.

1.The **unit of analysis** used for the study (circle answer and describe):

    Individuals
    Groups
    Organizations
    Artifacts
    Social interactions

2.The **dependent variable** under study was:

3. The **theoretical approach** used to conduct the study was (specify):

4. The **purpose/aim/intent/goal/objective** (circle one and elaborate about the concept under examination) is to:

    Discover

    Explain or seek to understand

    Explore a process

    Describe the experience

    Examine the nature of the experience

    Develop

5. The **grand-tour research question** was (elaborate):

6. The supporting **subquestions** were (identify):

---

3. Locate the W.K. Kellogg Foundation's *Evaluation Handbook* by going to the Web site www. wkkf.org. Conduct a search by typing in "Evaluation Handbook." Once you have found the document, read "Recommendation Two: Question the Question" (found on page 18 of the document) and "Chapter 5: Planning and Implementing Level Evaluations" paying particular attention to "Step 1: Identify Stakeholders" (beginning on page 54) and "Step 2: Developing Evaluation Questions" (picked up on page 57). Identify one thing you learned, from this reference, about defining the scope of a study.

4. For *each* of the following statements: (a.) Schematically (see Figure 2 in this chapter for an example) identify the independent and dependent variables; (b.) Specify the nature of the relationship between the two variables (by using a "+" or "-" sign); and (c.) Write, if possible, an alternative hypothesis.

A. Amount of unstructured playtime children experience/week and children's creativity.

B. Income and frequency of playing golf.

C. Parents' leisure attitudes and individuals' leisure attitudes.

D. Stress and number of times of exercise every week.

E. Weight and walking speed of adults.

F. Number of hours per week participated in structured campus recreation programs/activities and students' boredom.

G. Extent of participation in "Working with People with Physical Disabilities" Workshop and attitudes about persons with physical disabilities.

H. Reaction time and amount of alcohol consumed.

I. Challenge level experienced when participating in an activity and satisfaction derived from that activity.

J. Number of leg weight-lifting repetitions performed/week and size of leg muscle.

K. Amount of time adolescents play video games/week and school grades.

L. Swimming ability and number of swim class sessions attended.

5. Read about the efficacy of visitor education programs on litter bugs and depreciative visitor behaviors on public lands by locating Reid and Marion's 2003 paper published on the subject. An online version of the paper that is available at the Leave No Trace Center for Outdoor Ethics Web site at www.lnt.org. Select "Programs" and do a search using "Reid and Marion." Use what you learned from the paper to sketch out a research proposal related to this topic.

Purpose statements, research questions, and hypotheses don't have to be complex and elaborate, but they should narrow in on what useful information needs to be generated from the study. Venice, Italy. *Copyright © 2008 Carol Cutler Riddick*

STEP 5: Explain Study's Significance

Making a Case for Significance
Improve Professional Practice/Service Delivery
Address a Social Problem
Contribute to Scientific Knowledge

Significance Statement

Strong reasons make strong actions.
William Shakespeare

The last step of the *Getting Started* phase is addressing a study's significance. Research studies take time and cost money to conduct, so it is crucial that the study's significance is considered. We may have to answer why:

- An organization should get involved in a study?
- A thesis or dissertation committee should approve a proposed study?
- Someone should fund or publish a study?

We believe research should be transformative (Kielhofner & Fosey, 2006). ***Transformative research*** refers to inquiry that ultimately brings about change in some situation, improving social realities and people's lives. (Case 1).

Case 1. Transformative Research Makes a Difference.

Henderson, J. (2005). Responding to natural disasters: Managing a hotel in the aftermath of the Indian Ocean tsunami. *Tourism and Hospitality Research, 6,* 89-97.

This case study described the experiences of the general manager of a luxury resort hotel on the island of Phuket in Thailand in the days immediately following the Indian Ocean tsunami of 2004. Although the property escaped physical damage and there were no fatalities among guests and staff, the management had to deal with an unprecedented crisis caused by a disruption to tourism. Recovery efforts were outlined. The discussion centered on the long-term impacts on business and the challenges of restoring confidence and returning normalcy to the tourism industry.

Making a Case for Significance

Significance has the quality of being important. Depending on its purpose, a study can be significant for any number of reasons. Usually, a case can be made for a study's significance by using one of the following three strategies. Namely, a study could be significant because it has the potential to:

- Improve professional practice/service delivery.
- Address a social problem.
- Contribute to scientific knowledge.

Improve Professional Practice/Service Delivery

One compelling argument is that a study has the potential to help practitioners learn of ways to enhance or improve professional practice and/or leisure service delivery (Case 2). For example, from what was discussed in Step 1, the study's significance could address how the study will provide insights regarding program need, design, process, impact, or economics.

Case 2. Example of a Study's Significance to Professional Practice.

McKinney, W., Bartlett, K., & Mulvaney, M. (2007). Measuring the costs of employee turnover in Illinois public park and recreation agencies: An exploratory study. *Journal of Park and Recreation Administration, 25,* 50-74.

The intent of this study was to examine employee turnover within a cost analytical framework. The study was deemed important because employee turnover is both an unavoidable and expensive part of most public park and recreation agency operations. Findings suggest that the employee *separation costs* (such as payments for unused vacation time) are about two to three times larger than *replacement costs* (such as for advertising for the position). Therefore, the challenges confronting managers facing employee turnover is to control unused vacation and sick pay, losses in production, and overtime paid to existing staff. Based on the findings, a model was proposed to assist park and recreation agencies accurately quantify their employee turnover costs.

Address a Social Problem

In some cases, a study is significant in its potential for addressing a social problem. That is, the study is important in solving an injustice, void, excess, and/or issue facing a community or society. Social problems result from a loss in the ability of individuals/groups/ communities to perform their function in society (Case 3).

Case 3. Example of a Study's Social Importance.

Thapa, B., Graefe, A., & Meyer, L. (2006). Specialization and marine based environmental behaviors among SCUBA divers. *Journal of Leisure Research, 38,* 601-615.

The purpose of the study was to explore the relationship between recreation specialization (such as certification level) and marine-based environmental behaviors among SCUBA divers. The *Introduction* sets the scene for the study's significance by addressing the need to alter divers' behaviors given the degradation of underwater environments over time, and also how this problem affects major tourist dependent communities that specialize in dive tourism.

> Coral reefs are a major attraction for SCUBA . . . divers. . . . It has been estimated that there are 5-7 million active divers worldwide. . . . Recent accounts have projected that 60% of the world's reefs are currently under threat . . . while 27% have already been lost. . . . inappropriate behaviors . . . lead to irreversible damages or death of the coral. . . . lack of knowledge about the marine ecosystem and environmentally responsible behaviors all contribute to negative impacts. (pp. 601-602)

For instance, if drug use is a problem among college students, it could reasonably be argued that setting up alternative, drug-free leisure programs on weekends has social significance. Or, if urban sprawl has denigrated the quality of life in a community, developing social space and pedestrian rights-of-way have social significance. Studies could be carried out to confirm each of these social problem solutions.

Research that answers the question of what promotes conservation behavior in children could be significant in solving the social problem of pollution. *Copyright © 2008 Ruth V. Russell*

Typically, research that is important to solving social problems uses three kinds of numbers to confirm the existence of a problem. Societal problems are often stated using prevalence, incidence, or at-risk need statistics (Rossi, Lipsey, & Freeman, 2004).

Prevalence is the number of *existing* cases in a particular geographic area at a specified time. An example of prevalence would be to say, "In 2006, the prevalence of the adult Canadian population, who reported not participating in weekly physical exercise, was 46% (or 46 out of 100)."

Incidence is the number of *new* cases of a particular problem in a specified geographic area and during a specified period of time. An illustration of an incidence statement is, "In the first quarter of 2007, there were 50 reported cases of vandalism within the Montgomery County park system."

Sometimes prevalence or incidence is stated as a rate. Although rate is described in greater detail in Step 14A, a sneak preview is that *rate* is an expression of the number of existing or new cases in a geographic area during a given period of time to some base, usually per 100 or 1,000 persons. For example, statistics suggest the rate of binge drinking (or 5/4 consecutive drinks among men/women in about two hours), in 1997, among American college students was 43 out of 100 (Harvard School of Public Health, 1998).

At-risk need, sometimes referred to as a *population in need,* is a group of individuals in a specified geographic area that currently is in jeopardy of experiencing an identifiable condition or problem of concern. For instance, *latch-key children* are elementary school-aged children who return to an empty home, after school, when no adult is present. Latch-key kids are typically considered a population in need because they are entering an environment devoid of adult supervision.

To make claims about a study's significance using statistics usually requires consulting secondary data sources. In fact, any number of statistical sources is available to buttress an argument for the prevalence or incidence of social problems that potentially can be impacted by recreation, park, tourism, or sport services. The *Idea* box below provides some leads on some of these.

Idea . . . Using Secondary Data Sources to Help Make the Case for a Study's Significance.

Check out these sources of statistical information for assistance in developing a rationale for your study. These sources are free, and chocked full of amazing facts.

- The *Bureau of Justice Statistics* (www.ojp.usdoj.gov/bjs/) provides information about crime and victims, drugs and crime, criminal offenders, the justice system in the United States, law enforcement, prosecution, etc.
- The *Centers for Disease Control* (www.cdc.gov) Behavior Risk Factor Surveillance System identifies and reports (at national and state levels as well as for selected local areas) the prevalence of selected health behaviors (e.g., health status, leisure-time physical activity, chronic conditions).
- The *National Center for Health Statistics* (www.cdc.gov/nchswww/nchsome.htm) contains the results of the National Health Interview Survey, the National Health and Nutrition Examination Survey, and the Epidemiological Catchment Area Study—all which provide facts on illnesses, impairments, health behaviors, and mental health.
- *National Statistics Online* (www.statistics.gov.uk) contains social and economic data related to the United Kingdom with links to other statistical agencies around the world.
- *Statistical Abstracts of the United States, State and Metropolitan Area Data Book,* and the *County and City Data Book* publish social indicator statistics and are available online (http://www. census.gov) or at local libraries.
- The *Substance Abuse and Mental Health Services Administration* (www.samsha. gov) reports on usage, abuse, and treatment facts by state.
- *United Nations Statistics Division* (http://unstats.un.org/unsd/demographic /products/indwm/) provides official national and international statistics and indicators on women and men in these fields of concern: population, families, health, education, work, and political decision-making.
- The *U.S. Bureau of the Census* (www.census.gov) provides demographic, social, and economic information broken down by state and county.
- The U.S. Department of Health and Human Services' (www.healthypeople2010. gov) *Healthy People 2010* document is a national health promotion agenda that identifies leading disease and health-related focus areas. This is a must read!
- The *World Bank* (www.worldbank.org) has information on social indicators around the world.
- *World Tourism Organization* (http://www.unwto.org/statistics/index.htm) reports national and international arrival/departure statistics and the economic measurement of tourism.

Contribute to Scientific Knowledge

Every piece of research should be framed within a review of literature (Schutt, 2006). This means a literature review (Step 2) should have been conducted that reveals what has already been learned about the topic under consideration. This sort of grounding enables us to understand the scientific relevance of the study. Thus, a study can be significant for how it helps scientists understand the puzzling relationships among phenomena or to fill holes or gaps in our knowledge (Case 4).

Case 4. Example of a Study that Adds to Our Scientific Knowledge Base.

Marsh, P. (2007). *Backcountry adventure as spiritual development: A means-end study.* Unpublished doctoral dissertation, Indiana University.

The purpose of this study was to establish an understanding of what is meant when someone describes a backcountry adventure as spiritual. Open-ended interviews were conducted with 63 backcountry users in the region of Teton Pass, Wyoming. The study's findings identified the spiritual values of backcountry activities as reflecting: transcendent experience, increased awareness, and a sense of fulfillment. Why is this important? From the study's abstract the study's significance was provided:

> The rationale for this study lies in the small pool of leisure and recreation research that has identified spiritual outcomes from backcountry adventures. Prior studies have not defined the term spiritual, or fully explored the meaning of these spiritual experiences. (p. iii)

Significance Statement

We maintain that all studies, at the very onset, should contain a significance statement. This is the opportunity, indeed the responsibility, of the researcher(s) to point out the potential importance of the study. Some refer to this as addressing the *practical significance* of the study, meaning explaining how findings can or will be useful (Leedy & Ormrod, 2005).

The *significance statement* establishes a context for why the study is important. A well-written significance statement should point out the worthiness of the research. Why is it worth doing? The significance statement is the researcher's best chance to highlight or call attention to a " . . . substantive area that is important" (Schutt, 2006, p. 56).

The challenge before the investigator, then, is to convince others in both the proposal and final report about the merit(s) behind the study. Here's a story to illustrate our point. One of the co-authors of this text is a first-generation college graduate. She vividly recalls trying to explain to her family what her dissertation was going to be about. After dutifully listening to a long-winded recitation, her mother, trained as a lab technician, offered her the following advice, "Pretend your explanation is subjected to the following litmus test. Would you be able to phone me long distance, paying $100 a minute, to answer the question, 'So why is this study important?' in terms I would understand and accept?" Wow, talk about not beating around the bush!

In summary, every research project needs a written statement of significance. Case 5 offers several examples of statements of significance.

Since inevitably a significance statement must be prepared, we suggest the sooner it is drafted the better. In conclusion, if you're embarking on a study, we implore you early on to convincingly address the question of why your research is significant.

Case 5. Examples of Significance Statements.

Importance to:	Significance Statement	Citation
Professional Practice/ Service Delivery	For over a decade, the scientific community and park professionals have recognized that climate change will have critical implications for park conservation policy and management. . . . The implications of global climate change for nature-based park tourism have only recently begun to be assessed.	Jones, B., & Scott, D. (2006). Climate change, seasonality and visitation to Canada's national parks. *Journal of Park and Recreation Administration, 24,* 42-62.
Society	As the attraction to professional sport and college scholarships becomes more and more prominent, competition and winning at all costs in youth games are beginning to replace the development of skills and values, building friendships, and respecting the sportsmanship aspects of the game. . . . Further, this decline in sportsmanship may be correlated to the decline in participation. By the time children reach age 13, approximately 70% will have stopped participating in youth sport completely . . .	Arthur-Banning, S., Paisley, K., & Wells, M. (2007). Promoting sportsmanship in youth basketball players: The effect of referees' prosocial behavior techniques. *Journal of Park and Recreation Administration, 25,* 96-114.

Importance to:	Significance Statement	Citation
Scientific Knowledge	The leisure experiences of non-dominant cultures are receiving more attention as a focus of study and further understanding, yet little of this research has attempted to explore interrelationships between personality, affect, and motivational style and leisure for all but European American individuals. The rationale for this . . . investigation stems from the pressing needs to extend our understanding of leisure, further inform our efforts to conceptualize leisure and theorize about its natures, and our broader mission to more fully understand the experiences of leisure beyond those in the mainstream of society.	Barnett, L. (2006). Accounting for leisure preferences from within: The relative contributions of gender, race or ethnicity, personality, affective style, and motivational orientation. *Journal of Leisure Research, 38*, 445-474.

Your Research

1. **In what way is your research project meaningful? That is, does it have the potential to:**
   A. **Improve professional practice or service delivery?**
   B. **Address a social problem?**
   C. **Further science?**
2. **Write a significance statement for your research project.**

Review and Discussion Questions . . .
What have you learned about explaining a study's significance?

1. Define the term *transformative research?*
2. Why is a *significance statement* important?
3. Identify the three perspectives that can be used as a study's rationale when writing a significance statement.

Exercises

1. Did you know that every year people from a variety of backgrounds are awarded the Ig Nobel Prize for accomplishments in physics, medicine, and other disciplines? These awards are sponsored by the Annals of Improbable Research and focus on "research that makes you laugh and then think." The Ig Nobel Prize honors accomplishments that are both educational and funny. For example, a 17-year-old won based on her research on the "five-second rule," or the health

risk of eating food that has fallen on the floor (less than five seconds on the floor, it's eatable!). Also, a physicist figured out how Hula Hoops stayed up and won the prize.

    A. Read more about how Ig awardees have shown how scientific methods can be applied to problems that aren't normally thought of as being important by going to the Ig Nobel home page, http://www.improb.com/.

    B. Identify an award-winning topic you found both humorous and significant.

    C. Why do you think the topic you chose is significant?

2. Read about drinking patterns among college students by going to Harvard's School of Public Health's web site at www.hsph.harvard.edu/cas and click on the "College Alcohol Study." Look at the most recent articles to determine:

    A. Alcohol abuse among college students. What statistics impress upon you that alcohol abuse is a problem on American college campuses?

    B. Does the magnitude of alcohol consumption on college campuses suggest there is a need for alternate and constructive recreational activities for this population?

    C. If a research study was designed to provide alternative, drug-free recreational activities for college students, how significant would you consider this study to be? Why?

3. If not assigned a research article, find one that has been published in the past five years on a topic of interest to you. Rate (using "Excellent," "Good," "Fair," or "Poor" ratings) the significance of the research project in terms of implied or explicit arguments made at the beginning of the article regarding the study's importance to:

    A. Improving professional practice.

    B. Addressing a social problem.

    C. Contributing to scientific knowledge.

Research worth doing has significance for improving professional practice, addressing social problems, and/or contributing to scientific knowledge. Vintgar Gorge, Bled, Slovenia. *Copyright © 2008 Carol Cutler Riddick*

Part III: Developing a Plan

STEP 6: Select a Sample

Population and Sample

Probability Sampling
Sample Size
Simple Random Sampling
Systematic Random Sampling
Stratified Random Sampling
Cluster Sampling

Nonprobability Sampling
Volunteer Sampling
Quota Sampling
Expert/Key Informant Sampling
Snowball Sampling

**New knowledge is the most valuable commodity on earth. The more truth
we have to work with, the richer we become.**
Kurt Vonnegut, *Breakfast of Champions*

Let's review the steps in the research process up to this point. A topic area has been identified; a literature review has been conducted; a theoretical framework has been adopted; a purpose
statement, hypotheses and/or a research question have been crafted; and a statement of significance has been declared.

Attention must now be turned to bridging the gap between a ***strategy of inquiry*** and a ***plan
of action.*** The first order of business in this plan of action is to select a sample. To help us understand how to select a sample, this chapter is divided into three major sections. In the first section,
a review of what is meant by population and sample is distinguished. Next, the two major types
of sampling are explained.

Population and Sample

It is important to determine whether you are studying a population or a sample. A ***population*** consists of the entire set of entities for a situation. Examples of populations are all sports
management undergraduate majors attending colleges in North America during the 2006-2007
academic year, all youth hostels located in London, all children with documented developmental
disabilities attending public elementary schools in Houston during the past school year, and all
government-owned hiking trails in Slovenia. These examples demonstrate that populations vary
by size and location.

Conducting a study of a large-numbered population, technically known as a *census*, is often
impractical. For example, it would be quite time-consuming and expensive to determine all the
tourism undergraduate majors in North America. Instead, it is more efficient to study a sample of
the population. A ***sample*** is a subset or subgroup of the population. Technically, individual cases
or entities in the sample are referred to as elements or ***units of analysis*** (Step 4). A listing of all
elements in a population is referred to as the ***sampling frame.***

Two approaches are used in selecting a sample: probability sampling and nonprobability
sampling. Studies based on a quantitative framework use either probability sampling or nonprobability sampling. On the other hand, studies that pivot around a qualitative framework rely on
nonprobability sampling.

Probability Sampling

Probability sampling is when every unit of a population has the same chance of being
chosen for the sample. Stated another way, in probability sampling every member of the population has the same chance of NOT being chosen for the sample. In other words, no inherent or
systematic bias is used in choosing who is or who is not selected to be in the study.

A sample that is selected using probability sampling is a **representative** or **unbiased sample.** A representative sample " . . . 'looks like' the population from which it was selected in all aspects that are potentially relevant to the study" (Schutt, 2006, p. 138).

Probability sampling can be carried out any number of ways. Among the more popular techniques are simple random sampling, systematic random sampling, stratified random sampling, and cluster sampling. There are advantages and disadvantages of each probability sampling technique, of course, and these are summarized in Figure 1.

Figure 1. Advantages and Disadvantages of Different Types of Probability Sampling Techniques.[1]

Sampling Technique	Possible Advantages	Possible Disadvantages
Simple Random	• Easy to implement • Sampling error can be approximated	• Requires knowing all members of the population • When a large sample must be generated, cumbersome to do by hand
Systematic Random	• Convenient when population units are arranged sequentially • Easy to use when a list of sample names is available (e.g., registrants)	• If not randomly selected, a biased or non-representative sample is drawn
Stratified Random	• Represents subgroups	• Requires knowing all members of groups within the population • Requires weighting or drawing appropriate percentage of each subgroup
Cluster	• Useful when dealing with populations spread out across a wide geographic area or among different organizations • *Sampling error* (or the difference between the characteristics of a sample and the characteristics of a population) decreases as the homogeneity of cases per cluster increases	• Expense • Sampling error increases as the number of clusters decreases

[1]Adapted from Schutt (2006).

Sampling

Probability Sampling

non probability Sampling

Sample Size

Before delving into these probability sampling techniques, our attention first must be shifted to a question that must be dealt with early on. Namely, when conducting a study involving probability sampling, it is important to decide on the **sample size** or the number of units selected.

Mathematicians have issued guidelines for a desirable sample size when the population size is known. Figure 2 identifies the sample size (represented by columns headed with the universally accepted "*n*" notation) needed when the population size (represented by columns headed with the standard "*N*" notation) is identifiable.

N = population   n = sample size needed

Figure 2. Given Finite Population Sizes (N), What is the Recommended Sample Size (n)? [2,3]

Law of Diminishing Return

N	n	N	n	N	n
10	10	220	140	1,200	291
15	14	230	144	1,300	297
20	19	240	148	1,400	302
25	24	259	152	1,500	306
30	28	260	155	1,600	310
35	32	270	159	1,700	313
40	36	280	162	1,800	317
45	40	290	165	1,900	320
50	44	300	169	2,000	322
55	48	320	175	2,200	327
60	52	340	181	2,400	331
65	56	360	186	2,600	335
70	59	380	191	2,800	338
75	63	400	196	3,000	341
80	66	420	201	3,500	346
85	70	440	205	4,000	351
90	73	460	210	4,500	354
95	76	480	214	5,000	357
100	80	500	217	6,000	361
110	86	550	226	7,000	364
120	92	600	234	8,000	367
130	97	650	242	9,000	368
140	103	700	248	10,000	370
150	108	750	254	15,000	375
160	113	800	260	20,000	377
170	118	850	265	30,000	379
180	123	900	269	40,000	380
190	127	950	274	50,000	381
200	132	1,000	278	75,000	382
210	136	1,100	285	100,000	384

[2]At + .05 precision of estimate
[3]From R. Krejcie and D. Morgan (1970, p. 610). Reprinted with permission of Sage Publications.

One interesting thing to note is that as the population size increases, sample size does not proportionally increase. This statistics principle is known as ***diminishing returns*** and is reviewed in greater depth in the following *Something to Remember* box.

Something to Remember!   Sampling frame : population on a list

In general, there is a point of ***diminishing returns*** when it comes to choosing how many persons to sample from a known population size. To demonstrate this point, consult Figure 2. Determine how many persons are needed in a sample when the known population size is:

• 300?
• 600?

The correct answers are 169 and 234 persons, respectfully. Did you notice that the sample size did not increase that much, even though the population size was doubled? This illustrates the statistical concept of ***diminishing returns*** in sample size.

Simple Random Sampling

In order to accomplish simple random sampling, you first must have the ***sampling frame*** or list of names of all individuals or elements in the population under scrutiny. Examples of sampling frames include a list of: participants in a county's youth soccer program during the season that just concluded, current adult members of a chain of health clubs, pottery class registrants for the past five years for an arts center, newspaper articles written about a public recreation agency last year, and all RV pad sites at a state park campground.

Randomly selecting units from the sampling frame can be carried out a number of different ways. If the population size is not too large, the "pull out of the hat" technique is used. Yes, the name of each person or element in the population is recorded on a separate slip of paper, the slip is folded so the name is hidden, and it is put into a container (such as a hat, fishbowl, bag, or envelope). The slips of paper are mixed up (by hand or by shaking the container) and then someone reaches into the container and one at a time draws a name out of the container until the desired number of sampling units has been identified.

As demonstrated in Case 1, when a large number of unites exist in the population, a popular way to implement a random sample is to rely on a table of random numbers (Figure 3). Alternatively, computer programs can be used to generate random numbers.

Case 1. Simple Random Sample.

Suppose a Department Chair wants to conduct a survey, using simple random sampling, of students enrolled in an introductory evaluation course. The course has 100 students. According to Figure 2, 80 names need to be randomly selected. The 80 people identified will receive a questionnaire to complete. The steps for selecting the 80 names follows:

1. Alphabetize (by last name) all students registered for the course. Then assign each person in this list a unique number, beginning with the number "001."
2. Decide to move through the table of random numbers (Figure 3) in a downward fashion, using the first two digits in a number array. Close your eyes, arbitrarily pointing to a number in the table of random numbers. Pretend your finger lands on Row 8, Columns 16 and 17, revealing the number 58. Record the number selected.
3. Now, move downwards through Figure 3, until you identify 80 people from the class list to become part of your sample. The next few numbers that appear are 83, 62, 15, 46, 73, 60, 43, 93, 89, etc. NOTE: If you encounter: (a) a number that is not assigned or (b) the same number array twice, skip the number and continue until you have identified the names of 80 different persons.

Figure 3. Table of Random Numbers.[4]

Row #	1	2	3	4	5	6	7	8	9	10	11	12	13	14	15	16	17	18
									Column #									
1	2	1	0	4	9	8	0	8	8	8	0	6	9	2	4	8	2	6
2	0	7	3	0	2	9	4	8	2	7	8	9	8	9	2	9	7	1
3	4	4	9	0	0	2	8	6	2	6	7	7	7	3	1	2	5	1
4	7	3	2	1	1	2	0	7	7	6	0	3	8	3	4	7	8	1
5	3	3	2	5	8	3	1	7	0	1	4	0	7	8	9	3	7	7
6	6	1	2	0	5	7	2	4	4	0	0	6	3	0	2	8	0	7
7	7	0	9	3	3	3	7	4	0	4	8	8	9	3	5	8	0	5
8	7	5	1	9	0	9	1	5	2	6	5	0	9	0	3	5	8	8
9	3	5	6	9	6	5	0	1	9	4	6	6	7	5	6	8	3	1
10	8	5	0	3	9	4	3	4	0	6	5	1	7	4	4	6	2	7
11	0	5	9	6	8	7	4	8	1	5	5	0	5	1	7	1	5	8
12	7	6	2	2	6	9	6	1	9	7	1	1	4	7	1	6	2	0
13	3	8	4	7	8	9	8	2	2	1	6	3	8	7	0	4	6	1
14	1	9	1	8	4	5	6	1	8	1	2	4	4	4	2	7	3	4
15	1	5	3	6	7	6	1	8	4	3	1	8	8	7	7	6	0	4
16	0	5	5	3	6	0	7	1	3	8	1	4	6	7	0	4	3	5
17	2	2	3	8	6	0	9	1	9	0	4	4	7	6	8	1	5	1
18	2	3	3	2	5	5	7	6	9	4	9	7	1	3	7	9	3	8
19	8	5	5	0	5	3	7	8	5	4	5	1	6	0	4	8	9	1
20	0	6	1	1	3	4	8	6	4	3	2	9	4	3	8	7	4	1
21	9	1	1	8	2	9	0	6	9	6	9	4	2	9	9	0	6	0
22	3	7	8	0	6	3	7	1	2	6	5	2	7	6	5	6	5	1
23	5	3	0	5	1	2	1	0	9	1	3	7	5	6	1	2	5	0
24	7	2	4	8	6	7	9	3	8	7	6	0	9	1	6	5	7	8
25	0	9	1	6	7	0	3	8	0	9	1	5	4	2	3	2	4	5
26	3	8	1	4	3	7	9	2	4	5	1	2	8	7	7	4	1	3

[4]From Patten (2007). Reprinted with permission from Pyrczak Publishing, Inc.

Systematic Random Sampling

Systematic random sampling is a variation of simple random sampling. After choosing the initial person or element in a random fashion, a logical and organized method is used to select the remaining sample members. In particular, a sampling interval is calculated and used. A *sampling interval* is the total number of units in the population divided by the number of units required for the sample (Case 2).

Case 2. Systematic Random Sampling.

A study is being conducted on opinions that **master's athletes** (or people age 55 years and older) hold about a track and field competition. Approximately 1,200 individuals registered for the event. Consulting a table of recommended sample size (Figure 2), it is determined about 300 individuals need to be part of the systematic random sample. The steps for conducting a survey of these individuals using systematic random sampling would be the following:

1. Number each person registered in the track and field competition. The list of names can first be alphabetized and then numbered or you can number names in the order of registration date. Regardless, in progressive order, assign a number to each person beginning with the number 0001 and ending with the number 1,200.
2. Calculate a sampling interval, which in this example equates to 1,200 divided by 300, which equals 4. This means every fourth individual who registered needs to be surveyed.
3. Close your eyes and randomly choose a number from the table of random numbers (Figure 3). This number identifies the first case or person to be sampled.
4. After the first person has been chosen for the sample, the name of every fourth person down on the registration list from the previous person selected is identified. This step repeats itself until the desired 300 names have been identified.

Stratified Random Sampling

A *stratified random sample* involves randomly sampling different categories or subgroups of persons represented in a population. Technically, these categories or subgroups are known as *stratum*. Examples of stratum are gender (males and females), undergraduate matriculation level (first year, sophomores, juniors, and seniors), and residency (by zip code).

The rationale for examining subgroups within a population is that the dependent variable(s) under study are believed to differ between or among the identified *strata* (NOTE: *strata* is the plural of *stratum*). Thus, the dimension used to divide the population into subgroups should be relevant to the problem under study.

The most common use of stratified sampling is proportionate stratified sampling. *Proportionate stratified sampling* assures that the different subgroups are represented in the sample in the same proportion they are found in the population. For example, if the population contains 60% females and 40% males, a proportionate stratified sample for gender would include 60% females and 40% males too. Case 3 provides another example of proportionate stratified sampling.

129

Case 3. Stratified Random Sample of Undergraduates at a University.

A study is being set up on the leisure interests and values of undergraduates at a university. Previous research results indicate that a year in college has a profound effect on one's leisure lifestyle. The university's undergraduate enrollment is about 10,000. A breakdown by matriculation year appears in the figure immediately following.

University's Undergraduate Student Population ($N = 10,000$).

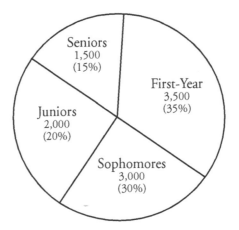

You know by consulting a table of recommended sample size (see Figure 2), you need a sample size of about 370. Therefore, you ask the Registrar's Office to generate (using a computerized random number generator) 370 names across the four matriculation rank strata using the same proportions found in the university's undergraduate student population. The numbers and respective percentages of those randomly selected appear in the following pie chart.

Proportionate Stratified Random Sample Selected from the Population of the University ($N = 370$).

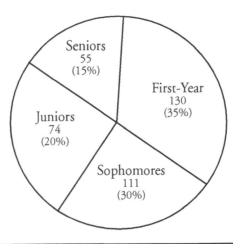

Cluster Sampling

Cluster sampling involves dividing the population into a set of smaller groups or clusters and then randomly choosing one or more clusters for inclusion in the sample. For example, suppose at a Florida retirement community residents have moved from such clusters as Canada, Michigan, Ohio, Illinois, and Pennsylvania. Randomly selecting two of these locales (such as Michigan and Illinois) from which to draw a sample is an example of cluster sampling.

For those clusters randomly chosen, either every person in the cluster is sampled or a random sample of cluster members is used. Cluster sampling is used when it is difficult or impossible to obtain a sampling frame list of all members of a population.

Typically, cluster sampling is carried out in waves using a multistage approach. A *multistage approach* consists of identifying a series of samples. It begins by breaking down a large-sized cluster into a group of smaller clusters. Within each of these smaller clusters one or more subsets are randomly chosen (Case 4).

Case 4. Multistage Cluster Sampling.

Suppose a study is designed to survey the opinions of people who visit parks located in American metropolitan areas. It has been decided to focus on parks located in geographic areas whose population numbers 50,000 or more persons. Implementing cluster sampling would require the researcher to follow the multistage approach described below:

1. Divide the United States into five regions, East, South, Midwest, Southwest, and West.
2. Randomly select three states from each of the five regions, amounting to selecting a total of 15 states.
3. Randomly select two metropolitan areas from each of the 15 states selected, thus totaling the identification of 30 metro areas.
4. Randomly select visitors to survey from each of the 30 metropolitan park systems that have been identified.

Nonprobability Sampling

The distinguishing difference between probability sampling and nonprobability sampling centers on how people/units are selected to be in the study. Recall that probability sampling involves random selection of study participants, meaning everyone in the population has been given the same chance to be included or excluded.

Contrastingly, *nonprobability sampling* does not rely on random selection; instead, people or units are selected accidentally or due to convenience. When nonprobability sampling has been used, a *nonrepresentative* or *biased sample* has been chosen.

At first glance, using a biased sample may seem to be a bad thing. There are, however, defensible reasons for using nonprobability sampling. First, situations where it is impossible to identify all members of a population beforehand, dictate the use of nonprobability sampling. And second, there are instances, such as ethical concerns, where it becomes impossible to rely on probability sampling.

Nonprobability sampling may be carried out a number of ways. Four of the common methods used to conduct nonprobability sampling are: volunteer sampling, quota sampling, expert sampling, and snowball sampling. Each of these techniques has possible advantages and disadvantages (Figure 4).

Figure 4. Advantages and Disadvantages of Different Types of Nonprobability Sampling Techniques.[5]

Sampling Technique	Possible Advantages	Possible Disadvantages
Volunteer Sampling	• Ease of implementation	• Biased, not representative
Quota Sampling	• Potential of providing insights from different groups	• In order to set the correct quotas, must know the proportion characteristics fall across the entire population • Biased, not representative
Expert/Key Informant Sampling	• Insightful if informants are knowledgeable, willing to talk, and representative	• Biased, not representative
Snowball Sampling	• Useful when no sampling frame exists and members are interconnected • When sampling is repeated through several waves, the composition of the sample comes closer to being more representative	• Biased, not representative • Difficulty in identifying and/or soliciting cooperation from hard-to-reach individuals • Initial contacts may shape the entire sample or prevent access to some members of the population of interest

[5]Adapted from Schutt (2006).

~~Volunteer~~ *Convenience* Sampling

Volunteer sampling is also known as convenience, accidental, or haphazard sampling. Basically, in ***volunteer sampling,*** a person is chosen to be in the sample because of expediency. She or he is readily available or accessible (Case 5). Volunteer sampling has been referred to as the "take-them-where-you-can-find them" method of obtaining participants (Cozby, 2006 p. 132).

Case 5. Volunteer Sampling.

A theme park wants to find out about visitors' experiences. When people purchase an admission ticket, they are given a business size card that solicits their participation in an online survey. Individuals 18 years of age or older are instructed to log on to a Web site and complete a questionnaire.

Quota Sampling - like police officers

Quota sampling is the nonprobability equivalent of stratified sampling. You identify the various subgroups of interest, set a target about the number of individuals needed for each subgroup, and then by "hook or crook" find the requisite number of people for each subgroup. In other words, in a nonrandom manner, people are studied who satisfy each identified strata or subgroup of interest (Case 6).

Case 6. Quota Sampling.

Suppose a university wants to conduct a survey about the school's intramurals (IM) program. Administrators want to learn about the opinions IM users have about the program, as well as reasons for non-use. There are about 1,000 students registered at the school and records reveal that about 30% of the student body participates in the IM program. A table is set up in the student union to recruit students to complete a short questionnaire. In particular, a quota is set. Those staffing the table are told to gather completed questionnaires from 83 students who report participating in the IM program and 195 students who say they did not participate in the IM program during the school year. [Do you follow where all these numbers came from? First, consulting Figure 2, it was determined the sample size should be set at 278. Second, quotas were set for the proportion of the sample that should be IM users (30% IM participation rate multiplied by 278 equals 83 individuals) and the proportion of the sample that should represent non-IM users (70% multiplied by 278 equals 195)].

Expert/Key Informant Sampling
Target

An *expert sample* consists of targeting individuals who are knowledgeable about the issue under study. Individuals with known or demonstrated expertise and/or experience are called upon to serve as a member of the sample group (Case 7).

Case 7. Expert/Key Informant Sampling.

Vandalism has been a reoccurring problem in a state park system. Maintenance supervisors are invited to attend a workshop to share ideas on vandalism prevention and remediation.

Snowball Sampling

Snowball sampling could be viewed as an adaptation of expert sampling. In *snowball sampling*, one person is found who meets study criteria and then that person is relied on to identify another person meeting the same criteria.

Snowball sampling is used when trying to reach members of groups who are hard to locate or hard to reach and no sampling frame exists. The premise behind snowball sampling is that individuals belonging to a certain group are interconnected and the researcher's only hope is to gain access to one member of the group, who in turn will open the doors or put the researcher in touch with other members of the group (Case 8).

Case 8. Snowball Sampling.

A study is being undertaken on female teenage gang members. The investigator meets a gang member during an in-line skating contest. She asks the individual if she would be willing to be interviewed later in the week. The teenager shows up at a park and agrees to answer some questions. At the conclusion of the interview, the researcher asks this gang member if she would identify another girl in the gang who might be willing to be interviewed. The following day the first girl shows up at the park with another female, teenage gang member, and she is interviewed. At the conclusion of the interview, the second person is asked if she could enlist a third gang member to be interviewed and so the cycle continues.

If we asked six players on each pool volleyball team to complete a questionnaire rating recreation services at a Florida retirement community, what form of sampling would we be doing? *Copyright © 2008 Ruth V. Russell*

Your Research

1. Define the population and the sample you plan to use for the study.
2. Will you be relying on probability or nonprobability sampling? Identify the specific sampling technique you plan to use.

Review and Discussion Questions . . .
What have you learned about selecting a sample?

1. What is the difference between a *population* and *sample?*
2. How is *probability sampling* distinguished from *nonprobability sampling?*
3. How do you go about deciding the *sample size* for a probability sample?
4. Explain each of the techniques for implementing probability sampling: *simple random sampling, systematic random sampling, stratified random sampling,* and *cluster sampling.*
5. Explain each of the techniques for implementing nonprobability sampling: *volunteer sampling, quota sampling, expert/key informant sampling,* and *snowball sampling.*

Exercises

1. Examine an article that either has been assigned by your instructor or that you choose.
   A. Was probability or nonprobability sampling used? Specify the exact type of sampling technique used.
   B. How many individuals were involved in the sample? Explain whether or not the sample size was adequate.

2. Read Robert Wood Johnson's "Planning and Using Survey Research Projects" available at www. rwjf.org (click "Publications & Resources," then "How-To Tools," and then "Research Guidance"). List one additional point you learned about each of the following topics: "Probability Sampling Methods," "Sample Size," and "Over-Sampling," and "Response Rates."

3. Learn more about randomization by going to the Research Randomizer Web site at www. randomizer.org.
   A. Complete "Lessons I: Random Sampling of . . . ," "Lesson 2: Random Assignment . . . ," and "Lesson 4: Random Sampling of 100 Phone Numbers." What did you learn from each of these tutorials?
   B. Suppose you are asked to conduct a study dealing with the leisure pastimes of college age students. In order to do the study, you decide to rely on cluster sampling. To begin, write an alphabetical listing of the names of the 50 states; then number this alphabetical listing. Click on the "Randomization Box" and reset "How Many Numbers" to "10" and also reset the "Sort Numbers" to "Least to Greatest." What numbers were generated and which states were consequently identified for inclusion in your study?

4. Read about the experience sampling method (ESM) by going to an article authored by Barbara Schneider and Linda Waite entitled, "Timely and Timeless: Working Parents and Their Children" found at the University of Maryland's Web site www.popcenter.umd.edu/events/nichd/papers/scheider.pdf.
    A. Write a one-paragraph description of this sampling technique.
    B. Does ESM rely on probability sampling or non-probability sampling?
    C. How does ESM differ from time diaries?

5. Spend about an hour (or whatever imposed time limit) trying to construct a snowball sample of people who play paintball or some other uncommon activity identified by your instructor. See if you can find someone who engages in the unusual activity, then ask that person to introduce you to another person who takes up the same unusual activity.
    A. How many people were you able to identify within the time limit?
    B. Explain how this exercise is easier or more difficult than you expected.

6. If you feel you need or want to learn more about topics reviewed in this chapter, check out information presented on the following Web sites:
    A. For sampling and design, go to the International Consortium for the Advancement of Academic Publication's "Resources for Methods in Evaluation and Social Research" web page that is at http://gsociology.icapp.org. Click on "Sites About Sampling."
    B. Another reference for sampling and design is William Trochim's web page for *Research Methods Knowledge Base* at www.socialresarchmethods.net/kb/contents.htm. Click on "Sampling."
    C. For snowball sampling, go to the Department of Sociology, at the University of Surrey, Social Research Update's web page at www.soc.surrey.ac.uk/sru. Click on Issue 33, "Accessing Hidden and Hard-to-Reach Populations: Snowball Research Strategies."

Sampling individuals, groups, organizations, artifacts, social interactions, etc. can be accomplished either via probability or nonprobability methods. Burano, Italy. *Copyright © 2008 Carol Cutler Riddick*

STEP 7: Choose a Design

Quantitative Approaches
Experimental Designs
Quasi-Experimental Designs
Pre-Experimental Designs
Single-Subject Designs
Non-Experimental Designs
Sample Size Guidelines
Response Rate
Criteria for Choosing a Quantitative Design
Internal Validity
External Validity
Sample Generalizability

Qualitative Approaches
Case Study
Critical Theory
Ethnography
Grounded Theory
Narrative
Phenomenology
Rigor in Qualitative Designs

Mixed-Methods Approaches
Concurrent Design
Sequential Design

The more alternatives, the more difficult the choice.
Abbe' D'Allanival

As previously discussed (Step 3), the theoretical approach adopted for your study has implications for how it will be designed. In other words, the theoretical lens that has been identified brings into focus the options available to structure the research (Figure 1).

Figure 1. Overview of Design Options.

Theoretical Framework Adopted		
Quantitative Approach	**Qualitative Approach**	**Mixed-Methods Approach**
• Experimental • Quasi-Experimental • Pre-Experimental • Single-Subject • Non-Experimental	• Case Study • Critical Theory • Ethnography • Grounded Theory • Narrative • Phenomenology	• Concurrent Design • Sequential Design

So, at this step, the challenge is to choose a way to design or structure the study to support its theoretical framework (Case 1). Choosing a design depends on other factors too. Available designs, whether quantitative or qualitative, are also based on the (Weiss, 1972, p.4):

- Research purpose and question (Step 4).
- Information needs of the users of the study.
- Program and organization needs and constraints.
- Protection of human subjects.

Case 1. Choosing a Quantitative or a Qualitative Design.[1]

Think of a research project you'd be interested in undertaking. Perhaps it is the one you're doing as a class assignment. In order to figure out which kind of design to adopt for the research, answer the following four questions:

1. Do I want to measure numerically what I am interested in?
2. Am I mostly concerned about using measurable "facts?"
3. Am I mostly concerned about individuals' explanations of what is happening?"
4. Do I think that the "truth" is different for each individual?

If you answer "Yes" to the first two questions and "No" to the last two questions, then you're likely to choose a quantitative design. If you answer "No" to the first two questions and "Yes" to the last two questions, then you're likely to adopt a qualitative design. And finally, if you answer "Yes" to all four questions, you're headed towards a mixed-methods design.

[1]Adapted from Gratton and Jones (2004).

In order to introduce you to your design choices, the chapter is divided into three parts. The first section deals with quantitative design options. The second part reviews popular ways to structure a qualitative inquiry. And lastly, designs associated with a mixed-methods approach are reviewed.

Quantitative Approaches

Designs related to a quantitative framework have been labeled *fixed designs* (Robson, 2002) and can be divided into five major categories. These are experimental, quasi-experimental, pre-experimental, single-subject, and non-experimental designs.

Fixed designs vary in practicality, cost, and level of technical skill required to implement (Rossi, Lipsey, & Freeman, 2004). This is why choice of design is dependent on the realities of the research situation, including the focus of the research question. For example, with one exception, fixed designs are used to measure the impact of a program or treatment intervention. The exception, non-experimental designs, are used when the focus is on surveying individuals or groups.

Experimental Designs

Before reviewing experimental designs frequently used in recreation, park, tourism, and sport research, some historical perspective will help our understanding. In the 1800s, researchers in the physical sciences began using what is known as the *classic experimental design.* This design has five distinguishing qualities: random selection, experimental group, random assignment, pretest, and post-test. Figure 2 highlights the scientific notation typically used for each of these experimental elements. This notation system will come in handy when you read about the different designs a bit later.

Figure 2. Qualities and Notations of the Classic Experimental Design.

Quality	Notation[2]
Random selection from study population	*RS* = random selection
Experimental group (or group offered or exposed to the program intervention) and a *control group* (or group not participating in program intervention)	Group that experiences the treatment or *program intervention* (*X*) is the experimental group; group without the *X* notation is the control or comparison group
Random assignment to either the experimental group or the control group	*RA* = random assignment
Pretest or baseline data collected on the two groups before the program intervention is introduced or experienced	*OX,* with *O* = observation or measurement and since *O* comes before or is to the left of the *X* this indicates a time order of events with the pretest occurring before *X* is introduced or experienced

Quality	Notation[2]
Post-test or data collected on the two groups after program intervention is completed by the experimental group	***XO,*** with ***O*** = observation or measurement and since ***O*** follows or is to the right of the ***X*** this indicates a time order of events with the post-test occurring after ***X*** is introduced or experienced

[2]This notation system was developed by Campbell and Stanley (1967).

When studying human beings in social contexts, random selection and random assignment are often difficult to accomplish. Some people refuse an invitation to participate in a study after they have been informed that they were randomly chosen. Others refuse to be randomly assigned to a control group, even if promised the treatment once the experiment is over. Thus, in identifying a design for research in our field, one or more of the distinguishing five qualities found in the classic experimental design will be dropped.

Nonetheless, experimental designs used in social research do attempt to control the environment and measure the effects of controlled change. Three of the more commonly used experimental designs are the pretest-post-test control group, the post-test only control group, and the Solomon four-group designs (Figure 3).

Figure 3. Popular Experimental Designs.

Design Name	Schematic	Summary	Comment
Pretest-Post-test Control Group	RA O---X---O RA O--------O	• Participants randomly assigned to one of two groups • Both groups receive a pretest and a post-test • Treatment only given to experimental group	• Able to determine if two groups are in fact equivalent at the beginning of the experiment
Post-test Only Control Group	RA X---O RA ---O	• Participants randomly assigned to one of two groups • Treatment only given to experimental group • Both groups receive a post-test • Controls for confounding effects of a pretest	• Assumes at the beginning of the experiment the two groups were equivalent/did not differ in any systematic way • Appropriate to use this design when pretesting is illogical (e.g., if evaluating the teaching effectiveness of swimming instruction on toddlers, it makes no sense to do a pretest!)

Design Name	Schematic	Summary	Comment
Solomon Four-Group	RA O---X---O RA O--------O RA X---O RA O	• Random assignment to one of four groups • Whether or not a group receives a pretest and/or treatment varies • All groups receive post-test • Can assess the effect of pre-testing sensitiza-tion and experimental mortality	• Relative to other experimental designs, requires more research participants • Logistical work required since four groups need to be set up

Quasi-Experimental Designs

In comparison to experimental designs, quasi-experimental designs are considered more practical. In *quasi-experimental designs,* study participants are not randomly selected to be involved in the study; and if a control group is featured in the quasi-experimental design, individuals are not randomly assigned to one group or the other (i.e., the experimental or the control group). Often, researchers turn to a quasi-experimental design because of difficulties associated with trying to implement the random selection and random assignment features of experimental designs.

There are a number of quasi-experimental designs available to us. Three of the most commonly used are identified in Figure 4 as the nonequivalent control-group, single group interrupted time series, and control group interrupted time series.

Figure 4. Popular Quasi-Experimental Designs.

Design Name	Schematic	Summary	Comment
Nonequivalent Control-Group	O---X---O O--------O	• Both groups are selected without using random selection or random assignment • Both groups take pre- and post-tests • Only experimental group receives treatment	• Used when random assignment to the two groups is impossible • In order to address equivalency of the two groups at the pretest phase, matching should be considered
Single-Group Interrupted Time-Series	O-O-O-O-X-O-O-O-O	• Individuals not randomly selected • Only one group or the experimental group • Multiple pretests and post-tests	• Number of pretests and post-tests can vary • Pretest trend score is estimated and compared to post-test trend score

Design Name	Schematic	Summary	Comment
Control-Group Interrupted Time Series	O-O-O-X-O-O-O O-O-O-O-O-O-O	• Two groups, not randomly selected or assigned • Treatment is received by only experimental group • Multiple pretests and post-tests	• Number of pretests and post-tests can vary • Pretest trend score is estimated and compared to post-test trend score

Additional discussion of the first quasi-experimental design listed in Figure 4 above, non-equivalent control-group design, is useful. Matching is often used in an attempt to overcome one challenge associated with using this design. *Matching* involves pairing persons in the experiment and control groups on the basis of similarity of age, gender, or some other characteristic (Case 2). Matching essentially is an attempt to equate selected characteristics of individuals in the experimental group to those possessed by the control group (Schutt, 2006).

Case 2. Matching of Experimental and Control Group Members in Study Designed to Measure the Impacts of Video game Play on Nursing Home Residents.

Suppose you've decided to introduce a novel activity to nursing home residents: video game play. You want to adopt a nonequivalent control-group design to conduct the study. The challenge confronting you is how to identify two groups, the experimental and control, for the study. Below are your options for matching individuals belonging to the two groups.

Approach to Matching	Application
1. *Intact group matching.* Locate a second group, usually in a different geographic location, whose demographic characteristics and/or pretest scores are anticipated to resemble experimental group.	Choose to implement the study in two nursing homes owned by the same chain in the same town.
2. *Individual matching.* Each control group member is selected because he or she is a close or perfect match, in terms of having the same pretest score on the independent variable (or variable that is strongly related to the dependent variable), as his or her corresponding experimental group member. Individual matching can be time consuming and, if a number of variables are matched, difficult to implement.	If length of time living in the nursing home is considered an important matching variable, each person in the control group would be an equivalent match to an experimental group member. For instance, if an experimental group member had lived in the facility for five years, then there would be a control group equivalent who had lived in a nursing home for five years.

Approach to Matching	Application
3. *Aggregate matching.* The overall "average" on important pretest variable scores, for the experimental and control groups, are matched. Aggregate matching is deemed less desirable to use than individual matching.	If age is deemed an important matching variable, the control group would be constituted so that their "average" age matched the experimental group though the range of ages in the two groups would vary. For instance, suppose the age of experimental group members spanned between 70 and 80 years; whereas control group members age spread was from 74 to 76 years. One concern, however, is that although both groups' mean age emerged as 75, one group relative to the other group had much younger and older members.

Originally, matching emerged as an alternative technique to randomization. In reality, matching can only be performed when individuals are matched on one or two characteristics. Thus, matching is actually a poor alternative to randomization. This is because other characteristics, that were unmatched, may ultimately influence outcomes.

Pre-Experimental Designs

Four pre-experimental designs are frequently used. These are: one-group pretest-post-test, static group comparison, one-time post-test, and alternative treatment post-test only with non-equivalent groups (Figure 5). Simply put, pre-experimental designs lack the rigor found in experimental and quasi-experimental designs. In other words, problems arise when not using random selection and random assignment, as well as not using a pretest and/or a control group. Interpreting results and drawing conclusions, when these designs have been used, becomes problematic (see Figure 5, "Comments" column).

Figure 5. Popular Pre-Experimental Designs.

Design Name	Schematic	Summary	Comment
One-Group Pretest-Post-test	O---X---O	• One group, or the experimental group, receives pretests and post-tests	• Any noted changes from pretest to post-test does not necessarily stem from the intervention
Static Group Comparison	X---O O	• Both experimental and control groups receive a post-test	• No assurance that the two groups were equivalent at the beginning of the experiment

Design Name	Schematic	Summary	Comment
One-Time Post-test	X---O	• Experimental group receives intervention followed by a post-test	• Provides no information regarding any change study participants experienced
Alternative Treatment Post-test-Only with Nonequivalent Groups	X_1---O X_2---O	• Two different treatments (X_1 and X_2) are compared using two different groups • Only post-tests are used	• Not able to know if noted differences between the two groups stems from non-equivalency at the beginning of the experiment or is due to differences in the interventions under study

Experts advise that pre-experimental designs are best suited for a pilot study or test (discussed in greater detail in Step 12) (Patten, 2007). Nevertheless, even with their known disadvantages, many people opt to use a pre-experimental design when conducting a program evaluation because these designs are much easier to implement.

Single-Subject Designs

Single-subject designs, also referred to as *A-B designs,* deal with multiple observations of a single individual. Single-subject designs evaluate the relationship between an intervention and a study participant's behaviors. These designs are especially popular in therapeutic recreation since they can be used to document program intervention success. Nevertheless, it is important to note that single-subject designs work best when there is a stable baseline period and the effect from the intervention is relatively large (Stangor, 2006).

In single-subject designs, *baseline data* or multiple pretests of the target behavior (or *A*), are administered over a period of time, and a pretest trend score is calculated. Then the intervention, along with multiple assessments of the target behavior (or *B*), is administered over time (Case 3). Four common single-subject designs, that are an elaboration or variation of the A-B design, are single-subject withdraw/reversal design, multiple baseline design, multiple probe design, and alternating treatments design (Dattilo, Gast, Loy, & Malley, 2000).

Case 3. Single-Subject Withdraw/Reversal Design.

Wolfe, B., Dattilo, J., & Gast, D. (2003). Effects of a token economy system within the context of cooperative games on social behaviors of adolescents with emotional and behavioral disorders. *Therapeutic Recreation Journal, 37,* 124-141.

A single-subject reversal design was used to examine the effects of cooperative games and a token economy program on the social behaviors of three adolescents with emotional disorders. In particular, each participant was introduced to the following sequence of events, $A-B_1-BC_1-B_2-BC_2$ with:

A = Free Play.
B_1 = Cooperative Games.
BC_1 = Cooperative Games and Token Economy System.
B_2 = Cooperative Games.
BC_2 = Cooperative Games and Token Economy System.

When cooperative games were introduced, adolescent behaviors remained stable and unchanged. When a token economy system was introduced in combination with cooperative games, there was an immediate increase in the number of prosocial behaviors.

Non-Experimental Designs

In non-experimental studies, a program intervention per se is not the focus of the study. Instead, individuals or groups are studied as they are. Two examples of non-experimental designs are the survey and ex post facto design.

Survey design, typically implemented by using probability sampling and questionnaires, examines individuals' self-reported attitudes, beliefs, preferences, and/or behaviors. In the past, survey research has been the most popular design used in studies published in recreation and leisure journals (Bedini & Wu, 1994; Riddick, DeSchriver, & Weissinger, 1991).

Surveys can be used to study people at one point in time or at several points in time. When the latter approach is adopted, it is because there is interest in monitoring age differences, age changes, or both age differences and age changes.

If age is used as the basis for selecting different groups, a one-time administration of a questionnaire is known as a *cross-sectional survey.* A cross-sectional survey measures age differences. If the same age group is surveyed at different times, this is known as a *longitudinal survey* or *panel study,* and produces a measure of age changes. Several age groups studied over time but with different persons used to represent each age group is known as a *time-lag survey.* An excellent reference explaining these three kinds of survey designs is Hooyman and Kiayk (2004).

The *ex post facto design,* sometimes referred to as a *correlational design,* is a variation of the survey design. The aim of ex post facto research is to explain after-the-fact linkages found among a specified set of variables (Case 4).

Case 4. Ex Post Facto Study on the Relationship Between Heat and Aggression in Major League Baseball.

Reifman, A., Larick, R., & Fein, S. (1991). Temper and temperature on the diamond: The heat-aggression relationship in major league baseball. *Personality and Social Psychology Bulletin, 17,* 580-585.

The purpose of the study was to investigate if there is a relationship between hot temperatures and pitchers' aggressive acts during a game. Microfilm copies of major daily newspapers were consulted to obtain details, over a three-year period, on air temperatures and number of batters hit during daytime major league baseball games. Results indicated a link between air temperature and aggression. When games were played in 90 degrees Fahrenheit or higher, batters had a two-thirds greater chance of being hit by pitchers than when games were played in 80 degree weather. Even fewer batters were hit by the pitchers when temperatures were below 80 degrees. Findings are discussed in the context of support of the vascular theory of emotional efference (or brain temperature may underlie heat-aggression effects). It was concluded that baseball games should be played at night and inside domed stadiums.

Sample Size Guidelines

For studies using experimental, quasi-experimental, and pre-experimental designs, experts tell us a minimum of 10-15 individuals is needed for each experimental group and each control group in the study. This is only a guideline. A number of other considerations that are beyond the scope of this book (such as effect size, levels of power, and alpha level) can come into play; thus, consulting a statistician or statistical reference (such as Hedrik, Bickman, & Rog, 1993; Henry, 1990) is advisable.

The sample size for survey designs, when the size of the population is known, was reviewed in Step 6. For ex post facto designs, statisticians provide some guidance on the desirable sample size as well. One guideline is that 35 individuals are needed for each independent variable in the study (Kerlinger & Lee, 2000).

Response Rate

If using a non-experimental design, it is good practice to report the response rate of individuals who received a questionnaire or were interviewed. *Response rate* is the percentage of people who essentially cooperate or respond to the posed questions.

Something to Remember!

It is important to report the response rate to a survey. The reason is that non-respondents may differ from respondents in a systematic way related to the research question.

Response rate can be calculated using one of two formulas:

1. Number returned or completed surveys divided by the number in sample and multiplied by 100.
2. Number returned or completed surveys divided by the number in sample minus non eligible or unreachable individuals and multiplied by 100.

Experts are not in agreement on what constitutes an acceptable response rate. Some maintain a response rate should fall between 75% to 90% (Rossi, Lipsey, & Freeman, 2004). In comparison, Figure 6 summarizes another authority's guidelines for judging response rate.

Figure 6. Report Card for Response Rates.[3]

Response Rate	Grade
> 70%	Very Good
> 60% to < 69%	Good
> 50% to < 59%	Adequate
< 49%	Unacceptable

[3] Adapted from Babbie (2004).

Criteria for Choosing a Quantitative Design

In choosing the best research design to use you also need to consider how you intend to use the findings. In other words, you need to decide which of the following applies to your situation: internal validity, external validity, or sampling generalization.

Internal validity and external validity affect experimental designs, quasi-experimental designs, pre-experimental designs, and single-subject designs. Sampling generalization, on the other hand, becomes relevant when dealing with non-experimental designs.

Internal validity. Most research in our professions centers on ***internal validity*** or determining whether a specific recreation program or activity works, or has had positive impacts on a specified group of program participants. Internal validity is sometimes referred to as ***causal validity*** or ***causal effect.***

If changes are due to something other than the program or intervention, then the internal validity of the study is said to be threatened. A ***threat to internal validity*** is "a mislabeling of the cause of an effect" (Reichardt & Mark, 1998, p. 196). Threats to internal validity are also called ***alternative explanations,*** meaning something other than the program or intervention could be responsible for the effect.

The major types of threats to the internal validity of studies relying on experimental, quasi-experimental, pre-experimental designs, and single-subject designs, are summarized in Figure 7. Figure 8 catalogs how the six quantitative designs stack up to these threats.

Figure 7. Threats to Internal Validity.

Source of Threat	Explanation	Example
Maturation	People change due to natural development (e.g., grow stronger or wiser with age).	Was participation in a school year-long after-school arts program or the developmental process responsible for improved fine motor skills of nine-year-olds?

Source of Threat	Explanation	Example
History	Events, other than the intervention, can affect change between the pretest and post-test.	Do the attitudes toward drug use by teenage athletes change due to their participation in an anti-drug education program or because a young and promising athlete dies from a cocaine overdose?
Repeated Testing	The first testing educates or sensitizes people, thus the initial pretest or observation becomes the change agent.	Prior to participating in a friendly companion program, a group of "temporarily able-bodied" teenagers completes a pretest on prejudice towards individuals with a physical disability. Did the pretest sensitize or trigger these individuals to recognize the negative stereotypes they hold and motivate them to change their ways of thinking?
Instrumentation	Between pretesting and post-testing there is a change in the way observations or testing is defined or recorded.	Judges, as a result of their pretesting experiences, have become more skilled in observing behavior.
Regression to the Mean	Individuals with extreme high or low scores on the pretest will tend to have scores closer to the mean on the second testing.	A group of teenage females hospitalized for anorexia is offered a therapeutic recreation program. A significant increase in the group's average body image score is recorded (i.e., the group's average pretest body image score was extremely low; whereas the post-test score increased by 10%). Were these changes inevitable or was indeed the treatment program effective?
Experimental Mortality	Also known as ***attrition or drop out.*** Attrition happens for many reasons. People do not complete a post-test because they exert their right to quit the study, move away, become ill, die, etc.	Do drop-outs from a research project skew results? The nagging question is whether any noted changes are due to the intervention program or due to experimental mortality?

Source of Threat	Explanation	Example
Selection Bias	Not relying on randomization to select people for a study; instead, "intact" groups or volunteers are used who bring with them unique learned (e.g., attitudes) and inherent characteristics (height, etc).	Do recreation majors, completing a leisure attitudes survey in their research methods class, accurately reflect the sentiments of undergrads on campus?
Selection Bias Interaction	Selection bias interacts with another threat (see points immediately above).	Counselors at Camp A, the experimental group, are returning staff and have previously taken the environment awareness inventory test; whereas Counselors at Camp B, the control group, are all first time counselors.

Figure 8. Report Card on the Threats to Internal Validity of Selected Research Designs.[4]

Design	Threat to Internal Validity							
	Maturation	History	Repeated Testing	Instrumentation	Regression to the Mean	Experimental Mortality	Selection Bias	Interaction
Pretest-Post-test Control Group	+	+	?	?	+	+	+	+
Solomon Four-Group	+	+	?	?	+	+	–	+
Nonequivalent Control Group	+	?	?	?	?	–	–	–
One-Group Pre-test-Post-test	–	–	?	?	?	–	–	–
Static Group Comparison	–	–	+		?	+	–	–
One-Time Post-test	–	–	+		?	+	–	–

[4]Adapted from Van Dalen (1979).

NOTE: A plus (+) symbol denotes the factor is not a threat to the design, a minus (-) symbol designates the design fails to control for the threat, a question mark (?) indicates the factor could be a threat, and a blank symbolizes the factor is not relevant.

A number of strategies can be adopted to improve the internal validity of a study. Depending on the research question, one or more of the following tactics may be prudent to adopt (Leedy & Ormrod, 2005):

- Conduct the study in a controlled laboratory setting.
- Conduct a ***double-blind study,*** meaning neither study participants nor the people administering the methods (program leaders, research assistants, etc.) know what the hypotheses are and/or which program or intervention is expected to be more effective.
- Use a ***non-reactive*** or ***unobtrusive measure*** (Step 8), which means examining "naturally" occurring information (such as installing electronic counters on hiking trails in order to measure hikers' use of different hiking trails).

In summary, if internal validity is a concern, then use the strongest design possible given the realities of the research situation. For example, if maturation and history threats to internal validity are of particular concern, the pretest-post-test control-group or Solomon four-group designs are likely your best choice.

Which quantitative design is best in terms of maximizing internal validity? Figure 9 presents popular design options in decreasing order of preference for maximizing internal validity.

Figure 9. Hierarchy of Designs for Maximizing Internal Validity.[5]

1. Classic experiment design (randomly selected, randomly assigned to one of two groups, pretest and post-test)
2. Pretest-post-test control-group design
3. Classic experiment design minus pretests (randomly selected, randomly assigned to one of two groups, post-test
4. Post-test only control-group design
5. Solomon four-group design
6. Nonequivalent control-group design
7. Quasi-experimental design with pre- and post-tests but no control group (randomly selected to be in experimental group, pretest and post-test)
8. One-group pretest-post-test design
9. Static group comparison
10. One-time post-test design

[5]Adapted from Green (1976).

External validity. Every so often individuals are concerned with conducting a program evaluation that emphasizes external validity. ***External validity*** is the ability to generalize study findings beyond the study group, to other individuals or groups, or to the "rest of the world" (Babbie, 2004).

Suppose, for example, a significant decline is noted in the arrest records of individuals after they get involved playing midnight basketball in a community. Consequently, someone suggests that if midnight basketball programs were introduced in other towns, arrest records will drop there too. Whether one is entitled to generalize or to what extent generalizations are justified, is a question of external validity, and the answer evolves around the research design that's been used.

There are at least three situations when an emphasis on external validity becomes critical. These are:

- Study results will be used to decide whether or not an expensive (in terms of monetary costs) program/intervention will be duplicated or set up in other locations.
- The program being evaluated is controversial in nature.
- The program being evaluated has been set up to remedy or manage a serious condition.

Threats to external validity are factors that stand in the way of being able to extend study results to other situations. In other words, threats are obstacles that preclude having conclusions extended or generalized to other contexts.

The major threats to external validity are summarized in Figure 10. Then Figure 11 highlights threats to external validity that exist for six designs frequently used in recreation, park, sport, and tourism research.

Figure 10. Threats to External Validity.

Source of Threat	Explanation	Example
Selection Bias	See Figure 7 above.	See Figure 7 above.
Reactive Effects of Experiment	Observations or responses recorded in an artificial environment/lab do not indicate what happens in a natural setting.	Responses recorded inside a batting cage are not the same ones used when playing a game of softball.
Repeated Testing	See Figure 7 above.	See Figure 7 above.
Multiple Treatment Interference	Study participants are exposed to several different programs/interventions, thus making it difficult to "tease" out how each unique program has affected them.	A group of adjudicated youth participates in a one-month high adventure camp. Which of the program offerings (bungee jumping, survival camping, white water rafting, etc.) is responsible for notable changes in mental and social health?

Source of Threat	Explanation	Example
Instrumentation	The instrument used to measure the variable is no good and/or there is an inadequate operational definition of dependent variable(s).	Sport management majors are asked on a paper and pencil test "Do you aspire for a white-collar or blue-collar job upon graduation?" Individuals have no idea what the question means and guess an answer.
Hawthorne Effect	People consciously and subconsciously react to being tested. The act of being measured affects outcome, the so-called *"guinea pig effect"* (Webb, Campbell, Grove, Schwartz, and Sechrest, 1981).	Some employees opt to participate in a stress reduction seminar. All employees at the agency take a pre- and post-test measuring their perceived stress. Both stress reduction seminar participants and nonparticipants experience decreased stress levels over a three-month period.
Selection Interaction	Selection interacts with another threat (such as with reactive effects of the experiment, multiple treatment interference, etc.).	A study is undertaken to measure the effectiveness of a new lifeguard training program. If the people volunteering for the program change, is the change due to self-selection into the study, knowledge that he or she will be observed during work hours, or because of what was learned in the course?

Figure 11. Report Card on the Threats to the External Validity of Selected Research Designs.[6]

Design	Selection Bias	Reactive Effects	Repeated Testing	Instrumentation	Hawthorne Effect	Selection Interaction
Pretest-Post-test Control Group	+	?	?	?	?	+
Solomon Four-Group	-	?	?	?	?	?
Nonequivalent Control Group	-	?	?	?	?	?
One-Group Pretest-Post-test	-	?	?	?	?	-

Design	Selection Bias	Reactive Effects	Repeated Testing	Instrumentation	Hawthorne Effect	Selection Interaction
Static Group Comparison	-	?	+	?	?	-
One-Time Post-test	-	?	+	?	?	-

[6]Adapted from Van Dalen (1979).

NOTE: A plus (+) symbol denotes the factor is not a threat to the design, a minus (-) symbol designates the design fails to control for the threat, a question mark (?) indicates the factor could be a threat, and a blank symbolizes the factor is not relevant.

Two strategies are used to boost the external validity of a research project. One tactic is to rely on a representative sample (Green, 1976). The other strategy is to **replicate** a study a number of times. If similar studies are done in different contexts and the same findings and conclusions are reached, then one can argue there is an indirect case for external validity.

When all is said and done, which quantitative designs are best in terms of maximizing external validity? Figure 12 highlights, in descending order of preference, designs that maximize external validity.

Figure 12. Hierarchy of Designs for Maximizing External Validity.[7]

1. Classic experimental design (randomly selected, randomly assigned to one of two groups, pretest and post-test)
2. Modified classic experimental design (randomly selected, randomly assigned to one of two groups, post-test) but no pretest
3. Nonequivalent control-group design
4. Randomly selected individuals who experience intervention and pre- and post-testing
5. Randomly selected individuals who experience intervention and post-testing
6. Choices 1, 2, 4, and 5 but with no random selection

[7]Adapted from Green (1976).

Sample generalizability. If you're using a non-experimental design (i.e., survey or ex post facto design) and want to generalize from the sample to the population from which the sample came, you're engaged in **sample generalizability.** Recall that the rationale behind using probability sampling is to be able to **generalize,** or assert that findings from the sample apply to the population from which the sample was selected.

The ability to generalize hinges on sampling error. Simply put, **sampling error** relates to the quality of the sample (Case 5). Samples with larger sampling error are of less quality. This means, "The larger the sampling error, the less representative the sample and thus the less generalizable the findings" (Schutt, 2006, p. 136). Therefore, a quality sample is highly representative of its population.

Case 5. Do the Experiences of Grand Canyon Visitors Represent Those of Visitors to Other National Parks?

Often at the beginning stages of defining your population you are faced with the necessity of having to ***delimit*** the population base. This means you wind up defining the population more narrowly than initially planned. For instance, a population for a study may have started out as being defined as any-one visiting a U.S. national park during the current calendar year. When it is realized that it would be difficult, if not impossible, to secure the names of the millions of people visiting all the national parks, the population may be redefined so as to apply to a particular park, say Grand Canyon visitors. The problem with delimiting the population is that you lose the ability to ***generalize,*** meaning the ability to conclude that what you find in one population group extends to other population groups. Thus, in this example, would it be appropriate to extend findings from a satisfaction survey of randomly chosen Grand Canyon visitors to other national park visitors? We advocate that study conclusions, at best, apply only to Grand Canyon visitors. Indeed, it would be premature to conclude that satisfac-tion levels found at the Grand Canyon mirror what is occurring at other national park sites because the visitors to specific parks may have unique characteristics.

So what affects sampling error? As a rule, sampling error is reduced when:

1. The population, from which the sample was selected, is known. If the population cannot be identified or defined, the possibility of sampling error becomes astronomical.
2. The population is homogenous or is alike regarding key characteristics. Our confidence regarding the representativeness of the sample decreases when there is a lot of variation in the population concerning the variable(s) examined.
3. Probability sampling has been used.
4. The size of the sample increases. As the sample size increases, our confidence that the sample represents the population also increases.

Qualitative Approaches

A number of designs, sometimes referred to as ***flexible designs*** (Robson, 2002), are available for qualitative inquiries. As when choosing the quantitative approach, a qualitative study design will initially depend on its theoretical framework (Step 3) and unit of analyses (Step 4).

Six of the more popular qualitative designs, by unit of analysis, are outlined in Figure 13. Examples of how these designs have been used are cited in Case 6. A summary of each of these designs then follows.

Figure 13. Popular Options for Structuring Qualitative Research by Unit of Analysis.[8]

Unit of Analysis	Design Option					
	Case Study	Critical Theory	Ethnography	Grounded Theory	Narrative	Phenomenology
Individual	√	√		√	√	
Group	√	√	√	√	√	√
Organization	√	√	√	√	√	√
Artifacts	√	√	√	√	√	√
Social Interactions	√	√	√	√	√	√
Community	√	√	√	√	√	√
Event	√	√	√	√	√	√
Time period	√	√	√	√	√	√

[8]Adapted from: Cozby (2006); and Creswell (2003).

Case 6. Reported Research Using Some of the More Popular Designs for the Qualitative Approach.

Designs Available for Qualitative Research	Example of Published Research Using the Design
Case Study	Stevenson, C. (1999). The influence of nonverbal symbols on the meaning of motive talk: A case study from masters swimming. *Journal of Contemporary Ethnography, 28,* 364-388.
Critical Theory	Daniels, M., & Bowen, H. (2003). Feminist implications of anti-leisure dystopia fiction. *Journal of Leisure Research, 35,* 423-440.
Ethnography	Fortier, A. (1998). Gender, ethnicity and fieldwork: A case study. In C. Seale (Ed.), *Researching society and culture* (pp.48-57). London: Sage Publications. NOTE: This is a study of two Italian social clubs. The author points out that the word "fieldwork" in the title is to be used as a synonym of ethnography.
Grounded Theory	Kiewa, J. (2001). Control over self and space in rock climbing. *Journal of Leisure Research, 33,* 363-382.
Narrative	Noy, C. (2004). This trip really changed me: Backpackers' narratives of self-change. *Annals of Tourism Research, 31,* 78-102.

Designs Available for Qualitative Research	Example of Published Research Using the Design
Phenomenology	Shannon, C., & Shaw, S. (2005). "If the dishes don't get done today, they'll get done tomorrow": A breast cancer experience as a catalyst for changes to women's leisure. *Journal of Leisure Research, 37,* 195-215.

Case Study

Case study entails the concentrated descriptive study of a specific unit of analysis in order to explain *why* certain things are happening (Stake, 1995). Thus, recalling the units of analysis reviewed in Step 4, case studies can become in-depth descriptions of individuals, groups, organizations, artifacts, social interactions, communities, events, or time periods.

Studying a single unit of analysis (such as a program participant, a program, an organization, or a community) is typically done when some new phenomena is of interest. For example, a case study of the experiences of tourists on a European tour the first time it is offered, would help determine if adjustments to the itinerary and hospitality sites need to be made for future tours.

A case study evaluating the precamp training of counselors at a residential camp is conducted for the full week of its duration. *Copyright © 2008 Ruth V. Russell*

For case studies, there is no experimental manipulation of an independent variable, rather the goal is to comprehensively report what happened. There are two unique features to remember about case studies. First, regardless of the unit studied, the case study takes place in its "natural setting," rather than in an artificial or contrived environment. Second, the case is usually studied over an extended period of time.

Critical Theory

Critical theory incorporates a subjective and interpretative view of social reality through meanings and interpretations provided by individuals (Matchua, 1997). In other words, this design seeks to empower research participants by examining reality through their self-reflections and insights. Understanding gained from the study can be used to provide a vision of how social institutions and public policies can be improved (Tyson, 2006).

As an example, feminist theory is a popular subset of critical theory (Kinlock, 1997). As originally articulated, the *feminist theory* approach asserted that women occupy an inferior status in capitalist and patriarchal societies, meaning that women's experiences are shaped by social, economic and political forces, or inequities, rather than individual choices. Over time, feminist theory has become more expansive, and today this design examines experiences from gender, race, and social class subjective and interpretative perspectives.

Ethnography

An *ethnography* is an in-depth study of a group, culture, or situation by a researcher who is immersed into its natural setting for an extended period of time (LeCompte & Schensul, 1999). Ethnography is used when the purpose is to understand the behaviors, circumstances, or culture of a group through the perspective of members of the group themselves. The emphasis is on portraying the regular, everyday experiences of the group or situation by extensively observing and/or interviewing intensely over a sustained period of time (Miles & Huberman, 1994). Researchers use an ethnographic approach in order to comprehend as much of what is going on as they can; that is, to understand the "whole picture" of a recreation, park, tourism or sport situation (Fraenkel & Wallen, 2005).

Ethnographic studies have two unique features (Miles & Huberman, 1994):

1. *Discovery process,* meaning the evaluator observes and/or interviews for a period of time, develops some initial conclusions that in turn lead to additional observations and/or interviews, observes/interviews again, and so on.
2. *Descriptive enterprise* or reaching across the multiple sources of information to uncover what is typical about the setting or situation studied. The emphasis is on depicting "how things are."

Idea . . . If You're Searching for an Ethnographic Data Base.

> Considering an ethnographic study? One secondary ethnographic data base that exists is Yale University's *Collection of Ethnography* stored in the *Human Relations Area Files.* These cross-cultural studies contain anthropologists' descriptions organized by culture and subject classification. Access is available through institutional (universities, colleges, public libraries, museums, high schools, etc.) or individual membership. For more information go to www. hraf@yale.edu or phone 1.800.520. HRAF (or 4723).

Grounded Theory

Grounded theory is an approach designed to construct theory from qualitative data (Glaser & Strauss, 1967). That is, the term *grounded* refers to the aim of having theory emerge from, or be grounded in, the data collected. The theory that is developed is a generalization about the data.

The process unfolds following a defined set of procedures for data collection and analysis, which is without direction from existing theories. In the first wave, open-ended questions are used to generate insights. Responses are then studied to identify emerging categories. These emerging categories are studied collectively in order to induce a theory.

The drafted theory is challenged through another round or two of data collection that involves other group(s) or individuals, and subsequent data analysis guides the refinement of theory (Strauss & Corbin, 1998). Ultimately, the successive refinements of theory " . . . ensure the theory is grounded within the data" (Gratton & Jones, 2004, p. 99). This process is referred to as *constant comparison,* in which each new piece of information (attitude, behavior, opinion, etc.) is compared to other data as it is gathered.

While a grounded theory design can undoubtedly be informative, there is at least one disadvantage. As you can probably surmise, the major challenge confronting grounded theorists is it usually takes a lot of time to complete the design.

Narrative

Narrative research involves the researcher asking one or more individuals to provide stories about some aspect of their lives (Clandinin & Connelly, 2004). The story is " . . . retold or restoried by the researcher into a narrative chronology" (Creswell, 2003, p. 15).

The following three distinct narrative types have emerged:

1. *Personal stories* or autobiographical accounts of an individual's own personal history (Reissman, 1993).
2. *Dominant cultural narratives* or stories about persons, places, or things that contain consistent storylines and thematic content. These narratives are transmitted through social institutions (e.g., mass media) and in conversation (Richardson, 1990).

3. **Community narratives** or descriptive and historical accounts that represent the collective knowledge and experience of a specific group. These narratives are also identified through consistent themes that emerge from personal stories (Rappaport, 2000).

Phenomenology

Phenomenology is "both a way of doing research (method) and a way of questioning and conceptualizing thought (philosophy)" (Luborsky & Lysack, 2006, p. 335). This makes for a complex and multifaceted endeavor, but at its most basic level, phenomenology focuses on everyday life and gives prime attention to the ordinary that is experienced and expressed by people (Moustakas, 1994). As a researcher you reflect on what you identify as the "essence" of lived human experiences (Creswell, 2003).

Admittedly, one way of systematically discovering the ordinary is through the narrative approach mentioned above. However, the primary question researchers using phenomenology ask is, "Over time, what is the meaning of the recreation, park, sport, or tourism experience and how does that individual interpret it for him or herself?"

Phenomenology is unique from other qualitative research approaches in that it regards the lived experiences and meanings provided by study respondents as paramount. Only those who share an experience are fully knowledgeable about the experience under study. That is, researchers are limited in their ability to grasp the meanings of the experiences of other people. Thus, in this qualitative approach, as with the narrative design, researchers do not apply much analysis to the data collected. Rather, the researcher presents the findings in the form in which they are originally expressed.

Rigor in Qualitative Designs

Regardless of the qualitative design chosen, findings from research should be accurate (Creswell, 2003). This notion of **rigor**, meaning findings will not be so subjective that they cannot be trusted, is important when choosing a qualitative design. Sometimes rigor is referred to as **trustworthiness.**

Trustworthiness or rigor requires that the designs possess the following three criteria (Lincoln & Guba, 2005):

1. **Truthfulness** refers to the "truth" value of the results from the study. Truthfulness is somewhat parallel to the internal validity of quantitative designs.
2. **Applicability** refers to how useful the evaluation findings are to other situations. Applicability is parallel to the external validity of quantitative designs.
3. **Consistency,** or dependability, means the findings from the study are reliable.

Idea . . . for Maximizing the Rigor in Qualitative Designs.

Strategies for increasing trustworthiness in qualitative designs are:

1. *Truthfulness* = Aspire for truthfulness by using:

   • *Prolonged engagement* or lengthy and intensive contact with respondents or phenomena in the field in order to develop in-depth understanding and avoid the distortions of comprehension that can accompany concluding too quickly.
   • *Peer debriefing* or when the findings and conclusions are shared with a disinterested, professional peer whose role is to review and ask questions about the study so as to "keep the inquiry honest."
   • *Member checks* or the process of continuous, informal testing of information that is acquired by soliciting reactions of the respondents themselves—asking respondents if the researcher's understanding of the phenomena matches what was told to him or her.

2. *Applicability* = Achieve applicability by using *thick descriptions,* meaning the written report is richly developed, with the context and descriptions so thoroughly presented that judgments about the fit of findings may be made by others who wish to apply them to other situations.

3. *Consistency* = Obtain consistency by conducting an external audit. In an *external audit,* a competent outside person (the external auditor) examines the process and results of the study to make sure the interpretations made by the evaluator are confirmed. In order to have an external audit, the evaluator must leave an *audit trail* or notes and materials that help the auditor trace how the evaluator arrived at the conclusions.

Mixed-Methods Approaches

As mentioned in Step 3, more researchers today are using a mixed-methods approach for implementing their studies. Again, *mixed methods,* or *triangulation,* refer to integrating elements of both qualitative and quantitative designs so that the strengths of each can be maximized. A mixed-methods approach to research can be executed in one of two ways: that is, a concurrent or sequential strategy can be used.

Concurrent Design

The *concurrent mixed-methods strategy* is more frequently used and involves collecting both quantitative and qualitative data at the same time. Results from the two approaches are then integrated when interpreting the findings (Case 7).

Case 7. Mixed-Methods Research Using a Concurrent Approach.

Bonadies, V. (2004). A yoga therapy program for AIDS-related pain and anxiety: Implications for therapeutic recreation. *Therapeutic Recreation Journal, 38,* 148-166.

The purpose of the study was to evaluate how an eight-week yoga intervention impacted the pain and anxiety of individuals who were HIV positive and/or had AIDS. The yoga program was originally developed by Iyengar for individuals with disabilities. The intervention was offered twice a week for an hour each session. Four individuals participated in the study. Pre- and post-session self-reported pain and anxiety ratings were collected. Requested pain medication (known as "PRN" meds) was also monitored. Additionally, videotaped interviews were conducted with study participants following the conclusion of the intervention. Participants were asked to share their perspectives about the utility of the yoga intervention on improving their health and well-being. Interviews were also conducted with interdisciplinary staff members involved with participants' care. Quantitative findings indicated that yoga was effective in decreasing self-perceptions of pain and anxiety as well as the use of PRN pain medications. Qualitative comments by study participants included the following (pp. 160-161):

> "Yoga helped to get rid of the jitteriness."
> "I was not excited about starting the yoga program. But I saw the benefits which it made me more motivated to attend."
> "Yoga works if you are willing to give it a try."

Sequential Design

The *sequential mixed-methods strategy* consists of conducting the study in two waves in order to either elaborate or expand upon initial findings (Case 8). An example of sequential mixed methods used for elaboration purposes is conducting an initial study with a sample of people using a quantitative methods approach. Case studies, again a qualitative strategy, involving a few people from the original sample are next undertaken in order to provide a more detailed exploration of the topic.

Case 8. Mixed-Methods Research Using a Sequential Expansive Approach.

Davenport, M., Borrie, W., Friemund, W., & Manning, R. (2002). Assessing the relationship between desired experiences and support for management actions at Yellowstone National Park using multiple methods. *Journal of Park and Recreation Administration, 20,* 51-64.

The purpose of the study was to gain knowledge of visitor experience preferences and perceptions of proposed management actions needed for Yellowstone National Park (YNP). Initially a quantitative study was conducted. The names and addresses of visitors to four YNP entrances were systematically gathered. About 70% of the 1,500 persons who were sent mail questionnaires returned completed surveys. Data analyses revealed some contractions about wildlife priorities in YNP. Thus, the following winter a qualitative study was undertaken " . . . to provide the depth of understanding that the initial survey lacked" (p. 56). In-depth interviews with 93 persons provided insights regarding why visitors believed wildlife was at the heart of the YNP experience, and why they were unlikely to support management actions aimed at protecting the bison herd in the YNP.

Sequential mixed methods can also be used to expand upon what is initially learned. An illustration of this is setting up the first study as an exploratory study, using qualitative methods, with a small number of participants. The insights learned from the original study can then form the basis of a follow-up study using quantitative methods with a large number of participants.

Your Research

1. Are you undertaking a quantitative, qualitative, or mixed-methods study?
2. Accordingly, identify the research design you are planning to adopt for your study.
3. About how many persons/units do you anticipate having in your study? Provide a rationale for this number.
4. Is your study focused on internal validity? External validity? Sample generalizability? What are the threats or limitations associated with the design you've chosen?
5. Or, is your study focused on rigor? If so, what strategies could you use to increase truthfulness, applicability, and consistency?

Review and Discussion Questions . . .
What have you learned about choosing a design?

1. Identify the five elements of the classic experimental design. Which of these elements are more difficult to execute in recreation, park, sport, and tourism research?
2. Illustrate the popular experimental designs: pretest-post-test control-group design; post-test only control-group design, and Solomon four-group design.
3. Diagram three popular quasi-experimental designs: nonequivalent control-group design, single-group interrupted time-series design, and the control-group interrupted time-series design.
4. Give a hypothetical example of the following four popular pre-experimental designs: one-group pretest-post-test design, static group comparison design, one-time post-test design, and alternative treatment post-test-only with nonequivalent groups design.
5. Describe the single-subject design.
6. Contrast the two popular non-experimental designs used in leisure research.
7. Delineate how the following two criteria influence quantitative design choice: internal validity and external validity.
8. How does sampling error affect sample generalizability? And, what four factors reduce sampling error?
9. Compare and contrast the following qualitative designs: case study, critical theory, ethnography, grounded theory, narrative, and phenomenology.
10. List the three strategies for increasing trustworthiness in qualitative designs.
11. What is the difference between a concurrent versus a sequential mixed-methods strategy?

Exercises

1. Examine an article that has been assigned by your instructor or you locate.
   A. Was a quantitative, qualitative, or mixed-methods approach used for the study? Identify exactly how the study was designed or structured.
   B. How many individuals were involved in the sample? Explain whether or not the sample size was adequate.

C. If a non-experimental design was used, what was the response rate? And was this response rate sufficient?

D. If a quantitative design was used, provide a rationale regarding how confident you are in the findings having internal validity? External validity?

E. If a qualitative design was used, what efforts were directed at ensuring: Truthfulness? Applicability? Consistency?

2. Read about the American Camp Association's research study, *Directions: Youth Development Outcomes of the Camp,* by going to American Camp Association's Web site at www.acacamps. org (click on "Research," under "Camp Outcome Study" click on "Directions" and then click on "View the Final Results").

A. What was the sample size for the study?

B. What was the response rate?

C. What research design was used for the camper survey? Parent survey? And staff observation?

D. Do findings have internal validity? What are some of the threats to the internal validity of the study?

E. Do findings have external validity? What are some of the threats to the external validity of the study?

3. Find out if you understand threats to internal validity by going to a tutorial written by Drs. Polson, Ng, Grant, and Mah at Athabasa University that is found at http://psych. athabascau. ca/html/Validity/index.htm. If need be, review the threats to internal validity presented in Part I. Then go to Part II and decide if each of the 36 hypothetical experiments has internal validity and if it does not, decide what threats exist to compromise the noted findings.

4. Participate in an online social psychology experiment by going to www.socialpsychology. org/expts.htm.

A. Choose to participate in one of the experiments.

B. Was a quantitative, qualitative, or mixed-methods approach used to conduct the study?

   i. If a quantitative approach was used, what research design was used?

   ii. If a qualitative approach was used, how was the study structured?

   iii. What kind of sampling technique was used to conduct the study?

   iv. From what you surmised about how the study was conducted, would you argue that findings have: Internal validity? External validity?

5. Try your hand at undertaking some abbreviated qualitative studies using the following designs and scenarios. After completing each assignment, share your feelings about the design used, including a reaction to whether it was easier or more difficult to implement?

A. **Case Study:** Conduct about a 30-minute tape or video-recorded interview with an individual regarding his/her favorite recreation activity. Ask the open-ended question, "Please tell me about the kind of emotions and social psychological benefits you experience when you're participating in your favorite recreation activity." Type up the recorded interview, and in a paragraph explain how this was a case study.

B. **Critical Theory:** As an individual project, observe for 30 minutes a campus sport activity for both genders (co-ed). Take field notes that include a description of the: setting, event, people, and things seen. Were gender inequities noticed in terms of how the sport was played or refereed? After the observation period, conduct a brief interview with one of the participants in the sport event. Indicate to him/her what you observed about gender inequities during the activity (either the nature of what you observed to be inequities or the nature of what you observed as an absence of inequities). Request comments about this finding from your interviewee. For example, has she/he experienced gender inequities in co-ed campus sports? In a paragraph explain how this was a critical theory design.

C. **Ethnography:** Conduct a 30-minute observation of what goes on in a group you're part of (e,g., sport team, residence hall floor, college course). Take field notes that include a description of the setting, event, people, things heard, and non-verbal interactions. In a one-page paper, interpret and provide some personal impressions of what was observed. Also, explain in a paragraph how this was an ethnographic study.

D. **Narrative:** Find an individual who has an unusual hobby and is willing to discuss it for about 30 minutes. Conduct a tape- or video-recorded interview asking the individual to tell you the "story" behind how she or he got introduced to the leisure time activity. Type up the recorded interview. Include a paragraph about how this approach was a narrative design.

6. If you feel you need or want to learn more about topics reviewed in this chapter related to the quantitative approach, check out information presented on the following Web sites:

A. Go to the International Consortium for the Advancement of Academic Publication's "Resources for Methods in Evaluation and Social Research" Web page that is at http://gsociology.icapp.org. Click on "Statistics, Design."

B. Another reference for design is William Trochim's Web page for *Research Methods Knowledge Base* at www.socialresarchmethods.net/kb/contents.htm. Click on "Design."

C. Learn more about experimental designs, quasi-experimental designs, pre-experimental designs, sources of invalidity, and/or sampling, by going to Professor Germain's (at California State University Long Beach) Web page located at www.csulb.edu/~msaintg Web page and click on "PPA 696 Research Methods."

7. Suppose you were asked to identify a means to test the research question, "How do teenagers use their leisure time?" Identify a mixed-methods approach to implement the study.

How studies are designed reflect, in large part, the purposes and theoretical framework(s) that have been adopted for the research. Venice, Italy. *Copyright © 2008 Carol Cutler Riddick*

STEP 8: Consider Measurement

Logic of Measurement

Points to Consider When Choosing a Measure
Kind of Measure
  Reactive Measures
  Non-Reactive Measures
  Psychophysiological Measures
Multiple Variable Measures
Single versus Multiple-Item Measures
  Index
  Scale
Instrument Validity
  Construct Validity
  Criterion Validity
Instrument Reliability
  Inter-Rater Reliability
  Test-Retest Reliability
  Split-Half Reliability
  Inter-Item Reliability
Normative Data

Resources for Locating a Good Instrument

Assignment 4: lecture (handwritten)

**Even with the best maps and instruments, we can never
fully chart our journeys.**
Gail Pool

Knowing the basics of measurement is a must for today's recreation professionals. This holds true regardless of whether you are a practitioner, a student completing an honors paper, thesis, or dissertation, or a full-time researcher. A fundamental understanding of measurement basics " . . . is not only a prerequisite to providing appropriate interventions to the clients that we serve, but is an integral part of dictating the efficacy of services" (Zabriskie, 2003, p. 330).

Logic of Measurement

As introduced in Step 4, defining the scope of a study involves identifying concepts and variables of interest. In actuality, this is just the beginning of a sequence of actions that has been dubbed the logic of measurement (Dixon, Bouma, & Atkinson, 1987). The *logic of measurement* consists of specifying four things (Figure 1):

- First, identify each *concept* or construct under examination. Remember, these concepts or constructs can be found in the research question, objective, or hypothesis.
- Second, select a *variable*(s) that reflects each concept's working definition, officially known as the *nominal definition*. nominal = name of something (handwritten)
- Third, choose or devise a measuring *instrument,* technically known as the *operational definition,* for each variable.
- Fourth, specify *units of measurements* for each variable in the instrument. In other words, a system for categorizing answers must be adopted or devised.

Figure 1. Logic of Measurement.

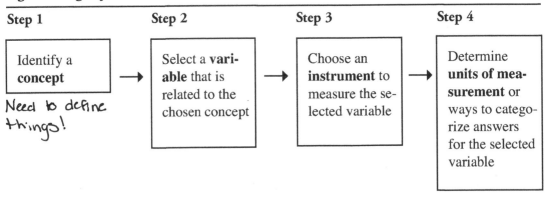

Step 1	Step 2	Step 3	Step 4
Identify a **concept**	Select a **variable** that is related to the chosen concept	Choose an **instrument** to measure the selected variable	Determine **units of measurement** or ways to categorize answers for the selected variable

Need to define things! (handwritten)

Logically planning a study, from identifying a concept in the purpose statement, to selecting a variable(s) to signify the concept, and finally to determining an instrument to measure and categorize the variable(s), is often referred to as *operationalizion*. Crucial to the logic of measurement, then, is the adequacy of operationalizing a definition for each variable to be studied. This requires selecting at least one measuring instrument or indicator for each variable.

Idea . . . Interchangeable Words.

Some words are used interchangeably in research. For example, when you read about ***instruments, instrumentation, measurement, and measures,*** or even ***operationalization,*** all refer to the measuring instruments that were used in the study. To illustrate, research reports are organized by some conventional labeling rules (introduced in Step 11 and covered in more detail in Step 16). That is, usually the measuring instruments used to collect information for a study are described as a subsection in the "Method(s)" section of a report. This subsection may be titled any number of ways, including: "Instruments," "Measures," "Measurement," "Assessment," "Dependent Variables," and "Independent Variables." Incidentally, please note that the report section labeled "Method(s)" should never be called "Methodology." This is taboo because methodology means the study of methods and not the methods themselves.

The ideal is to attain a high level "***goodness-of-fit***" (Grosof & Sardy, 1985) between the concept and the operationalized variable. See if you agree that there is a goodness of fit between the concepts and corresponding measurement instruments highlighted in Figure 2.

Figure 2. Examples of the Logic of Measurement: Is There a Goodness of Fit?[1]

Concept	Variable	Measurement Instrument	Units of Measurement
Mental Ability	Intelligence	College Grade Point Average	Zero to 4.0
Social Support Network	Best Friends	Self-Reported Count	Zero to hundreds!
Body Composition	Body Density	Underwater or Hydrostatic Weighing	Lean-Fat Ratio
Good Life	Quality of Life	Time devoted to walking, hiking, playing outdoors, and engaging in sports	Minutes

[1]Adapted from Scitovsky (1976).

At this step in the research process, you must locate an appropriate measuring instrument. Searching for an instrument is analogous to shopping at the grocery store. At the concept level you've decided to buy a beverage to drink, but after a few minutes, you realize you have a hankering for fruit juice, the "variable" of choice (Figure 3). You enter the store, walk to the aisle containing juice drinks, and search for the shelves storing the various juice brands. Now, you must ponder on what to purchase and drink. You narrow your choice between a 32-oz container of the store brand or a 12-ounce concentrate made by Welch's™. The "instrument" of choice, for satiating your thirst and taste preferences, ends up being the store brand concentrate.

Once variables are named stick to those names!!

Figure 3. Linkage Among Concept, Variable, and Instrument: Grocery Shopping Analogy.

Beverage Aisle **AKA Concept**

Juice Shelves
AKA Variable

Store Brand Juice
AKA Instrument

There are basically two ways to operationalize concepts—either adopt an already existing measuring instrument used by other researchers or create your own instrument. In order to teach you more about picking instruments, the remainder of the chapter is broken into two parts. In the first section, an overview of points to consider when choosing an instrument is provided. Second, resources for finding instruments are presented.

Points to Consider When Choosing a Measure

A number of instruments may exist for the variable you are considering measuring. Indeed, you'll want to choose a "good" one, but may feel overwhelmed choosing one instrument from among all those available. To help alleviate this anxiety, keep in mind there are at least six things to consider when choosing an instrument: kind of measure, multiple variable measures, single versus multiple-item measures, instrument validity, instrument reliability, and existence of normative data.

Kind of Measure

One way to classify measuring instruments is to label them as a reactive measure, a non-reactive measure, or a psychophysiological measure. Each of these kinds of measures provides unique information, yet each has its own limitations. Ultimately, a decision must be made to adopt one or more of these types of measures when carrying out the research project.

Reactive measures. Instruments that both create and measure responses are known as ***reactive measures*** (Webb, Campbell, Schwartz, & Sechrest, 2000). When you ask people questions (via interviews or questionnaires) or observe them, you can make them aware that you are studying them. When people know their words or actions are being measured, they may not always respond or behave normally or truthfully. In other words, they may portray behaviors, attitudes, preferences, beliefs, or behaviors in ways that are socially acceptable.

Non-reactive measures. On the other hand, **non-reactive measures** examine "naturally" (Webb et al., 2000, p. vii) occurring information. A non-reactive measure can be quite literally anything that does not tamper with the nature of the measured response. There are two types of non-reactive measures: physical traces and documents/records (Webb et al., 2000).

Reactive measures operate the same as taking a person's photo. These photo subjects know their picture is being taken, so they "pose" for the camera. *Copyright © 2008 Ruth V. Russell*

1. ***Physical tracing*** is finding and recording visible evidence or traces of behavior that are not specifically produced for the research project, but are nonetheless available to measure. Physical traces are inconspicuous and anonymous; those who left them behind have no knowledge of their potential for use in an evaluation project. There are two broad classes of physical traces: erosion and accretion (Webb et al., 2000).

   A. ***Erosion physical traces*** deal with the degree of selective physical wear on objects or the environment. Such measures can be an index to popularity. Examples of erosion physical traces are the wear patterns on floor tiles in front of various museum exhibits and short cut paths in the grass that deviate from paved sidewalks in a park.

   B. ***Accretion physical traces*** involve the deposit or accumulation of material. Examples of accretion physical traces are the amount of garbage found on a beach (as a measure of the level of compliance with the city's no litter policy) and number of alcohol containers left in the stadium after a football game (as a measure of compliance with a no alcohol policy).

2. ***Documents/records,*** sometimes referred to as ***archival data,*** can be categorized into two types (Figure 4). One category consists of public records. ***Public records*** are materials created to provide unrestricted information or accounting. Among other things, public records can help determine an organization's priorities and concerns, financial resources, values (such as commitment to diversity), operating processes (such as evaluation of staff), and consistency of policies (Neuendorf, 2001).

Figure 4. Examples of Documents/Records.

Kinds of Documents	Examples
Public Records	• Advertisements • Annual reports • Board meeting minutes • Books • Bulletin board postings on the Internet • Census data • Course or activity registration records • Mission statements • Newspaper articles/editorials • Organization and program budgets • Policy manuals • Promotional videos • Songs • Speeches • Strategic plans • Television show or programs • Visitor and convention bureau records • Web pages

Kinds of Documents	Examples
Personal Documents	• Appointment calendars • Children's drawings • Email messages • Diaries • Personal letters • Photographs • Scrapbooks

The second type of document is a personal document (Figure 4). ***Personal documents*** are first-person accounts of events or personal experiences (Merriam, 1997). People keep all sorts of personal documents, and by examining these documents, a researcher can begin to understand how the person views his or her experiences.

Psychophysiological measures. ***Psychophysiological measures*** assess the physiological functioning of the body's central nervous system and autonomic and somatic nervous systems (Cacioppo, Tassinary, & Berntson, 2007). Instruments that have been used as proxy indicators of psychophysiological concepts include blood pressure, heart rate, skin temperature, respiration rate, and muscle tension. These kinds of measures are used almost exclusively in sport studies, though there have been a few exceptions in the recreation literature (cf. DeSchriver & Riddick, 1990; Riddick, 1985).

Multiple-Variable Measures

Another important point to remember in choosing measuring instrumentation is to select multiple variables for each concept studied. At best, each measure of the same concept can be viewed as only a partial glimpse of what is happening, but taken together they provide a "truer" whole picture. That is, each variable contributes a different perspective of what is studied—they are unique nominal definitions of a concept. This is often accomplished by measuring multiple dependent variables. Figure 5 illustrates how individual slices of dependent variables capture a fraction of the larger concept of affect. That is, to measure the psychological effects of physical fitness training, one would measure depression, anxiety, and happiness.

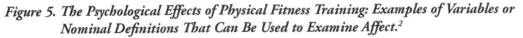

Figure 5. The Psychological Effects of Physical Fitness Training: Examples of Variables or Nominal Definitions That Can Be Used to Examine Affect.[2]

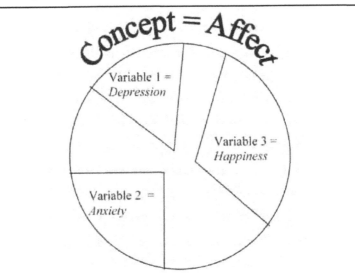

[2]Adapted from Folkins and Sime (1981).

Single versus Multiple-Item Measures

In addition to measuring multiple variables for each concept, consideration must be given on whether or not to use single or multiple items to measure the variable under scrutiny. Here's an example of what we mean. For demographic variables, a single question is popular. For example, we know the variable of age can easily be measured with the one question "What is your age?" Variables that are multifaceted or complex, on the other hand, need to use a multiple-item instrument. For instance, how many different perspectives should be considered when measuring the variable of happiness? The challenge is to find or develop an instrument that delivers the comprehensive information you need in as short a time as possible. There are essentially two types of multiple-item measures. These are an index and a scale.

Index. An **index** is created when a number of questions are used to measure one variable. The responses then are tallied together to get a sum or average (Case 1). It is generally accepted that an index is a more complete measure of a variable than any single question can provide.

Case 1. Fitness Leader Index.

Suppose you are a supervisor and want to develop a short form that asks members of a fitness class to rate their instructor. You feel that a good leader (the concept) should exhibit three attributes (the variables) equally or be: prepared, able to communicate, and able to maintain a safe environment during the workout. Consequently, class members are asked to complete the following form.

Please rate your leader on the following three points (draw an arrow to each of your answers):

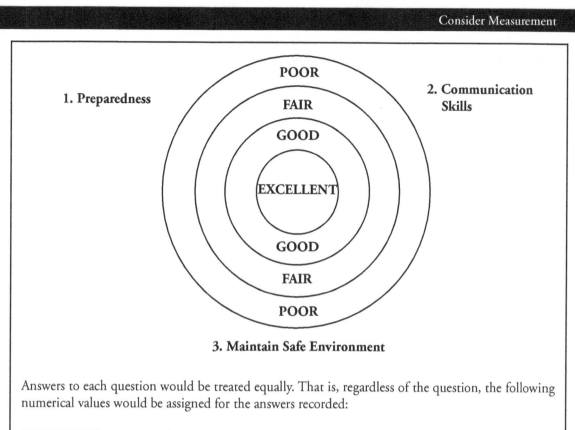

1. Preparedness
2. Communication Skills
3. Maintain Safe Environment

Answers to each question would be treated equally. That is, regardless of the question, the following numerical values would be assigned for the answers recorded:

EXCELLENT ------------> Score of 4 points
GOOD --------------------> Score of 3 points
FAIR ----------------------> Score of 2 points
POOR --------------------> Score of 1 point

Given the scoring system, the range of scores for the Fitness Leader Index could be 3 – 12 points. (Remember, each answer is converted to a number, or 1, 2, 3, or 4 points). So a good instructor will receive a higher number of points than a marginal instructor.

Creating an index is difficult to do well. The goal is for each question to measure the same thing but from a different angle. If you have succeeded in measuring one variable with several different questions, people's responses to the various questions should show some consistency. A special statistic, called an *internal consistency reliability statistic* (described below), is available to determine if the questions comprising the index are "holding together" to measure the same variable.

Occasionally, an index is created containing questions that cluster together to measure different aspects of the variable. Technically, this is known as a *multi-dimensional index* (Case 2).

Case 2. Examples of Multidimensional Indices.

Martens, R., Vealey, R., & Burton, D. (1990). *Competitive anxiety in sport.* Champaign, IL: Human Kinetics Publishers.

The Competitive State Anxiety Inventory-2 is a 27-item self-report test designed to measure overall competitive state anxiety as well as three independent competitive states in high school and college athletes: cognitive state anxiety, somatic state anxiety, and confidence.

Marsh, H., Richards, G., Johnson, S., Roche, L., & Tremayne, P. (1994). Physical self-description questionnaire: Psychometric properties and a multitrait-multimethod analysis of relations to existing instruments. *Journal of Sport & Exercise Psychology, 16,* 270-305.

The Physical Self-Description questionnaire is a 70-item test designed to measure adolescents' physical self-concept on 11 multi-dimensions: strength, body fat, activity, endurance/fitness, sports competence, coordination, health, appearance, flexibility, global physical self-concept, and global esteem.

Scale. Sometimes responses to questions in an index are given different weights before an average score is calculated. Responses to one or more questions may be counted in the calculation of the overall scale score as worth twice (or higher) times as much as responses to another item. Technically, weighting answers in an array of questions used in an index is referred to as a *scale* (Case 3). Normally, extensive testing is used to assign the weighing.

Case 3. Fitness Leader Scale.

Remember Case 1? Suppose the supervisor revisits how to assess a fitness leader. Because of a rash of accidents that have happened during classes, the supervisor wants to double-weigh safety assessments.

Suppose Ms. Lily assigns her fitness instructor the following scores:

Attribute	Rating
Preparedness	EXCELLENT
Communication Skills	EXCELLENT
Maintains Safe Environment	FAIR

Converting Ms. Lily's answers would result in her instructor receiving 12 points out of a possible 16 points. Given that the range of scores could be between 4 to 16 points, a score of 12 isn't awful but it isn't great either! This one score suggests the instructor has room for improvement. Do you follow how this scale was calculated? In other words, one attribute, safe environment, got double points. That is, the initial rating was multiplied by two, due to its importance.

Attribute	Rating	Points Assigned	Weighting	Sub Total
Preparedness	EXCELLENT	4	1	4
Communication Skills	EXCELLENT	4	1	4
Maintains Safe Environment	FAIR	2	2	4

Instrument Validity

Instrument validity refers to the accuracy of a measuring instrument. In other words, does the instrument capture its intended variable (Monette, Sullivan, & DeJong, 2005)? There must be a logical relationship between the way a variable is nominally defined and the way it is operationalized. For instance, if we propose to measure intelligence on the basis of hair color, we most assuredly would have an invalid measure of intelligence.

There are basically two approaches for establishing the validity of an instrument. That is, the validity of an instrument can be documented by using either construct validity or criterion validity. Figure 6 summarizes the various approaches we can use to establish either the construct or criterion validity of a measuring instrument.

Figure 6. Approaches Used to Assess the Validity of an Instrument.

Type of Validity	Description
I. Construct Validity	Allegedly measures the variable it is designed to measure.
Face Validity	"Appears" to measure what is intended.
Content Validity	Deemed to include relevant content.
II. Criterion Validity	Correlates with objective evidence (or pre-selected standard).
Concurrent Validity	Groups of people score differently on the construct in expected ways.
Predictive Validity	Foretells a future outcome or event.
Convergent Validity	New measure is correlated to a previously validated instrument that was designed to measure the same variable.
Discriminant Validity	New measure does not correlate with a previously validated instrument designed to measure a different variable.

Construct validity. Because it is the easiest way to address validity, construct validity is frequently used to establish validity of an instrument. *Construct validity* consists of making a subjective judgment regarding the adequacy of the instrument. Two ways used to establish construct validity are face validity and content validity.

Face validity is a subjective judgment that the instrument appears to be an adequate measure of the variable. Someone or a group has decided that the variable (or nominal definition of the concept) has been captured in the operational definition provided by the instrument. Normally the researcher makes this determination. In other words, "on the face of it" the instrument appears to measure what it is supposed to measure.

As an example of determining face validity, pretend someone is trying to figure out how to measure a variable called leisure attitude. Items on a questionnaire that are initially considered for measuring this variable include "I often feel nervous when faced with what to do in my free time" and "I learned how to tie my shoes when I was five." Because the first item, relative to the second item, appears to be more closely related to leisure attitude, it is chosen to be used in the instrument designed to measure leisure attitude. In other words, the item is deemed to have face validity.

Face validity alone is not able to demonstrate the validity of an instrument. Indeed, it has been pointed out that "Appearance is not a very good indicator of accuracy" or meaningfulness (Cozby, 2006, p. 90). Face validity, however, is a good place to start when you are trying to create items for an instrument, but once the instrument is completed, other ways of determining its validity should be pursued.

Content validity examines the content of an instrument to determine it contains " . . . an adequate, or representative, sample of all content or elements" (Monette, Sullivan, & DeJong, 2005, p. 114) of the variable of interest. For instance, if someone was attempting to create a new leisure-satisfaction measure, a review of literature would reveal that satisfaction derived from leisure can affect various components of life, including psychological, social, and physical satisfaction. Therefore, if all the statements used in the instrument dealt with only psychological satisfaction, then this instrument would not demonstrate content validity because it didn't include various angles or aspects of leisure satisfaction according to the literature.

Face and content validity can be established either by an individual or by a jury. *Jury opinion* consists of asking a group or panel of knowledgeable persons or experts to review and verify that the selected items do indeed measure the concept. Jury opinion, though subjective, is considered superior to an individual researcher's declaration that an instrument has face or content validity.

Criterion validity. In **criterion validity,** comparisons are made between the newly developed instrument and some objective evidence, such as a pre-selected standard that is known or believed to accurately measure the variable. Unlike content validity approaches, criterion validity involves collecting information that substantiates the validity of an instrument. Criterion validity can be established four ways: concurrent validity, predictive validity, convergent validity, and discriminant validity.

The criterion used for establishing **concurrent validity** is determining whether two or more groups of people score differently on a concept in expected ways (Cozby, 2006). For instance, someone has developed an appreciation of nature scale. The scale creator expects that people, active in the outdoors, will score higher on the scale than those who report little or no involvement in the outdoors. If this is found to be the case, then the concurrent validity for the newly developed instrument has been established.

Predictive validity is the ability of a measure to predict or foretell something. For example, validity for the SAT was established by determining its ability to predict graduation from college. Similarly, predictive validity for Zuckerman's (1979) Sensation Seeking Scale was established when it was determined that people who scored high on the scale behaved differently from individuals who scored low on the scale. High sensation seekers, relative to low sensation seekers, were found to engage in more dangerous activities, such as driving faster.

Convergent validity occurs when a new measure is found to be related to another previously validated instrument that was designed to measure the same concept. In other words, in convergent validity the new instrument is compared against a previously validated instrument that is known to measure the concept of interest. If the new and old comparable instruments are administered to a group of individuals, both tests should basically yield the same results—people who score high on one measure should score high on the second measure; likewise, people who score low on one measure should score low on the second measure. Many consider correlations in the range of .40 to provide evidence of convergent validity (Stangor, 2006).

An example of convergent validity for an instrument would be if a person thought of a new way to measure perceived leisure functioning. The developer of the new test asks a group of 100 persons to complete both the new test and Witt and Ellis' (1985) Leisure Diagnostic Battery (LDB), a previously validated test that measures perceived leisure functioning. Convergent validity would be documented if test scores on the two tests coincided. That is, if a respondent scored high on the LDB, he or she would also attain a high leisure functioning score on the newly created test.

Discriminant validity is established when the new measure is found not to be related to another instrument that has been documented as validly measuring a different concept. The new " . . . measure should discriminate between the construct being measured and other unrelated constructs" (Cozby, 2006, p. 92). For instance, it is expected that individuals, who scored high on a previously documented valid test of aggressiveness, will have different scores (i.e., low scores) on a newly developed measure of passiveness. If this happens, then the new test is deemed to have discriminant validity.

Instrument Reliability

Another goal of scientific inquiry is to use measurement instruments that are reliable. *Reliability* is the " . . . consistency with which a measurement instrument yields a certain result when the entity being measured hasn't changed" (Leedy & Ormrod, 2005, p. 29). In other words, instrument reliability deals with stability or constancy of responses on an instrument. Several factors can result in unreliable data (Creswell, 2005, p. 162):

- Questions are ambiguous and unclear.
- Administration procedures for the instrument are inconsistent.
- Respondents are tired, anxious, and/or misinterpret or guess at questions.

Reliability of an instrument is expressed as a ratio. Technically, a reliability ratio is the variance of the "true score" to the total variance observed on an instrument (Kielhofner, 2006). The value of this ratio is referred to as the ***reliability coefficient,*** and it ranges from 0.0 to 1.0. A reliability coefficient of 1.0 indicates perfect reliability with no error. If your instrument has a reliability coefficient of .90, this means that 90% of the differences that are measured are true for the variable, and the likelihood of making an error in determining this is only 10%. So, a reliability coefficient of .90 reveals that the instrument is quite reliable.

There are four approaches for documenting an instrument's reliability: inter-rater reliability, test-retest reliability, parallel-forms reliability, and internal consistency. These techniques are summarized in Figure 7.

Figure 7. Approaches to Assess Instrument Reliability.

Approach	Description	Look for a Reliability or Correlation of:
Inter-Rater Reliability	The ratings of two or more judges correlate with each other.	$\geq$ .60[3]
Test-Retest Reliability	Scores on the same instrument, administered at two different times, correlate with each other.	$\geq$ .80[4]
Split Half Reliability	Scores on similar instruments, administered at two different times, correlate with each other.	$\geq$ .80[3]
Inter-Item Reliability	Items used in an index are measuring the same concept as revealed by correlations between the items.	$\geq$ .80[5]

[3] Patten (2007).
[4] Fisher and Corcoran (2007).
[5] Shannon and Davenport (2001).

Something to Remember!

In Figure 7, did you notice the signs used in the last column? Many people get confused about what the "<" and ">" mathematical notations mean. Here's your key:

< = "less than."
> = "more than."

To remember this, think about writing numbers across the page, moving from left to right, beginning with the number 0, 1, 2, 3, 4, and so on. Imposing "<" anywhere on this line of

numbers points to numbers that are going down in value. Likewise, placing the ">" somewhere on this line points to numbers that are going up in value.

A spin-off of the notations above are:

$\leq$ = "equal to or less than."
$\geq$ = "equal to or more than."

The addition of the straight line below the arrow equates to meaning "equal to."

Inter-rater reliability. **Inter-rater reliability,** sometimes referred to as inter-observer reliability, involves two or more observers independently rating some phenomena at the same time.
These ratings, typically centered on assessing behavior, are compared to determine the degree of
agreement. If the raters' ratings are relatively consistent or in agreement, then inter-rater reliability has been established.

One way to determine reliability among raters is to calculate an **inter-rater reliability
coefficient.** For instance, two individual swimming experts can be asked to independently judge
whether 30 individuals achieved proficient swimmer status at a course's culmination. Suppose for
25 individuals in the class the two judges are in complete agreement (i.e., their ratings for each
of the 25 individuals are the same), and for the remaining five, the two judges are not in uni-
son. This means that the inter-observer reliability correlation coefficient is .83 (or 25 out of 30
is equal to 83% agreement). Experts tell us that an inter-rater reliability coefficient should be at
least .60 (Patten, 2007).

Test-retest reliability. To measure **test-retest reliability,** the phenomena is measured with the
same instrument, at two different points in time, and then these two sets of results are compared.
For example, Yang (2004) wanted to know the reliability of the smiley face assessment test. The
test was administered to children with disabilities attending Camp Koinonia. The same children
took the same test twice, on April 10 and then again the following day. Test-retest reliability was
then checked to determine if the campers were consistent in their use of smiley faces to rate their
camp experience. A **test-retest reliability coefficient** of .80 and above suggests the instrument is
stable over time (Fisher & Corcoran, 2007).

Split-half reliability. In **split-half reliability,** sometimes referred to as equivalent forms reliability, two versions of the same instrument are developed. Each version is designed to be inter-
changeable with the other. The same content is supposedly covered in both forms, even though
the questions are different. You've probably been on the receiving end of a split-half test. Often
times, in large lecture college courses, two different versions of an exam are given to measure the
same content knowledge.

Split-half reliability is established by administering one form (for example, the long adult
version of the Leisure Diagnostic Battery) of the test to a sample and a few days later administering the second form (or the short adult version of the Leisure Diagnostic Battery) to the same
sample. Thus, each respondent will have two scores and these scores are used in a reliability

coefficient to determine the split-half reliability. ***Split-half reliability coefficients*** above .80 are needed to consider the equivalent forms as consistent (Patten, 2007).

Inter-item reliability. When multiple items are used to measure a single construct, it is important to determine if the items are indeed measuring the same construct. ***Inter-item reliability,*** or internal consistency, verifies that items used in an index really do belong together. The answer provided to one item is paired successively to answers provided on all remaining questions. If items are a consistent measure of the same construct, then the items themselves should be highly and positively reliable. The stronger the relationship or association between each pair of items, the higher the inter-item reliability.

Cronbach coefficient alpha is the statistic commonly used to measure inter-item reliability. ***Cronbach coefficient alpha*** determines the extent to which each item used in the instrument measures the same concept. Cronbach alpha coefficients should be > .80 (Fisher & Corcoran, 2007). In the course of calculating this statistic, items that don't belong in the index are identified when inter-item correlations are < .50, or when negative inter-item correlations are found (Shannon & Davenport, 2001).

For example, suppose socioeconomic status (SES) is measured using the traditional approach of asking about the respondent's educational attainment, occupation, and income. Most likely the Cronbach alpha for this index would be higher than .80 since previous research has repeatedly indicated responses to these three questions are highly inter-related. That is, people with higher levels of educational attainment typically hold more prestigious jobs and subsequently earn higher incomes. If for some reason, we decided to try to measure SES by asking about a respondent's education, occupation and height, then the Cronbach alpha for this index would most likely fall below .80 because the three questions are not measuring the same construct. Indeed, common sense tells us it is ludicrous to envision height as having any bearing on SES, unless you are tall enough to play at the National Basketball Association level!

In review, it is important to know a measuring instrument's reliability and validity. Actually, measurement reliability is a prerequisite for measurement validity (Figure 8). An instrument cannot have measurement validity if it does not have measurement reliability. An instrument can be: (1) invalid and unreliable, (2) invalid but reliable, or (3) valid and reliable.

Figure 8. Thinking of Instrument Validity and Reliability as Marksmanship Ability.

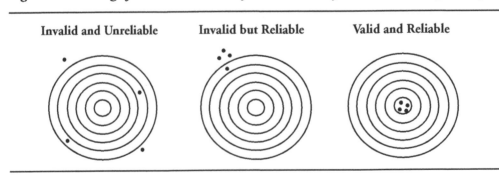

| Invalid and Unreliable | Invalid but Reliable | Valid and Reliable |

The point is that we cannot assume that if an instrument has been documented as reliable, then it must automatically be valid. Reliability alone is an insufficient criterion for selecting an instrument. For instance, an inaccurate bathroom scale might consistently report your weight as being 10 pounds lighter than your true body weight. This inaccurately calibrated scale could be described as consistently reliable but invalid. Remember, in order for an instrument to be useful, it must be both valid and reliable. Because it is easier to establish, many instruments we use in our fields have documented reliability but no documented validity.

Normative Data

Finally, a "good" instrument ideally has normative data. ***Normative data*** means that many studies have documented the way the instrument works in a specified population. This is technically known as ***standardization.*** That is, the instrument has been administered under controlled circumstances to a well-defined large group, and this group's average performance has been recorded (Case 4). For example, we know what the normal body weight is given a person's age, gender, and height.

Case 4. Leisure Diagnostic Battery's Normative Data.

Witt, P., & Ellis, G. (1985). *Leisure diagnostic battery users manual.* State College, PA: Venture Publishing.

The Leisure Diagnostic Battery (LDB) consists of two parts. The first part contains scales (perceived leisure competence, perceived leisure control, leisure needs, depth of involvement in leisure, and playfulness), which when added together measure perceived freedom in leisure. The second part assesses barriers to leisure experiences, leisure preferences, and knowledge of leisure opportunities. The LDB is available in four forms, a short and long form for children and a short and long form for adults. Documentation is available on the LDB's validity (content, predictive, convergent and discriminant validity) and reliability (alpha coefficients).

Extensive testing of the long-form versions of the LDB, with hundreds of individuals, has resulted in the creation of normative data for a variety of groups. These groups include: junior high students; university students in a rehabilitation/therapeutic recreation class; university students voluntarily participating in physical education activity classes; hospitalized asthmatic adolescents; adolescents who have been hospitalized for emotional disturbances; veterans who have been hospitalized for drug dependency; individuals who are physically disabled, emotionally disturbed, or mentally retarded; and high school students attending regular or special education classes who have been classified as either educable mentally retarded, learning disabled, emotionally disturbed, or non-disabled.

If you use an instrument that has established normative data, you are able to compare a group you've collected information on, to the norms that have been reported for the measure (Case 5). Such a comparison can establish the relative need for a program or the relative effectiveness of one program against another. It is unfortunate that few standardized instruments have yet to be developed to assist leisure service professionals.

Case 5. Establishing the Need for a Leisure Counseling Program for Individuals Hospitalized for Chronic Psychiatric Illness.

Wolfe, R., & Riddick, C. (1984). Effects of leisure counseling on adult psychiatric patients. *Therapeutic Recreation Journal, 18,* 30-37.

This study examines how a leisure counseling program affected participants' leisure attitudes and self-esteem. The program was offered to individuals who had experienced long-term hospitalization for psychiatric problems and were scheduled for discharge. Pretest data, collected before the program started, revealed participants' leisure attitudes and self-esteem scores were considerably lower than norms established and anticipated for adults. This finding was interpreted as underscoring the need for the intervention, since participants' scores were lower than what was expected for an "average, normal adult."

Resources for Locating a Good Instrument

A multitude of instruments to measure a variety of concepts have already been developed for us by other researchers. When sifting through what is available, you should be mindful of what we've just discussed: kind of measure, multiple-variable measures, single versus multiple-item measures, instrument validity, instrument reliability, and availability of normative data.

Locating tests, surveys, or scales can be challenging and very time consuming. Sometimes you find that a published instrument must be purchased directly from its publisher. In instances where part or an entire instrument is published within a research article, it is necessary to contact the author(s) to secure inspection copies of the instrument and/or seek permission to use their test.

To help, a variety of sources exists for locating instruments you can use when conducting research related to recreation, park, tourism, and sport settings. Secondary print sources for finding measuring instruments are cited in Appendix 4.

Additionally, a review of three of the major leisure science journals *(Journal of Leisure Research, Journal of Park and Recreation Administration, Therapeutic Recreation Journal)* during the year 2000 through 2006 uncovered the reporting of newly created instruments, measuring an array of leisure-related phenomena (Figure 9). Also, keep in mind that other excellent sources for identifying potential measurement instruments include articles or books published in other disciplines and abstracts of professional conferences and symposia.

Figure 9. Articles, Reporting on the Development of Instruments Related to Leisure Phenomena, Appearing in Three Journals, 2001-2006.[6]

Baldwin, C., & Caldwell, L. (2003). Development of the free time motivation scale for adolescents. *Journal of Leisure Research, 35,* 129-151.

Boothman, S., & Savell, K. (2004). Development, reliability, and validity of the measurable assessment in recreation for resident-centered care. *Therapeutic Recreation Journal, 38,* 382-393.

Cavnar, M. et al. (2004). Evaluating the quality of recreation facilities: Development of an assessment tool. *Journal of Park and Recreation Administration, 22,* 96-114.

Green, G., Hatch, K., Betz, C., & DiStefano, C. (2006). Construction and validation of the national survey on recreation and the environment's lifestyles scale. *Journal of Leisure Research, 38,* 513-535

Hurd, A. (2005). Competency development for entry level public parks and recre-ation professionals. *Journal of Park and Recreation Administration, 23,* 45-62.

Hurtes, K., & Allen, L. (2001). Measuring resiliency in youth: The resiliency attitudes and skills profile. *Therapeutic Recreation Journal, 35,* 333-347.

Jones, C., Patterson, M., & Hammitt, W. (2000). Evaluating the construct validity of sense of belonging as a measure of landscape perception. *Journal of Leisure Research, 32,* 383-395.

Kaczynski, A., & Crompton, J. (2004). Development of a multidimensional scale for implementing positioning in public park and recreation agencies. *Journal of Park and Recreation Administration, 22,* 1-27. (NOTE: This instrument was developed to enable public park and recreation agencies to identify the issues deemed most important in the community, and to measure stakeholders' perceptions of the performance of these agencies and their "competitors" in addressing these issues.)

Kaczynski, A., Crompton, J., & Emerson, J. (2003). A procedure for improving the accuracy of visitor counts at state parks. *Journal of Park and Recreation Administration, 21,* 140-151.

Kloseck, M., Crilly, R., & Hutchinson-Troyer, L. (2001). Measuring therapeutic recreation outcomes in rehabilitation: Further testing of the leisure competence measure. *Therapeutic Recreation Journal, 35,* 31-42.

Kyle, G., Mowen, A., Absher, J., & Havitz, M. (2006). Commitment to public leisure service providers: A conceptual and psychometric analysis. *Journal of Leisure Research, 38,* 78-103.

Madrigal, R. (2006). Measuring multidimensional nature of sporting event performance consumption. *Journal of Leisure Research, 38,* 267-292.

Manning, R., & Freimund, W. (2004). Use of visual research methods to measure standards of quality for parks and outdoor recreation. *Journal of Leisure Research, 36,* 557-579.

Petick, J. (2002). Development of a multidimensional scale for measuring the perceived value of a service. *Journal of Leisure Research, 34,* 119-134.

Shapiro, D., & Yun, J. (2003). Sport motivation questionnaire for persons with mental retardation. *Therapeutic Recreation Journal, 37,* 315-325.

Widmer, M., Ellis, G., & Munson, W. (2003). Development of the Aristotelian ethi-cal behavior in leisure scale short form. *Therapeutic Recreation Journal, 37,* 256-274.

Yuen, F. (2004). "It was fun . . . I liked drawing my thoughts": Using drawings as a part of the focus group process with children. *Journal of Leisure Research, 36,* 461-482.

[6] Based on a review of articles published in the *Journal of Leisure Research, Journal of Park and Recreation Administration,* and *Therapeutic Recreation Journal.*

There are also many excellent Internet resources for locating tests, surveys, or other research instruments. Some examples of these follow in Figure 10.

Figure 10. Web-Based Instrument Sources.

___

ERIC/AE Test Locator (http://www.ericdigests.org/1996-1/test.htm.). The ERIC Clearinghouse on Assessment and Evaluation (ERIC/AE), the Educational Testing Service (ETS), the Buros Institute, and Pro-Ed (publishing) have collaborated to produce a comprehensive test locator service. The Test Locator service is located in a subdirectory of the ERIC/AE gopher site, and contains several searchable testing databases, tips on how to best select and evaluate a test, information on fair testing practices, and connections to library catalogs that may be of assistance to anyone searching for specific test information.

Finding Tests, Surveys, and Questionnaires (http://www.biomed.lib.umn.edu/ help/guides/test). Instrument leads from the University of Minnesota's Bio-Medical Library.

Performance Evaluations and Performance Appraisal for Management Employees. Available at the California Park and Recreation Society's Web page at http://www.cprs. org. Click on "Training/Education Resources," then "Information and Referral," and go down to "Creating Community: VIP Planning Tools" and look at "Performance Evaluations" and "Performance Appraisal for Management Employees."

Tests and Measures in Social Sciences. Available at University of Texas, http://libraries.uta.edu/helen/ test&meas/testmainframe.htm.

Tests Reviews Online (http://www.unl.edu/buros/). The Buros Institute of Mental Measurements presents reviews and information on 4,000 tests.

___

Your Research

1. Have you chosen reactive, non-reactive, and/or psychophysiological measures for your study?
2. Do you plan on using multiple variable measures?
3. Will you be using single or multiple-item measures?
4. For each measure you've chosen, provide documentation regarding its validity and reliability.
5. Do normative data exist for any of your chosen instruments? If so, provide a brief profile of the group that was used to establish the normative data.

Review and Discussion Questions . . .
What have you learned when considering measurement?

1. Recall the four steps associated with the *logic of measurement.* Cite a recreation/parks/ sport/tourism management example using these steps.
2. Define and differentiate between *reactive, non-reactive* and *psychophysiological* measures.
3. Why is it important to use multiple *variable measures*?
4. Identify how an *index* differs from *a scale.*
5. Provide a brief definition *of instrument validity,* and then illustrate the concept by drawing a representation of validity and lack of validity on an archery target.
6. Explain the two ways used to establish *construct validity: face validity* and *content validity.*

7. Describe the four approaches used to determine *criterion validity*: *concurrent validity*, *predictive validity*, *convergent validity*, and *discriminant validity*.

8. Define what is meant by *instrument reliability*; and then illustrate the concept by drawing a representation of reliability and lack of reliability on an archery target.

9. Explain the four ways instrument reliability can be documented: *inter-rater reliability*, *test-retest reliability*, *split half reliability*, and internal consistency.

10. Recall the minimum *reliability coefficient* value that suggests acceptability for: inter-rater reliability, test-retest reliability, split half reliability, and inter-item reliability.

11. What does it mean when it says *normative data* exist for an instrument?

Exercises

1. If your instructor doesn't provide you with a research article, find an article on a topic you are interested in that has been published in a refereed journal. Answer the following questions:

   A. What was the logic of measurement used in the study? That is, identify each concept examined, as well as corresponding variable(s) and instrument(s).

   B. For the dependent variables under examination, were reactive, non-reactive, or psycho-physiological measures used? Were multiple measures used to examine each concept of interest? Were single or multiple-item measures used?

   C. What was the documented validity and reliability for the respective measures? Be specific regarding how the instrument's validity and reliability were established. Record your answers in a grid you have prepared.

   D. Were norms available for any dependent variable under study? Again, fill your answer in a prepared grid.

2. If you feel you need to read more about instrumentation, go to:

   A. William Trochim's Web site at www.socialresearchmethods.net/kb. Click and read about: "Measurement," "Construct Validity," Reliability," "Survey Research: Constructing the Survey," and "Scaling."

   B. Alison Galloway's Web site at www.tardis.ed.ac.uk/~kate/qmcweb/qcont.htm. Click on "Question Types," "Question Order," and "Dealing with Problem Questions."

   C. Wilderdom's Web site at www.wilderdom.com/tools/html. Learn more about instruments that evaluate the impacts of psycho-social training and intervention programs by clicking on "Index to Instruments," "Summaries of Instruments," and "Links for Finding Research Instruments."

Accurate measurement requires choosing instruments that assess multiple variables, as well as multiple items, and that are nonreactive, valid and reliable. Whether or not normative data exist for the measure is also an important consideration. Entrance to Doge's Palace, Venice, Italy. *Copyright © 2008 Carol Cutler Riddick*

STEP 9: Specify Data-Collection Tools

Triangulation

Data-Collection Tools for Quantitative Studies
Structured Interview
Questionnaire
Observation
Projective Methods

Data-Collection Tools for Qualitative Studies
Unstructured In-Depth Interview
  Descriptive Information Interview
  Discovery Interview
  Problem-Solving Interview
Focus Groups
Participant Observation
  Passive Participant
  Marginal Participant
  Complete Participant
Document/Record Review

Interviewing Mechanics

Questionnaire Mechanics

Focus Group Mechanics

Observation Mechanics

Document/Record Review Mechanics

> **I was brought up to believe that the only thing worth doing was to add to the sum of accurate information in the world.**
> Margaret Mead

Triangulation

Every researcher is faced with the decision of exactly how to collect the information needed for a study. An important initial consideration in choosing data collection tools is to consider triangulation (an idea previously introduced to you in Steps 3 and 7). *Triangulation* can also be applied to data-collection efforts (Case 1). That is, multiple measurement tools can be used to determine if findings are supported or contradicted (Miles & Huberman, 1994). Triangulation in this step, therefore, suggests you can include both quantitative and qualitative data-collection tools in the same study.

Case 1. Data-Collection Triangulation for an Evaluation of a Resort Beach Program for Kids.

Using several data-collection tools in the same study can provide invaluable insights on program impact. For example, suppose we want to evaluate a beach program for the children of resort guests. The study could be implemented using the following triangulation of data collection tools:

- Conduct open-ended interviews with the parents of beach program participants, asking them questions about their perceptions of how their children benefitted from the program.
- Ask the beach program staff to complete a questionnaire about the effectiveness of the program in accomplishing the resort's guest relations goals.
- Observe the beach program participants for an hour on two different days, recording information about their enthusiasm for participating in the program.

Our belief is that, if possible, you always should carry out a study using data-collection triangulation. Figure 1 summarizes the reasons for using triangulation at the data-collection step. If you desire to learn more about a particular data-collection tool, Appendix 5 contains supplemental references.

Figure 1. Reasons for Using Data-Collection Triangulation.[1]

- **Facilitates convergence of results.** The expectation is that different data-collection methods yield the same results.
- **Is complimentary.** Overlapping and unique facets of a phenomenon emerge.
- **Is developmental.** One method may help inform a second method. For example, insights learned from a focus group could help shape interpretations of data obtained from a quasi-experiment.
- **Is inventive.** Contradictions and fresh perspectives emerge.
- **Is expansive.** Breadth is added to the study.

[1]Adapted from Greene, Caracelli and Graham (1989).

What sorts of data-collection tools are available to us? The next two sections of the chapter presents a roster of popular data-collection tools associated with both quantitative and qualitative approaches. And, the final sections, presented in the chapter, highlights the important mechanics of using these tools.

Data-Collection Tools for Quantitative Studies

A number of data-collection tools exists for conducting quantitative studies, including the use of structured interviews, questionnaires, observations, and projective methods. Popular ways to carry out structured interviews are to use either a face-to-face or telephone interview. Likewise, questionnaires are frequently used and are distributed to a group, by mail, or via an Internet site.

Before discussing these quantitative data-collection tools more, Figure 2 compares interview and questionnaire alternatives. Then, the advantages and disadvantages of observation and projective methods appear in Figure 3.

Figure 2. Comparison of Structured Interview and Questionnaire Data-Collection Tools.[2]

Criteria	Face-to-Face Interview	Telephone Interview	Mail Questionnaire	Internet Questionnaire
Administrative Factors • Cost • Data-collection period • Geographic distribution of sample	High ~ 4-12 weeks Must be in close proximity	Low-medium ~2-4 weeks May be wide	Low ~10 weeks May be wide	Low ~1-3 weeks May be wide
Question Issues • Length • Complexity • Ability to handle sensitive topics	Long (~30-60 minutes) May be complex Fair	Medium-long (~15-35 minutes) Simple Fair-good	Short-medium (~4-12 pages) Simple-moderate Good	Short (< 15 minutes) Simple-moderate Poor-fair
Data Quality Issues • Sampling frame bias • Response rate • Response bias • Quality of recorded response	Low Low Low Good	Low Fair-good Low Good	Usually Low Poor-good Medium-high Fair-good	Low-high Poor-good Medium-high Fair-good

[2] Adopted from: Czaja and Blair (2005); and Rea and Parker (2005).

Figure 3. Advantages and Disadvantages of Observation and Projective Data-Collection Tools.

Data-Collection Method	Advantages	Disadvantages
Observation	• Realistic • Insightful	• Access may be difficult • Expensive
Projective Methods	• Non-threatening	• Valid predictor of behavior?

Structured Interview

Interviews typically allow a researcher to collect information that leads to a broader and more integrative view of the constructs studied. There are several ways to carry out data-collection interviews; they vary only according to the amount of pre-planned structure they contain. That is, interviews can be categorized as a structured interview, a semi-structured interview, or an unstructured interview. The structured interview will now be discussed.

Dr. Elizabeth Barrie, Research Associate for the Eppley Institute for Parks and Public Lands, waits to interview visitors to the Chincoteague National Wildlife Refuge for a study about future plans at the visitors' center. *Copyright © 2008 Ruth V. Russell*

Structured interviews contain a set of pre-established questions that follow strict administration and scoring rules. The researcher reads the questions to the study participant from an **interview schedule,** or a form containing the questions.

Additionally, the structured interview uses closed-ended questions that provide specific options for responding. These **closed-ended questions** are also labeled **structured** or **fixed-choice questions.** Response categories for closed-ended questions typically are structured in the specific formats listed in Figure 4. When deciding on which response format to use, remember to stay alert to the intended purpose of the question, the theory related to the constructs being measured, and the population to whom the data-collection tool will be administered.

Figure 4. Popular Closed-Ended Question Response Options.

Response Options	Example
Dichotomous or a question offers two choices.	Did you work out in the University's exercise room yesterday (circle one answer)? **YES**　　　　　　**NO**
Likert scale or the respondent is asked to show the amount of agreement or disagreement with a statement.	Generally speaking, after working out, I feel better about body image (circle the extent you agree with this statement): STRONGLY AGREE AGREE NEITHER AGREE NOR DISAGREE DISAGREE STRONGLY DISAGREE
Semantic differential or a scale is set up between bipolar words and the respondent selects the point that represents the direction and intensity of his/her feelings.	Put a check mark in the space on each line below to show your opinion of the quality of the food served at the snack bar. **EXPENSIVE:__:__:__:__:__:__:__:INEXPENSIVE** **GOOD:__:__:__:__:__:__:__:BAD** **FRESH:__:__:__:__:__:__:OLD**
Forced ranking involves asking the respondent to rank each option that applies.	Indicate, in rank order, the times you prefer the University's exercise room to open up on the weekends, by putting '1' next to your favorite opening time through '5' for your least favorite opening time. <u>Opening Time</u>　<u>Rank</u> *5 A.M.*　　　____ *6 A.M.*　　　____ *7 A.M.*　　　____ *8 A.M.*　　　____ *9 A.M.*　　　____
Adjective checklist is used to ask respondents to rate or judge something.	Please put a check mark in the space behind the word that best describes your opinion of your personal trainer (check as many as apply)?: **PLEASANT**　____ **DEMANDING** ____ **REASONABLE** ____

Response Options	Example
Multiple choice is when a question offers two or more choices.	What weekdays do you typically exercise (check as many as apply)? **MONDAYS** ____ **TUESDAYS** ____ **WEDNESDAYS**____ **THURSDAYS** ____ **FRIDAYS** ____
Smiley face continuum provides an array of faces ranging from happy to sad.	Now, I'm going to ask you about various camp activities. Please point to the face that shows how you feel when you finish going to: **ARCHERY** **CANOEING**

There are advantages and disadvantages associated with closed-ended questions. Figure 5 summarizes some of these pros and cons.

Figure 5. Advantages and Disadvantages of Closed-Ended Questions.

Type of Question	Advantages	Disadvantages
Closed-Ended	• Quick to answer • Easy to assign a numerical score	• If all possible answers are not anticipated, responses can be misleading • Respondent can't qualify answer

The exact questions used in a structured interview schedule (and for that matter in a questionnaire) come from three sources. First, questions from an already existing instrument are used (see Step 8). Second, questions are created or written specifically for the study at hand. Third, and probably the most common way, is that the interview contains **blended questions,** meaning some questions are borrowed and some are new.

Idea . . . References for Writing Questions.

If you're faced with the task of writing questions for interviews or questionnaires, check out the following references. These resources may prove to be invaluable.

Czaja, R., & Blair, J. (2005). *Designing surveys: A guide to decisions and procedures* (2nd ed.). Thousand Oaks, CA: Pine Forge Press.

Fowler, F. (1995). *Improving survey questions: Design and evaluation.* Thousand Oaks, CA: Sage Publications.

Rea, K., & Parker, R. (2005). *Designing and conducting survey research: A comprehensive guide* (3rd ed.). San Francisco: Jossey Bass.

Dunn, J., Bouffard, M., & Rogers, W. (1999). Assessing item content-relevance in sport psychology scale-construction research: Issues and recommendations. *Measurement in Physical Education and Exercise Science, 3,* 15-36.

Schuman, H., & Presser, S. (1996). *Questions and answers in attitude surveys: Ex-periments on question form, wording, and context.* Thousand Oaks, CA: Sage Publications.

As already mentioned, there are two ways to conduct a structured interview: face-to-face or via telephone. A *face-to-face interview* is when the interviewer and interviewee meet one-on-one. Face-to-face interviews may be conducted in a variety of places, including a leisure service setting, at the respondent's home, or at some neutral site (e.g., a cafe). One possible problem associated with face-to-face interviews is the *Halo effect.* That is, a respondent may feel the compulsion to provide answers that are more socially acceptable. Once the interviewee has personally met an interviewer, there may be some subtle pressure to provide less than truthful answers since the interviewee feels his/her anonymity has been lost.

As the name implies, in a *telephone interview,* the researcher communicates with the respondent via the phone or Teletype (TTY)/Telecommunications Relay Service/Sorensen Videophone. The obvious limitation of phone interviews is that people who do not have telephones are excluded, producing bias in the results. Another limitation of phone interviews is that certain response options (such as the smiley face continuum) cannot be used.

Questionnaire

Keep it short & sweet!! K.I.S.S.

A very popular device for collecting data in the recreation fields is the questionnaire. Technically, a *questionnaire* is a self-administered structured interview (Grosof & Sardy, 1985). In fact, many of the principles for constructing a questionnaire and a structured interview are the same. Questionnaires are either mailed to respondents, directly administered at a group meeting, or presented online. Questions in a questionnaire can be either closed-ended, open-ended, or a combination of both a closed-ended and open-ended.

We've already discussed closed-ended questions, so let's now consider open-ended and combination questions. *Open-ended questions,* sometime referred to as *unstructured questions,* consist of asking a question and then not providing any possible answer choices. The respondent provides his/her own responses to questions. An example of an open-ended question is, "In your own words, please explain why you signed up for this trip?"

Typically, open-ended questions are used for several reasons. These kinds of questions come in handy when exploring unknown subjects or when it is downright difficult if not impossible to anticipate all possible response categories. Open-ended questions are also used to ask respondents to explain why they chose a particular answer option in an earlier question. And finally, open-ended questions are posed in situations where a precise piece of information is needed and can easily be recalled (such as the answer to the question, "What is your age?").

A **combination closed-ended question** asks a question and then provides some possible answers along with option(s) to provide another answer. An example is the following:

Identify the major reasons you use the university's exercise room (check and/or supply the requested information):

___ STRESS RELEASE
___ MAINTAIN or IMPROVE PHYSICAL HEALTH
___ MEET PEOPLE
___ OTHER (specify): _____
___ OTHER (specify): _____

There are a number of disadvantages, as well as advantages, associated with closed-ended and open-ended questions. Figure 6 identifies these.

Figure 6. Advantages and Disadvantages of Open-Ended Questions.

Type of Question	Advantages	Disadvantages
Closed-Ended	• Quick to answer • Easy to assign a numerical score	• If all possible answers are not anticipated, can be misleading • Respondent can't qualify answer
Open-Ended	• Doesn't limit responses. • Greater freedom of self-expression	• Demanding on respondent • Time consuming to analyze and interpret • Response rates can be low

Observation

Observation is gathering firsthand information by watching people, events, or geographic areas. Sometimes, observation is aided by using such electronic devices as videotaping, still photography, time-lapse photography, or aerial photography. Observation is most successful when there is tangible behavior, physical evidence, outcome, or a product that can be seen or heard.

Observational tools for data collection are suited to both quantitative and qualitative studies when the aim of the study is to answer questions about behavior and/or the physical environment. When used from the perspective of the quantitative approach, observation relies on pre-structured observational guides. **Observational guides** are printed forms that provide specific ways to record what is seen or heard. These guides could include structured checklists, rating scales, or structured note taking fields. Case 2 below illustrates an observational guide.

Case 2. Example of Observation Form Developed to Collect Quantitative Data.[3]

Guide for Observing the Social Behaviors of Deaf Adults Participating in a Group Session:[3]

Name of Patient _____   Date _____

Receptive Skills: Mark the number of times a behavior is exhibited during activity session:

1. <u>Alertness</u>:

Paying attention _____

Sleeping _____

Uninterested _____

2. <u>Eye Contact</u>:

Eyes open and maintain eye contact with group leader/speaker _____

Eyes open but no eye contact with group leader/speaker _____

Eyes closed _____

3. <u>Facial Expressions</u>:

Smiling _____

Unexpressive or flat _____

4. <u>Attentive Listening</u>:

Oh-I-See sign _____

Nodding of head (up and down motion) in agreement with person talking in the group _____
_____

Nodding of head (sideways) in disagreement with person talking in the group _____
_____

Twitching of nose (signifies agreement) _____

[3] Riddick and Baron-Leonard (2003).

There are a number of situations where observation may be appropriate in recreation, park, tourism, and sport research. These include recording (Veal, 2006; Taylor & Kielhofner, 2006):

- Children's play characteristics (e.g., inattention, hyperactivity, fatigue, engagement).
- Adult leisure behaviors (e.g., level of endurance, task completion).
- Spatial use of recreational sites and environmental circumstances (e.g., objects and their arrangement).
- Program participants' communication (e.g., what a person says to others, how a person acts toward others).

Projective Methods

Projective methods indirectly examine people's attitudes, beliefs, and perceptions (Case 3). These methods are used whenever direct questioning is inappropriate or whenever the true purpose of the study cannot be revealed (Bailey, 1994).

Case 3. Using a Projective Method to Assess Children's Feelings About Age-Appropriate Leisure Activities.

Riddick, C., Ansello, E., & Seefeldt, C. (1987, October). *Children's perceptions of the age appropriateness for participation in selected leisure activities.* Paper presented at the 1987 National Recreation & Park Association's Leisure Research Symposium, New Orleans.

The purpose of this study was to assess children's perceptions of age-appropriate leisure activities. Black and white charcoal drawings were used as a way to have children project ageism stereotypes they may have already formed and possessed. Five- to seven-year-old children were asked to review artist drawings that depicted a man at four stages of the life cycle (young adult, middle-aged, young-old, and old-old). During an interview, the child was asked to indicate which man was most likely to do a specified leisure activity "a lot" of the time. Data analyses revealed that the interviewed children had already formed strong opinions regarding what is and what is not "appropriate" leisure activity engagement across four periods in the life cycle. Older persons were stereotyped as engaging in more sedentary activities; whereas younger persons were type cast into participating in energy-demanding leisure activities.

Word association, cartoon/drawing/photograph tests (Case 3), and sentence completions are examples of projective methods. One sort of projective method that has emerged is the vignette technique. The *vignette technique* is a method that has been used to " . . . elicit perceptions, opinions, beliefs and attitudes from responses or comments to stories depicting scenarios and situations" (Barter & Renold, 1999, p. 2). An intriguing example of this sort of research is a study in which 30 children, in third, fifth and eighth grades, were asked to interpret the *Gunman in Town* comic book (Pallenik, 1976).

Data-Collection Tools For Qualitative Studies

Essentially, there are four tools for gathering qualitative data. These are individual unstructured in-depth interviews, focus groups, participant observations, and record reviews. The way the qualitative study is designed (Step 7) will have ramifications for which of these data-collection tools is best (Figure 7).

Figure 7. Interface Between Qualitative Design Approaches and Data-Collection Tools.

Approach	Unstructured Interview	Focus Group	Participant Observation	Record Review
Case Study	√	√	√	√
Critical Theory	√	√		√
Ethnography	√		√	√
Grounded Theory	√	√	√	√
Narrative	√	√		√
Phenomenology	√		√	

Of course, each data-collection tool used in a qualitative study has both advantages and disadvantages. Figure 8 highlights the major pros and cons of each method.

Figure 8. Advantages and Disadvantages of Qualitative Data-Collection Tools.

Data-Collection Tool	Advantages	Disadvantages
Unstructured In-Depth Interview	• Useful when have few people to interview • Appropriate when variability exists among study participants • Can "inform" quantitative research	• Expensive • Doesn't work if unskilled interviewer is used • Halo effect • Cannot compare responses
Focus Group	• Collect data quickly and at less cost compared to individual interviews • Obtain large and rich amounts of data in respondents' own words • Useful for collecting data from children or individuals who are not literate • Can "inform" quantitative research	• Limited generalization to a larger population • Biased if dominated by an opinionated member • Difficult to summarize and interpret results • Requires a skilled and practiced facilitator

Data-Collection Tool	Advantages	Disadvantages
Participant Observation	• Insightful, provides information on what actually is happening in a particular situation • Can "inform" quantitative research	• Difficulty gaining admittance to the group or social setting being studied • Doesn't work if observer doesn't possess good attending and observing skills • If a covert role has been assumed, there is difficulty recording information • Time consuming • Extra care needed to maintain ethical responsibilities
Record Review	• Unobtrusive • Triangulates with data collected from other methods	• Access may be a problem • Reporting bias of author • May be difficult to interpret

Unstructured In-Depth Interview

Again, an interview is a personal, face-to-face meeting between the researcher and a study participant. An *unstructured in-depth interview* consists of the interviewer asking open-ended questions of the interviewee during a meeting.

For in-depth interviews, the unstructured format is used to delve more deeply into a particular event, issue, or situation. Interview lengths range along a continuum from an hour, to several hours, to across multiple days. An unstructured in-depth interview can be tape-recorded, and then a verbatim transcript is prepared of the tape recording.

Unstructured in-depth interviews, depending on their purpose, are divided into three kinds. These are descriptive information interview, discovery interview, and problem-solving interview (Cunningham, 1993).

Descriptive information interview. A whole range of data can be collected in the descriptive information interview (Figure 9). In particular, during a *descriptive information interview,* the interviewee is asked about attributes, facts related to behavioral experiences, and self-evaluative information (such as attitudes, preferences, beliefs, and reactions to hypothetical situations). The time frame reference for a descriptive information-gathering interview may either be the past, present, or future.

Figure 9. Example of Data Collected from a Descriptive Information Interview.

Type of Information Requested	Question Example
Attributes	• What is the highest grade of school you have completed?
Facts Related to Behavioral Experiences	• During the past month, what programs have you participated in at the recreation center?
Self-Evaluative Information A. Likes and Dislikes (Attitudes)	• What program has our recreation center offered that you enjoyed best?
B. Preferences	• Would you be supportive of having a potluck dinner scheduled before the Friday night dances held at our recreation center?
C. Strengths and Weaknesses (Beliefs)	• How might our recreation program change to better meet your needs? The needs of citizens in our county?
D. Statement of Goals/Philosophy (Beliefs)	• What are your fitness goals for the upcoming year?
E. Hypothetical Statements	• What would you do if ...

Discovery interview. The **discovery interview** is used to identify impressions, concerns, suggestions, and/or ideas. This sort of interview emerges as a valuable tool for generating both problems and solutions for an organization as perceived by its patrons or potential clients (Case 4). The goal of a discovery interview is to find out about issues and perspectives shared by those being queried.

Case 4. Example of Questions for a Discovery Interview About a County's Bike Trail System.

Montgomery County Recreation Department is interested in knowing your impressions and ideas about the county's bike trail system. As a member of a bike club:

1. What are some of the positive things you can say about the public bike-trail system in Montgomery County?
2. Which one biking trail system feature is most important to you and why?
3. What are some of the problems you have experienced with the bicycle trail system in Montgomery County? For each problem you identify, tell me your ideas for how the problem could be solved or prevented?
4. What are some of the goals that might guide us in making a better bicycle trail system in the county? What things should the county try to improve within the upcoming year? The next five years?

Problem-solving interview. The ***problem-solving interview*** responds to the mutual interests of the interviewer and interviewee, with a focus on specific problem solving or goal setting. The interviewer attempts to develop a climate where there is mutual interest in sharing ideas for problem solving.

Problem-solving interviews are most commonly used in personnel situations, where personal growth and change are the objective of management (Case 5). The purpose of the problem-solving interview in these situations is to aid the employee or volunteer staff member to identify ways to change and improve. The interview provides a context where the individual can work out a solution to a problem or issue and begin to take action to resolve the situation.

Case 5. Data that May Be Collected in a Problem-Solving Interview.[4]

Imagine you are the supervisor of an employee who continuously fails to meet deadlines. Questions that could be asked of this employee, during a problem-solving interview, are:

1. What effect does your failure to meet report deadlines have on others?
2. If our roles were reversed (i.e., you were the supervisor and I the employee), what would you expect of me in terms of punctuality?
3. How, as your supervisor, may I help you do a better job meeting deadlines?
4. What can the organization do to help you do a better job in meeting deadlines?

[4]Adapted from Cunningham (1993).

Focus Groups

Focus groups are planned group interviews done in a meeting setting. The goal of focus groups is to do exactly what the name implies—focus on one or more purposes, while also capturing spontaneity and synergism (Figure 10).

Figure 10. Purposes of a Focus Group.

Focus groups serve a variety of purposes. For example, they are used to (Higgenbotham & Cox, 1979):

- **Obtain general background information about a topic.** Focus groups provide the means for exploring the potential ways respondents think and talk about issues.
- **Generate hypotheses.** Ideas emerging from focus groups could be reworked into hypotheses, which are tested in additional research using a quantitative approach.
- **Provide insights on how to structure a new program or make changes to an existing program.** These ideas may be the basis for questions used in structured interviews or questionnaires, or other research questions explored later in quantitative studies.
- **Confirm results collected by another data-collection method.** As introduced at the beginning of this chapter, this is known as triangulation of data-collection tools.

A focus group generally has six to 12 members who discuss a particular topic under the direction of a facilitator (Stewart, Shamdasani, & Rook, 2007). Members of the group may or may not know each other. Most of the time only one focus group is convened, and the session lasts from one and a half to two hours. Sometimes when the research question is complex, three or four focus groups may be assembled to provide broader insights about the issue or the same group might meet more than once. Most often focus group discussions are taped or video recorded, and then a summary of the recording is prepared.

In order to stimulate and manage the group discussion, the interviewer acts more as a facilitator (Case 6). In fact, the focus group facilitator is the key to assuring the group interview goes smoothly. The facilitator's role is to guide the discussion, making sure all aspects of the topic are covered, and ensure that everyone in the group contributes to the discussion and no one monopolizes the conversation. Thus, the facilitator must be well trained in group dynamics and interview skills.

Case 6. Examples of Questions and Tactics to Use with a Focus Group.[5]

Suppose you are convening a focus group to gain insights into your hotel's aquatic center. Various questions and tactics, as noted below, could be posed to the group during the meeting.

Type of Questions/Tactic	Purpose	Example
Main research question	Broadly focuses on issue being studied.	The topic today is to explore how you feel about the services provided at our new aquatic center.
Starter question	Get the group talking and comfortable with everyone.	Please take the index card in front of you and write down one idea that comes to mind about how services at the aquatic center could be improved.
Leading question	Carry the discussion to deeper meanings.	Why do you say that?
Testing question	Find the limits of an issue, then pose an extreme yet tentative question.	Are you saying that the food in the aquatic center is unfit for human consumption?
Steering question	Nudge the group back onto the main research question.	Well, to return again to overall reactions to the aquatic center, can you tell us . . .
Obtuse question	Help the group go into territory it may find uncomfortable by asking a question in an abstract form.	What do you think a first-time guest at the hotel would think of the aquatic center employees?

Type of Questions/Tactic	Purpose	Example
Factual question	Requires a factual answer that can be answered easily.	About how many times did you swim at the center while staying at the hotel?
Silence	Often the best question is no question!	Simply wait and allow group members time to respond.

[5]Adapted from Wheatley and Flexner (1988).

Focus groups are only one of several techniques that can be used with groups. You should be aware that a number of other group data-collection tools exist, including Nominal Group technique, Delphi technique, brainstorming sessions, and leaderless discussion groups (Stewart, Samdasani, & Rook, 2007). Sometimes, several of these techniques are combined. For instance, the Delphi technique has been used in combination with focus groups in order to explore constraints experienced by African Americans and Latino visitors and nonvisitors to U.S. national parks (Roberts, 2003).

Participant Observation

As people's actions are a central aspect in any inquiry, an obvious technique for collecting information is to observe what they do. *Participant observation* is " . . . a process in which an investigator establishes and sustains a many-sided and situationally appropriate relationship with a human association in its natural setting for the purpose of developing a social scientific understanding of that association" (Lofland, Snow, Anderson, & Lofland, 2006). In other words, participant observation consists of watching the naturally occurring actions of people.

Participant observations differ in terms of the duration of the observation. Observing the actions of others may take place in a single event over a brief time frame. At the other extreme, observations may be done over a very long term with repeat observations. The duration of the observations should be determined by the research question behind the study. More broadly focused questions will take longer to answer through participant observation than narrowly focused questions.

Participant observation places considerable responsibility on the observer(s). The data produced through this tool are the interpretations by the observer of what was observed. Therefore, an observer needs special training in order to know what to view, say, and record. Incidentally, one device observers use to record what is being observed is known as memory sparkers (see *Idea* box below).

Idea . . . Using Memory Sparkers When Engaged in Participant Observation.[6]

One of the areas of required skill for the observer is in recording what is observed. Even with the most unstructured and casual observation situation, it is important to have a system that allows you to capture information unambiguously and as faithfully and fully as possible.

Memory sparkers are a record of what is observed on the spot and during the action itself. In other words, jotted notes are made about the physical scene, the people involved, various activities of the people, and time sequencing. Memory sparkers consist of phrases, quotes and key words that are written down during the observation and at inconspicuous moments. As soon as possible, these memory sparkers are flushed out into a detailed written description (see Step 14B).

To illustrate, memory sparkers were used in an observational study of what adults did during a personal-goods auction (Glancy, 1987).

[6] Adapted from: Barker (1988); and Lofland, Snow, Anderson, and Lofland (2006).

The amount of participation by the researcher also varies along a continuum. As illustrated in Figure 11, the amount of participation ranges from minimal or passive participant involvement to a complete participant. The first two categories, passive and marginal participant, have been branded as the "outsider" participant researcher role; whereas, the complete participant has been dubbed the "insider" participant researcher role (Lofland, Snow, Anderson, & Lofland, 2006).

Figure 11. The Participant Observation Continuum.

Passive Participant	Marginal Participant	Complete Participant

Lowest amount of participation <-----------------------------> Highest amount of participation

Passive participant. A *passive participant* is someone who is present at the scene of the action but does not participate or interact with other people to any great extent (Spradley, 1980). About all you need to do to be a passive participant observer is to find an observation post from which to observe and record what is happening (Case 7).

Case 7. Passive Participant Observer.

Geller, E., Russ, N., & Altomari, M. (1986). Naturalistic observations of beer drinking among college students. *Journal of Applied Behavior Analysis, 19,* 391-396.

The beer-drinking behaviors of 308 university students at five drinking establishments were observed. Observations were made only of individuals drinking at tables and were made over three consecutive summer months. One or two research assistants served as observers and " . . . attempted to remain as inconspicuous as possible by sitting at tables and behaving as normal patrons" (p. 392) without directly interacting with the students being observed. Observer reliability checks were performed. Among the findings were: (a) Females, relative to males, drank less beer and stayed in the bar longer; and (b) Patrons drank significantly more beer when drinking in groups and when purchasing beer in pitchers, rather than in glasses or bottles. Findings were discussed relative to developing interventions to prevent alcohol-impaired driving.

Marginal participant. The *marginal participant* adopts the role, via behaviors and dress, of a peripheral, though completely "accepted" participant. The marginal participant assumes limited or cursory interactions and involvement with the persons being observed (Case 8).

Case 8. Marginal Participant Observer.

Snow, D., Robinson, C., & McCall, P. (1991). "Cooling out" men in singles bars and nightclubs: Observations on the interpersonal survival strategies of women in public places. *Journal of Contemporary Ethnography, 19,* 423-449.

The intent of this study was to understand the survival strategies used by women in public places. In particular, females were observed in singles bars and nightclubs as they fended off male advances. Data were collected using participant observation and informal conversational interviews with a non-random sample of 33 bar patrons and bar employees. Participant observations were conducted over a three-month period. Two of the authors visited nine nightclubs and drinking establishments (singles bars, country-western dance clubs, disco and rock clubs, and a topless club). On each occasion the participant observer(s) stood or sat where she could hear, see, and chat with other women. Three sets of strategies were used by females to *cool out,* meaning a process where the individual finds herself involved in encounters with males she wants to disengage from or to avoid altogether. First, initial cooling-out tactics consisted of polite refusal, excuses, and joking. Second, defensive, non-empathetic cooling-out tactics included studied seriousness, defensive incivility, and self-evident justifications. And finally, avoidance tactics consisted of *tie signs* (or signaling attachment or commitment to another person), non-verbal cues of disinterest, and flight.

Complete participant. The **complete participant** role means the observer becomes a full member of the group being studied. As a complete participant, the observer may assume either an overt or covert role. In an **overt complete participant** role, there is full disclosure of the identity of the observer (Case 9). Contrastingly, in a **covert complete participant** role, the observer's intentions are not disclosed to the group being studied (Case 10). If the observation is covert, then ethical considerations must be addressed.

Case 9. Overt Complete Participant Observer.

Jimerson, J. (1999). "Who has next?": The symbolic, rational, and methodical norms in pickup basketball. *Social Psychology Quarterly, 62,* 136-156.

The purpose of the study was to analyze the conversations among males waiting to play an informal game of basketball. The principal investigator had sporadically played in the same gym, which was the setting for the study, for 15 years and thus knew many of the players being observed. The players were informed the principal investigator was conducting a study. A video camera was set up in plain sight and over 20 hours of conversations between waiting players were recorded. Transcriptions of players' utterances were done using the conventions of conversation analysis. Results included a description of norm usage regarding who should play with whom, when, and where. No one paradigm explained pickup basketball behaviors. Instead, it was concluded that a unified theory of norms that uses three frameworks (internalization, rational calculation, and code) is a more realistic description of the reality of the world of pickup basketball. That is, players come to the gym with norms in mind, invoking them selectively to maximize playing time and game quality. Players often discussed among themselves, in coded language, whether and how to apply norms.

Case 10. Covert Complete Participant Observer.

Robins, D., Sanders, C., & Cahill, S. (1991). Dogs and their people: Pet-facilitated interaction in a public setting. *Journal of Contemporary Ethnography, 20,* 3-25.

The goal of the study was to examine how pet dogs facilitate interaction and development of relationships among previously unacquainted persons in a public place. The primary investigator, over a three-month period, visited the same park with his puppy and presented himself as "just another dog owner." Field notes were written in the evening following the park visit. Findings revealed that dogs exposed their human companions to: (1) Encounters with strangers through a "checking-out" process; (2) Probationary membership that included bounded interactions or conversations that deal only with dog-related topics, regulars' greetings and farewells of newcomers, and normative behaviors for negotiating trouble caused by the dogs; and, (3) Membership norms for regulars (e.g., the expectation the dog and its owner would be frequent park visitors and the content for closing salutations).

Document/Record Review

Sometimes researchers are interested in analyzing the contents of a document or record that already exists. This **secondary data analysis** (recall the *Overview* chapter) of the contents of a recorded communication is known as a **document or record review** or **content** or **document analysis** (Case 11).

Case 11. Record Review of Wimbledon Tennis Championship Commentary.

Fishwick, L., & Leach, K. (1998). Game, set and match: Gender bias in television coverage of Wimbledon 1994 in S. Scranton & R. Watson (Eds.). *Sport, leisure identities and gendered spaces* (pp. 31-44). Eastbourne: Leisure Studies Association.

Using secondary data, the purpose of the study was to find out whether or not there was gender bias in the British Broadcasting Company's commentaries of the Wimbledon Tennis Championships. Video recordings by commentators from the tournament were analyzed. Regarding *what* was being said, it was found that commentators referred to male players by their first names a total of 12 times through the tournament; whereas female players were referred to by their first names 589 times. Also, an analysis of *how* the commentary was being delivered revealed that the: (1) Men's tennis was considered superior to the women's game and (2) Women's tennis was almost always judged in relation to the men's game.

Something to Remember!

Don't get confused with the following terminology:

Secondary data = Available information that already exists for another purpose, such as information contained in documents.

Primary data = New information collected by the researcher.

Historically, record review has meant using a systematic, objective, and quantitative count of document content. In recent years, however, content analyses are often approached from an interpretive framework and/or a triangulation approach (Lysack, Luborsky, & Dillaway, 2006).

Here's an example of a triangulation approach to studying secondary data. Suppose you are interested in predicting the outcome of a new recreation bond initiative in an upcoming election. You might rely on the numerical counts of words in campaign speeches and advertisements as evidence of the support (or lack of support) for the ballot measure. Additionally, in order to prepare a targeted marketing strategy, the meaning of the words conveyed in the speeches and advertisements could be examined.

Some intriguing content analyses have been conducted through the years. Case 12 lists some examples of these.

Case 12. Examples of "Unusual" Content Analyses.

Topic	Citation
Citation analysis of reported leisure research	Samdahl, D., & Kelly, D. (1999). Speaking to ourselves: Citation analysis of *Journal of Leisure Research* and *Leisure Studies. Journal of Leisure Research, 31,* 171-180
Whale watching codes of conduct	Garrod, B., & Fennell, D. (2004). An analysis of whalewatching codes of conduct. *Annals of Tourism Research, 31,* 334-352.
Computer bulletin board	Correll, S. (1995). The ethnography of an electronic bar: The lesbian cafe. *Journal of Contemporary Ethnography, 24,* 270-299.
"Old South" life as portrayed in period literature	Harper, W., & Hultsman, J. (1992). Interpreting leisure as text: The whole. *Leisure Studies, 11,* 233-242.
Disney movies and theme parks	Rojek, C. (1993). Disney culture. *Leisure Studies, 12,* 121-136.
Heavy metal rock music	Straw, W. (1999). Characterizing rock music culture: The case of heavy metal. In S. During (Ed.), *The cultural studies reader* (2nd ed.) (pp. 451-461). NY: Routledge.
Australian newspapers' coverage of women's sport	Rowe, D., & Brown, P. (1994). Promoting women's sport: Theory, policy, and practice. *Leisure Studies, 13,* 97-110.
Print media coverage of women's Olympic Gold-winning teams	Jones, R., Murrell, A., & Jackson, J. (1999). Pretty versus powerful in the sports pages. *Journal of Sport and Social Issues, 23,* 183-192.

Topic	Citation
Photo albums	Walker, A., & Rosalind, K. (1989). Photo albums: Images of time and reflections of self. *Qualitative Sociology, 12,* 183-214.
Changes, as recorded by photographs, in a small farm community	Schwartz, D. (1989). Visual ethnography: Using photography in qualitative research. *Qualitative Sociology, 12,* 119-154.
Postcards	Cohen, E. (1993). The study of touristic images of native people: Mitigating the stereotype of a stereotype. In D. Pearce & R. Butler (Eds.), *Tourism research: Critiques and challenges* (pp. 33-69). London: Routledge.

Interviewing Mechanics

Now we conclude the chapter with some specific tips on how to use the data-collection tools just presented. We begin with interviewing. The most important thing to remember when designing the questions for an interview is to know the reason behind each question (Figure 12). Each question should be linked to a hypothesis or research question (Step 4).

Figure 12. Principles for Writing Questions for Interviews and Questionnaires.

These principles should be followed when writing questions for interviews or questionnaires:

1. **Use simple language.** Questions should use wording appropriate to the educational and cultural background of the respondents. Respondents should be able to understand all the words used in the question and answers. An example of a question violating this advice is, "Now, can you succinctly tell me how often you utilized parks within the geographic boundaries of our state?" A better way to pose the question would be to ask, "Did you visit a state park in Maryland during summer 2007?"
2. **Avoid jargon.** Questions should not use acronyms, or if they do, make sure they are spelled out the first time. Never assume respondents automatically know abbreviations that seem common to you. One of the authors worked in a hospital and observed a patient being asked, by a therapeutic recreation professional, if he had a "SOB" background. The perplexed patient took exception to the question and at this point was hastily informed "SOB" stood for "shortness of breath."
3. **Pose questions that are not "leading" or too personal.** A leading question sets an expectation that becomes socially difficult to counter or rebut. An example of a leading question is, "Of course, everyone makes time every week in his/her schedule for leisure, so now I want you to tell me about your leisure routine." Similarly, questions that are invasions of privacy should be avoided. An example of a question possibly perceived by respondents as insensitive is, "Tell me about your dating preferences."
4. **Ask questions that permit only one interpretation.** Avoid using words that are ambiguous or open to multiple interpretations. For example, the following response categories, "A lot," "Frequently," and "During the Last Year" are examples of answers that will cause confusion since individuals differ on what they mean. And, asking people, "How often do you participate in sport-

related activities?" is vague, since people may differ on how they define "sport." Instead, asking, "How often did you play any of the following sports during the past month?" is preferable.

5. **Raise questions that ask for knowledge the respondent possesses.** Don't fall into the trap of asking a question that either requires too precise or demanding of an answer or is being posed to the wrong person. Consider, for example, the specificity called for by the question, "How many times did you go for a walk during the last six months?" An example of directing the question to the wrong person is to ask a mother, "What does your teen do in his/her free time?" Instead, it would be more appropriate to ask the adolescent what she or he does during free time.

6. **Steer clear of double-barreled questions.** A double-barreled question contains two or more questions within the same question. "Do you agree that video games are a bad influence on today's youth and thus should be banned from municipal recreation centers?" asks two questions yet allows for only one answer.

Also, our experience is that when it comes to developing an interview schedule, there is a tendency to move too quickly and without deliberation. Thus, it is important to ask others to review and critique the drafted schedule. Seek feedback on question content, order, and amount. The more people who review it, the more suggestions you receive for additional or modified questions to ask. Other factors also enter the equation for pulling off a successful interview. Some of the mechanics of interviewing are highlighted in Figure 13.

Figure 13. Pointers for Setting Up and Conducting Interviews.

1. **Be careful about scheduling and executing a phone interview.** If possible, send a letter out beforehand alerting the respondent you will be conducting a phone interview. Calls should be placed on weekdays (forget Fridays) in the early evening between the hours of 7 p.m. to 9 p.m. If weekends must be used for calling, phone after noon and before 9 p.m. Make sure you are talking to the correct person and that this is a good time to conduct the interview. If not, schedule a time for a follow-up call.

2. **Begin the interview with some introductory remarks that have been pre-scripted.** These introductory remarks may be along these lines:

   > "Our research methods class is conducting a survey of weight room users. Would you mind answering a few questions about your experiences and ideas about ways to improve the weight room? It shouldn't take more than 10 minutes of your time and your answers will be anonymous. You will never be asked your name or identified."

3. **Have prepared questions (for a structured interview) or a question guide (for an unstructured interview) written out beforehand.** For a structured interview, make sure you ask each respondent the same questions and provide the same possible answer categories. For an unstructured interview, shape the question according to the circumstances of a particular interview (Veal, 2006). Questions should be based on the conceptual framework and informational needs identified for the study.

4. **For unstructured interviews, use attending and responding behaviors.** This means when vague, one-word, or unclear answers have been provided, use probes to ask for clari-

fications, and provide feedback phrases. Examples of standard probes, clarifications, and feedback phrases are (Weisberg, Krosnick, & Bowen, 1996):

Probes for Vague or One-Word Answers
- What do you mean?
- Would you tell me a little more about . . . ?
- Could you elaborate on . . . ?

Clarifications
- I'm not sure I understand what you mean. Would you mind elaborating a little more?
- Let me see if I understand what you mean. To summarize what I think I heard you say . . .
- I want to make sure I heard you right. (Repeat answer.)

Feedback Phrases
- That's interesting.
- That's useful/helpful information.
- Remember, there are no right or wrong answers.

5. **Avoid agreeing or disagreeing.** The interviewer should listen, not engage in debate!
6. **Avoid suggesting answers.** If you need to probe, ask "Why" rather than suggesting an answer. For instance, if you find the respondent does not go to local parks, don't lead the respondent by asking, "Is this because the parks are located too far away from your home?" Instead, ask a more open question, such as, "Why don't you visit your local parks?"
7. **Don't be afraid of silence.** Sometimes people need time to think. Don't try to fill the silence with verbiage. Allow the interviewee time to think and ask if he or she needs an explanation of the question posed.

Finally, recall that interviewers can have a profound influence on whether the interview is successful in gathering the information needed for a study. Whenever possible, interviewers should have characteristics similar to those interviewed. These include sharing gender, race and/or ethnicity, age, dress, mannerisms, and speech and language pattern characteristics (Bailey, 1994).

Questionnaire Mechanics

Responses to questionnaires are affected by a number of factors. When using a questionnaire as a tool to collect data, it is critical to put sufficient time into its design and layout. At best, you will only have one opportunity to make an impression, so the questions must be clear and have an easy flow or tempo.

Furthermore, a cover letter or introductory statement that is individually signed should be used in conjunction with the mail questionnaire. Points that should be addressed in the cover letter (as illustrated in Figure 14) are (Dillman, 2007; Slant & Dillman, 1994):

- Identify the organization conducting the study.
- Identify what the study is about or its purposes.
- Explain the study's social usefulness, using terms and language appropriate to the individual receiving the questionnaire or being interviewed.
- Make a promise of confidentiality.
- If appropriate, offer a token reward for participation, such as money or a prize.
- Tell the potential study participant what to do if questions arise—whom to contact and how.

Figure 14. Example of a Cover Letter Used to Recruit Study Participants.[7]

GALLAUDET **G** UNIVERSITY

DEPARTMENT OF PHYSICAL EDUCATION AND RECREATION

KENDALL GREEN
800 FLORIDA AVE. NE
WASHINGTON, DC 20002-3695

February 15, 2005

Dear Gallaudet Student,

As a student at Gallaudet University, one of the services offered to you is the Intramurals (IM) Program. Some people participate in IM, while others do not. The IM Program is interested in learning what barriers may exist to hinder student participation in their program.

Your are one of a small number of students being asked to provide insights into barriers you may be confronting in using the IM program. Your name was randomly drawn from the list of full-time Spring 2005 students. In order that the results of the study truly represent the thinking of students, it is important that you consider participating in this study.

The questionnaire will take about 10-15 minutes to complete. As an incentive, each person completing the survey will receive $5.

The study has been approved by Gallaudet's Institutional Review Board. If you are interested in participating, please complete and return the attached informed consent form. Once I receive that, you will be sent the questionnaire.

You may be assured of completed confidentiality. The questionnaire will have an identification number for mailing purposes only. This is so we may check your name off the mailing list when your questionnaire is returned. Your name will never be placed on the questionnaire itself.

I would be happy to answer any questions you may have about this study and may be reached at Joseph.Kolcun@gallaudet.edu. Furthermore, if you are NOT interested in participating in this study, I'd appreciate it if you would send me an e-mail.

Thank you very much for your assistance.

Joseph
Joseph Kolcun, M.S. in Leisure Services Administration Candidate

Carol
Carol Riddick, Ph.D. & Graduate Coordinator

[7] Adapted from Kolcun (2005).

There are a lot of things that factor into a successful questionnaire. Some of the critical points to consider regarding questionnaire mechanics are highlighted in Figure 15. Additionally, pointers unique to Internet questionnaires are presented in Figure 16.

Figure 15. Pointers for Developing Questionnaires.[8]

Among the things to consider regarding questionnaire mechanics (many of which are illustrated in Case 13) are:

1. **Print the questionnaire in a booklet format with an interesting cover.** Booklets that have an attractive cover page and make use of front and back pages so that length is somewhat downplayed, appear to work best.
2. **Questions should be related to the stated purpose(s) of the study.** The questions (sometimes called *items*) must be relevant to why the study is being carried out.
3. **List questions in descending order of perceived usefulness.** That is, place questions the respondent is most likely to see useful first and those least useful last. Demographic questions always appear as the <u>last</u> section of a questionnaire (and an interview). Putting background questions at the end will result in most people not finding them objectionable, because at this point you have established some rapport.
4. **Put related questions together and use transitions between sections of questions.** Keep questions similar in content together. When shifting subject content, use one- or two-sentence transitional statements. *Transitions* help prepare respondents for a change in the nature of questions coming up—they enable them to become mentally prepared that the nature of questions is about to be altered.
5. **Use branching questions.** *Branching questions* provide filters that determine if succeeding questions apply. If the question does not apply, the respondent is asked to skip the question(s) and move to another part of the questionnaire. An example of a branching question is:

   Have you participated in the Personal Discovery Program before (circle answer)?

   YES -----------------> Go to Question 2
   NO -----------------> Skip to Question 3

6. **Choose paper color and weight.** Some studies have suggested an off-white (yellow or beige) paper color is good since it prevents the questionnaire from getting lost on desks and at the same time is not viewed as an obnoxious color. If printing is going to be done on both sides, use 16-pound paper so print does not bleed through.
7. **Use first-class mailing.** If the questionnaire is to be mailed, always use first-class postage, with a personalized address label. This approach yields a higher response rate than bulk mailings with computer-generated mailing labels.
8. **Include a pre-addressed, postage-paid return envelope.** This is also a must to bolster questionnaire returns.
9. **Time the mailing.** The entire month of December should be avoided when sending out questionnaires. And questionnaires should be mailed on a Monday or Tuesday so they arrive the same week as mailed.

---

[8] Adapted from: Bailey (1994); and Dillman (1978).

Case 13. Sections from Kolcun's (2005) Mail Questionnaire.[9]

Gallaudet University's Intramural Program

The purpose of this research is to identify barriers affecting participation in the Intramural (IM) Sports Program. Specifically, we are trying to determine:

1. The reasons people don't participate in IM.
2. Barriers that stand in the way of greater IM participation.

You are one of the select few who have been randomly chosen to provide us with insights on this topic. Thus, it is important we hear from you. Results might ultimately improve the IM program. Regardless, we would be happy to provide you with a copy of study results. Please note, this research project has been approved by Gallaudet's Institutional Review Board. If you'd like to receive study results and/or have questions, contact: Joseph.Kolcun@gallaudet.edu.

Section III: The next set of questions ask about how your friend(s) or partner might have influenced your IM program participation in Spring 2004 and Fall 2004.

Read each question and indicate the extent you agree with the statement by choosing one of the following responses:

STRONGLY AGREE ⟶	Circle 1
SOMEWHAT AGREE ⟶	Circle 2
UNDECIDED ⟶	Circle 3
SOMEWHAT DISAGREE ⟶	Circle 4
STRONGLY DISAGREE ⟶	Circle 5

My friends(s) and/or partner:

31. Lived too far away to join me in IM activities	1	2	3	4	5
32. Didn't have time to join me in IM activities	1	2	3	4	5
33. Couldn't afford IM registration costs	1	2	3	4	5
34. Weren't interested in participating in the IM program.	1	2	3	4	5
35. Had too many obligations to join me in IM activities.	1	2	3	4	5
36. Didn't have the physical skills to participate in IM activities.	1	2	3	4	5
37. Didn't have transportation to get to IM activities	1	2	3	4	5
38. Other ways your friend(s) and/or partner influenced your IM participation (please specify):_____ _____...1		2	3	4	5

Any other comments you have about barriers you experienced participating in the IM program?
_____
_____

Thanks! Have a great day! ☺

---
[9] Adapted from Kolcun (2005).

Figure 16. Pointers for Developing Web Questionnaires.[10]

Some hints about putting together a Web questionnaire are:

1. **Take care in what you choose to put on the subject line.** Consider using the name of the sponsoring organization or a generic subject line related to the study (e.g., "Your Experiences at Sports Camp").
2. **Use a pre-notification that the Web-based survey is coming.**
3. **Provide prospective respondents with a password that permits them exclusive access to the questionnaire.** This step ensures integrity of the data.
4. **Include personalized e-mail cover letters.**
5. **Adopt simple layout formats.**
6. **Use at least a 13-point font and limit the display line length to approximately 70 characters.**
7. **Use colored headings and small graphics when appropriate** (adds interest and appeal).
8. **Due to time efficiency for the respondent, use *multiple-item screens* (or similar questions on the same screen) as opposed to a single item on each screen.**
9. **Consider using open-ended questions as optional questions at the end of the questionnaire.**
10. **When using open-ended questions, the text box should be multilined with enough space to accommodate the maximum amount of text expected.**
11. **When the respondents click on the "Submit" icon, make sure a brief thank-you note pops up onto their screens.**

---

[10] Adapted from: Couper, Traigott and Lamias (2001); and Young and Ross (2000).

To maximize response rates for mail and Internet questionnaires, one idea is to use a ***tailored design strategy*** (Dillman, 1978, 2007). This means having up to three follow-up phases. For example, for a mailed questionnaire, one week after the initial mailing a postcard reminder is sent to everyone. Three weeks after the initial mailing a replacement questionnaire is sent to non-respondents. And seven weeks after the initial mailing, non-respondents then receive a certified mail questionnaire replacement. For Internet questionnaires, e-mail reminders should be sent. Other factors that affect response rate are highlighted in Figure 17.

Figure 17. Factors Affecting Response Rate to a Questionnaire.[11]

Factors that affect the response to a questionnaire:

1. **Cover letter contents.**
2. **Respondent's interest in topic.**
3. **Questionnaire length.**
4. **Questionnaire design.**
5. **Reward(s) for responding.**
6. **Provision of postage-paid reply envelope** (for mailed questionnaires).
7. **Number and timing of follow-ups.**

---

[11] Adapted from: Solomon (2001); and Veal (2006).

Focus Group Mechanics

It's been noted that focus groups are " . . . not a freewheeling conversation among group members" (Stewart, Shamdasani, & Rook, 2007, p. 45). Some ideas for setting up and running focus group meetings are featured in Figure 18.

Figure 18. Pointers for Convening a Focus Group.[12]

1. **Take time to define the research question.** The question should clearly identify the topic of interest and the relevant population. The question should relate to the purpose of the focus group—to inform a decision, provide a solution to a problem, etc. Payne (1980) is an excellent reference for learning how to write questions for focus groups.
2. **Develop a focus group interview guide in collaboration with all parties interested in the research.** Remember to order questions from: (a) General to the more specific; and from (b) Most relevant to the research question to least.
3. **Choose an accessible, convenient location for the focus group meeting.** Possible sites for the meeting may be a community center or a mall, hotel, or agency conference room.
4. **In general, schedule the focus group meeting towards the end of the workday or early evening on a Tuesday, Wednesday, Thursday, or Monday (least desirable).** Research indicates these times of the day and days of the week are likely to increase participation.
5. **Take care about who you recruit for the focus group.** The most common method is to draw focus group members from a convenience sample. If you do this, make every effort to identify individuals who are more or less representative of the population group of interest.
6. **Consider using a multistep process in recruiting a focus group member.** The initial contact with potential group members should be done by mail, e-mail, telephone, or in person. Identify the general topic that will be discussed by the group and let them know they will be expected to share their opinions. If potential group members show interest, inform them of specifics, such as when and where the focus group will be meeting and the incentive for participating, if any. Finally, confirm (by telephone) the meeting 24 hours ahead of time.
7. **Carefully choose the focus group facilitator.** Research findings suggest the group's facilitator affects the group's success. Along with his or her educational and experiential background, personality characteristics (animated, sense of humor, empathetic, genuinely interested in people, articulate, etc.) can work for or against the group's deliberations. The facilitator also needs to be able to shift among several roles during the meeting, being supportive, directive, participative, and achievement-oriented at various times. Some facilitators prefer to take notes themselves, while others may want to identify an assistant who handles the note taking and/or video or audio recording.
8. **The group's facilitator should begin the meeting by creating trust and openness within the group.** The challenge is to create a non-threatening and non-evaluative environment that promotes expression of thought by focus group members.

[12]Adapted from Stewart, Shamdasani, and Rook (2007).

Observation Mechanics

The choice of **data site** or setting to conduct the observation is a critical issue. A potential site should be evaluated in terms of its (Lofland, Snow, Anderson, & Lofland, 2006):

- **Appropriateness.** Is there a good fit between the research question(s) and the setting?
- **Access.** Is your observation post natural and legitimate? And, do you possess the same attributes as those you'll be observing?
- **Physical and emotional risks.** What are the physical dangers and risks associated with the potential site for you the researcher and for those observed?
- **Ethics.** The critical question that must be examined is, "Is it fair and right that this particular group, setting, or situation is being observed?"

As noted earlier in this chapter, observations may be recorded and analyzed quantitatively or qualitatively. Regardless of which approach is used, as Figure 19 demonstrates, the steps to observing human behavior are the same.

Figure 19. Observation Pointers[13]

If you're observing human behavior, consider using the following check list to help:

1. **Decide on what to observe** (visitor characteristics, numbers in party, behaviors, etc.).
2. **Find or develop an observation recording sheet.**
3. **Choose study site(s).**
4. **Choose viewing vantage point(s).**
5. **Choose calendar date(s) for observations.**
6. **Decide on continuous observation,** (e.g., from 9 a.m. to 5 p.m.), **intermittent observations** (such as on the hour beginning from 9 a.m. and ending after the 5 p.m. observation), **or random observation** (e.g., for 20 minutes at different times and on different days).
7. **Conduct the observation, taking field notes.** *Field notes* are a running description of the setting, events, people, things heard, and interactions among and with people.
8. **No later than the morning after the observation period, fill in your field notes** (see Step 14). Getting a full record of what was observed may take as long as the original observation! Filling in the details should include:
    - A. *Running Descriptions* = Specific, concrete descriptions of events.
    - B. *Recall of Forgotten Material* = Things that come back to you later.
    - C. *Interpretive Ideas* = Notes offering an analysis of the situation.
    - D. *Personal Impressions* = Your subjective reactions.
    - E. *Reminders to Look for Additional Information* = What you will look for during the next observation session.

---

[13]Adapted from: Lofland, Snow, Anderson, and Lofland (2006); and Veal (2006).

Document/Record Review Mechanics

When undertaking a content analysis of some form of recorded communication, be aware of a couple of issues. First, it may take considerable time to identify and locate the appropriate document. Second, if the document being analyzed is a newspaper, you may want to check the accuracy of the reporting by cross-checking the first newspaper report with coverage in a second newspaper (Gratton & Jones, 2004). Sometimes document or record reviews lend themselves to a triangulation approach (Case 14). Regardless, for pointers on how to implement a record review, see Figure 20.

Case 14. Multi-Method Content Analysis.

Auster, C. (1985). Manuals for socialization: Examples from Girl Scout Handbooks 1913-1984. *Qualitative Sociology, 8,* 359-367.

The purpose of this study was to conduct a content analysis of Girl Scout manuals over a 71-year time frame. Both a manifest and latent content analysis were conducted. Regarding manifest content analysis findings, it was found that in 1913 close to one-fourth of the badges centered on home life; whereas only seven percent of the badges in 1980 were on this theme. One of the latent content findings was that over time there was a shift in uniform, from skirts to pants. Another latent content finding was the emergence of new badges such as "Ms. Fix-It," "Math Whiz," "Computer Fun," and "Science Sleuth." Findings underscore societal expectations for family, career, sexual behavior, social stratification, and gender roles across time. One conclusion reached was, "The shift from skirts to pants may reflect an acknowledgement of the more physically active role of women as well as the variety of physical images available to modern women" (p. 362).

Figure 20. Record Review Pointers.[14]

When undertaking a record review remember to:

1. **Identify the population of documents.** This will tie into the research question. Are you interested in all newspapers published in North America, Disney movies, or Girl Scout manuals? For how many years? If you're dealing with newspapers, remember LEXIS/NEXIS archives newspapers. Check your campus library.
2. **Pinpoint the unit of analysis.** For instance, if a newspaper has been selected as the source text, you must decide on whether you're focusing on the entire newspaper or examining columns, paragraphs, or lines.
3. **Select a sample of units from the population.** If you can determine the entire population, then you need to decide if you're going to use simple random sample of documents or a stratified sample. For example, if your unit of analysis is newspapers, you might want to stratify on the basis of size of cities, weekday, or Sunday papers. If the population of interest cannot be determined, then non-random sampling methods are used to conduct the content analysis.
4. **If undertaking a quantitative study, decide on categories or codes, then place each unit of analysis into the appropriate category, and analyze the patterns that emerge.** When setting up these codes, decide on if you're going to code *manifest content* or visible surface content and/or *latent content,* meaning underlying meaning (see Case 14). The codes may be taken from existing

theory or are ones you make up. Codes may be broad or narrow. Explicit coding rules are needed to ensure coding consistency. Note, special dictionaries can be developed to keep track of how categories of interest are defined (Weber, 1990).

5. **If undertaking a qualitative study, a *summarizing content analysis* can be performed**. This entails two steps: (a) Review the document and paraphrase what is read or seen (known as the ***first reduction***); and (b) Re-review the paraphrases and bundle similar paraphrases together and summarize (known as the ***second reduction***).

[14]Adapted from: Babbie (2004); Flick (2006); Gratton and Jones (2004); and Schutt (2006).

Your Research

1. Are you using data-collection triangulation for carrying out your study? If not, why not?
2. What data-collection tool(s) are you using to implement the quantitative part of your study?
3. What data-collection tool(s) are you using to implement the qualitative part of your study?
4. If you're planning on using an interview: (a) When will the interviewing occur?, (b) Draft introductory remarks to kickoff the interview, and (c) Write out the questions that will be posed during the interview.
5. If you're using a questionnaire: (a) Draft a cover letter, and (b) Draft the questionnaire.
6. If you're using quantitative observation: (a) Develop an observation recording sheet; and, (b) Identify study site(s), vantage points at the site(s), date(s) and time(s) for observation(s).
7. If you're using participant observation, will you be a passive, marginal, or complete observer? How will you carry this out?
8. If you'll be relying on a focus group: (a) What is the research question you propose using with the group? (b) Describe the types of individuals you want to include in the focus group; and (c) How would you go about recruiting these individuals?
9. If you're conducting a record review develop a: (a) Quantitative coding sheet and, (b) Summary content sheet to record paraphrases of what is being reviewed.

Review and Discussion Questions . . .
What have you learned about specifying data collection methods?

1. What is meant by data-collection triangulation? Why is it used?
2. Explain four data-collection tools used in quantitative studies: Structured interview, Questionnaire, Observation, and Projective methods.
3. Distinguish the difference between a closed-ended question versus an open-ended question. Provide an example of each.
4. Write questions that illustrate each of the following response options: dichotomous, Likert scale, semantic differential, forced ranking, adjective checklist, multiple choice, and smiley face continuum.
5. Distinguish among three ways unstructured interviews are carried out: Descriptive information interview, Discovery interview, and Problem-solving interview.

6. What purposes can be fulfilled by using a focus group? Describe the characteristics of focus groups and the reasons why such groups are convened.
7. What is participant observation? What are the three kinds of participant observer roles? Cite an example of each of these roles.
8. Define document/record review.
9. Recall three mechanical rules for conducting interviews.
10. List three mechanical rules for developing questionnaires.
11. Outline three mechanical rules for setting up a focus group.
12. Identify three mechanical rules to use when conducting an observation.
13. Name three points regarding implementation of a record review.

Exercises

1. For each item in the list below, identify: (a) What data-collection method you would use to collect the information and (b) Explain the rationale behind your choice.
    A. Children's impressions of a class trip to a museum.
    B. College students' leisure pastimes.
    C. Ideas for alleviating crowding at a national park.
    D. Reasons why children have not learned how to swim.
    E. Coverage of the Deaf Olympics.
    F. Stair climber machine usage at a health club.

2. Different questions, different information. There is almost always more than one way to ask for information. The point of this activity is to illustrate that the way you ask for information, in part, determines the kinds of information you get. This can be easily noticed in the questioning we typically use for a structured interview as compared to an unstructured interview.
    A. Select a friend to interview. First, ask your friend these questions as a structured interview, recording the answers.
        i. Have you ever been a leader? "YES" or "NO"?
        ii. Do you consider your leadership to be successful? "YES" or "NO"?
        iii. Has your leadership experience been in a recreation, work, or school situation?
        iv. What do you think are the most important qualities of good leadership? Choose among: intelligence, creativity, communication skill, and/or group management.
    B. Now, repeat the interview, only this time use a more unstructured interview approach, again recording the answers.
        i. Can you describe a specific example of when you've been a leader?
        ii. In what ways would you describe this as successful leadership?
        iii. In what types of situations do you most often exhibit leadership?
        iv. What do you see as the most important qualities of good leadership?
    C. Discuss with your friend the differences in the interview experiences. See if together you can identify the different sorts of information received from the two approaches. Did you or your friend prefer the structured or unstructured interview experience? Why? Write up your conclusions in a one-page paper to present to your class.

3. Go to the University of Surrey's Web site at http://qb.soc.surrey.ac.uk
    A. Read General Guide for "Survey Questions," "Information" and "Measurement."
    B. If not assigned a topic by your instructor, undertake a search for questions dealing with one of the following topics, "Recreation," "Parks," "Tourism," or "Sport." Find and critique 10 questions (using principles reviewed in this chapter) that have been used in surveys.

4. Go to the American Camp Association's Web site at www.acacamps.org. Under "Camp Outcomes Study," click "Research," then click "Directions" and under "Camp Director" click on "Camper Post-Camp Survey," "Parent Post-Survey," and "Staff Observation" checklist. Critique these three forms using the principles reviewed in this chapter.

5. Learn more about:
    A. Questionnaire design by going to the University of Edinburg Web site, www.tardis. ed.ac.uk/~kate/qmcweb/qcont.htm.
        i. Read about "Question Types," "Instructions in Questionnaires," "Question Order," "Layout of the Questionnaire," "Dealing with Problem Questions," and "Checklist for Questionnaires."
        ii. Under "Checklist for Questionnaires," click the "Activity" box at the bottom of the page. Print the questionnaire. Per the instructions: (a) Identify as many problems with the survey as you can by circling the problem; and (b) Make notes in the margins of the page regarding what pitfall or land mine the questionnaire's author fell into.
    B. Question types by going to:
        i. *PHP Surveyor* at www.phssurveyor.org and click on "Question Types."
        ii. *Insiteful Surveys* at www.insitefulsurveys.com and click on "Question Types."
        iii. *Survey Monkey* at www.surveymonkey.com, then under "Tell Me More," click on "Guided Tutorial," then "Creating a New Survey (with audio)."

6. Go to Professor Boeree's "Qualitative Methods Workbook for PSY 405" at Shippensburg University's Web site, www.ship.edu/~cgboeree/qualmeth.html. Complete the exercise listed for each of the following three chapters, "Observation," "Participant Observation," and "Non-Directive Interviewing." For the Observation exercise the instructor might assign the class one television show to watch. Regardless, tape the program you watch.
    A. Provide a written description of the results of each exercise (just follow the directions noted on the Web site).
    B. What appreciation and insights did you have about adopting a passive observer role? Complete participant role? Non-directive interviewing?

7. This exercise demonstrates how the focus group method may provide insights. Your task is to design a question that measures people's attitudes or beliefs about a particular issue. Think of a topic that involves some degree of controversy. Examples of topics include: "Allowing the Use of All-Terrain Vehicles in State Parks," or "Selling Beer at City-Owned Concession Stands."
    A. Design several questions with specific closed-ended responses about the topic you've chosen.

B. Now convene a small group (with classmates or a few friends) and ask the questions WITHOUT offering the response options you've also developed. Pay attention and see if your response alternatives match the answers provided by the group.

C. Near the end of the session, share your preconceived answers with the group. Ask the group how well your expectations captured their opinions.

D. What did you learn from this exercise?

8. Practice passive participant observation by using a camera to record five examples of neglect, damage, and/or litter to a recreational site. If the site is not identified by your course instructor, choose a site.

A. Write an essay regarding what you found and attach the five photographs you took.

B. What were the advantages and disadvantages of this data collection method?

9. If not assigned a Disney cartoon film, choose one yourself. Discuss the film using points made in the article written by Rojek (1993). That is: determine if the movie demonstrates quantitatively and qualitatively the following themes often found in Disney films and Disney parks:

A. Individual versus collective forces make things happen.

B. Social strife and conflict are temporary.

C. Every day must by a "Zippidy-doo-da-day."

D. Disney heroes are associated with characteristics of leisure, or choice, self-determination, and flexibility.

E. Inanimate objects become animate.

F. Characters conform to patriarchal stereotypes: the female is submissive, passive, and incapable of problem solving; whereas, the male is powerful, independent, and a problem solver.

G. There is a division between work and leisure.

H. Villains are represented by working-class accents and mannerisms.

10. Try your hand at conducting a record review.

A. Acquire from your local park, recreation, sport, or fitness organization a copy of recent program offerings. Sometimes these are in flyer or booklet form and copies can be found at branches of the local library.

B. If not directed by your instructor, choose two or three categories and corresponding levels that can be used to analyze the material. For instance, some of the category and corresponding levels that could be considered are:

Category	Levels
Program Location	Indoors versus Outdoors
Program Type	Art, Dance, Fitness, Music, Sport, Other
Time of Day	Morning, Afternoon, Early Evening, or Late Evening
Day of Week	Weekday, Weekend, or Holiday

Category	Levels
Participant's Gender	Males, Females, or Coed
Participant's Age Group	Toddler, Children, Teens, Young Adults, Middle Aged Adults, or Seniors
Cost	Free, Less than $25, $26-50, $51 or more
Program Length	One day or less, One Week, One Month, Two Months, Three Months or Longer
Required Ability Level	All Ability Levels, Restricted to Beginners, Restricted to Intermediates, or Restricted to Advanced

C. Set up a form that helps you tally the number of programs that fit in each category level.

D. Fill in the form by counting the number of programs according to the category levels.

E. Examine the findings. What are the tendencies for each category?

11. Here's another way to practice a record review. Go to the Web site of the American Association of Leisure and Recreation: http://www.aahperd.org/aapar. Familiarize yourself with this professional organization, then from the top banner, select "Programs & Events," and from the drop-down menu select "National Family Recreation Week." Finally, select "Activity Calendar." For purposes of this assignment classify or code each activity listed as falling into one of the following three categories: "Outdoor Recreation," "Sport," and "Arts and Humanities."

A. How many family week activities fell into each of the three categories?

B. Did you have difficulty placing any activity in one of the three given categories? Why? What other category heading would you have included this activity?

C. Did certain activities appear more popular than others?

D. What do you tentatively conclude about what this professional organization considers to be family recreation?

Both quantitative (such as a questionnaire) and qualitative (for instance, observation) data-collection tools, each with their own requirements for use, are available for leisure research projects. The London Eye Millennium Observation Wheel. *Copyright © 2008 Carol Cutler Riddick*

STEP 10: Address Ethical Responsibilities

What are Ethics?

Research Ethics

Ethical Principles to Guide Research
Nonmaleficence
   Physical Harm
   Psychological Harm
   Loss of Privacy
   Loss of Confidentiality
Beneficence
Respect
Honesty
Justice
Competence

Rather fail with honor than succeed by fraud.
Sophocles

There are many ways to "mess up" when conducting research. One way is by violating any of the expected ethical research behaviors.

What Are Ethics?

Ethics deal with moral duty and obligation and what is proper and improper behavior (Reese & Fremouw, 1984). Ethics operate on two levels. First, individuals develop their own personal ethics. Second, there are professional ethics. When we join a profession, we face the challenge of blending our personal ethics with professional ethics.

In fact, one of the earmarks of a profession is that it has established a professional code of ethics (Stumbo, 1985). A *professional code of ethics* is the norms, values and principles that govern professional conduct and relationships with clients, colleagues, and society (Kornblau & Starling, 2000; Strike & Ternasky, 1993). It has been noted,

> Professions are moral institutions because their policies and practices are intended to contribute to a good society. The quintessential element of professionalization, then, is ethics, which guides professional practice in the right spirit toward the right ends using the right means. (Sylvester, 2002, p. 315)

Ethical behavior applies to all aspects of how a profession operates. For example, therapeutic recreation professionals are encouraged to embrace and practice four kinds of ethics: virtue ethics, feminist ethics, ethics of care, and communicative ethics (Sylvester, 2002). *Virtue ethics* refer to maintaining a morally sound character that includes insight, imagination, and sensitivity. *Feminist ethics* mean creating environments for clients that are inclusive and incorporate the experiences of women and others whose concerns have been marginalized in the past. *Ethics of care* emphasize sustaining human connectedness and caring relationships. Finally, *communicative ethics* entail open listening and conversation.

Research Ethics

Ethical behavior also extends to research activities. *Research ethics* encompass the principles that are expected when designing, conducting, and reporting research. In large part, society's confidence in and support of research revolves around trusting the integrity and ethics of researchers.

For example, what should you do about a teen who mentions during an interview that she uses drugs at the recreation center? Should the police be notified? Or, is it fair in testing the effectiveness of a new aquatics treatment program in the rehabilitation center that control-group clients are denied access to the program? Or, what if evaluation results reveal that a stress-reduction program for a corporation's employees has failed? Do you have to report these results to the company CEO?

Professional organizations, in an attempt to standardize and regulate researchers' actions, have identified acceptable and unacceptable ethical research practices. These codes perform a useful function by alerting researchers to the ethical expectations of their work (Case 1).

Case 1. What Some Professional Codes of Ethics Say About Research.

American Academy of Management

"Prudence in research design, human subject use, confidentiality, result reporting, and proper attribution of work is a necessity" (American Academy of Management, 2000, p. 1296).

American Association for Public Opinion Research

"We shall recommend and employ only those tools and methods of analysis that, in our professional judgment, are well suited to the research problem at hand. . . . We shall not knowingly make interpretations of research results that are inconsistent with the data available. . . . We shall not knowingly imply that interpretations should be accorded greater confidence than the data actually warrant." (Retrieved November 9, 2005, from http://www.aapor.org)

Marketing Research Association

" . . . Clients and other users of opinion and marketing research and the general public should not be in any way misled about the reliability and validity of any Internet research findings" (Retrieved November 9, 2005, from http://www.mra-net.org).

" . . . Unsolicited email should not be sent to those requesting not to receive any further email" (Retrieved November 9, 2005, from http://www.mra-net.org).

National Intramural-Recreational Sports Association

" . . . Be true in writing, reporting and duplicating information and give proper credit to the contributions of others" (Retrieved March 30, 2007, from http://www.nirsa.org/about/documents/code_of_ethics.aspx).

Tourism Industry Association of Canada

" . . . Avoid activities which threaten wildlife or which may be potentially damaging to our natural environment" (Retrieved January 1, 2005, from http://www.geocities.com).

Ethical Principles to Guide Research

People involved in research must carry out research in a responsible manner. In other words, their actions must be beyond reproach. Ethical behavior in research is determined by adherence to the following six fundamental principles that are the "roots" to all human service codes of ethics (McCrone, 2002):

- Nonmaleficence
- Beneficence
- Respect
- Honesty
- Justice
- Competence

Nonmaleficence

Nonmaleficence deals with the doctrine of "do no harm" (McCrone, 2002). It is expected that a study is executed in a way that causes no unnecessary harm to participants. Investigators must anticipate and avoid those risks that are likely to result from their research. The potential risks to study participants include physical harm, psychological harm, loss of privacy, and loss of confidentiality.

Physical harm. Study procedures that could cause some physical harm to participants must be avoided. For instance, asking people to ski down a slope as fast as they can in order to measure the quality of snow produced by new snow-making equipment would be unacceptable and downright negligent.

Psychological harm. While physical harm frequently can be predicted and easily guarded against, inadvertent psychological or emotional harm may occur. For instance, asking people about unpleasant events in their lives can cause stress for some.

Loss of privacy. The **right to privacy** means people are reasonably shielded from public view. Individuals involved in a research study have the right to determine when, how, and to what extent information about them is communicated to others. It is acceptable to make observations of public acts that would normally be viewed by others (e.g., a baseball game). Yet, observations of activity that would be considered personal or sensitive would be considered an invasion of privacy.

While this principle sounds clear enough, it is easy to violate. For example, asking people about their attitudes or opinions may be in conflict with their right to privacy. To be ethical, the researcher must consider how sensitive the questions posed, or behaviors observed, are to the individuals or groups studied. There are types of information, such as one's body weight and annual personal income, many people perceive too private in nature to be asked let alone answered!

Loss of confidentiality. **Confidentiality** occurs when the researcher can identify a response or observation as belonging to a given person but promises not to do so. Many persons confuse confidentiality with anonymity. **Anonymous** means there is no way any given response can be connected with a given respondent. That is, no information (such as name, phone number, address, social security number) is asked or recorded that could be used to identify an individual study participant.

In observing the drinking behaviors of these boaters, will their right to privacy be violated? *Copyright © 2008 Ruth V. Russell*

In research, confidentiality is considered an extension of the right to privacy. Whereas privacy refers to persons, confidentiality refers to information. Once information has been collected for a study, there is an ethical responsibility to protect it (technically this is known as an act of **fidelity** or keeping a promise). The names of the respondents must be removed or never appear on interviews, questionnaires, or observation forms. Not even the evaluator or researcher should be able to link the data to a specific individual. Study participants should be assured that any information collected from or about them will be held in strict confidence. This means never revealing a study participant's identity in written reports, staff and professional meetings, and/or social situations.

Idea . . . How to Handle Confidentiality and Anonymity.

One technique for assuring confidentiality in research requiring follow up or research that requires individuals to be studied on multiple occasions, is to use a unique code number to identify each interview or questionnaire. The code could be an assigned number but not any sequential numbers related to a person's social security number, last name alphabetical order, etc. Commercial numbering machines are available that can repeat the same number multiple times before advancing. For instance, you can successively number a master list of address labels and the front of a questionnaire. One number will be assigned to one person's name appearing on the master list and then the same number will be stamped on the front of the questionnaire. The numbering machine's tumbler will then advance to a new number. The researcher keeps, under lock and key, the name assigned to each number as well as completed pretests, posttests, or survey results.

One way for assuring anonymity, when using a questionnaire in a group setting, is to have respondents place their completed questionnaire, without any identifying information, inside an envelope and then seal the envelope. These envelopes can be dropped into a collection box.

Beneficence

The ethical principal of **beneficence** refers to promoting the welfare of individuals (McCrone, 2002). Applying the principal of beneficence to research, it is expected that the study is conducted in such a manner that study participants receive some benefit from their involvement. The kind of benefits extended to people for participating in research can fall into one of three classification groups. These are a direct benefit, a material benefit, or a less tangible benefit (Figure 1).

Figure 1. Possible Benefits of Participating in Research.

Benefits	Examples
Direct Benefit	• Learn new skill • Treatment of a problem
Material Benefit	• Money • Non-monetary gift
Less Tangible Benefit	• Contribute to a profession's body of knowledge • Potential to improve future practices or policies

Respect

Respect recognizes the autonomy of people to make their own choices (McCrone, 2002). In research, the right of individuals to decide about whether, and to what extent, they want to participate in a study must be accepted (Case 2). The ethical expectation is that the researcher informs potential study participants about the purpose(s) of the study, the risks and benefits of participation, and their rights to refuse and cease participation in the study at any time without retribution. Any procedure that limits an individual's freedom to consent voluntarily is considered *coercion*.

Case 2. A Case of Respect?

Several years ago, a state tourism agency mounted a television marketing campaign. Paddlers on scenic state waterways were filmed and aired as public service announcements. One clip showed a male and female adult paddling joyfully down a stream. The problem that arose was that the filmed couple were married but not to each other. Did the actions of the state tourism agency demonstrate respect to those who were clandestinely filmed?

As an acknowledgement of a potential study participant's autonomy, ***informed consent*** has now become common practice. The idea behind using informed consent is that there is an ethical commitment to ensure that a potential study participant has enough information about the study to make a sound decision about participating (Figure 2). Typically, the form is printed for the participant to read and sign (Case 3). It is imperative that the individual reading the form understand what information is being presented.

Figure 2. Components to Informed Consent Form.

In the United States, federal guidelines specify the critical information that must appear on an informed consent form (United States Department of Health and Human Services, 2001). This form must contain:

1. A statement that says the study involves research, notes the expected duration of the participation, and identifies any experimental procedures used in the study.
2. A description of any reasonably foreseeable risks or discomforts to the participant.
3. A description of any benefits to the participant or to others that may reasonably be expected from the research.
4. A disclosure of appropriate alternative procedures or courses of treatment, if any, that might be advantageous to the participant.
5. A statement describing the extent, if any, to which confidentiality of records identifying the participant will be maintained.
6. For research involving more than minimal risk, an explanation as to whether any compensation is to be made and an explanation as to whether any medical treatments are available if injury occurs; and, if so, what they consist of, or where further information may be obtained.
7. An explanation of whom to contact for answers to questions about the research, about information on research participants' rights, and in the event there is a research-related injury to the participant.
8. A statement that states participation is voluntary, refusal to participate will involve no penalty or loss of benefits to which the participant is otherwise entitled, and that the participant may discontinue participation at any time without penalty or loss of benefits to which the participant is otherwise entitled.

Case 3. Sample Informed Consent Form.[1]

Project Title: "Effects of Animal-Assisted Therapy"
Principal Investigator: Randi Baron-Leonard, CTRS
Address: **Phone:**
                                                Email:

Faculty Sponsor: Dr. Carol Cutler Riddick
Gallaudet University's Department of Physical Education and Recreation

I am a Masters' Candidate in the Department of Physical Education and Recreation at Gallaudet University. As part of my thesis, I'm offering and evaluating an Animal- Assisted Therapy (AAT) program. I am a Deaf, Certified Therapeutic Recreation Specialist, who has advanced signing skills.

I would like you to consider volunteering to be a study participant for this research project. You will be asked to:

1. Participate in eight AAT sessions, each lasting about one hour. During these organized recreational therapy programs you will be interacting with a dog. These sessions will be offered two or three times a week over a three-to-four-week period.

2. Complete a questionnaire two times, once before the AAT program begins and again at the end of the eight sessions. The questionnaires ask about your experiences with pets, mood, and feedback about the AAT program. If needed, Randi Baron-Leonard will provide verbal instructions related to the questions appearing on the questionnaire. It should take about 15 minutes to complete each questionnaire.

3. Be videotaped at two of the AAT sessions. The videotapes will be used to record what happens during the group session. The videotape will be viewed by two raters, then the tape will be destroyed.

There is no more than *low* risk to individuals who participate in this study.[2]

Please note that the answers you give on the questionnaires, as well as the videotapes, will be handled with confidentiality. If your data is used in a publication or presentation, your name, picture or other identifying information will not be used. Once the questionnaires and videotapes have been analyzed, they will be destroyed.

Possible benefits from participating in this study include improved mood and improved social skills. You also would be contributing to our knowledge about the effectiveness of using AAT with individuals who are Deaf and have been hospitalized for a mental disorder.

Staff will also be asked to provide diagnoses for each person consenting to be in the research study. This information will only be used to describe the medical background of the study group.

Your participation in this study is voluntary. You will *not* receive any payment for participating in this study. You may withdraw from this study at any time, for any reason and without penalty. If you decide not to participate in the study or to withdraw from the study, it will not change your relationship to Gallaudet University or the Hospital.

Questions about the risk of participation in this study may be addressed to the researcher named at the top of this form, or the Chairperson of the Gallaudet University's Institutional Review Board for the Protection of Human Subjects (phone 202.651.5400 (v/tty) or email irb@gallaudet.edu). If you should have any questions regarding your rights, contact Gay Hutchen at the Maryland Department of Mental Hygiene (phone 410.767.8448).

I have read the Informed Consent Form and agree to participate in the study, "Effects of Animal-assisted Therapy" by Randi Baron-Leonard.

Your Printed Name: _____

Your Signature: _____

Printed Name of Staff Witness: _____

| Signature of Staff Witness: _____ |
| Date: _____ |

[1] As cited in Baron-Leonard (2004).

[2] NOTE: To qualify for the study, the head of each patient's medical team had to attest the individual had no known allergies to dogs, was not fearful of dogs, and had no history of animal abuse. The animal used for the treatment was a certified therapy dog.

Informed consent procedures become more complex when the research involves members of special populations such as minors, individuals with cognitive impairments, or patients in psychiatric hospitals. When dealing with minors, two kinds of consent forms are necessary. First, a written consent form signed by a parent or guardian is necessary. Additionally, the minor is also asked to sign an *assent* or agreement to participate in the study.

Consent forms should be written in simple, straightforward language that is devoid of jargon. It has been suggested that the consent form for adults should be composed at a sixth to eighth-grade reading level, something that can easily be checked under the "grammar check" feature available on text editing software (Cozby, 2006). The rationale for setting the reading bar at this level is that individuals must be perfectly clear on what they have consented to do, otherwise the consent is not valid (Berg & Latin, 2003).

Honesty

Honesty or *fidelity* deals with trustworthiness. In research, the major issue associated with honesty is deceptive practices. *Deception* is the misrepresentation of information.

Perhaps the most common mistake of novice researchers is the deceptive practice of failing to give proper credit for ideas found in their research proposal or final report. While a hallmark of research is building on the works of previous studies and the thoughts of others, it is important to give credit where credit is due. In other words, you need to avoid *plagiarism* by citing sources for the ideas or thoughts you used.

To appropriate the thoughts, ideas, or words of another—even if you paraphrase the borrowed ideas in your own language—without acknowledgement is unethical and highly circumspect. Honest researchers do not hesitate to acknowledge their indebtedness to others. (Leedy & Ormrod, 2005, p. 102)

Another way deception can creep into a study is not informing potential study participants about the purpose or nature of the study. Some codes of ethics, such as that of the American Psychological Association, allow for such deceptive practices as concealed observation when it is necessary for the research. Some social psychologists and psychologists maintain deception is needed when studying certain phenomena such as stereotyping and aggression. The rationale is that if participants in these situations are informed ahead of time about the true nature of the study, they will change their behavior and not act naturally.

Our position is that in the leisure fields deceiving people about the real purpose of the study is unacceptable for two reasons. First, it is wrong to mislead people (Case 4). Second, deceptive practices harm the reputation of reputable researchers and research in general.

Case 4. A Cheating Experiment.

Kahle, L. (1980). Stimulus condition self-selection by males in the interaction of locus of control and skill-chance situations. *Journal of Personality and Social Psychology, 38,* 50-56.

The purpose of this experiment was to investigate the factors that lead college students to cheat. Study participants, however, were misled about the true purpose of the study. A test was administered to students and the test papers collected. Then the papers were returned to the students for self-grading. In order for them to improve their test score, it was made easy for the students to change their answers on the exam. So what do you think happened? Many of the students took advantage of the opportunity to cheat, by changing their answers. Unbeknownst to the students, the experimenter had recorded their original responses prior to returning the tests. Thus, it was easy to discover how many students had cheated by changing their answers. What two ethical principles were violated with this experiment?

One alternative to using deception is to set up a simulation study. A *simulation study* is when study participants are informed about the purpose of the research and are asked to pretend they are in a real life social setting.

Another aspect of deception deals with the analyses and reporting of results. The expectation is that data-collection procedures, analyses, and reporting are done in a truthful manner. Researchers have an obligation to make known shortcomings or failures experienced in data collection. Additionally, researchers are expected not to commit any even unintentional mistakes in data collection, let alone falsify data.

Something to Remember!

According to the Institute of Medicine National Research Council (2002), the integrity of an individual research scientist embodies above all else a commitment to intellectual honesty and personal responsibility for one's actions. Practices that define *individual integrity* include:

• Protection of human subjects in the conduct of research.
• Intellectual honesty in proposing, performing, and reporting research.
• Accuracy in representing contributions to research proposals and reports.
• Fairness in peer review.
• Collegiality in scientific interactions, including communications and sharing of resources.

Unfortunately, honesty is sometimes breached because of social pressure. Such pressure may occur when researchers believe positive results must be obtained in order to protect a program or job or to get their study published. One form of misconduct is *scientific fraud* or the " . . . deliberate falsification, misrepresentation, or plagiarizing of data, findings, or the ideas of others.

This includes embellishing research reports, reporting research that has not been conducted, or manipulating data in a deceptive way" (Monette, Sullivan, & DeJong, 2005, p. 63). Regrettably, as Case 5 illustrates, scientific fraud occurs.

Case 5. Results Lacking Integrity: A Case of Scientific Fraud.

One researcher (Bixler, personal communication, July 15, 1997) shares the following story. Read it and see if you concur that the described actions demonstrate scientific fraud.

> "Something my wife and I saw while on vacation got me thinking about cheating in research. We were interviewed as part of a tourism study at the entrance to a museum. The interviewer did a good job interviewing us and used an Apple Newton Pad for data entry. Being a typical male, I finished the museum almost 30 minutes ahead of my wife, so I sat down and watched the interviewer as I waited. Since I knew the interview routine, which involved having the interviewee choose from lists on sheets of paper, it was quite clear that she was now sitting on a bench filling out surveys herself instead of doing other interviews. I suspect much of this sort of behavior comes from the social discomfort of approaching strangers, laziness, and a lack of understanding of the implications of such dishonesty."

Justice

The principle of *justice* has been defined as addressing "issues of fairness in receiving the benefits of research as well as bearing the burdens of accepting risks" (Cozby, 2006, p. 47) or "fair, equitable, and appropriate treatment in light of what is due or owed to persons" (Sylvester, Voelkl, & Ellis, 2001). Justice comes into play when selecting study participants. In particular, *equity* must prevail meaning any decisions to exclude or include certain people from a research study must be based on scientific merit. Therefore, if gender, age, ethnicity, sexual orientation, disability, social status, or any other characteristic is used to select or not select participants, there must be a legitimate scientific reason (Case 6).

Case 6. A Reprehensible Example of Injustice Done in the Name of Research.

Jones, J. (1993). *Bad blood: The Tuskegee syphilis experiment.* NY: Free Press.

In 1932, approximately 400 African Americans, were singled out and infected with syphilis. In order to track the long-term effects of the disease, medical treatment was withheld from these individuals for 40 years.

"Good" research practice frequently requires adopting a design involving one or more control groups. But what happens when a program or treatment emerges as being beneficial to experimental group members? Should people assigned to the no-treatment control group have equal access to the service or intervention offered to the experimental group (Case 7)? Legally, it appears the answer hinges on whether a treatment is being offered for a life-threatening situation. In these situations, once data reveal that lives are being saved or even improved by the treatment, the researcher must move control group members into the treatment group.

Case 7. You Be the Ethical Judge.

Riddick, C., Spector, S., & Drogin, E. (1986). The effects of video game play on the emotional states and affiliative behavior of nursing home residents. *Activities, Adaptation and Aging, 8,* 95-107.

In the following description of a study, what ethical principle has been "violated"?

> Researchers examined if video game play would improve, among other things, the affiliative behavior of nursing home residents. The research experiment was structured so that two nursing homes were involved in the study. Ten volunteers from one nursing home (the experimental group) played PacMan three times a week for up to three hours per session for a total of six weeks. Twelve other volunteers from a second nursing home (the control group) were not offered any opportunity to play video games. By comparing changes in the pre- and post-test scores of the two groups, it was found that the video game players experienced a significant positive change in their affiliative behaviors. Apparently, the stimulation of playing PacMan triggered social interaction. For example, several players were overheard saying, "Help! That pink critter is out to get me. What can I do?" (p. 105).

If after reading this description, you questioned whether the researchers acted fairly by withholding the treatment from the control group, you've earned an "A." Accordingly, the researchers were quite sensitive to upholding the ethical principle of justice. In fact, nursing home residents within the interested homes were recruited with the promise all study participants would eventually be offered the opportunity to learn how to play a video game. At the conclusion of the study period, as originally promised, the video game equipment was made available to residents in the second home, the control group, for six weeks.

Competence

Finally, researchers are expected to be competent. ***Competence*** means that an individual is qualified by training and experience to conduct the research study. Researchers must know their limitations, engage in continuous education activities, and seek assistance when necessary.

For instance, if your knowledge of statistics is restricted, you should consult with others who have expertise in this area. Likewise, if you plan to use measurement instruments that require special credentials (e.g., a degree or license in psychology, a certification or specialized training) then you need to attain these prerequisites or seek assistance from people who have these qualifications.

Your Research

1. **What are the ethical issues involved in your research project?**
2. **How will you ensure your research project will not violate any of the six ethical principles?**

Review Questions . . . What have you learned about addressing ethical responsibilities in research?

1. Provide definitions for *ethics, professional code of ethics,* and *research ethics.*
2. What is *nonmaleficence?* Identify four categories of maleficence risks that should be minimized when conducting a study.
3. Distinguish between maintaining *confidentiality* versus assuring *anonymity.*
4. Explain the term *beneficence.* What are three types of benefits that can be used in a study?
5. What does the ethical principal of *respect* encompass?
6. Identify three or more points that should be addressed in an *informed consent form.*
7. Define *honesty, plagiarism,* and *scientific fraud* as they relate to ethical research behaviors.
8. Do you support deceiving study participants about the real purpose behind a research project? If so, what do you think are the allowable limits of deception? If not, why not?
9. Characterize how *justice* should prevail in a research study?
10. How do you define *competence* as it relates to individuals involved in carrying out research?

Exercises

1. Examine a research article in one of your professional journals (or use one assigned by the instructor). Did the reported research demonstrate or adhere to the following ethical principles. How?
    A. Nonmaleficence?
    B. Beneficence?
    C. Respect?
    D. Honesty?
    E. Justice?
    F. Competence?

2. Search for research ethics in the news. Over a week or two time period, keep a scrapbook of newspaper clippings, magazine articles, research presentations, and television reports that deal with a research example of an ethical principle either upheld or breached. Organize this scrapbook according to the six ethical principles outlined in this chapter. Use a selection of your scrapbook contents to contribute to class discussions.

3. For each of the following scenarios, decide whether or not you think the research is ethical. Identify the ethical principle(s) that were violated and/or upheld. Discuss your decisions with classmates.
    A. Suppose you're interested in learning about conflict-resolution strategies used when children play. Accurate information on this topic could be obtained by hiding a video camera in a trash can centrally located on the playground.

B. Interviews on how boredom is related to drug use and abuse was conducted with a college class of 20 students. A detailed report on the findings was published. Even though fictitious names were used in the report, a majority of the 20 original study participants could read the report and identify who was being referred to.

C. A study was set up to identify what types of people were most likely to give money to a stranger at a jogging park. People at a public park were asked for money by an individual who said she had just lost her purse. No one was ever told that (s)he was part of a research project.

D. Suppose a beginning tennis instructor will give her students extra credit to be in a study. They are told the purpose of the study is to examine how well they serve and return a tennis ball over the course of the semester. In truth, individuals will be observed for frequency and intensity of losing their tempers while playing tennis.

E. As part of his thesis research, a graduate student was approved to survey students at his college. Random sampling was used to identify 200 individuals who, in turn, were invited to participate in the study. Over a three-day period the contacted individuals were supposed to stop by a table set up at the student union and complete a consent form and a 10-minute questionnaire. On the third day, only 35 students had completed the survey and the graduate student panicked. He walked around the student union pleading with people he saw to participate in the study. In the end, he wound up "finding" 40 more individuals to complete the questionnaire.

F. A recent recreation major graduate begins a new job at a health club. She has a black belt in karate. She proposes to her boss that she evaluate her beginning martial arts class. She thinks class members will be willing to help her when she tells them she is undertaking a scientific study and she will be able, at the conclusion of the study, to provide each person with group results. Her idea is to measure bilateral coordination and hamstring flexibility. Through her reading, she found a way to measure each of these dependent variables, using tests with which she was not familiar but seemingly appeared easy to administer. She proposed measuring bilateral coordination by the "Stork Balance" test (standing on one foot until balance is lost) and hamstring flexibility with the modified sit and reach test (in a sitting position with legs extended straight, the person tries to touch his/her toes with the tips of the fingers).

G. An in-home leisure education program is offered to older adults who had difficulty adjusting psychologically after a stroke. A randomized clinical trial design is used to conduct the study. That is, individuals were assigned to either a 10-week long experimental leisure education group or a 10-week placebo "friendly visit" group. Five weeks into the study, the first post-test was conducted and it revealed that those individuals receiving the leisure education program experienced substantive and significant reduction in depression. The decision is made to continue the study for another five weeks.

4. Visit the Web sites of two professional recreation, park, tourism or sport organizations that have their code of ethics available online. Summarize the important points, made at each site, regarding research ethics.

5. Read more about ethical issues revolving around data management, mentor and trainee responsibilities, and reporting and reviewing research by reading N. Steneck's *ORI Introduction*

to the Responsible Conduct of Research at the Office of Research Integrity's (ORI) Web site at the United States Department of Health and Human Services (http://ori.dhhs.gov/publications/ori_intro_text.shtml).

    A. Identify two data-management issues after reading "Part III. 6. Data Management Issues."

    B. Identify two mentor and trainee responsibilities after reading "Part III. 7. Mentor and Trainee Responsibilities."

    C. What are two things you learned after reading "Part IV. Reporting and Reviewing Research?"

6. Read "Part B: Basic Ethical Principles" of the Belmont Report by going to the National Institutes of Health's Office of Extramural Research OER Human Subjects Web site at http://grants.nih.gov/grants/policy/hs/ethical_guidelines.htm. Which of the three ethical principles do you feel is most important to observe when conducting research in recreation, parks, tourism, and sport settings? Explain your answer.

7. Develop an informed consent form. Beforehand, visit two Web sites. First, go to the University of Minnesota's Web-Based Instruction on Informed Consent at www.research.umn.edu/consent/orientation.html. Complete the five modules for the "Social and Behavioral Sciences" topic. Second, go to the American Association for Public Opinion Research at www.aapor.org and click on "Survey Methods," then "Institutional Review Boards," and then "Example Consent Documents and Forms."

The weathervane by which to judge research ethics is that a study is designed, conducted, and reported with integrity. Fortuna Weathervane Atop Dogana di Mare (Customs House), Venice, Italy. *Copyright © 2008 Carol Cutler Riddick*

STEP 11: Seek Proposal Approval

Approval Entities
Study Site
Thesis/Dissertation Committee
Institutional Review Board
    Expedited Review
    Non-Expedited Review
    Other Comments about IRBs
Funding Sponsors

Proposal Language and Writing Style

Proposal Content
Title Page
Table of Contents
Lists of Figures, Tables, and Appendices
Introduction
Theoretical Foundation
Hypotheses and/or Research Questions
Literature Review
Methods
    Research Design and Study Participants
    Intervention
    Instrumentation
    Data Collection
    Data Analyses
    Limitations
    Time Budget
    Financial Budget
References
Appendices

Judging the Proposal

You create your opportunities by asking for them.
Patty Hansen

All research projects require permission before they may be conducted. This usually requires preparation of a proposal. A ***proposal*** is a preliminary plan that contains essential information on what will be studied, why this is important to study, and how the study will be conducted. A written proposal serves as a contract or agreement between the researcher and supervising authority. Think of it as a road map to the research process that others could follow to carry out the project themselves.

Research proposals signal the researcher's intentions to such interested parties as agency staff, committees, review boards, and external funding groups. These gatekeepers judge the adequacy and usefulness of the planned research. Such checks and balances promote implementation of sound and useful scientific research and assure study participants will not be harmed. Seeking and attaining these approvals is a good thing for our professions.

Approval Entities

An important logistical arrangement to remember is to obtain the necessary permissions for conducting the study. Even though recreation, park, tourism, and sport areas are often public, approval to conduct research in these areas should be sought and acquired from the relevant authorities. In fact, never begin to collect data without the necessary permissions, even if you're sure it is forthcoming at any moment (Case 1).

Case 1. Fast Out of the Gate Yet Slow to the Finish!

Phil was a hard-working guy. In the first semester of his two-year masters program, he took a research methods course. Inspired, during the second semester, he began working on a thesis idea. He wanted to evaluate a softball skills clinic for adolescent girls. During the semester, he had several meetings with his advisor to discuss revisions to his proposal. Among other things, it was decided he would use a pretest-post-test design for the study. His thesis advisor told him he had a gem of an idea. The semester ended and Phil accepted a position to work at a summer softball skills camp. Phil thought he'd get ahead in his graduate program by going ahead and collecting data for his thesis. He only had a few days between finishing final exams, packing and driving to camp, and greeting the first group of campers. So he arrived at camp not being ready to collect pretest data—he hadn't copied the various assessment forms. Nevertheless, he felt compelled to proceed and collected post-test data from the campers. When he got back to campus in the fall, he met with his thesis advisor and told her what he had done. Guess what? He was informed that the data he collected could not be used for his thesis because he had never obtained approval for data collection from the camp, his thesis committee, or the IRB. He was crushed.

What are the necessary permissions? The answer is, "it depends!" If the study proposes assessing service constituent needs, interests, or impacts, the evaluator probably will need approval from the agency's policy makers and director. On the other hand, if the study will be used for college credit, such as in a thesis or dissertation, the researcher is accountable to a committee of professors and one or more institutional review boards. And, if the study is externally funded, there is a reporting responsibility directly to the grantor or the organization funding the study.

Study Site

Even if your study will assess a program for an organization you work for, you still need to clear data-collection methods and procedures with the appropriate supervisors. And if the study is to be carried out in an organization other than your own, contacting the appropriate officials for permission should be taken care of as early as possible. Moreover, if the research is being conducted in a public place, don't overlook obtaining approval from the appropriate government agencies. For instance, if you are surveying visitors to a public garden it only makes sense that you have prior approval from the organization that manages the garden.

Also, don't forget to inform the police, who have jurisdiction in the area you are working, about what you're up to. That way, in case someone contacts them about you or your study, these law enforcement entities know what is going on. Another reason for doing this, especially if you're carrying out an observation study, is you don't want to be suspected of loitering or something even more serious.

Thesis/Dissertation Committee

Most universities require a faculty member to supervise student research. If, for example, you are conducting a study as part of a course requirement, the course instructor is likely to be your supervisor.

On the other hand, if a study fulfills a degree requirement for a masters or doctoral degree, the student decides who serves on his/her committee. To begin, a faculty person needs to be identified who agrees to serve as chair of the thesis/dissertation committee. The **chair** serves as a mentor, or " . . . a person of competence who instructs a less experienced person in an area of mutual interest" (Mauch & Park, 2003, p. 43). The chair serves four roles: information source, sounding board, motivator, and approval authority. A student should work very closely with his or her chair throughout the entire research process. Therefore, it is crucial to identify someone who can provide the skills and knowledge needed to support your research project.

Something to Remember!

When choosing a research advisor, or thesis or dissertation chair, consider asking someone who will fulfill the following four roles:[1]

1. **Information source.** Your advisor or chair should have research experiences and skills to assist you in the completion of your project. Essentially he or she is your mentor, instructing you as you learn how to plan and conduct research.
2. **Sounding board.** You should be able to use your advisor or chair as a sounding board to help you think and write more clearly. Your advisor is invaluable as you shape your research topic and procedures into a manageable size, keeping your focus on track.

3. **Motivator.** Your advisor or chair should inspire you to complete the project. He or she evaluates your research and provides timely and useful feedback. Take notes when you meet with your advisor or chair, complete with dates, issues discussed, and tasks you've agreed to complete. This log will help you see your progress and keep you motivated.

4. **Approval authority.** Your advisor or chair tells you when you are ready to convene a proposal meeting. She or he is also responsible for issuing a grade for your research project and authorizing your graduation. In some universities, before a grade will be issued, student conducted research projects must also be examined by people external to the university, such as field professionals.

[1]Adapted from Polonsky and Waller (2005).

Besides the committee chair, two to five other professors also serve on a student's thesis/dissertation committee. The purpose of the committee is to review and provide guidance to the student researcher. This approval is discussed at a proposal meeting.

Before any data may be collected, a formal ***proposal meeting*** with the chair and committee is held to discuss the merits of the proposal and to seek permission to execute the study in the manner outlined in the proposal. At a proposal meeting, members of a thesis/dissertation committee usually make a determination about the following points (Mauch & Park, 2003):

• Is the study topic *suitable?*
• Is the study *appropriate* for the student's major?
• Will the study make a *contribution* to the literature and/or professional practice?
• Does the student have the *capabilities* necessary to complete the study?
• Is the study *manageable* in terms of how much time the student has to complete the work?

Figures 1 and 2 share some tips for experiencing a successful proposal meeting.

Figure 1. Getting Ready for a Proposal Meeting.

1. **Allow for plenty of lead in time before a proposal meeting.** Check with your committee members on how much reading time they need for your proposal. This can vary considerably, some members request receiving the proposal only three days in advance of the meeting, while others insist on a one-month reading time.

2. **If permissible, it may help to sit in on another person's proposal meeting beforehand.**

3. **Conduct a rehearsal.** Reread your proposal, making sure you understand each word and sentence you wrote. Anticipate the most difficult questions you can imagine and make sure you can deliver a brief and clear answer.

4. **During the meeting, take notes of requested changes.** At the end of the meeting, in order to make sure there is no misunderstanding, summarize the suggested changes.

5. **Understand how proposal committee meetings are conducted.** Meetings usually begin with the student's summary presentation, followed by questions and answers among the committee and student. When committee members have finished questioning, the student is excused. Without the student present, each committee member is polled about the proposal and asked to decide whether to reject, approve with conditions, or approve unconditionally. Do not be surprised if changes are suggested; this is the norm! Once the committee has made a decision, the student is

called back into the room and the chair reports the committee's decision. The chair and student meet afterwards to review revisions suggested in the meeting.

6. **Finally, get a good night's sleep before the meeting.** You've worked hard, so don't worry. Be confident, yet humble.

Figure 2. Handling Questions About Proposed Research.

When presenting a proposal you will sometimes experience perplexing questions. The secrets to success? Think before you respond. Organize your thoughts and answer questions as directly and simply as possible. If the questioner is long winded, take notes of what is being asked. You may also find the following strategies for replying helpful.

- **Responding to a question you don't understand,** "Gee, I don't get what you're asking, would you mind restating your question or point?"
- **Responding to a question when you don't know the answer,** "I've never thought about this point, what do you think?" or "I'm sorry, I don't know the answer to the question" or "I don't know the answer, will someone help me out?"
- **Handling a disagreement among those in attendance,** "I'm lost now. I hear different kinds of advice or conflicting requests. I'd appreciate it if we could spend a few minutes trying to reach agreement about what I'm being asked to do or change."
- **Responding to biting criticism,** "I did what I thought was best or warranted . . . now I understand what I did was wrong and I appreciate you correcting me."
- **Wrapping up the proposal meeting,** "Thank you all for taking the time to read and respond to the proposal. You've given me good constructive criticism. I'd appreciate receiving the written comments you made on my proposal, and I will earnestly try to address each and every concern raised."

Institutional Review Board

In the United States and Canada, governmental regulations require universities, hospitals, and other organizations receiving federal funding to establish review boards for research involving human subjects. These review boards are known as an *Institutional Review Board (IRB)* and are another common approval authority for your study.

The overall responsibility of IRBs is to determine if the researcher is treating study participants ethically. The criteria IRBs use in reviewing proposals are to determine that:

- Risks to research study participants are minimal.
- Benefits of participating in the study are greater than the risks.
- Vulnerable populations (such as children, institutionalized individuals) are carefully selected and sensitively dealt with.
- Participants are extended the right to informed consent.

There are two kinds of IRB reviews—an expedited and a non-expedited review. The IRB chair makes a determination as to whether the research proposal qualifies as an expedited or non-expedited review.

Culmination of a successful proposal meeting. *Copyright ©2008 Ruth V. Russell*

Expedited review. An **expedited review** occurs when the proposed study does not present more than minimal risk to human subjects and does not involve vulnerable populations or novel or controversial interventions or data collection techniques. Research involving the use of educational tests, surveys, interviews or observation of public behavior typically falls into the expedited review category. An expedited review requires only written approval from the IRB chair.

Problems with obtaining an expedited review emerge when:

1. Information is obtained or recorded in such a way that study participants can be identified directly or indirectly; and
2. Any disclosure of the study participants' responses outside the research could reasonably place them at risk of criminal or civil liability or be damaging to the participants' financial standing, employability, or reputation (American Association for Public Opinion Research, 2003).

Non-expedited review. A **non-expedited review** occurs when vulnerable subjects or controversial interventions or data-collection techniques are proposed. A study involving institutionalized individuals automatically triggers a non-expedited review. A non-expedited review requires a full IRB meeting with a quorum of members present. A majority of those members present at the meeting must approve the proposal.

Other comments about IRBs. The timeliness of submitting a proposal to an IRB is important. Most IRBs set up an annual schedule that may or may not identify monthly meeting times. Additionally, it is important to learn how far in advance a proposal needs to be received in order to be considered at an upcoming IRB meeting.

Depending on the nature of the study, the approval of more than one IRB may be required. One student we know of needed months to obtain approval from three separate IRBs—a university IRB, a state hospital IRB that hosted the intervention designed for the study, and a state Department of Mental Health that governed the hospital involved in the study (Baron-Leonard, 2004).

Funding Sponsors

Often individual researchers and leisure service organizations cannot afford to pay for a research project from their own budget. The expenses associated with carrying out a study may necessitate finding a funding sponsor (Case 2).

Case 2. Non-Monetary Sources for Leisure Research.

Many times, people limit themselves by only soliciting money to fund their research. If appropriate, think of how non-monetary donations may help in getting your project off the ground. For instance, in order to carry out a research project centering on video game play, the American Amusement Manufacturers Association was approached. As a way of showing support for the study, arcade games were loaned out for several months. The regional supplier even delivered and picked up the equipment at the senior center involved in the study. The supplier appreciated acknowledgement in the various presentations and papers written on the study (Riddick, Drogin, & Spector, 1987).

Another time, a student was interested in studying the exercise behaviors of pregnant women. In exchange for completing three surveys over the course of their pregnancies, study participants were given baby care products donated by a pharmaceutical company. In this instance, the company asked their name not be publicly identified.

Many universities have a small grants program supporting student research. Additional funding sources for studies in recreation, parks, sport, and tourism include foundations, government agencies, and corporations. Grant support may range anywhere from a few hundred dollars to thousands, or even hundreds of thousands of dollars. To be eligible for support, it is crucial to follow guidelines issued by funding sources regarding the content and timing of submission.

Something to Remember!

Many foundations use a two-stage grant application process. The first stage involves sending a prospectus. The **prospectus** is essentially a pre-proposal, usually no more than three pages, that provides an overview of the proposed study. Make sure you adhere, to the letter, to submission requirements. Foundations, and for that matter federal government agencies, receive hundreds if not thousands of prospectus submissions. An easy way for reviewers to narrow down the list is to reject those that do not follow submission directions and guidelines. If the foundation is interested in your idea, you'll be invited to submit a full-fledged, detailed proposal. This is the second stage. In most cases, if you've been invited to submit a full-fledged proposal, you may have a very short time period to turn things in, anywhere from one to two months.

Often, multiple external funding sources are used to fund an evaluative research study, especially a large-scale study. For example, *The Michigan After-School Initiative Survey* (Baker & Post, 2003) was funded by nine different agencies, including the Michigan Department of Education, Michigan State University, the Robert Wood Johnson Foundation, and the United Way.

Idea . . . Finding a Funding Source.

To find research funding sources, begin by asking other professionals or a university grants office for leads. Also, read government-issued Requests for Proposals (often referred to as **RFPs**) announced in the *Federal Registry,* consult foundation directory references available in libraries, and read the acknowledgements in research reports and journal articles. Additionally, commercial services exist, including *Community of Science,* that track federal, foundation, private and other funding opportunities.

There are also specialized funding sources. For example, if you're into mountaineering check out Mazamas (http://www.mazamas.org/your/adventure/starts-here/C99/). Mazamas (a Native American term for mountain goat) is a mountaineering organization that supports three grant programs: Graduate Student Research Grants, Standard Research Grants, and Youth Grants. The Graduate Student Grant program awards masters and doctoral candidates up to $1,500 for field studies that contribute to, among other things, conserving mountain environments (particularly in the Pacific Northwest), encouraging the scientific exploration of the natural world, and enhancing the enjoyment and safety of outdoor recreation.

If working with special populations is your interest, then look into the Special Olympics Health Professions Student Grants Program. Grants are awarded for short-term projects exploring issues that impact on the health and well-being of all persons with intellectual disabilities. Undergraduate and graduate students majoring in a health-related area can receive up to $3,500 to conduct studies on such things as: measurement of attitudes, opinions and behaviors of coaches and athletes, follow-up assessments of existing programs, and health promotion. To learn about specifics, access the Special Olympics Web site at www.specialolympics.org and in the "Search" box type in "Research."

The Robert Wood Johnson Foundation also supports promising new ideas that address health problems affecting society's most vulnerable people, including low-income children, frail older adults, adults with disabilities, the homeless, and those with severe mental illness. For details visit www.rwjf.org.

Finally, student and professional members of the American Park and Recreation Society (APRS) Branch of the National Park and Recreation Association (NRPA) can receive up to $1,000 in seed money for research projects that further document the benefits of park and recreation services. Learn more by going to NRPA's web site at www.nrpa.org and in the "Search" box type in "APRS Recreation Research Support Funds."

Proposal Language and Writing Style

Basically, four language and writing styles exist for the proposal (adapted from Gratton & Jones, 2004):

1. ***"Dry" and objective style.*** This style is written in a business or scientific-like tone, devoid of humor and personal pronouns.
2. ***"Down to earth" and informal style.*** The writing tone conveys information in an unpretentious manner.
3. ***"Long winded" and technical jargon style.*** This is a detailed and exhaustive portrayal of information using academic language.
4. ***"Chic" and blended style.*** This method uses a hybrid that mixes the objective and informal styles together.

Which style is best depends upon the audience for the project proposal. If the research proposal is needed to satisfy a degree requirement, then the convention is to use objective and/or technical jargon language, typically adhering to the American Psychological Association's (2001) style manual. Conversely, if the proposal is for laypersons, such as a recreation board of directors, then adopting a style that reflects a blend of objective and informal writing is more desirable.

Something to Remember!

One popular style manual, adopted by many professional journals and universities is the American Psychological Association's (APA) (2001) *Publication Manual.* Frequently asked questions, related to APA style, can be found at the APA Web site www.apa.org/ software/homepage.html (once at the site, select "APA-Style Tips," then "Specific Questions"). Also, consult: www.apa.style.org, www.psy-hwww. com/resource/apacrib.htm, www.wisc.edu/writing (click on "Writers Handbook), and www. diana.hacker.cdom/resdoc. There are two other APA style resources you may find helpful. First, there is the APA (2005) abbreviated version of the *Publication Manual* entitled *Concise Rules of APA Style.* Second, the software program *APA-Style Helper 5.1* is available to help create papers and articles following APA style guidelines.

The ***style manual*** you adopt should provide lots of detail and guidance on the various things that make up writing style, including organization, grammar, references, and table and figure set-ups. The following box summarizes some of the common style mistakes we have observed in proposals.

Something to Remember!

Our collective experiences indicate the following mistakes are frequently made in writing a proposal. (NOTE: For some of these rules, an APA [2001] reference marker has been noted parenthetically.)

1. **Writing a one-sentence paragraph.** A paragraph must, as a minimum, contain at least two sentences.

2. **Failure to seek copyright permission.** Copyright permission must be secured for quotations of 50 or more words and for tables and figures developed by someone else. Many times copyright permission requires paying the granting source a fee.

3. **Using ambiguous words related to time.** Avoid words, such as "currently," "presently," and "recently," since people don't agree about time frames that constitute the words and/or because time elapses between when the words are written and when the text is read.

4. **Not knowing the difference between the Latin abbreviations "i.e.," and "e.g.,".** The former (i.e.,) means "that is," and the latter (e.g.,) means "for example." Note that a period follows each letter and a comma appears after the second period. [Section 3.2 Latin Abbreviations]

5. **Not knowing when to spell out a number or record it numerically.** The rule is numbers less than 10 are spelled out and numbers 10 and higher are written numerically. An example is the following sentence, "There were 25 study participants, all of whom were eighth-grade students." [Section 3.42 Numbers Expressed in Figures]

6. **References used in the text do not show up in the *reference* section and vice versa.** Sit down and go page by page through your proposal, checking off references as they are encountered in the *reference* section. Also, make sure the spelling of reference names in the text correspond to what appears in the *reference* section. Ditto with the year of the cited publication as there should be an exact match between what is in the text and what is in the *reference* section.

7. **Not knowing when to use the ampersand sign ("&") in a reference.** The rule is if two or more authors are cited in the ***running text*** or narrative, you need to join the authors by the word "and." If the authors are cited ***parenthetically*** in the text (or inside the parentheses) then you connect authors' names with the ampersand sign. In the *reference* section two or more authors are joined together by the ampersand sign. [Sections 3.95 One Work by Multiple Authors and 4.13 Title of Work]

Proposal Content

For most of us, writing a proposal is a time-consuming and difficult endeavor. The good news is that once you're ready to write a proposal (Figure 3), with perseverance you should be able to produce a solid draft.

Figure 3. Checklist for Determining Readiness to Write a Proposal.

___ I have an understanding of the stages and steps involved in conducting a study.

___ I have read literature on my topic until my eyeballs are ready to pop out!

___ I possess the technical skills (e.g., knowing how to conduct a literature retrieval) and/or have resource people who can assist me with some of the technical aspects (such as using and interpreting statistics or qualitative data) needed to complete a proposal.

___ I am organized and have drafted an outline to guide me in the writing process.

___ I am motivated to complete a research study.

Idea . . . Getting the Most Out of Your Writing Sessions.

1. **Begin writing sooner rather than later.** Many proposal writers find it helpful to start with the "Purpose Statement," followed by the "Introduction" and "Literature Review" sections.

2. **Keep a research diary.** Record ideas and questions you have about the proposal as soon as you have them. By keeping these notes in one place you won't have to rely on your memory. As you review these notes later on, the answers may become evident, or you'll be prepared to ask for your advisor's or chair's advice.

3. **Recognize your writing idiosyncrasies.** What time of the day and location do you prefer to write? How can you minimize distractions? Do you need, for instance, to turn off Instant Messenger and post a sign on your door that reads, "Please DO NOT Disturb, Writer at Work!"?

4. **Follow a routine.** Know your "getting started" rituals—rearranging your desk, sharpening your pencils, playing a computer game, pouring yourself a cup of tea, or whatever. If you need these pre-writing rituals, allow for them.

5. **If you are stalled and have been working for a while, take a break.** When you come back, if you're still at a standstill, jot a note to yourself about what it is you're getting hung up on, and discuss the issue with someone whose advice you value.

6. **Get someone to read your drafts and provide meaningful feedback.**

7. **Cover the basics and then go back and "tighten" up.** Analogous to putting a new child's toy together, you first need to have everything in place before you tighten things down. When you think the content is okay, edit, and edit some more.

8. **Remember to proofread your work.** Initially, use the spelling and grammar check "Tools" on your computer software, but do not rely entirely on these. We heard about someone who wrote about a pheasant hunting study. The trouble was the writer mistakenly used the word "peasant" throughout and since "peasant" appeared in the word processing spell checker dictionary, the essay about peasant hunting was submitted for review.

9. **Plan on many revisions.** Realize an "acceptable" proposal will not be written after one, two, or even three efforts. It is not uncommon for a novice researcher to have 10 or more proposal drafts, so allow plenty of time for writing and revising. As well, it is a good idea to date each revision. Dating the various drafts will save you time and frustration in the long-run.

10. **Always have three updated backups of your text file.** Two of the proposal backups should be on two separate computer hard drives. For instance, store one on your school/office computer and one on your home computer. At least one of the copies should be on a portable device, such as a flash drive, CD, or floppy disk.

11. **Set up achievement milestones and reward yourself for accomplishing them.** If you feel that significant gains have been made, such as completing the first draft to the "Introduction" section, celebrate! Use positive reinforcement for your efforts—go on a hike, invite friends over for a pot luck dinner, or participate in some recreational activity you find gratifying.

Proposals often share common ingredients. Proposals differ, however, from final reports in that some information you expect in a final report is not initially presented in the proposal. Figure 4 makes this distinction.

Figure 4. Outline of What Typically Appears in a Proposal.

Final Report Headings	Contained in Proposal
Title Page	√
Abstract/Executive Summary	
Acknowledgements	
Table of Contents	√
Lists of Figures, Tables and Appendices	√
Introduction	√
Theoretical Foundation(s)	√
Hypotheses and/or Research Question	√
Literature Review	√
Methods	√
Results	
Discussion	
Conclusions	
Recommendations	
References	√
Appendices	√

It is important to further point out the content and organization of the proposal may be dictated by the group or organization receiving or sponsoring the research. Thus, prior to writing, you will want to find out what is required in terms of content and style.

Regardless of how you organize the proposal, it is imperative that you clearly delineate the various sections. To help, the American Psychological Association (2001) provides guidance on the mechanics of using heading and subheading captions in the proposal (Figure 5).

Figure 5. Headings and Sub Headings.[2]

One challenge in writing about research is how to use headings and sub-headings. The American Psychological Association's (2001) *Publication Manual* provides specific directions about this. For example, one way to think of headings and subheadings is to envision them as corresponding to the outline of your paper. First, decide on major ***headings*** or central points. Then, for each heading, decide if two, three, or more sub components or ***subheadings*** are needed.

The following five formatting styles can be used for organizing the hierarchy of headings and corresponding sub-headings for a proposal:

CENTERED UPPERCASE HEADING
Centered Uppercase and Lowercase Heading
Centered, Italicized, Uppercase and Lowercase Heading
Flush Left, Italicized, Uppercase and Lowercase Side Heading
Indented, italicized, lowercase paragraph heading ending with a period.

---

[2] Section "3.31 Levels of Headings" of APA (2001).

Now, let's consider each of the major headings in a research proposal.

Title Page

Four bits of information appear on the title page. Presented in order, these are:

- *Descriptive title.* The title should identify the major variables examined by the study and the study population. The trick is to use a title that is concise yet informative (Case 3).
- *Name of principal investigator(s)* (PI).
- *Organizational affiliation of the PI(s).*
- *Date proposal was submitted or distributed.*

Case 3. Title Possibilities.

You are planning to propose an evaluative research study to examine the impacts of an outdoor education course on college students. In particular, dependent variables of the study are self-esteem, problem solving, and nature appreciation. Brainstorming resulted in the following title possibilities and subsequent constructive criticism:

Title Possibility	Feedback
Evaluation of Outdoor Education Course	If written for lay people, the title is short and simple, but more specificity would be in order (such as identifying sponsor of the course). If written for a university requirement or professional publication, the title falls short. Final grade: So-So title!
Impacts of an Outdoor Education Course on Social Psychological Health	An improvement from the first title in that the reader is now learning what independent and dependent variables will be examined. Nevertheless, the title is vague, especially in the sense of not knowing who was involved in the study. Final grade: Better than first title!

Title Possibility	Feedback
A Mixed-Methods Investigation on How Participation in an Outdoor Education Course Affected the Self-Esteem, Problem-Solving Skills, and Nature Appreciation of College Students	The most descriptive title yet. A reader would learn a lot from this title, including the notion that mixed-methods were used, exactly what variables were examined, and the sampling frame used for the study. Final grade: Best descriptive title out of the three possibilities but admittedly very long!

Table of Contents

This section provides the reader with an overview of how the proposal is organized. The major headings and subheadings used in the proposal should be listed along with their respective page numbers. Having a "Table of Contents" can be of immense help to a reader who wants to revisit a particular section.

Lists of Figures, Tables and Appendices

It is always a good idea to incorporate figures and tables into your proposal. Why? They can provide mental relief to reading only narrative and provide a quick way to present or summarize information. Following the "Table of Contents," create separate lists for figures, tables, and appendices. Page numbers should be noted for each titled figure, table, and appendix.

Introduction

Introductory paragraphs that grab the reader provide background on the topic of the study. Years ago, one of us heard Mickey Spillane, a prolific mystery writer who has sold over 150 million books, comment that the first and last pages of a manuscript were extremely important. What was on the first page dictated if someone read on; whereas, the last page weighed in on whether or not the reader ever wanted to pick up anything else you wrote!

While all parts of the proposal are important, the introduction sets the stage and tone of the study for your readers—try to open with a statement about real people as opposed to referring to the work of others or statements dealing with past research.

The *Introduction* section is the point where you provide a logical transition into the study itself. Specific information that should be included in this section is:

- Background about the problem being investigated.
- Definitions of key concepts and variables.
- Purpose statement (Step 4).
- Explanation of the significance of the study (Step 5).

Theoretical Foundation

Information about the theoretical bases of the study (Step 3) should also be included in the proposal. Your writing task is to identify how the theoretical foundation relates to the independent and dependent variables, as well as the data collection methods.

Hypotheses and/or Research Questions

If used, hypotheses and research questions for the study are stated under this heading. Likewise, if triangulation or a qualitative approach is to be used, you need to state the research question(s) guiding the study.

Literature Review

As discussed in Step 2, this section presents a review and appraisal of previously completed studies that relate to your topic. At the proposal stage, the literature review is relatively brief (such as three to four pages). It is important to remember that when a reader finishes the review of literature section, it should be apparent there is a strong link between the literature presented and the objectives of your study.

Methods

The methods section provides detail about how the study is to be carried out. In order to help the reader follow the discussion, it is smart to use sub-headings for the various sub-components.

Research design and study participants. This subsection identifies the precise research design that will be used for the study and provides details about study participants (who will be selected and how) [Steps 6 and 7]. If you're conducting a survey, present the kind of sampling that will be used to identify potential respondents, the number of persons that will be contacted, and the rationale for how you went about identifying your desired sample size.

For qualitative studies, another point to make here is acknowledgement of how the investigator's biases can affect the study. This is known as *reflectivity* (Case 4).

Case 4. Reflectivity or Acknowledging Possible Biases in a Qualitative Study.

Burns, J. (2007). *A photo-elicitation study on the meanings Gallaudet University students derived from a weekend camping trip.* Unpublished master's thesis, Washington, D.C.: Gallaudet University.

A qualitative study was conducted on how a camping trip affected college students. Study participants were given cameras and asked to record memories of the three-day experience. Each camper was asked to select six photographs and describe, during an interview using probes, the meanings each photo held for them. All campers had either experienced congenital or adventitious deafness. The student conducting the thesis research acknowledged and reflected on how his background could have affected study findings. "The principal investigator is a male in his early thirties, was born with congenital deafness and grew up in Canada. . . . He attended a mainstreamed school from five years old to 18 years old" (p. 18).

Intervention. This subsection appears only if you are involved with evaluative research or a program evaluation study. If so, you provide a program description or information on program objectives, the content of the program, programming process, and length of each program session as well as the entire program.

Instrumentation. For a quantitative study, this subsection of the methods section identifies every instrument to be used to measure each independent and dependent variable under study. If adopting an already existing instrument, the tool is named and referenced and the number of items comprising the instrument is identified. If any of the variables are being measured by an instrument you are devising, then you need to explain how the instrument was developed, and provide a copy in the appendix. In either case, you also need to provide information on the validity and reliability of the instrument, coding of responses, and theoretical range of scores.

The details provided for the instrumentation section of a qualitative study will depend on the data-collection tool used. The main goal is to write a description that is as specific as possible about the open-ended questions that will be used in the unstructured interview, the research question(s) that will be posed to the focus group, the observation recording sheet that will be used in the observation, and/or the documentation regarding how the content analysis for a record review will be performed.

Data collection. This subsection begins, if relevant, with a statement of intent to apply for Institutional Review Board (IRB) approval. A copy of the informed consent you plan to use should appear in the appendix.

Details on the content and timing of communications with potential study recruits also needs to be outlined, with copies of the exact wording you plan to use in these contacts appearing in the appendix. If you are conducting survey research and are using a variation of the tailored design strategy (reviewed in Step 9), you need to identify the intended dates of your follow-ups as well as provide copies of these appeals in the appendix.

Additionally, you need to present information on your data-collection procedures (such as the questionnaire will be distributed in a group setting, through postal mail, or over the Web) and when data will be collected (for instance, playground observations will be made the first workday week in October, during the hours of 9 a.m. to 3 p.m.) (Step 9 details all of this). If using a group setting to collect data, you also need to supply a copy of the instructions to the group in the appendix.

Data analyses. Here you present information on the specific data analysis approach you will use. This would include specifications of the statistical analyses to examine each hypothesis and research question in a quantitative study, and/or detailing every data analysis step that will be used for interpreting each research question in a qualitative study. Such advance planning is important because if you give little or no thought to data analysis until after the information is gathered, you may discover it is impossible to analyze it in the way you wish.

Limitations. Shortcomings in research are sometimes identified in the proposal stage as a subsection of the "Methods" section. A *limitation* is something that may adversely affect the study (Mauch & Park, 2003). As noted earlier (see Steps 3, 6-9, and 14) limitations may stem from several sources, including the study's theoretical approach, sampling, research design, instrumentation, data collection, and/or data analyses.

Time budget. Sometimes inclusion of a time budget in the proposal can be beneficial, especially when the proposed study is going to be executed by other professional staff within an organization. A *time budget* projects both clock and calendar time needed to complete specified tasks for carrying out the evaluation. A time budget breakdown is accomplished by using a person-loading chart and a Gantt chart (See Step 13).

Financial budget. If a budget is needed for a study, usually a *line-item budget* is prepared. A typical model of a line-item budget submission is found in Figure 6. Figure 7 illustrates a line-item budget used by a student to solicit extra funding from a university to support his thesis.

Figure 6. Sample Line Item Budget for an Evaluation Project.

Budget Period: from month/day/year to month/day/year
Grant Period: from month/day/year to month/day/year
PROJECT YEAR   1   2   3   4   5   (circle)

I. PERSONNEL	Base Salary	FTE	Total	Internal Support	External Support
Position					
Principle Investigator	_____	_____	_____	_____	_____
Project Staff	_____	_____	_____	_____	_____
Administrative Staff	_____	_____	_____	_____	_____
Other Staff	_____	_____	_____	_____	_____
Fringe Benefits (@ __ %)			_____	_____	_____
SUBTOTAL			_____	_____	_____

II. OTHER DIRECT COSTS

Office Operations (phone, supplies, etc.)	_____	_____	_____
Communications/Marketing	_____	_____	_____
Equipment	_____	_____	_____
Travel Expenses	_____	_____	_____
Other	_____	_____	_____

SUBTOTAL   _____   _____   _____

III. INDIRECT COSTS (@ __%)   _____   _____   _____

GRAND TOTAL   _____   _____   _____

Figure 7. Proposed Budget for a Mail Survey Conducted for a Thesis.

Expenses/Direct Costs	Total Cost
Randomly Generated Address Labels from Registrar (N = 380)	$ 25
Department Stationery for Four Cover Letter Mailings (two reams)	$202
Paper for Two-page Informed Consent Form (four reams)	$24
Four-page Survey Booklet Professionally Photocopied, Collated, and Stapled (first, third, and fourth mailing replacement)	$214
Envelopes (4" X 6") for First, Third, and Fourth Mailings	$30
Envelopes (standard) for Second Mailing	$10
Payment to 300 Study Participants @$5/participant	$1,500
GRAND TOTAL REQUESTED	$2,005

Some funding organizations, such as the federal government, may require a second budget, known as a narrative budget. A ***narrative budget*** describes how the funds requested, for each line item, will be spent and how the amount was determined.

Typically, there are two major parts to a research budget—direct costs and indirect costs. ***Direct costs*** can in turn be broken down into personnel expenses and non-personnel expenses.

When personnel costs are identified in a budget as a direct cost, the norm is to list the base salary of each person needed in the project and then identify the percentage of time or effort that individual will devote to the project or the ***full-time equivalency (FTE).*** FTEs are noted in decimal form. For instance, if .25 is the FTE for the Principal Investigator, it means he or she is expected to devote 25% of full-time effort toward the research project.

Another important component of personnel costs is something known as fringe benefits. ***Fringe benefits*** are all federal, state and local taxes (for Social Security, worker's compensation, disability insurance), health insurance, life insurance and other benefits provided to employees. A percentage is used to calculate fringe benefits, which is usually dictated by the funding organization. For example, according to the Office of Sponsored Programs at Gallaudet University, fringe benefits at this institution average 22.5% to 26.5% (depending if the person is part-time or full-time) of the total costs calculated for salary (Christine Katsapis, personal communication, January 11, 2006).

Budgets submitted for funding consideration by other organizations also include facilities and administration costs, commonly referred to as indirect costs. *Indirect costs* are overhead expenses and include such things as utilities and custodial services. For most institutions of higher education, hospitals, and research centers, the negotiated indirect cost rate has been set at 38% of salaries and wages (Christine Katsapis, personal communication, January 11, 2006).

References

References, or any and all citations appearing in the proposal, must appear alphabetized in the *Reference* section. The way in which cited references are formatted will again depend on the style manual you have adopted. As well, your instructor or organization may provide more specific examples of a preferred reference list format.

Appendices

The appendix is used to present information dealing with technical details, such as copies of interview informed consent forms, copies of proposed correspondence to study participants, schedules, questionnaire or observation instruments, and directions to interviewers. All appendices you include at the end of the proposal should also be cited in the text.

Judging the Proposal

A written research proposal should be used to gather constructive feedback on a study's adequacy. In addition to the various approving entities who will judge your study via the proposal, you can also use the draft to determine the strengths and weaknesses of your own proposal.

Use the questions below (Figure 8) to re-examine your proposal before presenting it to the approving agents. You could also ask colleagues or friends to use this checklist for providing feedback after reading your proposal draft. Remember, every study has its shortcomings. The major concern is whether fatal flaws exist that will call into question the credibility and usefulness of study findings.

Figure 8. Judging a Proposal.

	Yes	No
INTRODUCTION		
1. Do the beginning paragraphs provide a logical transition to the study?		
2. Is the study purpose clearly stated?		
3. Is the purpose or problem researchable?		

	Yes	No
4. Have key concepts and variables been defined?		
5. Is the study population identified?		
6. Is what being proposed reasonable?		
7. Is the study significant? Does it discuss how results will: (a) Improve professional practice/service delivery, (b) Address a social problem, and/or (c) Contribute to scientific knowledge?		
LITERATURE REVIEW		
8. Is the literature review comprehensive? Relevant to study purpose or problem? Does it address the independent and dependent variables of the study?		
9. Have important previous studies been included?		
10. Have problems or flaws with earlier studies been noted?		
11. When possible, have primary sources been used?		
12. Is the review of literature up to date?		
THEORETICAL FOUNDATION		
13. Is a theoretical approach to the study acknowledged?		
14. Has a mixed-methods approach been adopted?		
15. Is a theoretical framework identified?		
HYPOTHESES and/or RESEARCH QUESTION		
16. Do hypotheses deductively flow from the theoretical framework?		
17. Do the hypotheses state expected relationships or differences?		
18. Are the hypotheses unambiguous, testable, and concise?		
19. Is the research question written as a desscriptive or normative question or a grand-tour question (with accompanying subquestion)?		
METHODS		
20. Overall, are the methods appropriate to the study's purpose?		
21. Is sufficient documentation provided so the study could be replicated?		
22. Is it clear that the principal investigator(s) has the necessary training, skills, and attitude to conduct the study?		
23. Considering the limitations of the study, are they so major that the proposed study should not be endorsed?		
Research Design and Study Participants		
24. Is the research design for the study identified?		
25. How many groups will be involved in the study?		
26. What sampling strategy is used to identify study participants and/or assignment to groups?		

	Yes	No
27. Does fairness prevail in terms of how study participants are selected and assigned to groups?		
28. Will the study be harmful to study participants?		
29. Will study participants benefit from the study?		
30. Is there an adequate number of study participants?		
31. Will study participants provide a credible answer to the research question? Are those being tapped as study participants appropriate?		
32. What threats to the truthfulness or internal validity of the study exist?		
33. What threats to the applicability or external validity of the study exist?		
Intervention		
34. Has an adequate description of the intervention been provided in terms of program content and process?		
Instrumentation		
35. Are the instruments appropriate in terms of the purpose or scope of the study, and study participants?		
36. Is information on the validity and reliability of all instruments provided? Does this information support using these instruments?		
37. Has the coding of possible answers been spelled out? Is the theoretical range of scores provided?		
38. Do normative data exist for the selected instruments?		
Data Collection		
39. Is IRB approval needed?		
40. Is informed consent an issue?		
41. Are the procedures for collecting data described in detail?		
42. Is a pilot warranted?		
43. Will the chosen data-collection method provide enough quality data for sufficient analyses?		
44. If used, are interviewers/facilitators/observers adequately trained?		
DATA ANALYSIS		
45. Will the proposed data analyses provide meaningful understanding?		
46. Is there a statistical and/or qualitative analysis plan to answer the hypothesis and research question?		
47. Are the proposed statistics or data-management plans appropriate?		
48. How will missing data be handled?		
49. Is the adopted level of significance fitting?		

	Yes	No
50. If confidential information is being collected, what provisions will be made to keep the responses or observations secure? Who will have access to the data?		
BUDGET		
51. Is the time budget sensible?		
52. Are the financial costs reasonable?		
POSTSCRIPT		
53. Has the author(s) committed any acts of plagiarism?		
54. Is the language and writing style acceptable?		

Your Research

1. Prepare a proposal on your research topic.
2. If appropriate, draft an IRB application for your proposal. If you are a university student, complete the forms issued by your institution's IRB.
3. Develop a small grants application to your university/agency. Include a line-item budget. Unless otherwise directed, follow the small grants guidelines available from the Robert Wood Johnson Foundation Web site at www.rwjf.org (click on "Grant Applications" and under "Unsolicited Proposals" click on "How to Apply" and then click on "Download Brief Proposal Form and Guidelines" and review the section entitled "Brief Proposal Application and Instructions").

Review & Discussion Questions . . . What have you learned about seeking proposal approval?

1. Why is it useful to obtain prior approval for a study?
2. Identify at least two *approval entities* with which a researcher must work.
3. Explain what functions are served by a *thesis/dissertation committee.*
4. Distinguish between an *expedited* and *non-expedited* Institutional Review Board (IRB) review?
5. What is a research *proposal?*
6. Recall the major headings presented in a proposal.
7. Name the major categories appearing in a *line-item budget* for a study.
8. Identify one question that determines the strengths and weaknesses of each of the following proposal parts: *Introduction, Literature Review, Theoretical Foundation, Hypotheses or Research Question,* and *Methods.*

Exercises

1. Read more about how to write and present a thesis or dissertation. After visiting two of the following sites, identify three useful things you learned about writing up a proposal.
    A. S. Joseph Levine's article, *Writing and Presenting Your Thesis or Dissertation,* available at http://www.wmich.edu/science/dissguid.pdf.
    B. *How to Write a Dissertation or Bedtime Reading for People Who Do Not Have Time to Sleep,* available at www.cs.purdue.edu/homes/dec/essay.dissertation.html.
    C. Mark Leone's Web site at Carnegie Mellon University offers tips on writing and publishing, research skills, and related topics and resources, available at www.cs.cmu.edu/~mleone/how-to.html.

2. As noted in an earlier chapter (Step 7), the bulk of research in recreation, parks, sport, and tourism settings has been focused on survey research. Read about how to protect study participants involved in survey research by consulting the American Association for Public Opinion Research's document entitled, *A Source Document for Institutional Review Boards,* found at www.aapor.org, click on "News and Issues," then "Statement for IRBs."
    A. Are written consent forms necessary or desirable in every research setting?
    B. Under what conditions may IRBs waive requirements for signed consent?
    C. How much should survey respondents be told about the study? Should they be informed, for example, of study hypotheses?

3. Learn more about IRBs by reading the *Code of Federal Regulations* posted at the United States Department of Health and Human Services' Office for Human Research Protections Web site at www.hhs.gov/ohrp/humansubjects/guidance/45cfr46.htm.
    A. What is the minimum number of people needed to serve on an IRB?
    B. What backgrounds or qualifications are needed to serve on an IRB?
    C. Under what circumstances does an IRB suspend or terminate approval of a research project?

4. Ask questions of a resource person (who possibly has been invited to one of your classes) familiar with how IRBs operate. For example:
    A. How are IRB openings publicized?
    B. Who chooses people to become IRB members?
    C. What factors are considered in extending an invitation to become an IRB member?
    D. What are common mistakes found in IRB applications?
    E. After a proposal has been approved, what oversight responsibilities does the IRB have?

5. Learn about resources available for grant seeking by visiting the W.K. Kellogg Foundation Web site at www.wkkf.org (click on the "Grant Seeking," then "Grant-seeking Tips"). Using the links appearing on the "Listing of Resources on the World Wide Web," briefly summarize what you learned from the National Institutes of Health's Web site and one other listed site.

6. Review another person's proposal.
    A. Identify which of the four writing styles (described in this chapter) the proposal used.
    B. Critique the language or clarity of the proposal.
    C. Rate the proposal's content. If your instructor does not identify evaluative criteria to use (such as the points listed in Figure 8), then use those listed appearing on NRPA's APRS Recreation Research Support Funds page which can be accessed by going to www.nrpa.org and typing "APRS Recreation Research Support Funds" in the "Search" bar. For each criterion used, decide whether the proposal deserves a "Satisfactory" or "Unsatisfactory" score.

Virtually all research projects require permission before they may be conducted. Typical overseers are managers of study sites, thesis/dissertation committees, institutional review boards, and funding sponsors. Murano, Italy. *Copyright © 2008 Carol Cutler Riddick*

Part IV: Implementing the Study

STEP 12: Conduct a Pilot Test

Purposes of Pilot Testing

Using Mixed-Methods in Pilot Testing

General Pilot-Testing Guidelines

Piloting an Interview

Piloting a Questionnaire

Piloting an Observation Plan

Anything that can go wrong, will—at the worst possible moment.
Finagle's Law of Dynamic Negatives

Is it finally time to actually collect information for the study? Many steps in the research process have already been accomplished. At this point the following tasks have been completed:

- Decided on a topic.
- Reviewed the literature.
- Identified theoretical underpinnings.
- Developed a scope of study.
- Explained the study's significance.
- Selected a sample.
- Chose a design.
- Considered measurement.
- Specified data-collection tools.
- Addressed ethical responsibilities.
- Sought proposal approval.

Seemingly, all the bases have been covered and we're ready to collect data. Well, almost. An important task remains ahead of us. At this juncture, we need to engage in pilot testing.

Purposes of Pilot Testing

Pilot testing is a small-scale, preliminary study to test either parts of a research plan or the entire plan. Think of a pilot test as a mini-version of a full-scale study. In essence, it is a confirmatory study that amounts to a "dress rehearsal," or "shakedown cruise."

While many purposes can be served by a pilot (see the *Something to Remember* box below), essentially it is a check of the effectiveness of your study proposal. That is, the feasibility of the instrumentation, procedures, intervention (if a program evaluation is being undertaken), and methods of analysis are examined (Case 1).

Something to Remember![1]

Many purposes can be served by pilot testing. Some are to:

- Establish whether the sampling technique is effective.
- Discover if the intervention is working as well as you hoped it would.
- Test the adequacy of data-collection instruments.
- Determine whether the procedures are realistic and workable.
- Assess interview time and/or response rate.
- Appraise the proposed data analysis techniques.
- Improve the data-collection skills of the research staff.
- Find out if resources (staff, time, funding) planned for the study are adequate.
- Assess the feasibility of a full-scale study.

• Convince funding groups and other stakeholders that: (a) The research team is competent; (b) The main study is worth funding; and/or (c) The main study is feasible.
• Identify politics that may affect the research process.

[1] Adapted from: Stangor (2006); and van Teijlingen and Hundley (2001).

Case 1. Piloting a Data-Collection Method.

Myllykangas, S. (2005). *Meaning of leisure: A case study of older women with HIV/AIDS and their female family caregivers.* Unpublished doctoral dissertation, Indiana University, Bloomington, IN.

One purpose of the study was to understand the meaning of leisure for older women diagnosed with HIV or AIDS. To collect this information, study participants were going to be asked to take photographs of the nature of their leisure both before and after diagnosis. To be sure this method of collecting information worked, a pilot test was first done. Disposable box cameras with automatic flash were given to a small sample of older men with HIV or AIDS. (The reason men were chosen for the pilot was because the entire population of older women with HIV/AIDS in the community was to be used in the main study.) After the photos were taken, debriefing interviews with the men revealed that the photo-taking instructions for the study needed to be modified. In particular, instructions given were altered in the main study by making the definition of "leisure" clearer. Additionally, the pilot revealed that respondents needed many more cameras than originally thought. Consequently, in the full-fledged study, each participant was given 16 cameras or one camera for each research question posed.

Pilot testing is a crucial element of "good" research because it helps you determine if things will work out in ways that are expected and to identify ways to refine the endeavor before it is launched in its entirety. Pilot test results can give advanced warnings about issues or flaws in the implementation of the research plan so that these can be corrected, and increase the odds of pulling off the main study without any major glitches (van Teijlingen & Hundley, 2001).

While a pilot study does not guarantee success for the larger-scale study, it goes a long way in assuring that it goes off as planned and delivers useful information. Thus, we are unabashed proponents of pilot studies. We view a pilot test as a precautionary maneuver. It is risky to undertake a study without one. In fact, a pilot study can be viewed as an inexpensive insurance policy; after all it's better to be safe than sorry!

Using Mixed-Methods in Pilot Testing

Pilot testing can be conducted for both quantitative and qualitative design approaches. In fact, even though the goal is to imitate the main study circumstances as much as possible, pilot testing can also be done using different methods than those in the main study. That is, a qualitative pilot test can prepare for a quantitative main study. Alternatively, a quantitative pilot can lay the groundwork for a qualitative main study. For ideas on how mixed-methods can be used in the pilot testing step, see the *Idea* box that follows.

Another way to understand the utility of a pilot study is to think of it as a "test drive." You wouldn't spend money on a car without taking it for a spin first to be sure it runs as you expect it to! *Copyright © 2007 Ruth V. Russell*

Idea . . . Using Mixed-Methods in Pilot-Testing Studies.

<u>Idea 1.</u> **Use one approach to develop another approach.** For example, in-depth unstructured interviews in a pilot could be used to identify points of view when preparing a questionnaire for a full-fledged study. As another example, a questionnaire could be piloted with a group. Responses with the highest percentages would then be used as indicators of the sort of questions to be posed in a subsequent qualitative study using focus groups.

<u>Idea 2.</u> **Use one approach to confirm another approach.** For instance, after a questionnaire is drafted, a focus group could be convened to identify misunderstandings appearing in the questionnaire. These "problem spots" could be corrected before the questionnaire is given to the main study respondents. As another example, a pilot study could be conducted with several individuals who have picked up flyers promoting different college majors from a hallway dispenser. As a way of confirming the conclusion that people selected the particular flyers they did because they were interested in those majors, they could be asked to complete a short questionnaire asking for the reasons behind removing the flyers.

General Pilot-Testing Guidelines

Some generic guidelines should be practiced during a pilot study regardless of what data collection methods are used. These principles are highlighted in Figure 1.

Figure 1. Pilot-Testing Tips.

1. **Seek and secure permission to conduct the pilot from your ethical review board.** A researcher's ethical responsibilities are identical for a pilot study as they are for the main study (Step 10).
2. **Use convenience sample selection.** Pilot respondents do not need to be randomly selected from the population group. Rather, pilot participants can be chosen based on their availability.
3. **Choose sample members who match the main study population.** It is important to select individuals for the pilot who, as much as possible, match the same social and cultural characteristics of respondents for the main study. It is critical to follow this principle because the point of the pilot is to see how things work. If pilot group members don't come close to representing the background characteristics (e.g., education, age) of individuals involved in the full-fledged study, the purpose behind a pilot test is defeated.
4. **Use a small sample size.** For a questionnaire, the pilot test should include about 15 to 20 individuals (Fowler, 1998). Fewer respondents can be employed in piloting interviews and observations.
5. **Do not use pilot respondents again in the main study.** The concern about including participants from the pilot test in the main study arises because these individuals will have experienced the study instruments and protocol an extra time. In other words, their extra exposure to the study *contaminates* the results.
6. **Do not merge pilot data into the main study's data.** The data collected from a pilot test should not be used to test a hypothesis or reported in the conclusions of the actual study. This is especially true when the pilot revealed problems with the research tools, and modifications had to be made accordingly.
7. **Acknowledge pilot testing in study reports.** Include information in the final report about the pilot testing. In particular, explicitly identify and defend the changes made in the directions, questions, observation and response categories, and/or data collection procedures. It is important that lessons learned are shared so that future studies and evaluators don't have to "re-invent the wheel." "Unfortunately, pilot studies are in general, under-discussed, underused and under-reported" (Prescott & Soeken, 1989, p. 60).

Piloting an Interview

Pilot-testing plans for a study using interviews is particularly useful. This advice applies to both close-ended interview scripts, as well as open-ended interview schedules. Even if casual and conversational interviews are held, it will make a big difference if the questions are practiced on a few people ahead of time.

An important goal of pilot testing an interview plan is to be sure the questions can and will be answered. This suggests the foremost consideration is checking out how comfortable and confident interviewees feel in answering the questions.

There are two approaches to use in soliciting feedback from a pilot of an interview. First, an interview can be piloted by asking one interview question and then soliciting feedback on the question (Figure 2). This cycle is repeated until all the questions appearing on the interview schedule are exhausted. Then some additional questions about the interview schedule can be posed.

Figure 2. Piloting an Interview.[2]

When conducting a debriefing interview with interviewees, begin by reminding them of the purpose of the pilot. Namely, the researcher is not interested in learning about their answers to posed questions; instead, the researcher is seeking advice on how to make the interview's directions, questions and possible answers (if provided) clearer. People involved in a pilot should be told that one question at a time will be posed, and then he or she will be asked several other questions about the question. That is, after explaining the pilot interview's purpose, follow the sequence below:

1. Pose one interview question.
2. Allow the respondent to answer the question and record the answer.
3. Then ask the respondent what was going through his/her mind during the questioning process.
4. Request the respondent to paraphrase his/her understanding of the question.
5. Raise another question and repeat steps two, three, and four above. Continue this loop until all questions have been asked.
6. After all questions have been asked, inquire if the sequencing of questions is logical; and if directions or transitions were used, were these clear?
7. Then ask how the introduction to the interview could be improved.
8. Finally, invite the individual to share any other thoughts on how the interview experience could be improved.
9. Wrap things up with an expression of gratitude for the interviewee's time and thoughts.

[2] Adapted from: Lessler, Tourrangeau, and Salter (1989); and Forsyth and Kviz (2006).

Alternatively, a second way to pilot an interview is to ask pilot respondents to complete a rating form. Figure 3 below highlights questions that can be posed on the rating form.

Figure 3. An Alternative Way to Pilot an Interview.

Some interviewers ask those involved in the piloting of an interview to fill out a brief rating form on each question (and response categories, if used) used in the interview (Fowler, 2002). In particular, individuals are asked to rate each question in terms of whether or not:

• It was easy to understand as worded?
• The question and/or possible answers needed clarification?
• The individual felt capable of answering the question?
• The individual felt willing to answer the question?

Ideally, if acceptable to the participants, pilot interviews should be video-recorded, or at least audio-recorded (Fowler, 1998). Studying these also helps determine changes or corrections necessary in the interview process and the interviewer's skill. As well, the interviewees themselves can be asked to judge the skills of the interviewer. For example, interviewees can be asked:

• Was the interviewer's body language appropriate?
• Did the interviewer ask the agreed-upon questions?

- Did the interviewer frequently interrupt?
- Did the interviewer use prompts, probes, and silence effectively?
- Was the interviewer capable in handling the recording equipment?

Since piloting an interview fine-tunes the process of interviewing, the interviewer(s) should be debriefed as well. From the pilot test you should be able to judge areas that need further improvement. Some of the questions posed to interviewers during a debriefing include:

- Did interviewees frequently check the clock or fidget?
- Were there questions for which the interviewees did not make eye contact with you?
- Which questions and possible answers did interviewees ask for clarification about or seem to have trouble identifying "what you wanted?"
- What comments do you have about the interview form? For instance, were the answers easy to record? Was there enough memory or tape to record all responses from the interview?

Piloting a Questionnaire

Questionnaire construction remains an imprecise science, therefore questionnaire drafts must be piloted in order to identify flaws and allow for corrections (Case 2). Pilot tests help to increase response rates, reduce the possibility of missing data, and obtain more valid responses on the final questionnaire (Schwab, 2005).

Case 2. Piloting a Questionnaire.

Chan, P-C. (2005). *Relevant attributes in assessment for design features of indoor games hall: The application of importance-performance analysis.* Unpublished doctoral dissertation, Indiana University, Bloomington, IN.

The purpose of the study was to evaluate the design features needed for a successful indoor games hall in Hong Kong, China. Prior to administering the questionnaire, a pilot study was conducted. Several participants of the Kowloon Park Indoor Games Hall were asked to complete the questionnaire under similar conditions that would be implemented for the main study. As a result of the pilot test it was determined that the questionnaire was reliable and feasible. Yet, the pilot testing also made it clear the questionnaire needed the following changes:

- Make a better distinction between the terms "importance" and "performance."
- Add "squash" and "tennis" to the list of recreational sports to choose from.
- Add a question about respondents' profession.

There are a number of things to be aware of when piloting a questionnaire. Figure 4 presents some tips.

Figure 4. Tips for Piloting a Questionnaire.[3]

1. **Administer the questionnaire in exactly the same way as it will be administered in the main study.** If it is a mail questionnaire, mail it along with the drafted cover letter and stamped, self-ad-

dressed, return envelope. If it is to be given out in a group setting, distribute the pilot in a group setting too.

2. **In pilot-testing Internet questionnaires, be sure respondents can access them.** Test the ease with which respondents can log onto a secure Web site and pull up the survey. Also, find out respondents' opinions about the subject line used. As mentioned in Step 9, first try using a subject line related to the study's topic, steering clear of using "Survey" and "Research."

3. **Ask respondents to provide feedback on: unclear directions, ambiguities or difficult questions or response categories, awkward transitions and questioning sequences, and design and layout.** Encourage members of the pilot group to write comments about the questionnaire in the margins of the questionnaire itself. Be aware that research indicates that the respondent's age will influence his or her perception that design and layout features are attractive.

4. **Check that all questions are answered.** If not, find out why the individual did not answer the question, was it because it was too personal? Also, pay particular attention to the frequency with which people record "Don't Know" or "No Response" to questions. A lot of answers in either of those response categories suggests the question does not get at the information needed and should be revised.

5. **Look to see if several answers are provided for the same question when only one answer was requested.** If so, obviously this problem needs to be addressed and resolved. For instance, are the possible answers to forced-choice questions mutually exclusive?

6. **Ask respondents to comment on whether or not the amount of time needed to complete the questionnaire was reasonable.** If not, shorten the questionnaire or experiment with making open-ended questions optional and placed toward the end of the questionnaire.

7. **Determine if data generated from the questionnaire are compatible with the data-analysis tools you plan to use in the regular study.** This means determining if data yielded from the pilot will answer the research question(s) and/or hypotheses (see Step 14).

8. **Rewrite difficult or problematic parts of the questionnaire.** Indeed, this is the ultimate point of conducting the pilot study in the first place!

---

[3]Adpated from: Couper (2004); Gratton and Jones (2004); and Peat, Mellis, Williams, and Xuan (2002).

Also, investigate whether set responses occur. A *set response* is the tendency to respond to questions from a particular perspective, usually due to social desirability. For instance, if young campers are asked how often they practice a list of desirable health habits while at camp (daily brushing of teeth, washing hands before meals, etc.), most likely they will tell you what they think you want to hear rather than the truth.

Idea . . . Consider a Second Pilot if Circumstances Warrant It.

If the first pilot reveals that substantial changes are needed in the questionnaire and/or methods used to collect questionnaire data, a second pilot study should be undertaken. All of this takes time, of course, and should be built into the timeline for the entire study. Nevertheless, taking up a second pilot is warranted when findings from the first pilot reveal the collected data do not match the study's purpose, research question and/or hypothesis testing needs (Neutens & Rubinson, 2002).

Piloting an Observation Plan

If observations will be used to collect information in the study, this method should be pilot tested as well (Case 3). Foremost, the ethical care given to the observation situation should be checked. Was there difficulty in gaining access to the observation site? What can and should be changed in the protocol to improve access? Did the subjects of the pilot observations behave in a usual way? Were observations recorded in the manner planned? Was an adjustment in the level of observer participation needed and warranted?

Case 3. Observing a Coffee Klatch.

A pilot observation study was undertaken of a coffee klatch program in a Florida *snowbird community* (or a winter sanctuary where northern residents go to escape cold weather). The investigator, one of the co-authors of this text, originally intended to use marginal participant observation in the main study. The pilot test revealed that the coffee klatch participants wouldn't allow for this. Instead, they insisted that the researcher become a bona fide member of the club! Thus, for the main study, she learned she had to adopt a complete participant observation role in order to complete the research.

Your Research

1. Now that your research study is planned and ready to go, will you conduct a pilot test of your data-collection tools and procedures, as well as data-analysis methods? If not, why not?
2. If you'll be undertaking a pilot, will you pilot the entire study or a specific data-collection tool?
3. When and how will the pilot test be carried out?
4. What do you actually want to know as a result of the pilot test?
5. How will you put what the pilot test reveals to use?
6. Will more than one pilot test be needed? Why or why not?

Review and Discussion Questions . . . What have you learned about conducting a pilot test?

1. What is meant by *pilot testing*?
2. What are at least three specific purposes of conducting a pilot test?
3. When are pilot tests usually carried out?
4. Are pilot tests used in both quantitative and qualitative studies? Why?
5. Can quantitative methods be used for a pilot test of a qualitative main study, and vice versa? How?
6. What are some guidelines for acquiring respondents for a pilot test? How large should a pilot test sample be?
7. Should pilot respondent data and/or pilot respondents themselves be used again in the main study? Why or why not?

8. Are the results of pilot tests reported?

9. What are at least three things to look for when piloting a questionnaire?

10. What are at least three things to look for when piloting an interview?

11. What are at least three things to look for when piloting an observation plan?

Exercises

1. The purpose of this activity is to demonstrate the sorts of things that can be learned from conducting a pilot study of an unstructured interview schedule (adapted from Janesick, 2003). Two different schedules seeking the same information are compared.

   A. Pair up with a classmate. Assign one member of the pair as "A" and the other as "B." Beforehand you (or your instructor) have made copies of Figure 5 (below). Distribute this figure so that person "A" receives a copy of schedule "A" and person "B" receives a copy of schedule "B."

   B. Once the interview schedules are distributed, individuals in each pair take turns asking and then answering the questions. That is, person "A" asks interview schedule "A" questions to person "B" who answers them, and then person "B" asks interview schedule "B" questions to person "A" who answers them.

   C. Afterwards, discuss within the pairs how the interviews went.

      i. Were there differences in the interview experience (asking and answering) between the two schedules?

      ii. How would you describe these differences for the interviewees? Did one schedule produce more information? Was one schedule more uncomfortable?

   D. In round-robin fashion have each pair share their experiences and impressions with their classmates and instructor.

Figure 5. Interview Schedules for Exercise 1.

I. Interview Schedule A:

1. Are you looking forward to winter/spring break this year?
2. What do you think you might do for winter/spring break this year?
3. How important is it to you to experience winter/spring break with friends? With family? Alone?
4. If you were to go to Cancun, Mexico this year with a group of friends, what sorts of things would you look forward to doing there?
5. During winter/spring break, some college students participate in dancing, socializing on the beach, meeting new people from other schools, and going to alcohol company-sponsored parties. What do you think of these sorts of winter/spring break activities?

II. Interview Schedule B:

1. For winter/spring break, some college students go to Cancun, Mexico to enjoy dancing, socializing on the beach, meeting new people from other schools, and going to alcohol company-sponsored parties. What do you think of these sorts of winter/spring break activities?

2. Have you ever observed other college students engaging in any of the activities noted in "1 (above)" during winter/spring break?

3. How did you feel about college students engaging the activities noted in Question 1 above?

2. The purpose of this exercise is to practice the steps for conducting a pilot study of a question-naire.

    A. Distribute copies of Figure 6 (below) to everyone in the class.

    B. Ask individuals to complete the questionnaire on their own.

    C. Form into discussion groups of no more than six persons. Within the discussion groups compare responses to the questionnaire and discuss the experience of taking the ques-tionnaire with each other. Respond to Questions 3-4, 6, and 8 appearing in Figure 4.

Figure 6. Questionnaire for Exercise 2.

1. Are you a male _____ or female _____?

2. Are you between the ages of 18 and 25?

3. What would you say is your favorite leisure pursuit?

4. Do you participate in this pursuit frequently? _____ YES _____ NO

5. What keeps you from pursuing your favorite leisure pursuit more frequently?

    _____ NO TIME
    _____ NO MONEY
    _____ NO ONE TO DO IT WITH

6. What is your annual income?

    Is it below $10,000? _____
    Is it between $10,000 and $20,000? _____
    Is it more than $20,000? _____

7. What other sports do you enjoy?

8. Why don't you participate in them more frequently?

    _____ NO TIME
    _____ NO MONEY
    _____ NO ONE TO DO IT WITH

9. Are the recreational facilities on campus good? _____ YES _____ NO

3. The points of this exercise are to practice observation and field note-taking skills and demonstrate the difference perspective can make in what is "seen" when using the observation data collection tool (adapted from Janesick, 2003).

    A. Arrange yourselves in a large circle (can be several layers deep) so that there is enough room for a small table in the center. On the table place four to six objects, for example, a vase of fresh flowers, a framed picture, a stack of magazines, a coffee mug, etc. Have everyone, from his or her seated vantage point, observe and record the objects seen on the table. Descriptive terms should be used in describing what is seen, such as color, space, shape, etc.

    B. After about five minutes, everyone changes seats, moving if possible as far away from their original location as possible. Repeat the observation for about five more minutes, again taking field notes on what is observed.

    C. Engage in a class-wide discussion of the differences in observation notes. Were these differences a result of vantage point? What does this activity demonstration about the importance of pilot testing an observation procedure?

Pilot tests are mini-versions of a full-scale study. Such "dress rehearsals" help establish if the sampling, data collection, and other study procedures will work. Street Minstrel, Venice, Italy. *Copyright © 2008 Carol Cutler Riddick*

STEP 13: Prepare for Data-Collection

Take Stock

Recruit, Hire, and Train Staff

Manage a Research Team

Be Prepared.
Boy Scout Motto

The previous chapter advised that before data for a study can be collected, pilot testing needs to be completed. Well, there is still one more step to be undertaken before data-collection begins, namely, preparing for data-collection! An analogy to this step is getting ready to cook your favorite meal—making sure you have on hand all the ingredients and cooking equipment you'll need.

Basically, preparing for data-collection requires paying attention to three things. First, time must be devoted to taking stock of materials, supplies, and equipment needed to conduct the study. Second, staff recruitment, hiring, and training must be tended to. And third, plans must be made for managing the research team.

Take Stock

Regardless of the nature of your study, you must make sure the materials, supplies, and equipment needed to collect the data are on hand and in good working order. For example, if special equipment is necessary to collect data, such as video cameras, audio recording devices, and laptops, then take time to check out the equipment. Is it in good working order? Are all attachments and accessories (e.g., microphones, spare batteries, connecting cables) in place and working? Similarly, are blank videos or audio cassettes in the supply cabinet and ready to be distributed, with extra backup available in case they are needed? Are the people assigned to use equipment proficient in their operation? Lastly, do you need to make sure equipment has been reserved for training purposes, as well as for actual data-collection times?

Idea . . . Heavy Duty Notebook Personal Computer (PC).

If face-to-face interviews are being conducted and you are using laptops to enter answers, consider investing in a notebook PC that is rugged or designed for road warriors (such as individuals involved in law enforcement, utility work, and emergency response). These PCs are wireless, have shock mounted hard drives, are built with anti-reflective, outdoor-readable LCD screens and backlit keyboards, and are housed in a heavy duty case that can withstand dropping. A number of different manufacturers make these sorts of notebook PCs, so shop around.

If data will be collected through phone interviews, then an obvious important detail to tend to is whether extra phone lines are needed. If so, make sure sufficient lead time has been allowed for so additional telephone lines can be installed. If questionnaires will be mailed, has the postage been purchased? If researchers will have to travel to data-collection sites, have arrangements been made for car rentals, lodging and meal reimbursements, and other travel-related costs?

As well, special computer software is sometimes required to conduct interviews or analyze data. The learning curve on mastering these programs can range from easy to steep. It may be that in order to master the software, one or more of the researchers need to register for special workshops or instruction. Regardless, make sure enough time has been allocated to master the software that will be used for the study.

Researchers prepare a mass mailing. *Copyright © 2008 Ruth V. Russell*

Assuring that the data-collection materials are ready also includes allowing enough time to have any necessary printed materials prepared, proofread, and reproduced (new staff orientation materials, release forms/informed consent, interview schedules, questionnaires, observation forms, cover letters, follow up letters, etc.). Commercial printing companies can be quite busy from Thanksgiving through New Years (printing holiday greeting cards and social invitations) and again in the spring (handling wedding announcements). Or, if printing is going to be in-house, then it is important to check on how much lead time is needed for you to obtain your printed material. Make sure you proofread your work prior to turning it over for duplication, and again when you pick it up from the printer.

Something To Remember!

> How to Avoid Proofreading Bloopers:
>
> - **Allow adequate time to proofread.** Write one day, and proofread the next. Better yet, get a second pair of eyes to read your draft.
> - **Proof it on paper.** If you think the copy is ready for mass or commercial printing, print and proof a paper version before sending it on its way.
> - **Have adequate reference materials available.** This includes a dictionary and a stylebook. Computer software can't be trusted to check spelling.
> - **Look for one type of error at a time.** Go through the draft and check first for grammar, then for punctuation, sentence structure, and spelling.

Finally, taking stock of necessary resources for data-collection includes addressing space needs. For example, is a quiet space for testing available? Does the basketball court need to be reserved for collecting data? Will extra file cabinets be needed to store and manage completed questionnaires? It is important that space, especially where interviews and group questionnaires are administered, be adequate to ensure confidentiality of respondents while maintaining optimal conditions for their participation.

Recruit, Hire, and Train Staff

Some research projects are simple enough to be conducted by a single person, without the assistance of additional staff. At other times, research studies require more than one person to be involved in collecting and managing data. Research assistants may need to be hired to conduct interviews, distribute questionnaires, or make observations for a study. These individuals are sometimes referred to as ***field workers.*** Occasionally, as well, individuals are hired to assist part-time or full-time with data entry into a computer or interview transcription.

If you find yourself in the position of hiring individuals to assist with a research project, it is important to interface with your agency's human resources unit. In particular, you need to be clear about regulations governing advertising, payment, supervision, and evaluation of hourly, part-time, or temporary full-time employees (Case 1).

Case 1. Hire Indigenous Workers.

> If you're in a position to hire research assistants, be expansive in your thinking about their qualifications. Often we spend a lot of time addressing the educational prerequisites for a job but give little thought about the "human dimensions" of hiring. We recommend that whenever possible you should hire people who have similar demographic characteristics as the group being sampled to conduct interviews, distribute questionnaires to groups, or make observations. In other words, hire people who are ***indigenous*** to study participants.
>
> We know of a university project that was funded by a state agency on aging. Graduate students were hired to conduct door-to-door structured interviews in an inner-city neighborhood from 9 to 5 p.m.

on weekdays. The graduate students canvassed the neighborhood, dressed up (ties worn by the males, females in dresses) and carried brief cases containing their interview forms. Not one of the interviewers was a person of color. Most of the time door knocks went unopened and the few times someone opened the door, and when the student began speaking, the door suddenly closed.

The people hired to work on the research project will need training and orientation. Lasting from a few hours to a few days, field workers should be paid for the time they are in training, and thus this expense should be budgeted to the project. Topics typically covered in training are outlined in Figure 1.

Figure 1. Field Worker Orientation.[1]

Some points to consider for the orientation of individuals hired or assigned to assist with a research project include:

- Provide an overview of the research project or its: purposes, significance, and methods.
- Distribute the interview, questionnaire, and/or observation forms that will be used.
- Discuss the importance of following interview, questionnaire, or observation instructions.
- Present tips for conducting and recording successful interviews, group questionnaires, and observations. For interviews and questionnaires, this includes how to greet and terminate contact with respondents.
- Emphasize the need for legibility.
- Demonstrate and practice administering interviews, questionnaires, and/or observations. Videotaping practice sessions will prove to be very useful for those being trained.
- Review policies for maintaining data-collection logs and submission of collected data.
- Discuss data verification procedures and consequences of falsifying data (see *Something to Remember* box below).
- Address dress and behavior codes.
- If the organization is providing transportation, announce policies and procedures for reserving motor pool vehicles.
- Outline procedures for submitting worked hours and travel-related expenses (mileage, per-diem lodging, and meal expenses).
- Disseminate emergency contact information.

[1]Adapted from: Alreck and Settle (2004); and Veal (2006).

The procedures that will be used to verify data should be reviewed during this orientation. Standard procedures, for dealing with completed interviews and questionnaires, are to review them for completeness, as well as to verify a proportion of the submitted data.

Something to Remember![2]

Field workers should be alerted that checks will be in place to determine the "quality" of the data they collect. The standard procedure is to have submitted interviews and questionnaires *sight-edited,* by another person, for completion.

Additionally, completed interviews and questionnaires are normally subjected to data verification. *Data verification* consists of contacting a proportion of those reported as completing interviews or questionnaires. Verification protects the data against ***arm-chairing***—to confirm the interview or questionnaire was completed by the field worker and not by the respondent. In particular, it is important to rule out that none of the following things happened:

• The interview or questionnaire was distributed to the wrong person or an unqualified individual.
• The interview or questionnaire was distributed at the wrong time or place.
• Parts, including questions the respondent refused to answer or the entire interview, were completed by the field worker.

[2] Adapted from Alreck and Settle (2004).

When conducting face-to-face interviews, there are two critical items that field staff must carry with them at all times. First, they must be provided with identity badges. Second, they need to carry letters of introduction.

Something to Remember!

Field workers should be in possession of two items at all times. First, they need identity badges. The identity badge should be worn around the neck or attached prominently on the left side (above the heart) of the worker and should contain:

• Name of sponsoring organization (and logo, if available).
• A picture identification of the field worker.
• The name and signature of the field worker.

Second, field workers must have a letter of introduction that specifies the:

• Identity of the sponsoring organization.
• Purpose of the study.
• Name and phone number of a contact person at the organization in case a question arises about the legitimacy of the project.

The letter of introduction should be laminated (to reduce wear and tear) and made available to the prospective study participant.

Manage a Research Team

In addition to recruiting, hiring, and training field workers to help with data-collection, there may be other people involved with carrying out the study. In fact, in large research studies you may be working with a team of people who have a variety of research-related skills and who make different contributions to the process. Figure 2 summarizes some of the key players on a research team, and their typical roles and responsibilities.

Figure 2. A Research Team.

Team Member	Typical Roles and Responsibilities
Principle Investigator (PI)	Responsible for all steps in the research process
Project Coordinator	Working closely with the PI, coordinates the implementation of all steps in the research process
Research Assistants/Field Workers	Primary data collectors
Statistician	Advises on data management and analysis
Administrative Assistant	Provides management and clerical support
Data-Entry Specialists	Converts raw data into electronic format

When a study is carried out using a team of evaluators, it is imperative that everyone's efforts are coordinated. Two different systems that aid in this are a person-loading chart and a Gantt chart.

A *person-loading chart* itemizes the individual/position assigned to each task and the estimated number of hours or clock time needed to complete the task (Figure 3). A *Gantt chart* presents, in illustration format, the calendar time projected for each task and the timing interface among the various identified project activities (Figure 4). The Gantt chart, once adopted, then becomes essentially a management tool or reminder of the various tasks that are suppose to be completed during an identifiable time period.

Figure 3. Person-Loading Chart (in hours) for Developing an Interview Schedule for Evaluation of a YMCA Youth Swim Program.

Task & Activity	Director	Youth Sports Coordinator	Personnel Personnel Business Manager	Lifeguard	Consultant
Choose/Design Instruments					
1. Specify data needs	10	5	2		20
2. Review existing instruments					
2.1 Locate instruments					30
2.2 Evaluate instruments	20	5		2	20
3. Modify existing instruments and/ or develop new instruments					
3.1 Develop interview schedule	4	4		2	20
3.2 Pilot interview schedule		4		4	4
3.3 Analyze and revise interview schedule	2	2			10
TOTAL	**36**	**20**	**2**	**8**	**104**

Figure 4. Gantt Chart for Developing Interview Schedule for Evaluation of a YMCA Swim Program.

TASK: Choose/Design Instruments

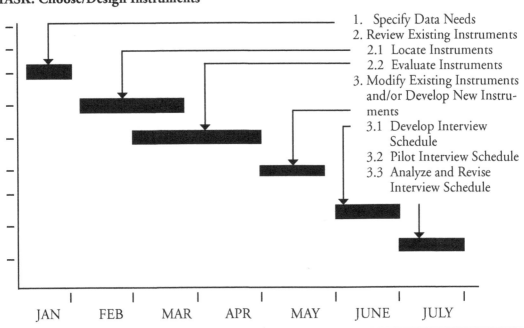

1. Specify Data Needs
2. Review Existing Instruments
   2.1 Locate Instruments
   2.2 Evaluate Instruments
3. Modify Existing Instruments and/or Develop New Instruments
   3.1 Develop Interview Schedule
   3.2 Pilot Interview Schedule
   3.3 Analyze and Revise Interview Schedule

JAN   FEB   MAR   APR   MAY   JUNE   JULY

Regardless of the size of a research project, at least one person within the organization should be designated as the "point person" for the research activity. This individual should be well versed on all the activities undertaken as part of the research endeavor; and thus, be able to field questions related to the research project.

Also, students should keep their thesis/dissertation chair current about developments related to data-collection efforts. If you are a student researcher conducting a program evaluation, then some basics about your project should also be shared with the staff working in your academic department.

In closing, find out how these different entities desire to be kept updated or briefed about the research project. Updates can be of a formal nature (a one-page summary) or given during informal meetings. Likewise, it is important to figure out how often these updates are needed.

Your Research

1. Make a comprehensive list of all the equipment (cameras, laptops, phones, software, etc.) and supplies (printed materials, etc.) you will need in order to carry out your study. Determine how and when you will acquire everything. Prepare a check-off list.
2. Will travel arrangements need to be made?

3. Who will be on your research team? What are their responsibilities? Who will serve as your "point" person?

4. Will you need to hire data-collection field workers? If so, how will you recruit and train them? What agency-required "human resources" paperwork and requirements will you need to adhere to in hiring extra research staff?

5. If more than one person will be involved in implementing your study, prepare a person-loading chart for each team member. Likewise, draft a Gantt chart for each major task associated with your research project

6. What data-verification steps will you adopt?

Review and Discussion Questions . . . What have you learned about preparing for data-collection?

1. Why is this seemingly easy step "Preparing for Data-Collection" so important to the research project?

2. What are some of the pieces of equipment and/or supplies that should be inventoried prior to data-collection?

3. Name at least two details that should be practiced when *proofreading*.

4. Why might it be useful to hire *indigenous* field workers to collect data?

5. Identify two things that are ruled out as part of a *data-verification check*.

6. Who typically are key players on a *research team*?

7. What is the difference between a *person-loading chart* and a *Gantt chart*?

Exercises

1. Go to the Resource Center at the Corporation for National and Community Services' Web site at http://nationalserviceresources.org. In the search box type, "A User's Guide for National Service Programs." Under the table of contents, click on "Data-Collection" and scroll down until you reach, "Step 4 Training Your Data Collectors." Identify three tips you learned about training data collectors.

2. Go to the American Association for Public Opinion Research's Web page (at www.aapor.org) and open up "Survey Methods", click on "Best Practices," then click on "Best Practices for Survey and Public Opinion Research"
    A. Read the following short passages, "Train Interviewers Carefully on Interviewing Techniques and the Subject Matter of the Survey" and "Maximize Cooperation or Response Rates within the Limits of Ethical Treatment of Human Subjects."
    B. Regarding the "Train Interviews" passage, identify three topics that should be covered in interview training.
    C. Regarding the "Maximize Cooperation" passage, identify:
        i. Three procedures to stimulate cooperation or participation in an interview.
        ii. Three strategies to deal with non-respondents and refusals? Do you agree with these strategies, why or why not?

3. Go to the American Association for Public Opinion Research's Web page (at www.aapor.org) and open up "Survey Methods", click on "Best Practices," then click on "Interviewer Falsification in Survey Research: Current Best Methods for Prevention, Detection and Repair of its Effects."

   A. What is **_interviewer falsification?_** Is there a continuum of severity of falsification?
   B. Identify five ways that organizations can assure data integrity in survey research.
   C. What are three things an organization can do to prevent interviewer falsification?
   D. What are five effective ways of detecting falsification?
   E. What are two effective actions to take when there is evidence of falsification?

An important step in research is preparing for data-collection. This entails getting all the materials, supplies, and equipment needed to collect data all lined up: recruiting, hiring and training staff, and making plans for managing the research team. Canal in "Little Venice," London, England. *Copyright © 2008 Carol Cutler Riddick*

STEP 14A: Analyze Quantitative Data

Levels of Numerical Measurement
Nominal Data
Ordinal Data
Interval Data
Ratio Data
Putting It All Together

Describing Numerical Information
Frequency Distributions
Rates, Ratios, Proportions, and Percentages
Measures of Central Tendency
    Mean
    Median
    Mode
Measures of Variability
    Range
    Standard Deviation
Selecting the "Best" Descriptive Statistic

Analyzing Relationships

Analyzing Differences

Statistical Software

Statistics can be made to prove anything—even the truth.
Author Unknown

Analysis of information does not happen in a vacuum between collecting data and interpreting it. In fact, thinking about how the data analysis might be carried out should be an integral part of the initial study design process. Otherwise you could end up with a mish-mash of information, which no analysis procedure can redeem (Robson, 2002).

Information that is initially gathered from interviews, questionnaires, case study notes, field observation journals, rating forms, and the like is not typically organized. Ordering and then analyzing such information is necessary because, generally speaking, data in their "raw" form do not speak for themselves.

When it gets down to it, the information that is gathered or measured in research is in one of two forms. First, there is **numerical data,** meaning information presented as numbers. Examples of numerical data include:

- Number of participants in an adult fitness program.
- Percentage of the black diamond ski trail users who prefer longer operating hours.
- Participants' accuracy of shot scores following a basketball clinic.

Information can also be presented in **non-numerical** or text form. Illustrations of non-numerical data are:

- Descriptive adjectives used by aquatics supervisors to describe lifeguards' performances.
- Ideas for new services voiced by infrequent health club users.
- Hand written notes of an observation of outdoor adventure leaders during a mountain climbing expedition.

This chapter focuses on making sense of numerical information, or **quantitative analysis.** The next chapter will examine how to handle non-numerical information collected in the research process, or **qualitative analysis.**

A vast extended family of quantitative data-analysis tools exists. This chapter will focus primarily on the more popular univariate statistics that are used to handle quantitative data. **Univariate statistics** focus on one variable at a time and are descriptive statistics that include such things as frequency distributions, proportions, ratios, rates, measures of central tendency, and measures of variability. Additionally, towards the end of the chapter, you will also be introduced to some **bivariate statistics,** meaning some of the statistical tools used to examine relationships and differences between two variables. Finally, we will round the chapter out by presenting some thoughts about computer statistical software.

→ Focusing on 2 variables

A forewarning is in order before we proceed. Please recognize that in this as well as the following chapter, we are only able to introduce you to a small selection of all the statistical tools available. Thus, we recommend that your professional preparation include a course in statistics, and/or that you ask for help from a consultant when analyzing data from your studies.

Levels of Numerical Measurement

In order to select the appropriate statistical tool, you first must know the level of numerical measurement that was used. Whenever a variable is measured four *levels of measurement* are used: nominal, ordinal, interval, and ratio.

As shown in Figure 1, the measurement levels can be ordered in a hierarchy according to the amount of specificity. This is because nominal and ordinal levels are categorical levels, which are more primitive measurements than interval and ratio levels, which are numerically continuous. If you read from top to bottom in Figure 1, you should see the precision increases when moving from nominal to ordinal levels and again transitioning between interval to ratio levels.

Figure 1. Levels of Measurement of Variables.

Level of Measurement	Defined	Example	Amount of Precision
Nominal	Categorical	Males, females Demographics	Least meticulous; no math can be used
Ordinal	Nominal with rank order	1st, 2nd, 3rd place finishers in a track meet	More meticulous than nominal yet no math can be used
Interval	Ordinal with equal distances between units of measurement	Water temperature	More meticulous than ordinal; math can be applied—yet because of a meaningless zero, ratios cannot be calculated
Ratio	Interval with meaningful zero	Minutes to swim first lap in race	Most meticulous; all math operations can be applied

Nominal Data

Nominal = categorical

The *nominal* level consists of measurement using labels or categorizes. The word nominal means "having to do with names" (Figure 2). Many demographic variables are measured nominally.

Every category gets a number!

Figure 2. Nominal Data Examples.

Variable	Nominal Measurement
Gender	Male or female
Ethnicity	African American, Asian, Hispanic, Caucasian, etc.
Residence	Rural, suburban, urban
Job titles	Department head, division head, supervisor, leader, assistant, volunteer.
Football player positions	Quarterback, lineman, linebacker, etc.

Since nominal data consist of discrete categorical distinctions rather than numerical distinctions, no arithmetic-based functions (such as addition and subtraction) can be applied. For instance, it would be inappropriate to "value" females with a score of "2" and males with a score of "1."

Ordinal Data

The *ordinal* measurement level ranks categorical information in terms of size or magnitude. As the word ordinal implies, data are arranged in rank order.

Examples of ordinal data are:

- A supervisor is asked to rank his playground leaders in terms of creativity. The resulting data indicate which leader the supervisor considers most creative, second most creative, and so on.
- The number of first-place, second-place, and third-place finishes for the swim club in the city meet.
- College class standing (first-year, sophomores, juniors, and seniors).

Like nominal data, ordinal data, while using numbers (1st, 2nd, 3rd, etc.), cannot be worked mathematically. The numbers just measure relative magnitude, meaning something is more or less.

This mathematical limitation for both nominal and ordinal data is overcome with interval and ratio levels of measurement. Interval and ratio data can be treated mathematically.

Interval Data ex: ruler

Interval data have the rank-order characteristic of ordinal data yet go one step beyond ordinal data. That is, for interval data, the distance between the numbers are equal units of measurement. What does this mean? Look at a ruler. A one-inch interval is the same size at every location on the ruler, so that the distance between two inches and four inches is equal to the distance between seven inches and nine inches. Examples of interval data are water temperature and air temperature.

Interval data provide a more highly refined level of measurement than nominal and ordinal, yet interval data also have a limitation. That is, a ratio cannot be determined with interval data because the zero point is arbitrary. While equal intervals between numbers reflect equal differences in magnitude, the interval level of measurement does not have an absolute zero point, or an absence of the quality being measured. For instance, zero degrees Fahrenheit for water temperature certainly doesn't mean you will feel an absence of temperature when you jump in! Guess you'd be ice skating!

It needs to be pointed out that when applying statistical procedures, some people wind up treating ordinal data as interval data. Admittedly, this practice has both proponents and critics (Case 1).

Case 1. Nearly Interval?

Researchers disagree about whether certain widely used measures, such as an attitude questionnaire, meet interval or ordinal data requirements. For example, suppose you ask respondents how much they favor an admission fee increase for the public pool. The following answer categories are used: "Strongly Agree," "Agree," "Neither Agree nor Disagree," "Disagree," "Strongly Disagree." Are these possible answers an example of ordinal or interval data? To be honest, in similar situations, some researchers treat the provided answers as an interval measurement level and then go on to use statistical tools that require interval data. Contrastingly, others consider these answers as exemplifying ordinal data and consequently turn to statistical tools that require an ordinal level of measurement. What do you think? Is this type of scale ordinal, interval, or "nearly interval?"

Ratio Data

The *ratio* level is the highest measurement level. This is because ratio data are defined as having a rank order, with equal units of measurement, and an absolute zero. You can think of ratio data as interval data but with the added characteristic of an absolute zero point.

An example of ratio data is annual salary. The difference between a yearly salary of $25,000 and $35,000 is the same as the difference between $90,000 and $100,000. Further, an annual salary of $0 is truly an absence of salary. This means that for information collected as ratio data we can apply mathematical operations, such as the salary of $100,000 is twice that of a salary of $50,000.

Putting It All Together

Knowing the level of numerical information measured is more than a textbook distinction. As discussed in the introduction to this chapter, the level of measurement directs the selection of descriptive statistics. As well, the level of numerical information collected has profound implications when testing hypotheses. In other words, the type of information collected for both the independent variable and dependent variable (Step 4), influences which statistical tests for hypotheses should be used.

Often, in the real world, researchers use several levels of numerical information in the same study. For example, in Case 2 below, investigators measured variables in the nominal, ordinal, and ratio levels.

Case 2. Example of Three Levels of Measurement Used in a Study.

> Shores, K., & Scott, D. (2005). Leisure constraints among military wives. *Journal of Park and Recreation Administration, 23,* 1-24.
>
> "Military wives" comprise a segment of the population who face all of the challenges of traditional family life as well as those associated with the hardships of military life. This study sought to understand the constraints military wives experience in leisure. Questionnaires were completed by 716 military wives living at the Fort Hood Military Housing Post in Texas. The questionnaire measured numerous variables that could help explain how military wives negotiate their lives in order to experience leisure. Variables used in the study were measured in terms of three of the levels of measurement. For example,
>
> • Wives' employment situation was measured using a nominal level of measurement (employed full-time, employed part-time, or homemaker).
> • Husband's military rank was measured using an ordinal level of measurement [using the Enlisted (E) or Officer (O) ranks of E1-E3, E4-E6, E7-E9, O1-O3, O4 or greater].
> • Age of youngest child living at home was measured using a ratio level of measurement.

Describing Numerical Information

Once the level of measurement used for a variable is understood, a decision can be made regarding the best way to describe the information. Describing main features of organizations, programs, clients, staff, etc. can be accomplished by selecting from a menu of descriptive statistics (Case 3). *Descriptive statistics* describe the variables that have been measured in a quantitative study.

Case 3. Choosing a Descriptive Statistic.

> Suppose you found yourself needing to describe a sample of children attending a summer camp serving kids with asthma. The following information is collected:
>
> • Age (ratio data).
> • Gender (nominal data).
> • Number of seasons attending the camp (ratio data).
> • Severity of asthmatic condition (ordinal data or mild, moderate, or severe).
>
> The first data-analysis activity is to describe these data. In other words, you need to choose and calculate descriptive statistics. Most likely you will focus on:
>
> • The most typical characteristics of the campers.
> • How diverse the campers are from each other.

Descriptive statistics about age, skill level, interest, etc. can be used to report on who participates in current programs, as well as to help plan future programs. *Copyright © 2008 Ruth V. Russell*

Frequency Distributions

The first descriptive statistical analysis tool, frequency distribution, gives a broad and general overview of the data that have been collected about a sample. With quantitative studies, you usually end up with pages of numerical information. The immediate analysis task is to organize these numbers into some understandable form so that any trends in the data can be seen easily. This is the function of frequency distributions.

A *frequency distribution* describes how data are distributed, meaning it is an arrangement of the values of a variable. A frequency distribution simply lists the variables and the number of responses or scores that correspond to it. A frequency distribution also shows us the location of any individual response relative to all the other ones in the data set.

Figure 3 provides an illustration of a frequency distribution. As you can see, now that the information is organized it becomes easier to draw conclusions. For example, do you notice a trend between the number of years in the basketball program and interest in continued participation in basketball programs?

Figure 3. Example of a Frequency Distribution.

Respondent Number	Age	Gender	Number of Years Participated in Basketball Program	Interest Level to Continue in Basketball Program
1	13	Female	2	Very Interested
2	15	Female	4	Some Interest
3	15	Female	1	Very Interested
4	14	Female	5	Not Interested
5	16	Female	4	Some Interest
6	12	Male	2	Very Interested
7	13	Male	3	Some Interest
8	15	Male	6	Not Interested
9	14	Male	1	Very Interested
10	13	Male	5	Not Interested

Often, frequency distributions are visually summarized in tables and graphs. These two presentation tools are discussed in Step 15.

Rates, Ratios, Proportions, and Percentages

Another way to describe collected information is to determine *relative comparisons.* Rates, ratios, and proportions are the most typical relative comparisons that are used. For example, reporting that the graduation rate for college student-athletes is 6.6 gives us a comparison of the graduation success of student-athletes relative to all students at the college, whose rate is 5.2. What do 6.6 and 5.2 mean? These descriptors are called rates; let's explore them more.

First, a *rate* is the frequency of occurrence of a particular outcome. Rates are calculated by dividing the actual number of occurrences by the number of possible occurrences (Case 4).

Case 4. Graduation Rate for Student-Athletes.

Let's suppose that for a college, the number of graduating student-athletes this year equaled 64. This number, 64, is the number of actual occurrences. Further, let's suppose that the total number of student-athletes who started college four years ago was 97. This is the number of possible occurrences. So, to calculate the graduation rate for student-athletes, the actual occurrences are divided by the possible occurrences. In this example, the rate is 64 divided by 97 = .66. This means .66th of a person graduated. Since it is hard to visualize this, the answer is usually multiplied by a "base." For example, suppose the base of 10 is chosen. Continuing the calculation using this base would result in .66 multiplied times 10 = 6.6. This means the graduation rate of student-athletes is 6.6 per 10 student-athletes.

Another relative comparison that can be used to describe information is a ratio. A *ratio* descriptive statistic is a simple comparison of the frequency of one response with that of another. To determine a ratio the elements in one response set (A) are compared to the elements in another response set (B) (Case 5).

Case 5. Outpatient Activity Therapy Ratio.

Suppose a comparison is wanted between reasons people miss outpatient activity therapy. Reviewing records, it is learned that 23 individuals missed therapy sessions last month because of "Not Being Able to Get Off Work;" whereas 10 participants missed sessions because they "Simply Forgot." The ratio of the "Can't-get-off-work reason (A)" to the "Forgetting reason (B)" is 23 divided by 10 = 2.3. Thus, the ratio of missing outpatient activity therapy due to "Work" versus "Forgetting" is 2.3. This means that for every one patient who missed the sessions because he or she forgot, 2.3 patients missed because they could not get off work.

Finally, a **proportion** is a ratio to the total. Proportions are used to compare the frequency of a response with the total frequency (Case 6).

Case 6. Proportion of Playground Injuries Due to Falls.

Suppose there is a need to determine the proportion of playground injuries due to falls from the play equipment. Let's assume it is known the total number of playground injuries is 68, with 41 of these injuries due to falls from the play apparatus and the other 27 due to other reasons. To determine the proportion of injuries due to falls from the apparatus you divide 41 by 68 = .60. Thus, the proportion of injuries due to apparatus falls is .60.

If a proportion is multiplied by 100 it is converted into a **percentage.** Percentages are the most commonly reported form of proportions. Continuing with the example from Case 6 above, dealing with playground injuries due to falls from play equipment, the percentage is .60 x 100 = 60%. Thus, 60% of playground injuries were caused by falls from the equipment.

Something to Remember!

- **Rate** = # of actual occurrences divided by # of possible occurrences, then multiplied by a base.
- **Ratio** of A to B = A is divided by B.
- **Proportion** = A divided by the sum of A + B.
- **Percentage** = A divided by the sum of A + B multiplied by 100.

Measures of Central Tendency

Another way to describe the information that's been collected in a study is to determine its "center." This calls for **measures of central tendency,** meaning a frequency distribution's center can be described with a single indicator. Let's discuss the three most commonly used tools for describing the center of data: mean, median, and mode.

Mean. The **mean** is an arithmetic average and is only appropriate for interval and ratio data. It is calculated by adding up all the scores in the distribution and dividing the answer by the number of scores (Case 7).

Case 7. The Mean Miles Jogged.

Suppose the number of miles jogged per week for four participants in our personal training program is three, seven, four, and six, respectively. The mean, then, is the total number of miles jogged by the four individuals divided by the total number of joggers. Breaking down the math to calculate the mean:

> Step 1 = 3 + 7 + 4 + 6 = 20.
> Step 2 = 20 divided by 4 = 5.

The mean is five miles jogged per week. You can think of it this way: the mean is the number of miles participants in our personal training program would jog per week if the miles were distributed equally among them. In other words, if all persons in the program were participating equally, they'd each jog five miles.

Median. The **median** is another descriptive tool for determining the centrality of information. It requires ratio, interval, or ordinal data. The median is defined as the actual middle value; half of the sample values will be larger than the median value and half will be smaller. The median, in other words, is the score that divides a frequency distribution exactly in half. To determine the median, the raw data are first arranged into ascending order, and then the value at the middle location is identified (Case 8).

Case 8. Calculating the Median With Odd Number of Scores.

Suppose the annual staff performance scores given by a YMCA manager are known. The rating scale was based on 0 to 25, with 25 representing perfect performance. To determine the median staff performance score, all the scores are first arranged in ascending order. Let's suppose these performance scores are:

5   7   8   8   8   9   12   15   17   19   23

By studying this ordered list of all scores it can be seen that the median performance score is 9. This is the middle score; it leaves the same number of values (or 5) to the left of it as to the right. This means that one-half of the staff had scores that are worse than a score of 9 and one-half of the staff had a better score than 9.

In the staff performance example in Case 8, there are 11 scores, so finding the middle position in the distribution is straightforward. Thus, the median can easily be visually determined. In situations where there are a large number of scores and/or an even number of scores, the median can be determined mathematically by first determining its position. To calculate where the median is positioned for an odd number of scores you total the number of scores, add "1" then divide by "2." If the distribution has an even number of scores, the median position is the average of the middle two positions (Case 9).

Case 9. Calculating the Median with Even Number of Scores.

Suppose we have the following 12 staff performance scores:

5   7   8   8   8   9   11   12   15   17   19   23

To calculate the median for the above scores you would:

Step 1 = Determine the number of scores, or 12.

Step 2 = Add "1" to the number of scores, or 12 + 1 = 13 .

Step 3 = Divide Step 2 answer by 2, or 13 divided by 2 = 6.5. This means the median score is at the 6.5th position in the array of numbers, or halfway between the scores of 9 and 11 in this case.

Step 4 = Calculate the mean position by adding 9 + 11 = 20, then divide by 2 = 10. This means the score of 10 divides the distribution exactly in half.

Mode. Finally, the mode is a measure of central tendency that is appropriate for all levels of measurement. The ***mode*** is defined as the most common response in a distribution. It is the most popular or most frequently occurring response category. It is what is typical for the distribution. In Case 9, for example, the mode equals 8. This score occurs more frequently than any other score.

Seems simple enough. But, be careful! The mode is always a score or category, not a frequency. For example, what is the mode for the distribution in Figure 4? Is it 22? No. Why not? Remember, 22 is a frequency. The mode in this distribution is the age of 20 because it is the most frequently occurring response in the distribution.

Figure 4. Age Distribution of Midnight Basketball Players, Spring 2007.

Player's Age	Number or Frequency
17	4
18	8
19	10
20	22
21	15
22	3
23	3
24	1

Something to Remember!

The three most popular measures of central tendency are mean, median, and mode. Each defines a distribution's center differently.

Mean = sum of X

          N

Median = the actual middle score in an ordered distribution

Mode = the most common response

Measures of Variability

The final descriptive statistical tools we'll discuss summarize the dispersion or spread of the individual responses in the data. These tools are known as measures of variability. *Measures of variability* provide a description of the degree to which responses are either close to or far from each other (Case 10).

Case 10. Illustration of the Concept of Variability.

Suppose the effect of a new pet-friendly policy at a resort is being studied. Before instituting the policy, information on how long guests stay in a single visit is collected. For the seven guests sampled, the number of nights they stayed at the resort was:

1, 2, 2, 2, 3, 3, 5

A new, pet-friendly policy is instituted. Small pet guests are now permitted. With payment of a $50 cleaning fee, human guests can have their pets stay with them in the room. Now, for a sample of seven guests, the number of nights stayed at the resort was:

1, 3, 5, 5, 7, 7, 10

After reviewing the two sets of data, a quick conclusion may be that guests tended to stay more nights after the pet-friendly policy was instituted. But, what else do the two data sets describe? Do the two data sets have the same "spread" of nights stayed? Notice that the distribution of number of nights stayed at the resort after the new pet-friendly policy was initiated is more spread-out. In other words, there is more variability in the data. Thus, it could be concluded that there is less variability in the number of nights stayed before the new policy was implemented relative to what occurred after the policy was implemented.

There are several ways of describing variability of scores with a single number. Two popular measures are the range and the standard deviation.

Range. The **range** can be calculated two ways. One way is the distance between the highest score and the lowest score in a distribution. The other way to calculate the range is to subtract the smaller score from the larger.

Thus, the range for nights stayed at the resort before the pet-friendly policy is 5-1, or 4. And for after the pet-friendly policy, the range of nights stayed is 10 -1, or 9. These single numbers (4 and 9) depict the spread of scores. Remember, the higher the range, the more dispersion is occurring in the sample.

Something to Remember!

To calculate the **range**, use one of the following formulas:

Range = X_1 (maximum score in the array of numbers) <u>to</u> X_2 (minimum score in the array of numbers)
OR
X_1 (maximum score in the array of numbers) <u>minus</u> X_2 (minimum score in the array of numbers).

A larger range indicates more variability, meaning that more of the responses differ from each other.

Nevertheless, the range can be problematic. It does a good job of showing the distance between the two most extreme values in the distribution, but ignores all the values in between. For example, suppose the nights stayed by a sample of resort guests are: 1, 1, 2, 2, 2, 2, 10. The range of 10-1 or 9 is equal to the range found with the new pet policy cited in Case 10. But the values in the two distributions are spread differently from each other and the range does not depict this.

Standard deviation. To account for the dispersion of all the scores in a distribution, a standard deviation is calculated. This is perhaps the most typically used measure of variability in research. The **standard deviation (SD)** uses the mean of the distribution as a reference point and measures dispersion between each score and that point. In short, the standard deviation can be thought of as the average distance from the mean.

When the *SD* is equal to 0, there is absolutely no spread of the scores (e.g., 2, 2, 2, 2, and 2). As the size of the standard deviation increases, the spread of scores around the mean increases.

While most calculators have a function for determining the standard deviation, following along with the hand calculation of a standard deviation shows exactly how it works (Case 11). These steps are:

1. Calculate the mean.
2. Subtract the mean value from each score. This is called the **deviation score.**
3. Square each of these deviation scores.
4. Add these squared deviation scores together.
5. Divide this sum by *N*-1 (where *N* represents the number of responses).
6. Take the square-root of this answer (Step 5 above).

Case 11. Calculation of the Standard Deviation for Nights Stayed at the Resort After the Pet-Friendly Policy.

Let's illustrate these steps to calculating the standard deviation with the distribution of nights stayed at the resort after instituting the pet-friendly policy:

1, 3, 5, 5, 7, 7, 10

1. Calculate the **mean:** 1 + 3 + 5 + 5 + 7 + 7 + 10 divided by 7 = 5.4 nights.
2. Calculate the **deviation score:** this is how far each value is from the mean (Figure 5, Column 3).
3. Square each deviation score: see Figure 5, Column 4.
4. Sum all the squared deviation scores: 19.4 + 5.8 + .2 + .2 + 2.6 + 2.6 + 21.2 = 52.
5. Divide the sum of the squared deviation scores by $N-1$: 52 divided by 6 (or the 7 responses minus 1) which equals 8.7.
6. Take the square root of the answer to Step 5: the square root of 8.7 = 2.9. Thus, 2.9 is the standard deviation for the nights stayed at the resort after the pet policy change.

Figure 5. Standard Deviation Calculations for Case 11.

Guest's Name	# of Nights Stayed	Deviation Score	Squared Deviation Score
Johnson	1	4.4 (5.4-1)	19.4
Allen	3	2.4 (5.4-3)	5.8
Cutler	5	.4 (5.4-5)	.2
Ramos	5	.4 (5.4-5)	.2
Oliver	7	-1.6 (5.4-7)	2.6
Smith	7	-1.6 (5.4-7)	2.6
Martin	10	-4.6 (5.4-10)	21.2

What does a standard deviation of 2.9 represent? Think of the standard deviation value as describing the typical distance of each night's stayed value from the mean of the distribution. That is, the average difference between individual guest values and the average for the sample is almost 3 nights.

Now you try it. Calculate the standard deviation for the number of nights stayed before the pet-friendly policy at the resort using the data from Case 10 above. Why should the answer you get be smaller than 2.9?

Something to Remember!

The formula for *standard deviation* is:

Square root of the sum of squared deviation scores divided by N-1.

Selecting the "Best" Descriptive Statistic

Now that you understand a variety of ways of describing numerical data, how do you decide which measure to use? The first answer is that it depends on your objective. Do you want to know the proportion, rate, ratio, or percentage? Or do you want to analyze the distribution's center or its spread?

The second consideration is the level of measurement that was used. Additional factors to consider, when dealing with measures of central tendency, are whether or not there are extreme scores and the sample size. Figure 6 summarizes these various considerations.

Figure 6. Which Descriptive Statistic is Best?

Descriptive Statistic	Objective	Level of Measurement Required	Comments
Rate, ratio, proportion, percentage	Describes relative comparisons	Interval or ratio	Typically understood by non-researchers
Mean	Describes the distribution center as an average of all values	Interval or ratio	Most precise measure of centrality, yet not useful when distribution has extreme scores
Median	Describes the distribution center as the middle value	Ordinal, interval or ratio	Less precise than mean, more precise than mode; useful when distribution in a small sample has extreme scores
Mode	Describes the distribution center as the most frequently occurring value	Nominal, ordinal, interval, or ratio	Least precise measure of centrality, yet the only choice for nominal data; useful when distribution in large sample has extreme scores
Range	Describes the spread of the distribution between the highest and lowest values	Ordinal, interval, or ratio	When want a simple indicator of variability; cannot be used with nominal data
Standard Deviation	Describes the spread of the distribution as the average distance of every value from the mean	Interval or ratio	Most precise measure of variability, yet not useful when distribution has extreme scores

Analyzing Relationships

Up to this point, every descriptive statistic that has been discussed applies to only one variable at a time. The relative comparison, center, or spread of individual variables such as age, staff performance scores, and jogged miles has been described. Now we turn our attention to another way of describing information, but this time it is about examining the relationships and differences between two variables. We have now entered the realm of *bivariate statistics.*

For example, a coach for a boys' basketball team is a firm believer that the more the boys practice, the more games they will win. So he calls lots of team practices. Is this true? Is there a relationship between practice and winning? Further, is the relationship such that more practice means more winning? Or, can we imagine the relationship going the other way—more practice means less winning?

Another kind of descriptive statistic that people are often interested in is the relationship between variables. For instance, one might be curious in finding out how the value of one variable (winning) changes when the value of another variable (practice) changes. The relationship between these two variables can be determined by computing a simple correlation coefficient.

A *correlation coefficient* is a numerical index that reflects the relationship between two variables. Actually, its formal name is the *Pearson product-moment correlation coefficient,* after its inventor, Karl Pearson (Salkind, 2002). The symbol "*r*" is used to denote this statistic.

Used only on variables in either the interval or ratio scale, the possible value of *r* ranges between −1 and +1. Correlation values tell you two things about the relationship. First, the positive and negative signs indicate whether variables tend to move in the same or opposite directions when they change. If variables change in the same direction, it is called a *positive correlation.* If variables change in opposite directions, it is called a *negative correlation.* As you can see from Figure 7, a negative correlation is not necessarily bad and a positive correlation is not necessarily good.

Figure 7. Directions of Relationships Between Variables.

What Happens to the Variables	Example	Direction of Correlation	Value
As one variable increases, second variable increases	The more you practice the more you win	Positive	.00 to +1.00
As one variable decreases, second variable decreases	The less you practice the less you win	Positive	.00 to +1.00
As one variable increases, second variable decreases	The more you practice the less you win	Negative	-1.00 to .00

What Happens to the Variables	Example	Direction of Correlation	Value
As one variable decreases, second variable increases	The less you practice the more you win	Negative	-1.00 to .00

The second thing the correlation coefficient value tells you is the *strength of the relationship*. The larger the correlation coefficient value, the stronger the relationship. That is, the closer the value is to 1.00 (known as a *perfect* relationship), the stronger the relationship. So, a correlation of -.70 is stronger than a correlation of +.50, because .70 is closer to 1.00.

A frequently made mistake with interpreting correlation coefficient values is the direction of the relationship is confused with the strength of the relationship. The rule is, when studying the direction of the relationship depicted in the coefficient value, pay attention to the plus or minus signs and ignore the actual number. Conversely, when studying the strength of the relationship depicted in the coefficient value, pay attention to the number and ignore the plus or minus signs.

So, if a computed correlation coefficient for the relationship between the amount of practice and winning basketball games is .22, it indicates that the relationship is in the positive direction and is weak. In other words, more practice makes for more winning only minimally. The relationship is positive, because the sign is (an implied) plus, and it is weak, because .22 is quite a long way away from 1.00.

Or, let's suppose a computed correlation between practicing and winning at basketball is -.73. This answer indicates that the relationship is in the negative direction, yet it is a strong relationship. That is, more practice pretty much means losing more games.

Now, we know you're asking, "How close to 1.00 does the value of the coefficient need to be to say it is a strong relationship?" There is a wide range of opinions on what constitutes a strong relationship! We prefer a fairly conservative approach as presented in Figure 8.

Figure 8. Interpreting the Strength of a Correlation Coefficient.[1]

Size of the coefficient	Interpretation
.8 to 1.0	Very strong
.6 to .8	Strong
.4 to .6	Moderate
.2 to .4	Weak
0 to .2	No relationship

[1] Adapted from Salkind (2002).

There is a much more precise way to interpret the correlation coefficient; namely compute the coefficient of determination. The **coefficient of determination** is expressed as a percentage. The percentage tells us the amount of change in one variable that is accounted for by the change in the other variable.

The coefficient of determination is computed simply by squaring the correlation coefficient. For example, if the correlation coefficient between practice and winning is equal to -.73 (a strong negative relationship), then the coefficient of determination would be calculated as follows:

Step 1 = .73 times .73 = .53.
Step 2 = .53 multiplied by 100 = equals 53%.

This means 53% of the basketball games lost can be explained by too much practice. Of course this also means that 47% of the losses are explained by something other than practicing! What we don't know is what things, other than practice, are influencing the team's losing record.

Something to Remember!

When dealing with correlation coefficients, recall the:

- Absolute value of the coefficient reflects the strength of the relationship.
- Sign attached to the value of the coefficient reflects the direction of the relationship.
- Coefficient of determination tells you how much change in the dependent variable is accounted for by change in the independent variable.

As you'll learn a bit later in this chapter, computer software is available to calculate the correlation coefficient (and the coefficient of determination), so we don't explain how to do this by hand here. If you, however, take an introductory statistics course, you will no doubt learn the computational steps for calculating the correlation coefficient.

Analyzing Differences

Finally, let's spend a bit of time with a concept that probably causes the most confusion in statistics. This is the concept of statistical significance. Above all, just remember that **statistical significance** is interested in differences between variables. To determine differences between variables we call up the help of inferential statistics.

Let's suppose we are interested in knowing if a high-risk rock-climbing program makes a difference in the self-confidence of participants. The research question is, "Are rock-climbing people different in their self-confidence than people who don't rock climb?"

Information is then collected about the self-confidence of both people in our rock-climbing program and people not in the program. Through the tools of inferential statistics, the self-confidence levels in these two groups is compared. If the statistic suggests that rock climbing does make a difference in self-confidence, then statistical significance will be present. Based on this, it can be "inferred" that the difference in self-confidence discovered in the study's rock-climbing sample would also be the case for the population of all rock climbers.

Let's define all this a bit more. First, ***statistical significance*** means the difference found between variables in the sample is greater than what would have been expected by chance alone. Second, think of ***inferential statistics*** as a big family of tools that help us determine statistical significance. Inferential statistical tools enable us to claim that differences between variables measured in samples can be estimated to exist in the population from which the sample was drawn. See Case 12 for some introductory insights of how this works.

Case 12. Anatomy of Statistical Significance for a Study.

Continuing with the illustration of how a rock-climbing program may affect self-confidence, let's dissect statistical significance.

1. The researcher selects a representative group of adolescents who are interested in learning how to rock climb.
2. A self-confidence questionnaire is administered to everyone in the group to see if there are any differences at the onset.
3. The researcher randomly divides the group in half, forming two samples.
4. The first sample of adolescents participates in a two-week rock-climbing program. The second sample of adolescents does not participate in the program.
5. After the program the self-confidence questionnaire is again administered to all adolescents.
6. A mean self-confidence score is calculated for each sample.
7. An inferential statistical test is applied to the two means to determine whether or not the self-confidence difference between the two groups is a result of chance (meaning some factor other than the rock-climbing experience), or the result of statistically significant, rock-climbing differences.
8. A conclusion is reached that the differences found/not found can be applied to the population of all adolescents.

Inferential statistics allow decisions about populations based on information about samples. (You can review populations and samples in Step 6.) There are many inferential statistical tools that help us make decisions about statistical significance, and computer software is certainly a big help in doing the actual calculations. But what's very important for you to master on your own is which tool is best for which research question. For example, such inferential statistics as the t-test, ANOVA, and chi-square are used in specific situations according to type of numerical information collected, the number of groups, and how many times the samples are measured, etc. As reminder, and at the risk of sounding like a broken record, you need to take a statistics course or consult someone knowledgeable in statistics to know how to proceed.

Statistical Software

As you probably know, computers can be used to analyze quantitative data. Many leisure service organizations, and all colleges and universities, have statistical software packages available that will carry out the calculations of descriptive and inferential statistics. For example, *SYSTAT,*

Minitab, and *SAS* are commonly used statistical packages. *SPSS for Windows* is probably the most powerful and widely used. And, it's easy! The menu-driven program asks you to type in the data, and then hit a key for the statistical test you want. It takes only seconds.

So we want to stress that undertaking statistical analyses and producing frequency distributions, measures of central tendency, measures of variability, coefficients of relationship, and inferential statistical tests are not, in themselves, that important. After all, a computer can do it! The parts that require human intelligence are being able to: (1) Choose the correct statistical tool for the research situation; and, (2) Understand what the numbers actually mean when the results are produced. We've tried to stress these two skills in this chapter.

Idea . . . For Assessing My Knowledge of Statistics and Empowering Myself.

Well, now we come to the moment of reckoning. Perhaps you have read this chapter with dread, and your self-talk declares, "I can't do this stuff." Or maybe you've avoided taking a statistics class because you are sure you'll fail it. Or worse, you've avoided learning about research because you're worried it includes statistics. Take heart! We're here to tell you that of all the quantitative "sciences," statistics is the easiest and most fun! And it is tremendously useful to determining what the evaluation information you collected means. So, get a grip, and ask yourself these questions:

1. When I read statistics in a research journal article, I usually do this _____. When I read statistics in a popular magazine or newspaper article, I usually do this _____. Is there a difference between your responses? Why?
2. What can I do today to make progress in understanding and using statistics in my future professional work?
3. What can I do next semester to make progress in understanding and using statistics in my future professional work?
4. In all honesty, what kinds of trouble would the leisure service professions be in if statistics weren't wisely used?

Your Research

1. Make a list of the variables about which you have collected quantitative information for your study.
2. For each variable in your list, determine the level of measurement. That is, are the data nominal, ordinal, interval, and/or ratio?
3. What sort of descriptive "story" would you like to be able to tell about your measured variables?
4. What descriptive statistics should you use to tell these stories? That is, for each quantitatively measured variable:
    A. Create a frequency distribution.
    B. Calculate a rate, ratio, proportion, and/or percentage, as appropriate.
    C. Calculate a measure of central tendency.
    D. Calculate a measure of variability.
5. Explain why you chose the statistical tools you did for Question 4 above.

6. What relationships and/or differences might be interesting to determine for your data? What type of statistics will help you determine these?

Review & Discussion Questions . . . What have you learned about analyzing quantitative data?

1. Name and define the four *levels of numerical information.*
2. What is a *frequency distribution*? How can it help describe numerical information?
3. What sort of *comparison* do rates, ratios, proportions, and percentages make?
4. How are the descriptions from calculating rates, ratios, proportions, and percentages different?
5. What sort of description do *measures of central tendency* provide?
6. How are the descriptions from calculating means, medians, and modes different?
7. What sort of description do *measures of variability* provide?
8. How are the descriptions for calculating ranges and standard deviations different?
9. What is the difference between *univariate* and *bivariate* statistics?
10. What does the *correlation coefficient* describe?
11. What is *inferential statistics*?
12. What does it mean when the result from a statistical test is statistically significant?

Exercises

1. Read Case 13 (immediately follows below). Determine what type of numerical data was used to report the sources of program funding.

Case 13. Type of Numerical Data Used.

Wilkins, N. (1997). Overtime is better than sudden death. *Parks and Recreation, 32,* 54-61.

The slogan "Overtime is Better Than Sudden Death" stretches across the gym walls in five Kansas City, Missouri, Night Hoops locations. In a world where connecting with youth is increasingly difficult, sports—basketball in particular— have become tools for reaching them. In Kansas City, the Mayor's Night Hoops program is not a panacea for preventing crime, but is a successful effort to relate to youth in a positive manner. The program is designed to expose youth in high-risk environments to new information and experiences. Through the program the lives of thousands of young people have been transformed by positive relationships with coaches and other members of their community. Approximately 160 young people participated in this summer activity it its initial year. Since then the program has expanded to five sites, serving more than 1,500 youth each year. As the program's reputation for results spread, community leaders began to get involved. Initially 80% of the Night Hoops program was funded by the Kansas City Parks and Recreation Department. The remaining funding was made up by private donations and grants from the state.

2. Following are actual data from a 2005 camper satisfaction survey conducted by a commercial nation-wide campground chain.

Camping Experience	Frequency (out of 438 total responses)
Overall experience was excellent	135
Would definitely return	151
Good value for the price	369
Clean campsite	295
Appealing recreational activities	421

A. What is the overall satisfaction with experience rate?
B. What is the ratio of "Would Definitely Return" to "Appealing Recreational Activities?"
C. What percentage of respondents consider the campground to be good value for the price?

3. Here are some made-up data about number of shore excursions a sample of passengers on a ship sailing the Panama Canal took during the two-week cruise.

$$2, 1, 0, 3, 3, 5, 2, 7, 4, 3, 2, 3, 4, 1, 6, 10, 3, 2, 3, 1, 3$$

A. Organize the data by creating a frequency distribution.
B. Calculate the mean, median, and mode for this distribution. Why are the answers to these measures of central tendency different or the same? Which measure is more "truthful" about the center of these data?

4. See if you understand measures of variability by going to the Web site at http://www.webster.edu/~woolflm/variability.html.
A. Select one of the four variability problems to work on.
B. Calculate both the range and the standard deviation (ignore the variance).
C. Check your answers by clicking on "Answer."

5. Following are some possible correlation coefficients. For each example, describe both the strength and direction of the relationships. And in which of the relationships is 85% of the change in one variable explained by the change in the second variable? What is this statistic called?
A. Number of years on the pro circuit and Masters Golf Tournament score in 2007, $r = .65$.
B. Body mass index score and self-esteem score, $r = -.35$.
C. Number of tennis players in the family and price willing to pay to join a private tennis club, $r = .15$.
D. Amount community annually spends on public recreation services and the community's quality of life index score, $r = .89$.
E. Number of years participating in Girl Scouts and number of truancy days in high school, $r = -.92$.

6. Copy a research journal article in your subject. Find the section of the article that reports the research results (usually called *Results*). By answering the following questions you should learn

something about yourself. Even though you may not feel that you've mastered the quantitative analysis tools reviewed in this chapter, you're probably impressed that you can at least recognize them!

    A. In the *Results* section, mark all the statistical procedures used to organize and analyze the data. How many of them can you identify?

    B. Was a mean or standard deviation reported?

    C. Was there a statistic that analyzed relationships between variables in the study?

    D. Did the researcher test for statistical significance?

7. Interview someone who uses statistics in his or her everyday work. It might be your instructor, a researcher who works for the recreation agency where you volunteer, a parent who is a market analyst for a company, a city planner, etc.

    A. Request that your interviewee explain the ways statistics are used in his/her work.

    B. What decisions do statistics help them make?

    C. Ask them to explain what they enjoy and don't enjoy about working with statistics.

    D. What have you learned about statistics from your interview?

The analysis of numerical data follows specific and prescribed statistical procedures that lead to deductively reasoned explanatory answers. Underpass, London, England. *Copyright © 2008 Carol Cutler Riddick*

STEP 14B: Analyze Qualitative Data

General Principles
Inductive Process
Cyclical Process

Managing Data
Expanded Accounts
Memos
Codes
Data Displays
   Matrices
   Networks
Computer Assistance

Making Tentative Conclusions
Strategies for Making Conclusions
   Clustering
   Subsuming Particulars into the General
   Counting
   Seeing Plausibility
   Making Metaphors
Holistic Understanding

Verifying Conclusions
Checking for Data Quality
   Representativeness
   Researcher Effects
Testing Explanations
   Replication of Findings
   Rival Explanations

Hamlet: Do you see yonder cloud that's almost in shape of a camel?
Polonius: By the mass, and 'tis like a camel, indeed.
Hamlet: Methink it is like a weasel.
Polonius: It is backed like a weasel.
Hamlet: Or like a whale?
Polonius: Very like a whale.
William Shakespeare, *Hamlet* (Act 3, Scene 2)

You'll remember that information gathered in research is based on either numbers or words. In the last chapter (Step 14A), ways of analyzing numerical information were discussed. Contrastingly, this chapter examines ways of analyzing information based on words.

In any research endeavor, raw data must be transformed into coherent, meaningful, and believable findings. Raw data produced from qualitative tools are more unstructured and unordered than the numerical data produced with quantitative tools. To help you practice the unordered nature of qualitative raw data, read Case 1 below and see if you can determine the two themes that *emerge* or surface. Since the answers are revealed in the last paragraph, cover this up before you begin reading.

Case 1. The "Unstructured" Nature of Qualitative Data.

Miller, J. (1996). *Female gang involvement in the Midwest: A two-city comparison.* Unpublished doctoral dissertation, University of Southern California, Los Angeles.

In-depth unstructured interviews were conducted with young women aged 13 to 18 who claimed affiliation with youth gangs in their communities. These interviews focused on the roles and activities of the young women in the gangs and the meanings they described as emerging from their gang affiliation. Following are some excerpts from different respondents taken from the interview transcripts (as reported in Miller & Glassner, 1997):

> "Well, I didn't get any respect at home. I wanted to get some love and respect from somebody somewhere else." (p. 107)

> "I didn't have no family . . . I had nothin' else." (p. 107)

> "Some of 'em are like me, don't have, don't really have a basic home or steady home to go to, you know, and they don't have as much love and respect in the home so they want to get it elsewhere. And, and, like we get, have family members in gangs or that were in gangs, stuff like that." (p. 107)

> "It was really, it was just normal life, the only difference was, is, that we had meetings." (p. 108)

> "[We] play cards, smoke bud, play dominoes, play video games. That's basically all we do is play. You would be surprised. This is a bunch of big kids." (p. 109)

What two themes surfaced from the interviews? If you identified that, among those interviewed, the two meanings emerging from the data were, "Gangs provide family" and "Gang members like to play" you've done a terrific job at your practice run in qualitative data analysis.

This chapter is organized into four major parts. First, a couple of general principles that should guide qualitative data analysis are reviewed. Second, pointers for managing data will be covered. Third, comments about making tentative conclusions will follow. And lastly, some ideas related to verifying conclusions will be discussed.

General Principles

There are many different ways to analyze qualitatively derived data. However, there are two general principles you should be aware of that govern all of these approaches. That is, it is important to remember that qualitative data analysis should be an inductive process as well as a cyclical process.

Inductive Process

Qualitative data analysis is primarily an inductive thinking process (recall Step 3). With an *inductive process*, patterns and relationships emerge from the data. That is, the idea behind an inductive analysis approach is to allow research insights to come to light from the study without being limited to pre-existing understandings or theories.

Contrastingly, as touched upon in Step 3, *quantitative data analysis* relies more on deductive thinking. With the *deductive process,* patterns and relationships are established before the study (usually in the form of hypotheses), and then data are analyzed to determine if there's support for these relationships.

The distinction between inductive and deductive thinking plays out in multiple ways in how qualitative and quantitative data are analyzed. Figure 1 compares these.

Figure 1. Differences Between Qualitative and Quantitative Data Analysis.[1]

Comparison Points	Differences Between
Conduct of analysis	• Quantitative analysis takes place at the end of data collection. • Qualitative analysis begins during data collection.
Treatment of raw data	• Quantitative analysis manipulates numbers, often to test hypotheses. • Qualitative analysis blends abstract concepts in the form of words often to explain or illustrate.

Comparison Points	Differences Between
Order of analysis	• Quantitative analysis is a linear procedure. • Qualitative analysis is a circular, iterative procedure.

[1] Adapted from Gratton and Jones (2004).

Cyclical Process

Basically, the qualitative data analysis process is a series of cyclical phases that moves among three areas (Figure 2). That is, data analysis moves back and forth between collecting and managing data and casting and recasting tentative conclusions. Gradually, more advanced levels of synthesis are achieved after each cycle.

Figure 2. The Cyclical Qualitative Data-Analysis Process.[2]

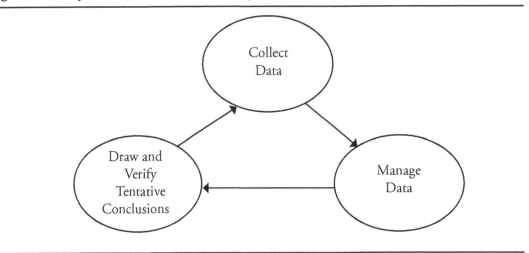

[2] Adapted from Miles and Huberman (1994).

Here's how qualitative data analysis works as a cyclical process. First, analysis begins as soon as the earliest bits of information are gathered. It continues in a parallel way throughout the collection of the rest of the data, because the analysis informs what is collected next. Thus, because you see a particular pattern emerging in the data, you set forth in your observations or interviews to find additional support for that pattern.

The analysis then proceeds by dividing the information into relevant parts, or units of meaning. These pieces of meaning are then categorized according to an organizing system, with all material ultimately belonging to a category. The organizing system emerges from the data. That is, the categories are informed by the information. Initially, these categories are preliminary and tentative, and remain as flexible working tools, rather than rigid rules.

We'll get more explicit about how to do all this a bit later in the chapter, but for now understand that the underlying intellectual activity throughout is comparison—comparing and contrasting every part of the data and assigning it to a category. Eventually, the tentative patterns are "checked" and if they seem logical, they become the conclusions of the study. Comparing, contrasting, and checking are the heart of the inductive and cyclical nature of qualitative data analysis.

Overall, analyzing qualitative data can be thought of as an intellectual puzzle. And, as with a puzzle, there is no one right way to get to its solution. As a researcher you must find your own "style of intellectual craftsmanship" (McMillan & Schumacher, 1993, p. 484). "Qualitative analysis can and should be done artfully, even playfully, but it also requires a great amount of methodological knowledge and intellectual competence" (Tesch, 1990, p. 97).

This means there is no single accepted theoretical approach that guides analyzing qualitative data in recreation, park, sport, and tourism. For example, as you may recall from Step 3, some researchers use **grounded theory,** which focuses on discovering theory from data (Glaser & Strauss, 1967). Others use a **framework analysis,** which is explicitly geared toward generating policy-

Qualitative data analysis requires an artful play of discovering the meanings of collected information. The researcher interprets what is reflected back by the data. *Copyright © 2008 Ruth V. Russell*

317

and-practice-oriented findings (Green & Thorogood, 2004). And, individuals engaged in inter-preting text materials often turn to ***componential analysis*** (Ryan & Bernard, 2005).

To review, regardless of which qualitative theoretical framework and which data-collection method(s) is used (Step 9) to guide the research, all qualitative approaches are based on the in-ductive intellectual activity of comparison. Now, let's focus on exactly how this is done. What are the actual procedures of qualitative data analysis? The procedures can be grouped as three basic steps: managing the data, making tentative conclusions, and verifying these conclusions.

Managing Data

To explain ***data management*** let's continue with the puzzle working analogy. Most people working a jigsaw puzzle usually begin by determining the nature and size of the pieces, and then putting the pieces into some kind of strategic order.

There is no single correct way to proceed with putting the jigsaw puzzle pieces in order, but one way might be to begin by laying all the pieces out onto the table face up. Then, pieces can be separated into groups. One grouping could be all the pieces with straight edges, or the puzzle's border. Another grouping could be pieces that are of the same color (the blue sky) or pattern (leafy).

Once the pieces have been grouped together we can begin to try out different puzzle pieces until we've fitted them together. Some puzzle solvers might begin by putting the border together, while others might work out the houses and people in the picture first.

This description of how jigsaw puzzles operate is analogous to what happens when managing data in qualitative analysis. Basically, when managing the words and images of raw data, meta-data are created. ***Meta-data*** are "data about data" (Peacock & Paul-Ward, 2006, p. 358). That is, new words and/or graphic products are created to represent key themes and relationships emerg-ing from the original data. The most common sorts of meta-data are:

- Expanded accounts
- Memos
- Codes
- Data displays

Expanded Accounts

Most qualitative data begin with words. Sometimes words have been collected in the course of making observation field notes, as transcripts of audio recorded interviews or focus group meetings, from respondents' personal documents, from descriptions of what is happening in photographs, etc.

318

Most likely the words that have been recorded are a ***condensed account,*** meaning phrases, single words, and unconnected sentences (Spradley, 1980). Even though condensed accounts don't record everything that went on or was said these notes are very useful. Annotations found in condensed accounts have enormous value because they were recorded on the spot and thus are rich in the information that has been recorded.

The next step after acquiring a condensed account is to expand it into a typed expanded account (Spradley, 1980). In an ***expanded account,*** details are filled in (Case 2). When creating an expanded account every effort is made to recall things not written down in the condensed account.

Case 2. Examples of Condensed and Expanded Accounts.

Kielhofner, G., & Takata, N. (1980). A study of mentally retarded persons: Applied research in occupational therapy. *American Journal of Occupational Therapy, 34,* 252-258.

The purpose of the study was to investigate the effects of deinstitutionalization. The sample consisted of adults with developmental disabilities who were deinstitutionalized from state hospitals into community residential facilities. The investigators were interested in how successfully these adults integrated into community life. Participant observation was the primary data collection method used. Following is an excerpt of a condensed account from one of the observation sessions in the local park:

Condensed Account

• D & M guitars
• Doris asked to play
• Others looking on
• Young male kid watching
• More kids approach
• Nervous, cautious, drawn in

After returning to the office following the observation session, this condensed account was converted into an expanded account. Here is an excerpt:

Expanded Account[3]

Daniel and Michelle had brought their guitars, so naturally Doris asked to play. Doris began to play and sing with Michelle accompanying her—both playing guitar and singing. I was sitting on top of a picnic table a few feet away and Tim sat beside me. From where I sat I could see not only Doris and Doreen, Bill, Shereen, Jess and the UCLA folks, but also the many kids in the background who had noticed us and were curiously looking on. Finally one brave soul (a young man who appeared 10 years old) approached the corner of the area and unobtrusively watched. He appeared almost mesmerized by the whole scene which included: a toothless lady with red skin and very obese, wearing a red wig playing a guitar and singing her soul out; Buddy, a 50-year-old with Down Syndrome, and Doreen whose appearance approximates Doris' but who seems older in a black wig. After the first young man had ventured into "our territory" more and more children began to approach. Those who were younger held expressions of curiosity, fear and intensity. They seemed nervous and cautious but were still drawn to the scene.

---

[3] Adapted from Peacock and Paul-Ward (2006).

Incidentally, taped interviews can be thought of as an expanded account. When the narrative or dialog of the taped interview is typed out this is called a ***transcript.***

Idea . . . Hire a Transcriber.

Should you type your own transcripts? Professional typists charge about $100 to transcribe a one-hour video or audiotape. One hour of taped interview is approximately 21 pages of single-spaced transcription.

As the amount of expanded account notes begins to grow, some early decisions about note management will be necessary (Miles & Huberman, 1994). More specifically, a filing system needs to be developed that enables:

- Keeping condensed and expanded notes organized and tidy.
- Cross referencing linked information from one file to another file.
- Labeling files in a way that they can easily be retrieved.

The *Idea* box below provides some specifics regarding ways for managing notes.

Idea . . . Managing Expanded Accounts![4]

Here are some recommendations for managing your notes. Choose the one best suited to you and your data.

1. **Cut notes up and put in folders.** Create a manila folder for each possible category of information. Cut the paper version of your expanded accounts apart and file them in the appropriate folder. Write a circled number on every expanded account piece of paper and keep a running directory of what notes are in what folder according to the numbering system.
2. **Use a file card system to retrieve relevant notes.** Each line on the expanded account transcripts is numbered consecutively. Record on each file card (such as 3" x 5" size) the relevant and corresponding phrase across the top of the card appearing in the original condensed accounts as well as the corresponding relevant lines found in the expanded accounts.
3. **Store information on retrieval cards.** These cards are available at college bookstores under the brands of McBee™ and Indecks™. Each card contains a large space where data are typed according to each paragraph or sentence. Each card comes with the same numbered holes around the rim. After each paragraph or sentence is typed on the card, cut off all holes except those that correspond to the number of the coding categories to which the paragraph or sentence pertains. There is a box for holding all the cards, and a needle-like tool for pulling same themed cards out of the box.

---

[4] Adapted from Bogdan and Biklin (2006).

Regardless of what system(s) is used to manage the pages of expanded accounts, remember the goal is to be able to locate specific data as the analysis proceeds. Also, it is important to have the ability to retrieve expanded accounts. Inevitably, as the data analysis progresses, there are times when you must go back and consult the expanded notes in order to gain greater appreciation of the meanings conveyed in these notes.

Memos

Another strategy for managing qualitative data is to use memoing. *Memos* are notes written by a researcher to him/herself that suggest explanations for the content of the expanded accounts. Memos become aids that assist in moving more easily from raw data to a conceptual level, building toward a more integrated understanding of events and interactions.

Memos are used to record ideas about patterns in the data. A memo is a sense-making tool. "Memo writing often provides sharp, sunlit moments of clarity or insight—little conceptual epiphanies" (Miles & Huberman, 1994, p. 74).

Why do we need these "conceptual epiphanies?" Memos provide an intermediate step between what comes next—coding and forming tentative conclusions about your information. Memos require you to stop and think about the data. "Memos keep the researcher writing, which is an essential element in the analysis itself" (Charmaz, 1999, p. 367). This means memoing should begin as soon as the first information starts coming in and usually continues right up to the writing of the final report.

Memos often start as notes in the margin of expanded accounts (Case 3). Then as analysis proceeds, they usually become longer and more complex. Eventually, memos are recorded on separate sheets of paper or in a journal.

Case 3. Example of Memoing.

Refer back to Case 2. The following memo was an idea handwritten in the margin beside the first several lines.

"There is a legitimizing effect that those who appear normal have in being associated with those who have obvious characteristics that lead to stigma."

Codes

In the early stages of qualitative data analysis, most all of the information you gather looks important. Coding helps keep the mounting quantity of information reasonable so that the truly meaningful patterns are able to emerge. *Codes* are tags or labels for assigning meaning to the information (Case 4). Codes are usually attached to phrases, sentences, or whole paragraphs in your expanded accounts. Codes capture the essential meaning to either the entire sequence or its parts.

Case 4. Coding a European Football Championship.

Maguire, J. & Poulton, E. (1999). European identity politics in Euro 96: Invented traditions and national habitus codes. *International Review for the Sociology of Sport, 34*, 17-29.

The purpose of this study was to examine the relationships between sport, national identity and the media during the 1996 European Football Championship. Data were collected about the event from news articles appearing in eight British newspapers. As a part of the data analysis of these expanded accounts, codes were developed. The coverage was ultimately analyzed as falling into the following codes, or categories:

• Invented traditions.
• Narcissistic language.
• National stereotypes.
• National symbols.
• Political issue in Europe.
• War vocabulary.

There are a couple of ways to create codes. One way is to adopt codes that have been proposed by others. An example of one such coding system appears in Figure 3.

Figure 3. Proposed Coding System for Expanded Notes.[5]

Event/Behavior	Code Label to Use
Information on surroundings	*Setting/context*
How people define the setting	*Definition of the situation*
Ways of thinking	*Perspectives of subjects*
Subjects' understanding of each other, outsiders, and objects in their world	*Ways of thinking about people and objects*
Categorizing events, changes over time, and flow	*Process*
Regularly occurring kinds of behavior	*Activities*
Specific activities	*Events*
Tactics, techniques, and other ways people accomplish things	*Strategies*
Behaviors not officially defined by the organization	*Relationships and social structures*
Categories of people in terms meaningful to the study	*Types of people*

[5] Adapted from Bogdan and Biklin (2006).

Another way to create codes is to return to your research questions, problem statement, or key variables that were determined at the beginning of the study and devise a ***start list*** of codes (Miles & Huberman, 1994). For example, if the research question is "To describe stereotypes included in recreation programming services provided for older adults" then a list of codes to begin with might be "Types of Stereotypes," "Incidence of Stereotypes," "Participant Reactions to Stereotype Programs," etc.

In actuality, a coding scheme is developed on an on-going basis. As new data are gathered, the units of meaning are both coded with the pre-planned system and used to initiate new code categories or merge old code categories. To keep track of your codes, prepare a ***code book*** (Case 5). This is simply a list of the codes and their translation. As you code subsequent expanded accounts, this code book reminds you of what the earlier codes mean, and will help you begin to see patterns in the data.

Case 5. Example of a Code Book.

Russell, R. (1991). [Observation of a hotel lobby]. Field notes.

A study was performed on how hotel lobbies are used. Using passive participant observation, the field notes were recorded and expanded. A codebook was devised and codes were then assigned to what was observed.

Code Book

Types of Lobby Users	Code
Local business people	BUS
Tourists	TOUR
Local people using the lobby as part of a recreational activity	REC

Amount of Time	
10 minutes	10MIN

Lobby Activity	
For processing hotel check-in procedures	CHECK IN
For meeting with others for another purpose	MEET
To relax or rest between activities	REST

Coding the Expanded Account

Code	Observation Notes
TOUR	Man and woman couple approach the end of the couch. They are dressed as tourists though conservatively. Woman sits down; man stands and studies tourist brochure. Woman rises after about 20 seconds to look at tourist map on wall. Hotel staff member (in yellow bellman-type jacket) approaches and exchanges some words (I can't hear).
10MIN	Both tourists sit down on the couch and resume study of brochure. After 10 minutes young man approaches (not in hotel uniform) and inquires "Mr. And Mrs. . . . ?", fingering folded sheet of paper.
MEET	Couple affirms and gets up and follows man out front door.

Postscript: The codes used in this case stemmed from suggestions found in the coding system presented in Figure 3. For example, the code "TOUR" uses the "Types of People" suggestion. The code "10 MIN" is from the "Process" suggestion, and "MEET" from the "Activities" suggestion.

How do you do coding? There are four steps involved:

1. Begin by carefully reading all the expanded accounts. Identify all statements relating to the research question.
2. Assign a code to each identified statement. Every relevant unit of meaning is organized under the code that best describes it.
3. Reread the expanded accounts to be sure the assigned code captures the themes.
4. Develop new codes if needed. For example, ask yourself:
   A. "Can I combine certain codes together under a more general code?"
   B. "Can I organize codes sequentially?"
   C. "Can I identify any causal relationships among the codes?"

Data Displays

A series of tools used in the initial analysis of qualitative data—expanded accounts, memos, and codes—have been reviewed in this chapter. Remember, all these efforts continue throughout data-collection. That is, we are continuously collecting data, converting our condensed accounts into expanded accounts, writing interpretation ideas as memos, and coding expanded accounts.

Here's a word of caution. Early in the analysis, things typically leap out as "the answers" to the research questions that have been posed. Comparisons of patterns and themes appear to be in sight. Be careful, though, because this early analysis is not enough. The researcher must resist the temptation to feel "finished" too early. In fact, one of the reasons data analysis begins while still collecting data is to improve data collection itself.

At this point, the data analysis advances by developing data displays. A *data display* is a visual chart that systematically presents information. The display is a narrowed view of the information—meaning you are able to see the full data set in a single format. Data displays present the reasons for why things are happening as they are. Ultimately, a data display helps develop and verify descriptive conclusions for what is being evaluated.

While there are various data display types, the two more popular are the matrix and network. Which one you use depends on what you are trying to understand.

Matrices. A *matrix display* is helpful for understanding the connections among bits of information since it offers "exploratory eyeballing," or a "thumbnail sketch" (Miles & Huberman, 1994, p. 93). A sample matrix display is presented in Case 6.

Case 6. Example of a Matrix Display Based on Observations made in a Hotel Lobby.[6]

Domain: Types of Hotel Lobby Waiters	Attributes of Waiting			
Solos	*Waiting Intensity*	*Posture*	*Emotion*	*Object of Waiting*
Watchers	Most intense/focused on waiting/can be distracted/increases with time	Often inert/lots of micro-flow/pacing/narrow range of motion	Anticipation/can be impatient	Other persons/transportation
Workers	Usually focus is not on waiting, but on work/rarely distracted		Patient/studious/contemplative	Other persons/a meal or meeting/transportation
Players	Not focused on waiting/occasionally distracted	Relaxed	Usually patient/preoccupied	Other persons/a meeting/transportation
Shifters		Posture shifts are first clue to this kind of waiting		
Groups	*Waiting Intensity*	*Posture*	*Emotion*	*Object of Waiting*
Socials	Varies	Often seated opposite or at right angles	Lighthearted/often animated	Other persons/transportation/a meal/social
Ad hoc Committees	More casual/less intense than a lobby-held working meeting	Highly animated		Other persons/transportation/a meal/the "business"

[6] Adapted from Russell (1991).

Notice in the matrix display in Case 6 that there are two lists. What are these? How do we get the two lists for a matrix? In a matrix display, the first list is of the domain ("Types of Hotel Lobby Waiters") and the second list is of attributes ("Attributes of Hotel Lobby Waiters").

The **domain** represents the "types" of something. For example, suppose we are studying television watching. A domain list could be prepared for a matrix according to types of TV programs. That is, there are news, comedy, talk, reality, sport, etc., types of programs. The domain list is placed down the left column of the matrix display.

Meanwhile, the domain of TV program types differs in a patterned way. Television programs might be differentiated according to the length of program, amount of prior scripting, accompanying type of commercial messages, and expected viewer reaction. This becomes a list of **attributes**. The attributes list is placed across the top row of the matrix display.

In summary, a matrix display presents domain and attribute lists. Figure 4 outlines the steps to building a matrix display.

Figure 4. Steps to Building a Matrix.[7]

1. **Identify a domain.** Identify a domain of interest that has emerged from data collection. For example, in Case 6 the domain is "Type of Hotel Lobby Waiters." The idea for this first appeared in the researcher's memos. The study did not begin with the purpose of studying waiting behavior; the initial research intended to assess how the lobby was used. It was during the memoing that "waiting" was formulated as the most common use. The identified domain and its categories become the ***subheads*** or row lists. You will find that a domain with less than 10 items or categories makes the process more manageable. However, the actual number of items in the domain does not matter all that much.
2. **Inventory your data and identify attributes of the chosen domain.** Review the coded expanded accounts searching for how the domain list can be contrasted. These contrasts, or attributes, should be distinguishable. For example, how is each domain item on the list unique according to its qualities? These attributes become the column headings in the matrix. In the hotel lobby study (see Case 6), "Attributes of Waiting" is the ***column spanner*** listed across the top.
3. **Prepare a matrix worksheet and fill it in.** The matrix worksheet contains the list of the domain types in the subheads on the left, and the list of attributes as the column spanner across the top. Technically, the matrix boxes are called ***cells.*** Leave enough room in the cells to write a short phrase of information. Now, complete the matrix by referring to the data in your expanded accounts and memos to fill in the cells.
4. **For information missing from the cells, prepare a list of contrast questions and then conduct additional data collection.** Notice in Case 6 above, several cells are blank. This is normal. That is, one of the biggest benefits of a matrix display is that it will quickly reveal the kinds of information you next need to collect (Spradley, 1980). Every blank space in the worksheet suggests the observations or interviews you still need to do.
5. **Complete the matrix.** The final matrix serves as an approximate outline for the final report. But it may not be the only outline. Some researchers using qualitative methods prepare a data display matrix for as many domains as possible, while others limit their study to one or just a few domains. Our suggestion is that you examine at least two domains, and thus prepare at least two separate matrices.

[7] Adapted from Spradley (1980).

Networks. A data display with a ***network*** format is useful in two situations. First, a network can be used when you want to focus on the order of things. Second, a network can be used when you want to examine three or more domains at the same time.

Case 7 presents a network display. With it, we are able to simultaneously display the domains of the workout series (lifter and trainer), along with their attributes (frequency, duration, and intensity), as well as the order in which it all takes place.

Case 7. Network Display of Amount of Weightlifter/Trainer Contact and Weight Room Use Timeline.

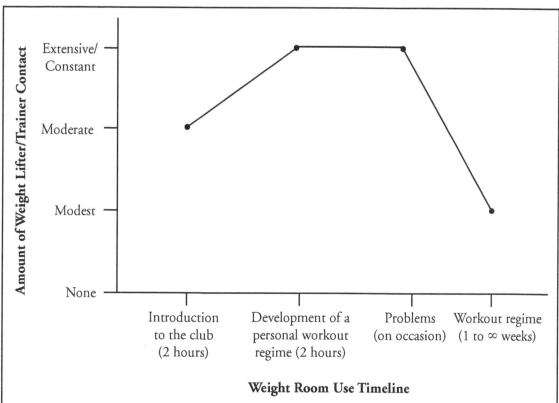

In a network display the points are events, and the line connecting the events have the implicit meaning of "is followed by" or "is related to" or "is a part of" (Miles & Huberman, 1994). The network is ordered and each point is labeled.

From studying a network display you should be able to detect any patterns or explanations about why things happen as they do. For example, in Case 7, the personal trainer's involvement with the lifter is an inverted "U." That is, it rises to a peak in the middle of the lifting program, meaning lifters have used trainers less before and after this point.

The steps to preparing a network (Figure 5) are similar to those for creating a matrix. The only difference is that instead of preparing two lists of categories (domains and attributes) as you do in a matrix, you identify major event patterns and qualities of the event patterns for a network display.

Figure 5. Steps to Building a Network.

1. **Identify major event patterns.** Identify a timeline pattern of events that has emerged from data collection. For example, in Case 7 the events are "Weight Room Use Timeline." In reviewing the coded expanded accounts the researcher notices each participant goes through an ordered series of ways of using the weight room. That is, there is the initial introduction and orientation, fol-

lowed by the development of a personal workout regime, etc. This ordered event pattern is partly established by the weight room program and partly by individual users. The identified pattern of events becomes the horizontal axis of the display.

2. **Inventory your data and identify qualities of the event pattern.** Review the coded expanded accounts searching for how the events can be contrasted. These contrasts should be distinguishable. For instance, in Case 7 "Weight Room Use Timeline," can be contrasted according to the "Amount of Weight Lifter/Trainer Contact." These contrasts become the vertical axis of the display.
3. **Prepare the network display.** Draw a graph with the major event pattern labels along the horizontal axis and the qualities labels along the vertical axis.
4. **Use dots to represent on the display the relationship between the events and the qualities.** For example, in Case 7 the "dot" for the event of the weight lifter's "Introduction to the Club" corresponds to the quality "Moderate" amount of involvement with a trainer.
5. **Connect the dots.** Linking the events with the qualities enables you to "see" the order of things in the data.

Figure 6 compares these two forms of data displays. Essentially, in both a matrix and a network, you are making choices about how to **partition** or separate the data. But remember (as the *Something to Remember* box below reinforces), a matrix and a network are not the same thing.

Figure 6. Commonly Asked Questions about Matrices and Networks.

Question	Answer
Where does the evaluator get ideas for a matrix or network?	Through inductive thinking, the ideas are a "translation" of the coded expanded accounts and the memos.
How many displays are needed?	It depends. You prepare as many networks and matrices as needed to understand your findings. And remember the contents of the matrices and networks will change and evolve throughout the analysis process.
When should a matrix or a network be developed?	Do it during the last phases of data collection. That way you can focus on what you know and don't know.

Something to Remember!

Recall when to use a matrix or a network by answering the following questions:

1. **Is the intent descriptive or explanatory?** Are you trying to lay out data to see what is there (matrix), or do you want to generate some explanations about why things happen as they do (network)?
2. **Do you need partial order or complete order?** Are you placing data in rows and columns that represent descriptive categories in a partial order (matrix) or are you completely ordering the categories in some specific way, such as by time, influence, intensity, roles, procedure (network)?
3. **Are you focusing on two domains or more than two domains?** Are you comparing and contrasting two domains (matrix) or more than two domains (network)?

In essence, formatting data into displays is a decision-making tool. It determines which understandings will be analyzed and in which ways. If a finding is not in the display, it will not be compared and contrasted to another finding. So, be careful not to let the display itself bully the data into shortcuts.

Computer Assistance

Every step in qualitative data analysis that has been presented in this chapter can be done "by hand" using paper and pencils and your own intellect as the analysis tools. Some researchers, on the other hand, use computer software to assist in qualitative data analysis. Indeed, specialized computer programs can help you with everything from taking notes in the field to transcribing, coding, and storing them (Figure 7). Software is also available for memoing, identifying codes, creating data displays, and even drawing conclusions. For example, using a software package such as NUD*IST allows you to import text data files that can be coded. Then the patterns are identified by the computer.

Figure 7. Examples of Qualitative Data-Analysis Software.[8]

Function	Commercial Software Available
Code-Based Theory-Builders	AQUAD, ATLAS.ti, HyperRESEARCH, NUD*IST, QCA
Code-and-Retrieve Programs	Ethnograph, HYPERQual2, Kwalitan, Martin, QUALPRO
Conceptual Network-Builders	Inspiration, MECA, Meta Design, Sem-Net
Text Retrievers	Metamorph, Orbis, Sonar Professional, The Text Collector, Word Cruncher, ZyINDEX
Textbase Managers	Folio VIEWS, MAX, Sam, Tabletop

[8] Adapted from: Neutens and Rubinson (2002); and Peacock and Paul-Ward (2006).

Popular qualitative data-analysis software programs also exist to support theory building. These programs help with the construction of explanations that are grounded in the qualitative data. For example, ATLAS.ti has a tool called a "Network Editor," which is a "graphic space" into which data and meta-data can be imported and linked to one another through semantic relationships. This feature permits the creation of conceptual maps or models that help interpret the meanings in the data.

All computer software that assists with qualitative data analysis begins with a preparatory step of ***data conversion.*** It is important to note that if this is done, it becomes the second data conversion, since condensed handwritten field notes were already converted to typed expanded accounts. Thus, computer-assisted qualitative data analysis converts the data again from that stored in a "hard" or analog form to a digital form. Such conversions then make it possible for the software to perform a variety of data management tasks.

Computerized data conversion can be a wonderful thing. But you should also appreciate two risks associated with using computer software for qualitative data analysis (Gratton & Jones, 2004). First, although computer analysis may allow for a much quicker, and seemingly more objective, analysis, the process of manually handling your data can give you insights about the findings that the computer won't have. You'll have a better feel for the information. This feeling cannot be underestimated because intuition and creativity are very necessary in qualitative data analysis. Do not assume that the quality of your own analysis is inferior to that done by a computer.

Second, much of the coding that is carried out by computer software requires words to be specified beforehand by the researcher, which, can often be just as time consuming as doing it all by hand. Time is also necessary to learn how to work with the software package. So, unless you'll be doing a considerable amount of qualitative research, it might not be worthwhile learning one of the statistical packages. You'll need to weigh the pros and cons of the usefulness of computer software to analyze your own qualitative data.

Making Tentative Conclusions

Now comes what for many researchers seems the hardest part. The procedures in qualitative data analysis that have been described so far (expanded accounts, memos, codes, data displays) are tools for finding meaning in the information gathered. There comes a time when these tools must finally produce the meanings.

These meanings are referred to as *conclusions.* Producing conclusions is not as difficult as you might think. We are all natural meaning-finders. After all, humans are always trying to make sense of things. Figure 8 outlines questions that can be asked in order to find the meaning in what has been learned.

Figure 8. Reflective Questions to Help Find Meaning in Qualitative Analysis.[9]

- What am I going to call this "meaning"?
- How am I going to define the nuances of this "meaning" as I look at different data?
- What are the examples of variations under the "umbrella" of this meaning?
- Why does this "meaning" matter?
- How well does this "meaning" answer the research question(s)?
---

[9] Adapted from Rubin and Rubin (2005).

Strategies for Making Conclusions

There are five strategies that can be used to draw conclusions. These techniques are (Miles & Huberman, 1994): clustering, subsuming particulars into the general, counting, seeking plausibility, and making metaphors.

Clustering. The data display tools (matrix and network) enable us to *cluster* or clump information into patterns or themes. By further clustering the information, patterns of similarities or differences emerge. The patterns identified in the data displays provide hunches for further pattern seeking, and thus, in drawing conclusions.

It is difficult to tell you exactly how to do clustering; if you use inductive thinking, the more complex patterns will jump out at you. One aid to accomplishing this, however, is to construct an **integrative diagram** (McMillan & Schumacker, 1993). This involves combining the matrices and/or networks you have already constructed. Case 8 presents a simplified integrative diagram example for a fictional study.

Case 8. Example of an Integrative Diagram: Becoming a Park and Recreation Professional.

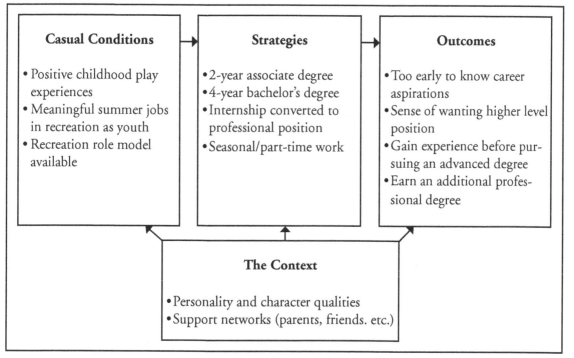

Casual Conditions

• Positive childhood play experiences
• Meaningful summer jobs in recreation as youth
• Recreation role model available

Strategies

• 2-year associate degree
• 4-year bachelor's degree
• Internship converted to professional position
• Seasonal/part-time work

Outcomes

• Too early to know career aspirations
• Sense of wanting higher level position
• Gain experience before pursuing an advanced degree
• Earn an additional professional degree

The Context

• Personality and character qualities
• Support networks (parents, friends. etc.)

Subsuming particulars into the general. Whereas clustering involves clumping things that go together and giving them a common label, there is a related approach that determines whether things are a part of a more general category. **Subsuming** is the process of drawing a conclusion by moving up a step on the abstraction ladder. According to Glaser (1978), this is a matter of looking for "basic social processes" that are more general in description than the specific things being analyzed. For instance, let's suppose the following behaviors of children were observed in a playground program: bullying, aggression, rule infractions, and defiance of authority. These behavior themes could be subsumed into a more general social process label called "incivilities."

Counting. Counting can also be useful in drawing conclusions for qualitative data. After all, when a pattern or theme has been identified, essentially, it is because it has been noted in the data a number of times. When we say a theme is important, we have come to that conclusion, in part at least, by making counts of its occurrence. For example, in a study suppose that 72% of the interviewees mentioned lack of child care as their reason for irregular participation in a fitness program. The frequency of this response tells us something important for improving the program.

Seeing plausibility. Conclusions also are derived from the act of determining what makes good sense, or what fits. This is the **plausibility** basis for conclusions, or "it just feels right." While we do not recommend this as the sole tactic for drawing a conclusion, there is no denying that many scientific discoveries at least initially appeared to their inventors in this way.

Making metaphors. Metaphors can be used in drawing conclusions. **Metaphors** are literary devices that involve comparing two things via their similarities, while ignoring their differences. For instance, the idea of the "empty nest" phase of a parent's life is a common metaphor for children growing up and leaving home. A metaphor from the hotel lobby example might be, "the lobby is the stage for a series of one-act plays, complete with entrances and exits . . . with the drama or comedy varying in terms of plot and performances" (Russell, 1991).

Holistic Understanding

All of these strategies for drawing conclusions involve shuttling back and forth in thinking among the coded expanded accounts, your memos, and the conceptual categories in the data displays. Making conclusions requires making discrete bits of information come together into a holistic understanding.

Now what? We are ready to move from our clusters, subsuming, counting, plausibility, and metaphors to constructs. That is, the findings of the study must be tied to the overarching explanations for the "how" and "why" of what has been studied (recall Step 3). **Constructs** are broader applications of the patterns or themes that have been noticed and focused on in the data. At last you have to ask yourself, "Do any broader constructs put these patterns together the way I am putting them together?" Your greatest ally in this will be your understanding of the research literature you conducted (Step 2) in the early stages of the research process. Are there any constructs from theories or models from the work of other researchers that your patterns fit?

The conclusions you make about the qualitative data can now be thought of as answers to the research question. In some circumstances, these solutions will become recommendations for how your leisure services organization changes or improves policies or service delivery practices. In other circumstances, the conclusions drawn from qualitative data analysis will be further developed into theory. As previously mentioned in this chapter and an earlier chapter (Step 4) this is called **grounded theory** because its conceptual rules are grounded in, or emerge from, the data. This means the term "theory" in this case does not refer to an existing theory of human behavior in the literature. Instead, it suggests that, via the inductive method of analysis, a better understanding of people's experiences has appeared.

Verifying Conclusions

Our last task in qualitative data analysis is to confront the issue of soundness. "Qualitative analyses (like quantitative analyses) can be evocative, illuminating, masterful—and wrong" (Miles & Huberman, 1994, p. 262). Therefore, conclusions must be verified. While there are many ways of double-checking conclusions, two will be featured: checking for data quality and testing explanations.

Checking for Data Quality

Checking for data quality means determining if the information upon which conclusions are based is "good." How do we do this? This can be done two ways or by examining: representativeness and researcher effects.

Representativeness. **Representativeness** entails determining if the gathered information is typical of the people, organization, or events that are being studied. For example, if only those people who can easily be contacted are interviewed, conclusions are likely to be based on non-representative information.

If it is suspected that the data are not representative what can be done? There are two common ways this is handled. First, a few more cases can be sampled in order to see if the findings from these match the conclusions. Second, two or three people from the study can be randomly selected and asked to judge the typicality of the conclusions. This is called **member checking**. That is, "members" of the observed or interviewed group are asked to read the tentative conclusions and to assess how closely their worlds have been captured.

Researcher effects. Another way to check for data quality is to determine if there are **researcher effects**, meaning the researcher's influence on data collected and/or analyzed for a study (Case 9). Unless completely non-reactive data-collection methods are used (Step 9), the researcher can alter the usual status quo, meaning creating behaviors in those studied that would not have occurred ordinarily. As well, the situation studied might affect the researcher. The investigator might form biased conclusions because something in the data struck him or her personally. Avoiding the effects of the researcher on the conclusions and the effects of the study on the researcher, requires keeping research questions firmly in mind and thinking conceptually and not sentimentally.

Case 9. Researcher Effect Dilemma.[10]

Recently, a programmer for a residential camp was conducting and taping interviews for a study designed to describe the quality of a federally funded music and arts program at the camp, with special focus on counselor effectiveness in the program. The five counselors were teaching and leading sculpture, painting, piano, voice, and composition to campers. The researcher conducted the interviews with all of the counselors over a two-month period and observed in seven of the music program sessions. He transcribed all the tapes and found that one counselor was totally neglecting her work as a music counselor. As well, all of the other counselors knew that one of their staff was a slacker, and that she was basically unqualified and rude to campers. The researcher showed these data to the camp director who would not accept them. The counselor in question was an old friend. The camp director asked the researcher to delete all comments referring to that counselor in case the data might jeopardize funding for the next summer. How would you handle this? What is the role of the researcher in this case?

[10] Adapted from Janesick (2003).

Testing Explanations

Next, in verifying conclusions we **test explanations.** There are two ways we might do this: replication of findings and checking rival explanations.

Replication of findings. Basically, findings are more dependable when other research studies are able to confirm them. This duplication of results is known as **replication of findings** (Miles & Huberman, 1994).

Replication of findings can be accomplished several ways. At the most basic level, the researcher in the course of a study is replicating as she or he collects new information from new respondents or from new events.

At a more rigorous level, conclusions can be replicated in additional studies by studying different respondents, cases, or situations to see whether the conclusions are repeated. For example, suppose the local authority for tourism development in a rural tourist site has been studied. To check conclusions made about one town, the study could be repeated in another town. The purpose of doing this is to look for matching patterns or a replication of findings.

Rival explanations. One last way to confirm the quality of conclusions is to check out rival explanations (Miles & Huberman, 1994). **Rival explanations** are conclusions that are opposite, or different from, the ones you determined from the study.

During data collection it is quite easy to get busy making sense of each bit of information. Later on, it is even easier to zero in on a particular conclusion. During data analysis hold on to several possible or alternative patterns or themes of explanation until one of them becomes increasingly more compelling. This strategy will help ensure conclusions are well grounded in the actual data.

Your Research

1. **Have you collected qualitative data in your study? That is, do you have written, verbal, or pictorial text data from interviews, focus groups, observations, or documents?**
2. **If so, how will you go from condensed accounts of these data to expanded accounts?**
3. **How will you provide memos for the expanded accounts?**
4. **What coding scheme will you use?**
5. **Will you use a network or matrix data display? How will you set this up?**
6. **What strategies will you use to draw tentative conclusions?**

7. Is there a computer software program available to you for analyzing your data?
8. What steps will you take to verify conclusions?

Review and Discussion Questions . . . What have you learned about qualitative data analysis?

1. In what ways is the analysis of qualitative data different from the analysis of quantitative data?
2. How does qualitative data analysis rely on *inductive thinking*?
3. When it is said that qualitative data analysis is a cyclical process, what does it mean?
4. What is *meta-data*? And what are the four common sorts of meta-data?
5. What is the difference between a *condensed account* and an *expanded account*?
6. What is *memoing*?
7. What is *coding*?
8. What is a *data display*? What are two types of data displays and how are they different?
9. Identify the five strategies often used to make *conclusions*?
10. What are four techniques that can be used to verify conclusions?

Exercises

1. Hopefully, you've enjoyed reading this chapter! Qualitative data analysis has a rather "intuitive" feel to it. You've probably also been making skeptical comments to yourself, such as qualitative data analysis seems too "loose." Ask yourself why you think both of these reactions occur and write a summary of your thinking in a one-page paper.
    A. In what ways do you already apply qualitative data analysis in your daily life?
    B. When I read the results section of a research journal article using qualitative data analysis, I usually do this _____. Why?
    C. What can I do today to make progress in developing expertise in qualitative data-analysis procedures in my future professional work?
    D. What can I do next semester to make progress in developing expertise in qualitative data-analysis procedures in my future professional work?

2. Using your library's on-line capabilities, create an annotated bibliography of the most recent (2003 to present) books and articles on how to carry out qualitative data analysis specific to the parks, recreation, sport, and tourism fields. Reading a selection of these books and/or articles will demonstrate the flexibility of procedures actually used in qualitative data analysis.

3. Carry out a brief interview with someone you know who enjoys playing a sport. Question them about their experiences of playing.
    A. Record condensed notes during this interview.
    B. Create an expanded account from your condensed account field notes.
    C. Now try to code the expanded account.
    D. Can you already see preliminary conclusions from your coding?

4. Review the steps in preparing a matrix form of data display and then create one yourself using the subject of television programs. Almost all of us watch television every day, but let's assume we are trying to understand this cultural phenomenon for the first time.

    A. As part of the "study" a matrix display is developed. It is determined that television programs have at least the following subject categories: News, Comedy, Talk, Sports, and Drama. Types of television programs become the domains for our matrix.

    B. While the domains are all types of television programs, they are unique in that they have their own attributes. What are the attributes for sports programs, for example? In what ways are these different from the attributes of comedy programs? Let's suppose we've identified two attributes that distinguish types of television programs: Length of program; and, Degree of prior scripting.

    C. Now, using these domains and these attributes to form the two lists of a matrix, sketch one out and fill it in from your own experience in watching television.

    D. What tentative conclusions can you make from studying your matrix?

5. Study the matrix example in Case 6. What patterns or themes jump out?

    A. Make a list of these themes.

    B. When you have finished, compare your list to those below, which were the actual ones that jumped out for the researcher in the study:

        i. Lobby waiting intensity varies greatly, but for the longer times, waiting can be quite focused.

        ii. The lobby often serves as a staging area for events elsewhere—both in and out of the hotel.

        iii. Waiting in a group is more pleasant than waiting alone.

        iv. Lobby activity *wraps around events*. That means lobby activity occurs before and after dining in the restaurant, before and after a meeting, or a tour departing from and returning to the hotel.

6. Using the list of available software packages applicable to qualitative data analysis from Figure 7, go online and check out a few so that you are introduced to the assistance they provide. Discuss the use of some of these software packages with university researchers who are using them. What are the pros and cons of using these from their perspective?

7. If not assigned a published qualitative research study, find one. Consider whether you found the report credible and interesting.

    A. What procedures discussed in this chapter did the researcher(s) use that contributed to your decision that the study was credible and interesting?

    B. What procedures discussed in this chapter did the researcher(s) *not* use that if they had would have made the study report more credible and interesting?

The analysis of qualitative data is a cyclical process using inductive reasoning to yield contextually descriptive answers. Wooden Bicycle, Ljubljana, Slovenia. *Copyright © 2008 Carol Cutler Riddick*

Part V: Reporting the Research

STEP 15: Present Results Using Visual Aids

Tables

Figures
Pie Graph
Bar Graph
Histogram
Line Graph

If I can't picture it, I can't understand it.
Albert Einstein

After collecting and analyzing raw data, the next task is to summarize the results. If, for instance, 100 people answer 20 questions each, then there are 2,000 responses. Your challenge is to summarize all these responses clearly and accurately so others can understand them. One way to do this is through *visual aids,* in particular tables and figures.

When developing a table or figure, there should be a clear vision about the purpose each visual aid is to serve. What exactly is it you are trying to convey with the table or figure? Visual aids should communicate important information (Case 1). This means they should complement rather than replace text. Never display a table or figure without discussing and referring to it within the body of the report or presentation.

Reporting the results of a study in a visual manner "speaks volumes." This photo is of the beginning of the weigh-in for the 2006 White Marlin Open Tournament in Ocean City, Maryland. Here you see the crowd paying rapt attention to the "data" being displayed on the scale. By the time the measurement of the fish's weight was finished the angler of this 78.5-pound white marlin took home a whopping $1.6 million. *Copyright © 2008 Ruth V. Russell*

Case 1. Data Analysis Involves Visual Understanding: Some Winners and Losers.

Michael Friendly, at York University, has put together a humorous Web page that contains *The Best and Worst of Statistical Graphics* (http://www.math.yorku.ca/SCS/Gallery/). Visit the site to learn why people's graphics have landed on the "Laurels" and "Darts" awards lists. Also, pause to review, on the same page, *ACCENT Principles for Effective Graphical Display.*

This chapter provides guidelines for developing tables and figures. For the most part, researchers in our professions have adopted the standards and styles supported by the American Psychological Association (see the *Idea* box below). We would, however, be remiss not to point out that every university, journal, and most agencies have their own explicit rules regarding tables and figures. So, you should check on these and draft your research report accordingly.

Idea . . . Great Resources for Figures, Tables, and Poster Presentations.

Two valuable resources, especially for graduate students, on how to create figures and tables (as well as poster presentations) are the following references:

Nicol, A., & Pexman, P. (2003). *Displaying your findings: A practical guide for creating figures, posters, and presentations.* Washington, D.C.: American Psychological Association.

Nicol, A., & Pexman, P. (1999). *Presenting your findings: A practical guide for creating tables.* Washington, DC: American Psychological Association.

Tables

There are essentially two types of tables. There are numerical tables and there are word tables.

The most basic way to illustrate data is through a **numerical table,** meaning data are presented as a frequency distribution. A **frequency distribution** involves tallying and representing how often scores occur (Table 1).

Table 1. Demographic Characteristics of Study Participants, Spring 2007 (n = 187).

Characteristic	N	%
Gender		
Male	80	43
Female	107	57
Age		
18 – 21	63	34
22 – 25	53	28
26 – 29	71	38

Characteristic	N	%
Year in college		
First-year	22	12
Sophomore	37	20
Junior	25	13
Senior	59	32
Graduate	44	23
Living Situation		
On-campus	109	59
Off-campus	78	41
Marital Status		
Single	157	84
Married	10	5
Partner	18	10
Divorced	2	1
Number of Children		
0	169	91
1- 2	13	7
3 or more	5	2

A frequency distribution can use ungrouped data, grouped data, or a combination of un-grouped and grouped data. A frequency distribution that uses **ungrouped data** reports every individual score for the variable. In instances where a wide range of answers appear for the measured variable, adjacent values are combined into a category and the number of responses in each category, or **grouped data,** are then reported. Reminders for developing the categories for a frequency distribution table are outlined in the *Something to Remember* box below.

Something to Remember![1]

When setting up a grouped frequency distribution table make sure to abide by the following rules for determining the categories:

1. **Use between three and eight categories.** If a table has too many groups, it defeats the purpose of summarizing the data. Conversely, if the table has fewer than three groups, it will not communicate much about how the data are distributed.
2. **Use mutually exclusive categories.** A score should only appear in one grouping. For instance, if you have established one group as ranging in age between 18-23 years and the second group falling between the ages of 23 and 28 years, you have violated this rule. The age "23" should appear in only one grouping.

[1]Adapted from: Nicol and Pexman (1999); and Torres, Preskill, and Piontek (2005).

Idea . . . For Collapsing Data.

Trying to figure out how to turn interval or ratio scores into nominal group categories? Consider using proportionate distribution to guide you in setting up the ***range of scores*** for grouping data. For instance, if you know you want to use four groups of scores, examine the frequency distribution of individual scores to determine logical groupings of scores. Using this principle, you might surmise that about one-fourth of the sample was between the ages of 18-21 years, one-fourth fell between 22-25 years, one-fourth fell in the 26-29 range, and the remaining one-fourth reported being 30 years or older. Using this rationale, you've saved space by successfully converting lots of individual scores into some "rational" groupings.

Usually the first table encountered in a research report is a frequency distribution of the demographic or social characteristics of the study sample (Table 1). Typically, this background table contains reported frequencies using ungrouped data (e.g., gender) as well as grouped data (such as age categories).

A number of guidelines exist for setting up both grouped and ungrouped frequency distribution tables. Some of the most important rules are reviewed in the *Something to Remember* box below.

Something to Remember![2]

There are a number of important things to keep in mind when creating frequency distribution tables. Most of the following points are illustrated in Table 1.

1. **Minimize table junk.** You don't have to use every function, every graph, and every feature a computer has to make your visual aid. Less is more. Simple is best.
2. **Numbering and Insertion.** In the report, assign numbers to tables, number tables consecutively and insert tables sequentially into the body of the report.
3. **Title.** Place the title immediately above the table. Title the table so it briefly conveys what information is being focused on, the data collection date, and total sample size. Regarding total sample size, the convention is to note this parenthetically using the standard "*(N =)*" with the appropriate sample size number inserted to the right of the parenthesis sign.
4. **Horizontal lines.** Use horizontal lines to mark different sections of the table.
5. **Headings.** Each row and column should have identifiable subject headings.
6. **Limit the number of words.** While you must label everything so there are no misunderstandings, too many words can detract from the visual message.
7. **Continuing a table to another page.** If a table spills over onto a second or multiple pages, repeat the table number and the row and column headings on the continuing page(s).
8. **Totals.** Totals should be shown, usually using whole numbers.

[2]Adapted from: Nicol and Pexman (1999); Salkind (2003); and Torres, Preskill, and Piontek (2005).

Idea . . . Handling Missing Data When Constructing a Table.

One issue many of us experience when creating tables is how to handle missing data. For instance, the *Statistical Package for Social Sciences* (SPSS) statistical software printout presented below reports the number of intramural activities college students participated in during the academic year ranged from zero to six. Additionally, the printout reveals that an answer to this question was missing for some persons; in particular, 20 people (or 4.7%) skipped or didn't answer the question.

Score	Frequency	Percent	Valid Percent	Cumulative Percent
0	102	24.0	25.2	25.2
1	266	62.6	65.7	90.9
2	15	3.5	3.7	94.6
3	7	1.6	1.7	96.4
4	6	1.4	1.5	97.9
5	4	1.0	1.0	98.8
6	5	1.2	1.2	100.0
Missing	20	4.7		
TOTAL	**425**	**100.0**		

If there were no missing data, then the values recorded in the percent and valid percent columns would be exactly the same. So the question confronting you is which percent should be used in the table you are constructing? Before answering this question note the differences among the three reported percentages. That is:

Percent = based on percentage of responses in a particular category relative to all other response categories, including missing or skipped answers.
Valid Percent = calculates percentage after dropping missing or skipped answers.
Cumulative Percent = running tally of valid percentages.

So which percent do you use? We suggest, unless a majority of the responses are "missing," reporting numbers from the "Valid Percent" column.

A second category of tables is word tables. *Word tables* present text on descriptive (Table 2) or qualitative information. Word tables typically summarize text narrative.

Table 2. Summary of the Physiological Parameters Used for Assessing the Effects of a Martial Arts Course on College Students.[3]

Concept	Variable	Test	Previously Documented Validity	Previously Documented Reliability
Range of Motion	Upper Extremity Flexibility	Shoulder Flexibility Test (Corbin & Lindsey, 1994)	Judgmental	None Found

Concept	Variable	Test	Previously Documented Validity	Previously Documented Reliability
Range of Motion	Hamstring Flexibility	Modified Sit and Reach Test (Hoeger & Hoeger, 2002)	Concurrent	Alpha = .98
Range of Motion	Total Rotation	Total Body Rotation Test (Hoeger & Hoeger, 2002)	Judgmental	Test-Retest = .75-.89
Balance	Static Balance	Stork Stand Test (Corbin & Lindsey, 1994)	Judgmental	Alpha = .85-.95

[3]Adapted from Jackson (2003).

Figures

A *figure* is ". . . any kind of graphic illustration other than a table" (Leedy & Ormrod, 2005, p. 285). Figures, like tables, graphically summarize data from a frequency distribution. Figures take many different forms; the most popular are pie graphs, bar graphs, histograms, and line graphs.

Many people find figures, when compared to a table, a visually more pleasing way to view results. Nevertheless, care must be taken to ensure that a figure accurately displays, rather than distorts, data findings. The *Something to Remember* box below features important considerations when drafting a figure.

Something to Remember![4]

Try to adhere to the following principles when setting up figures:

1. **One idea, one figure.** A figure should communicate only one idea. If you have more than one idea, use more figures.
2. **Numbering.** In a report, number each figure consecutively.
3. **Title.** Place the title immediately above the figure. The figure title briefly conveys the information of focus, the sample size, and the date data were collected.
4. **Font style and size.** All figures use the same font style, and font sizes within a figure should not vary more ± four font sizes.
5. **Insertion.** In the report, locate the figure as the next "paragraph" following where it is first mentioned.

[4]Adapted from: Nicol and Pexman (2003); Salkind (2003); and Torres, Preskill, and Piontek (2005).

Pie Graph

A *pie graph* (sometimes referred to as a pie chart) presents a circle or "pie" divided into sections that represent relative percentages (Figure 1). Pie graphs are used to represent nominal

345

categories of a variable. When creating pie graphs, apply the rules detailed in the *Something to Remember* box that follows.

Figure 1. Students Who Believe University's Weight Room Equipment is Generally Kept Clean, Spring 2007 (N = 186).

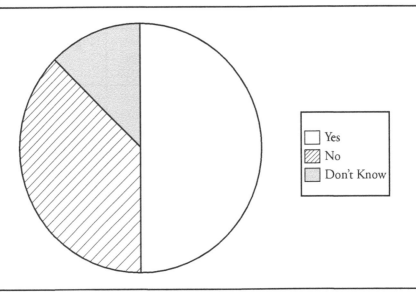

Something to Remember![5]

Some rules for creating pie charts:

1. Use five or fewer "slices" to present the findings.
2. Arrange the slices in descending order of magnitude. That is, the largest percentage should be placed at the 12 o'clock position. The second largest percentage should be next and so on, moving in a clockwise direction.
3. Use different shading, contrasting patterns, or color for each slice. Generally, color is used for live presentations (e.g., poster sessions and group presentations). And, due to the cost of color production, shading often is used for print versions of articles, reports, etc.
4. Report whole percentages (using decimal points provides too much detail and makes the visual too busy) and percentages should total 100%.
5. Place the percentage value inside the pie slice or outside the slice if the segment is proportionately very small.
6. Label the pie slices inside the slice itself or provide a key guide next to the pie.

[5]Adapted from: Nicol and Pexman (2003); and Torres, Preskill, and Piontek (2005).

Bar Graph

A ***bar graph*** uses non-touching columns to show the response categories for a variable, to compare variables, or to emphasize changes in groups over time (Figure 2). Nominal or ordinal data are represented in a bar graph. Guidelines for developing bar graphs are addressed in the *Something to Remember* box that follows.

Figure 2. Primary Reason Students Report Working Out at University's Weight Room, Spring 2007 (N = 186).

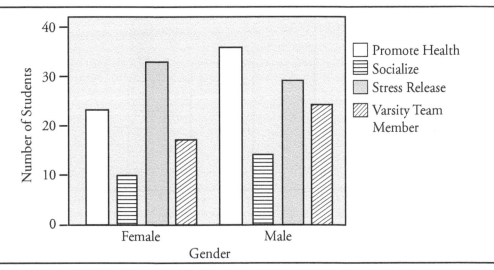

Something to Remember![6]

Some rules for creating bar graphs:

1. The vertical axis (technically known as the y-axis) is labeled and represents lower to higher frequency counts.
2. The horizontal axis (or the x-axis) is labeled with categorical groupings of the variable.
3. In any one grouping there should be no more than six bars.
4. Bars should have the same width size.
5. The entire graph is constructed so that its height (or y-axis) is approximately two-thirds to three-quarters the length of its width (x-axis). Failure to follow this rule will provide a distorted picture of the data.

[6]Adapted from: Nicol and Pexman (2003); and Torres, Preskill, and Piontek (2005).

Histogram

A *histogram* is similar to a bar graph. Histograms, however, are used to present interval and ratio data. Adjacent columns in the histogram (unlike a bar graph) touch (Figure 3). Cannons to follow when developing histograms are identified in the following *Something to Remember* box.

Figure 3. Hourly Rate Students Are Willing to Pay for a Personal Trainer, Spring 2007 (N = 186).

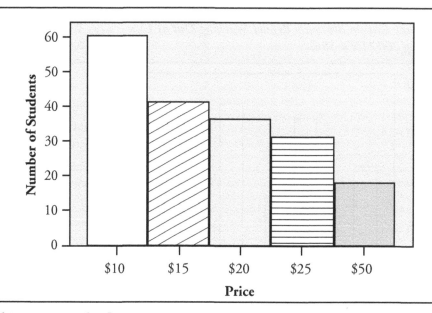

Something to Remember![7]

Some rules for creating histograms:

1. The horizontal axis depicts the variable category or score.
2. The height of the bar (vertical axis) denotes the frequency (or count) of the variable; and the values should increase when moving from bottom to top.
3. The entire graph is constructed so that its height is approximately two-thirds to three-quarters the length of its width.

[7]Adapted from: Nicol and Pexman (2003); and Torres, Preskill, and Piontek (2005).

Line Graph

A *line graph* uses a continuous line to connect data points over time (Figure 4). Line graphs are commonly used to examine rates of change and how fluctuations in an independent variable affect a dependent variable. Principles that should be used when creating line graphs are identified in the following *Something to Remember* box.

Figure 4. Body Index Scores of College Students Who Routinely Exercise Versus Those Who Do Not Exercise, Spring 2007 (N = 186).

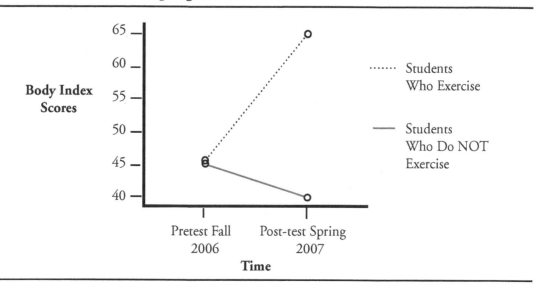

Some rules for creating line graphs:

1. The vertical axis represents the dependent variable and the horizontal axis represents the independent variable.
2. Use no more than three lines within the graph—otherwise it will be too confusing.
3. If printing in black and white, use a different shape or texture for each line. If using color, use a different color for each line, reserving the brightest color for the most important line.
4. The entire graph is constructed so that its height is approximately two-thirds to three-quarters the length of its width.

[8]Adapted from: Nicol and Pexman (2003); and Torres, Preskill, and Piontek (2005).

Your Research

1. What tables do you anticipate developing when reporting your research study? Why? Draft titles for each table you envision appearing in your study.
2. What is your plan for dealing with missing data when putting together your tables?
3. What figures do you think you'll be inserting into your study report? Why? Draft titles for each figure and indicate if the figure will be a pie graph, bar graph, histogram, line graph, or some other figure.

Review & Discussion Questions . . . What have you learned about presenting results?

1. Distinguish between *ungrouped data* and *grouped data* in a frequency distribution.
2. Identify two best practices for developing grouped data categories for *a table*.
3. Recall five rules for setting up a *frequency distribution table*.
4. Draw the differences in appearance of a *pie graph, bar graph, histogram*, and *a line graph*.
5. Identify three rules each for setting up a pie graph, bar graph, histogram, and a line graph.

Exercises

1. Consult the report, *Directions: Youth Development Outcomes of the Camp Experience,* that is available by going to the research pages of the American Camp Association's Web site www. acacamps.org/research/directions.pdf.
    A. What visual techniques were used to present the results?
    B. What did you like and dislike about the way results were presented?

2. Visit the following two sites, the University of Reading's *Informative Presentation of Tables, Graphs and Statistics* (at www.rdg.ac.uk/ssc/publications/guides/tgs.pdf) and Gary Klass', at Illinois State University, Web presentation, *Presenting Data: Tabular and Graphic Display of Social Indicators* (http://www.lilt.ilstu.edu/gmklass/pos138/datadisplay/). Identify three things you learned at each site regarding visual data presentation.

3. Referring to the data noted below, report the scores by creating a frequency distribution table, a pie graph, and a histogram. Figures can be created using any number of available commercial software programs. Most of these programs require entering the data and then selecting the type of chart you desire. Some options include *SPSS, Excel, Quattro Pro*, or *Access*.
    A. The data are the following exam scores for a research methods course: 92, 100, 65, 20, 90, 87, 86, 80, 88, 75, 75, 60, 65, 64, 92, 100, 0, 70, 80, 95, 91, 86, 71, 70, 88, 80, 88, 85, 98, 97, 76, 70, 85.
    B. Some Hints:
        i. For the *frequency table*, report grouped data using the following score groups: 91-100, 81-90, 71-80, 61-70, and ≤ 60.
        ii. For the *pie graph* convert scores using the following grading scheme: 90 - 100 = A, 80 - 89 = B, 70 - 79 = C, 60 - 69 = D, and < 60 = F.
        iii. For the *histogram*, use the listed absolute scores.

4. If not assigned an issue of a professional journal published in the past three years, choose one. Review the reported research articles.
    A. Identify where pie graphs, bar graphs, histograms, and line graphs were used. Make a photo copy of each.

B. Were there instances where the visual aid guidelines identified in this chapter were seemingly violated? Did these violations result in a distracting or misleading table or figure?

C. Identify points where narrative results could have benefited from being presented in a table.

In summarizing findings, visual aids are useful ways to complement orally and written communications about a study. Wall art, from debris gathered from the "Little Venice" waterway, London, England. *Copyright © 2008 Carol Cutler Riddick*

STEP 16: Prepare a Written Report

Types of Reports
Academic Report
Business Report

Final Report Sections
Title Page[1]
Abstract/Executive Summary
Acknowledgements
Table of Contents[1]
Lists of Figures, Tables and Appendices[1]
Introduction[1]
Theoretical Foundation(s) [1]
Hypotheses and/or Research Question(s)[1]
Literature Review[1]
Methods[1]
Results
Discussion
Conclusions
Recommendations
   Recommendations for Professional Practice and Policy
   Recommendations for Future Research
References[1]
Appendices[1]

Constructive Criticism on the Draft Report

Final Report Distribution

---

[1] Because these sections were previously covered in Step 11, they will not be reviewed again in this chapter.

For me, words are a form of action, capable of influencing change.
Ingrid Bengis

A research project without a report of its findings is considered unfinished business. You've completed the research cycle by identifying a topic and then collecting, analyzing, and interpreting information to gain new knowledge of the topic. You now have arrived at the point of having some answers. But until your research has been recorded in written and/or oral presentation form, it remains hidden and, thus, is completely useless. Preparing a good report, whether it is a written or oral report, is hard work. This chapter focuses on preparing the written final report.

Types of Reports

There are two basic kinds of reports, an academic report and a business report (Polonsky & Waller, 2005). Academic reports and business reports differ in terms of language and writing style, structure, and detail.

Academic Report

An *academic report* is used to present research to leisure scholars and managerial level professionals. Academic reports can be presented in any number of formats including a written thesis or dissertation, a written article appearing in a research journal, a report for discussion at an agency staff meeting, or a presentation at a professional conference (covered in Step 17).

The audience for an academic report is typically interested in the literature review, theoretical foundation, methodological details, findings, discussion, conclusions, recommendations, and references. Though an academic report may discuss the managerial implications of the findings, these are not typically the emphasis.

One good way to learn how to write an academic report is to study what others have done. If you're writing a thesis or dissertation, ask your committee chair to identify several written by other students to serve as models. If you're writing for a journal, choose one or two journals in which you'd like to see your work published and study the articles that have recently appeared there.

Business Report

In contrast, *business reports* focus on reporting evaluative research results to internal and external stakeholders of an organization. Business reports emphasize how the problem was examined and based on its findings, provide suggestions for practice. Unlike the academic report, a number of sections—theoretical foundation(s), hypotheses and/or research question, literature review, and methods—are presented in shortened form. Instead, in a business report the emphasis is on service provisions and/or organization management implications.

Final Report Sections

Regardless of report type, the final report is an extension of the proposal. In other words, the final report contains the sections outlined in the proposal, plus some additional sections. The structure of this final report is determined by the nature of the research project and its audience. However, there is a common format used for writing a report. One way to view this is to remember (as mentioned in Step 1) the major phases involved in carrying out research (Figure 1).

Figure 1. Hour-Glass Approach to Research.[1]

- Identify broad subject area

- Collect data

- Discuss and interpret results, state conclusions, and make recommendations

- Narrow topic and focus on concepts, instruments, and design

- Analyze data and present results

[1]Adapted from Trochim (2005).

By way of review, a comparison of the proposal and final report contents (as originally presented in Step 11) is reproduced in Figure 2. The remainder of this section will focus on parts that did not appear in that proposal step chapter but are expected to appear in the final report.

Figure 2. Outline of What Typically Appears in a Proposal and Final Report.

Heading	Contained in Proposal	Contained in Final Report
Title Page[2]	√	√
Abstract/Executive Summary		√
Acknowledgements		√
Table of Contents	√	√
Lists of Figures, Tables and Appendices	√	√
Introduction	√	√
Theoretical Foundation(s)	√	√
Hypotheses and/or Research Question	√	√
Literature Review	√	√
Methods	√	√
Results		√
Discussion		√

Heading	Contained in Proposal	Contained in Final Report
Conclusions		√
Recommendations		√
References	√	√
Appendices	√	√

[2] Sometimes copyright information appears on the title page or the page immediately after the title page. Theses and dissertations, written at American universities, do not need to be registered in order to be protected by copyright law. Other documents, however, must be registered for a small fee with the United States Copyright Office (www.loc. gov/copyright).

Abstract/Executive Summary

The *abstract* or executive summary, is a synopsis of the entire study (Case 1). It is arguably the most important part of the research report since its purpose is to help a reader decide whether to read the entire paper. Ultimately, more people will read an abstract than will go on to read the entire report. This is why abstracts should be written to "stand alone," that is to be understandable without reading anything more about the study (Kielhofner, Fossey, & Taylor, 2006). It takes practice and many revisions to write an effective abstract.

Case 1. Abstract / Executive Summary.[3]

Lai, P., Li, C., Chan, K., & Kwong, K. (2007). An assessment of GPS and GIS in recreational tracking. *Journal of Park and Recreation Administration, 25*, 128-139.

EXECUTIVE SUMMARY: This paper presents an assessment of the effectiveness of using Personal Data Assistants (PDA) equipped with Geographic Information System (GIS) and Global Positioning System (GPS) in field data collection of tourist movement. On-site questionnaire survey and GPS tracking of the leisurely walk of selective groups of park visitors were conducted between August 2005 and January 2006 at various entry points to the Pokfulam Country Park in Hong Kong. The results were examined by means of mapping, 3D visualization, and statistical analyses. Our results indicated that the time of survey and spatial locations influenced the reception of GPS signals. Environmental factors such as terrain, built structures, and tree canopies played an important role in the positioning accuracy. We managed to illustrate a workable method for tracking the flow of tourists and made recommendations on possible uses of such a practice in tourism planning and management.

[3] Reproduced with permission.

An informative abstract will describe the following (Brown, 1996; Hocking & Wallen, 1999):

- Why the study was conducted/the importance of the research topic.
- What was done in the study.
- Who the respondents were.
- What the main results/findings were.
- What the implications are for practice, theory, and/or future research.

Acknowledgements

In the final written report, those individuals who directly supported or cooperated with you during the planning and implementation phases of the study should be publicly acknowledged and thanked. Additionally, individuals as well as sponsors and/or organizations that provided funding for the study should be recognized.

Results

Results are also often labeled as ***Findings***. In this section of the report the analysis of the gathered information is presented. This will include the results of either qualitative or quantitative analyses, or both.

For a quantitative study, present the findings in the same order introduced in the *Introduction* and *Purpose Statement* and *Hypotheses* and/or *Research Question* sections. Remind the reader of each hypothesis or research question examined, then present descriptive and inferential statistics used to examine them (Case 2).

Case 2. Results Section of a Quantitative Study.[4]

The following passage exemplifies how the results from hypothesis testing were described in a *Findings* section.

> The second hypothesis stated that over the course of participating in a Hip-Hop dance program, adolescents will experience an increase in bilateral coordination. Comparing the pretest to the post-test, study participants increased the number of sidesteps they could accomplish in 30-seconds from 15.7 to 16.4 sidesteps, respectively. The change is significant, $t(17) = 1.57, p = .05$.

[4] Adapted from Gaines (2004).

Something to Remember!

When reporting statistics in the Results section, remember to:

- Restate the research question or hypothesis.
- Name the statistical test used.
- Report degrees of freedom (if pertinent).
- Cite the obtained test value.
- Identify the probability level associated with the reported value.

Consider presenting the results in several parts. Alert the reader to this organization by writing something similar to, "The results are presented in three sections. The first section reviews the reliability checks undertaken for the various instruments used in the study. The second section deals with descriptive findings. And the third and final section presents hypotheses testing results." Remember to use the present tense when examining results being discussed ("As Table 4 indicates the play therapy intervention is more effective ...").

Idea . . . Shifting from One Result to Another.

To help a reader journey through a written report, use headings and subheadings (see Step 11) as well as transitional words. Examples of **transitional words** are:

- "Turning to . . . "
- "Looking at . . . "
- "Examining . . . "
- "Concerning the . . . "
- "Regarding . . . "
- "When asked about . . . "
- "Furthermore"
- "Nevertheless"
- "However"
- "Turning attention to responses dealing with the question . . . "

Qualitative studies require presenting data in the report " . . . in such a way that they speak for themselves" (Leedy & Ormrod, 2005, p. 285). This entails providing a **thick description** or presenting data in such detail that the readers can envision the results (Case 3).

Case 3. Results Section of a Qualitative Study.

A study was completed on how youth sport coaches initiate rapport with their team members. Interviews were conducted with the coaches. Results indicated that initiating rapport was accomplished with strict attention to casualness. One of the coaches interviewed described this interaction:

"Just by introducing yourself individually to the player, by chatting along with him as you're doing things. . . . Asking them . . . questions about themselves . . . like do you like to play basketball? How do you like school? And then they'll sort of give you a clue . . . and actually then tell you about themselves . . . even though it's just general chit chat . . . " (Coach #4, Field notes on October 12, 2006).

Findings should be presented in a narrative style and from an emic-etic perspective (Padgett, 1998). First, use a **narrative style** to present the results as if you were presenting a story. This type of writing ushers readers through a journey of discovery and interpretation as if they were there at the study site. Also, an **emic-etic perspective** presents the results from the frame of reference of the research participant, rather than the researcher. The results are told in the participant's own words to add flavor and depth to the interpretation. Case 3 demonstrates the emic-etic perspective. The challenge before you is to " . . . think of your data as a jewel. Your job is to cut and polish this jewel, to select the facets to highlight, and to craft the best setting for it" (Judd, Smith, & Kidder, 1991, p. 454).

Idea . . . Regarding Different Ways to Refer to Numbers and Percentages.

Mix up how you report numbers or percentages in your report. For instance, the following thought can be said three different ways:

" . . . one-fourth of the respondents felt . . . "
" . . . 25% of the respondents reported . . . "
" . . . one out of four respondents expressed . . . "

Also, round out the results in the narrative. After all you don't want to lull your readers or listeners to sleep! Rather than report exact values in the text appearing in the *Results* section, consider using the following word choices:

"About"
"Almost"
"Roughly"
"Nearly"
"More or less than"
"Approaching"
"Approximately"
"Around"
"Rounding up"
"The modal response for"
"A majority" NOTE: When there is a percentage > 50%, it is technically correct to use the word "majority."

Finally, one additional point about the *Results* section of the report. Findings should be described without comment or discussion. Commentary, instead, should be saved for the *Discussion* portion of the final report.

Discussion

This section is all about interpreting your findings— discussing what they suggest or represent. Begin the *Discussion* section by summarizing the purpose, methods, and major findings, but resist the temptation to regurgitate the *Results* section again. Instead, focus on presenting a concise summary that systematically answers the questions originally proposed in the *Introduction* section of the report.

Next, compare and contrast the results with previous studies on the same topic. Do the findings agree with or contradict previously published research on the topic? If the findings are inconsistent with what has been reported earlier, discuss possible explanations for this.

As well, the *Discussion* section of the report relates the results to the theoretical reflection of the study. How can the findings be explained in terms of theoretical models? If a quantitative approach has been used, do the data support or not support the theory used in the study? If a qualitative approach was adopted, discuss the utility of your findings for developing theoretical understanding.

End by discussing alternative explanations for the findings. Highlight plausible competing explanations to what was found. Identify another theory or theoretical approach that might have provided better insights. Point out how some of the acknowledged limitations could have skewed reported results.

Idea . . . Rating Checklist for Discussion Section.[5]

For help in writing the *Discussion* section, consider using the following checklist. After you finish your draft, step back and rate yourself. You may also consider asking your research supervisor or someone knowledgeable about research to rate you.

Discussion	Excellent	Fair	Poor	Suggestions for Improvement
Study purpose and methods have been summarized				
Major results are systematically summarized and discussed in the order found in the *Introduction*				
Major results are integrated with previous research				
Plausible explanations for inconsistent results from previous studies have been stated				
Statement and brief narrative regarding support or non-support of theoretical approach was included or theory is constructed				
Alternative explanations to findings were discussed				

[5]Adapted from Mauch and Park (2003).

Conclusions

In this section of the written final report, begin by making concise concluding remarks about each research question and/or hypothesis examined in the study. Remember that each of these concluding statements must be backed by data presented earlier in the report.

Furthermore, interpretations of the findings should also appear in the *Conclusions* section. You need to talk about the meaning and importance of the results in terms of what was learned from the study (Case 4). Make sure concluding remarks identify how study results tie into theory testing and theory building. The challenge is to write a report that is " . . . faithful to the data but also finds meaning in those data" (Leedy & Ormrod, 2005, p. 282).

Case 4. Conclusions Contained in a Qualitative Study.

Meade, S. (2001). *"Look what boot camp's done for me": Teaching and learning in Lakev-iew Academy Boot Camp.* Unpublished doctoral dissertation, Iowa State University.

Paraphrasing the study, the concluding remarks included the following points:

- The research question was to determine whether attendance at a three-month boot camp was an appropriate method for teaching boys to avoid future involvement in juvenile crime.
- The keys to a positive camp experience were the relationships the boys developed while with both adults and other participants at the camp.
- Once leaving the camp, three of the four boys were unable to mend relationships with key individuals within their lives and experienced continued problems abiding by the law.
- Better aftercare is needed following release from boot camp. The amount and type of aftercare should be individualized depending on what the boy learned at camp; the amount of support he will receive, upon discharge, at home; and physical and emotional challenges confronting him.
- Another alternative would be to develop partial release programs. Namely, boys would participate in a boot camp during the day and return to home at night. This would enable them to practice newly learned skills in a life-like environment, while at same time receiving support during times of crisis and frustration.
- In order to reduce juvenile crime recidivism, interventions need to be designed that have been based on theories centering on learning, forgetting, and generalizing.

The concluding remarks should be carefully written. One common mistake is to overstate or understate the importance of the findings. Never state that the study is the definitive work on the topic. And, as discussed in Step 7, be particularly vigilant not to make extravagant claims and unwarranted inferences. As well, don't be too shy about the importance of your findings, stating them accurately is sometimes a difficult balance.

Idea . . . Rating Checklist for Conclusion Section.[6]

As you've done for the *Discussion* section, use the following checklist to check your draft of the *Conclusions* section. After you finish your draft, step back and rate yourself and also ask your research supervisor to score you.

Conclusions	Excellent	Fair	Poor	Suggestions for Improvement
A conclusion for each research question and/ or hypothesis has been clearly stated				
Conclusions are based on attained results				
Meanings and importance of results were explained and were framed within the limitations of the study				
Implications for theory testing or theory building have been mentioned				
Avoided making extravagant claims or inferences				

[6]Adapted from Mauch and Park (2003).

Recommendations

A major component of the report should consist of recommendations. ***Recommendations*** are the all-important action link from the present to the future. If evaluative research has been conducted, recommendations are especially important for professional practice and policy. If basic research is being reported, recommendations for future research are helpful.

Recommendations for professional practice and policy. Figure 3 summarizes how the research process ultimately leads to providing useful information by making recommendations for professional practice.

Figure 3. How the Research Process Leads to Recommendations.[7]

The flow behind program evaluation:

Ask Questions
↓
Seek Answers to the Questions
↓
Analyze Data
↓
Reflect on Results
↓
Act on What Has Been Learned, **Make Changes**!

[7]Adapted from Patton (1997).

This means recommendations stemming from a research project should be written in a manner that provides specific guidance for organizational actions (Case 5). To increase their likelihood of being used, be reflective and thoughtful when crafting professional practice and policy recommendations.

Case 5. Professional Practice and Policy Recommendation.

The Parks and Recreation Department of San Mateo, California conducted a study of how their recreation programs should be enhanced. An excerpt from the study's recommendations section follows:

> Recreation programming services will be managed more strategically within core program areas to ensure alignment with community demographics and lifestyle trends. An improved inventory of community recreation facilities that better support both program needs and revenue generation capabilities is needed. This includes the construction of a new, signature Lifestyle Recreation Center and indoor aquatics complex at Bay Meadows Park. (Retrieved January 28, 2005, from www.ci.sanmateo.ca.us /dept/parks/plan)

Something to Remember![8]

In order to enhance the acceptance of recommendations stemming from an evaluative research project, consider adopting the following strategies:

• **Be practical in what you're recommending.** The advice should be feasible, given the organization's available resources.
• **Recommendations should be compatible with each other.** For example, if you advocate for increasing services, then don't turn around and propose budget cuts.

> • **Share preliminary recommendations with stakeholders.** Don't assume that your version of the solution is the only "answer." You may need to modify recommendations after collaborating with the stakeholders.

[8]Adapted from Fullan (2007).

Idea . . . Writing Recommendations for Professional Practice and Policy.

It is important that practice and policy recommendations are understandable. To foster clarity, consider addressing as many of the following five points as possible:

What	Clearly state the recommendation. In other words, make a statement regarding a course of action.
Why	Provide a rationale for the recommendation, drawing on relevant information (e.g., research results, previous studies, theoretical suppositions).
Where	Specify exactly what programs, facilities, personnel, and departmental functions (such as marketing) should be involved in carrying out the recommendation.
When	Identify the desired time frame for carrying out the recommendation. If recommendations need to be phased in, identify a timetable and ultimate completion deadline.
Who	Earmark the roles of the individual(s) or entities who should be involved in carrying out the recommendation.

Recommendations for professional practice and policy may deal with any number of ideas. For instance, recommendations may call for a change in program operations, a new direction for a program, a change in personnel policies, a shift in resource allocation, an extension of services, or even a new philosophy or mission for the organization.

Recommendations should inform management decisions by identifying areas in which changes may be considered for future implementation. It may be prudent to advocate that changes take place over a period of time (Case 6). Regardless of the time frame used, anticipate and deal with controversial recommendations.

Case 6. Phasing-In Recommendation.

Here is an excerpt from the recommendations for perking up tourism in Hampton Beach, New Hampshire:

> For planning purposes, proposed action steps can be divided into three different time frames: short-term (1-2 years), mid-term (3-9 years), and long-term (10-50 years). For example, in order to extend the tourist season, Hampton Beach needs to create more activities and excitement in the "shoulder" months of April, May, September, and October. This can be accomplished in the short-term by establishing ongoing programs like a farmer's market or by having a seasonal, weekend-long festival such as a regatta or a hot-air balloon race. (Retrieved De-

cember 24, 2006, from www.hampton.lib.nh.us/hampton/town/masterplan/ mastplan4c.htm)

Recommendations for future research. Completed research should inform future research. You can do this by writing recommendations that fall into two areas of emphases.

First, outline your ideas for how additional research might improve upon what has been reported. That is, develop recommendations for future research that address your study's shortcomings (Case 7, first four recommendations). Start by acknowledging limitations of the study. Every study has limitations that have possible effects on the outcomes of the study. Be proactive by recognizing and admitting these criticisms rather than ignoring or trying to hide them. Remember, there is no such thing as a "perfect" study. Every research project has inherent weaknesses. Identify how future researchers can build upon your work by addressing some of your study's shortcomings, including flawed hypotheses as well as weaknesses related to the research design, sample selection, instrumentation, and statistical analyses.

Case 7. Recommendations for Future Research.

Jones, E. (2003). Reminiscence therapy for older women with depression. *Journal of Gerontological Nursing, 29,* 27-33.

Among the suggestions cited for future research are the need to:

1. Use larger sample sizes and random selection of participants.
2. Conduct longitudinal studies to determine the effects of reminiscence therapy over time.
3. Include qualitative methods to determine the perceived effect reminiscence therapy has on elevating overall mood and improving quality of life.
4. Determine the efficacy of reminiscence therapy with various elderly populations in a variety of long-term care settings.
5. Examine impact of reminiscence therapy on elderly: men, individuals experiencing cognitive decline, and adults from numerous ethnic and cultural backgrounds.
6. Verify the results of this study through replication.

Second, recommendations for future research should identify ways to extend the reported study. One possibility is to identify additional research questions (Case 7, point 5) and hypotheses suggested by your study's results. Another way is to call for replication (Case 7, point 6) and extension studies. It could also be advocated that alternative theoretical frameworks and conceptual maps (Step 3) be examined.

Idea . . . Rating Checklist for Recommendations Section.[9]

Draft the *Recommendations* section using the following checklist. Rate yourself. Then ask your research supervisor or someone knowledgeable about research to also score you.

Recommendations	Excellent	Fair	Poor	Suggestions for Improvement
Suggestions on how to improve service operations and/or management				
Ideas for future studies that address some of the present study's limitations				
Thoughts on how to extend the present study				

Constructive Criticism on the Draft Report

When you have carefully finished editing and proofreading your written research report, ask someone you trust to read it. After a while, it becomes increasingly difficult to read objectively what you have written. As a reminder, it is a big mistake to rely on computer spell and grammar checks to catch your errors. Not all mistakes are caught.

Next, you should share your draft with those who have a big stake in your research report. If you're a student, this initially will be your thesis/dissertation committee chair. If you're completing a program evaluation report, then you should share your draft with the staff program manager. Request a one-on-one meeting with these individuals after allowing a week or two for reading the report. Ask for constructive criticism and insights that can enhance the readability and acceptability of the report. Then, revise the report according to what you learned from these "sneak previews."

Final Report Distribution

Finally, you need to disseminate the final report. Research that is not publicly shared is incomplete. **Dissemination** refers to the processes by which researchers inform others about the study. Dissemination mechanisms should be chosen to ensure that your findings are effectively communicated and utilized (Patton, 1997). Who should know about the outcomes of the study? What information will be most relevant for them?

So, the research process is not finished until you think of ways to inform the various stakeholder groups both inside and outside your organization about the contents of the report. Among the actions that can be adopted are the following:

1. Conduct an "in response" campaign by implementing simple and quick ways to provide feedback to program participants (e.g., highlight the study's conclusions and changes the organization is making accordingly in "survey says" flyers located at the facility's front desk, posted on bulletin boards, and on the organization's Web site).
2. Prepare a popularized version of the report for a pamphlet, brochure, or booklet.

3. Issue a press release that is sent to local newspapers.
4. Present findings at professional meeting (see Step 17).
5. Publish a Web site or a link to the organization's home page.
6. Write an article about the study and submit the manuscript for publication consideration to a professional journal. For some guidance on how to do this, retrieve D. Bem's 2002 article, "Writing the Empirical Journal Article" from http://dbem.ws/WritingArticle.pdf.

"Dissemination" of the results of research can take many different forms. Notice how effectively the "message" is disseminated through art. Museum of Contemporary Art, Chicago. *Copyright © 2008 Ruth V. Russell*

Your Research

1. **Identify your target audience for the report.**
2. **Draft a report of your research project.**
3. **Review the drafted *Results* section by using the checklist found in this chapter.**
4. **Rate your *Discussion* section by using the checklist presented in this chapter.**
5. **Evaluate your *Conclusions* section by using the checklist presented in this chapter.**
6. **Review your *Recommendations* section. If appropriate, did you remember to address professional practices and policy? Did you provide ideas for future research?**

7. Review the draft making sure you have not violated any of the writing rules reviewed in this chapter.
8. What ideas do you have for disseminating your study outcomes?

Review & Discussion Questions . . . What have you learned about preparing a written report?

1. Distinguish between an *academic report* and a *business report.*
2. What major points are covered in the *abstract?* And what is the approximate word count of an abstract?
3. Who should be recognized in the *Acknowledgements?*
4. How is the *Results* section organized?
5. How is the *Discussion* section ordered?
6. What goes into the *Conclusion* section?
7. When crafting *policy and practice recommendations* for an evaluative research project, what five points ideally should be addressed?
8. Identify two emphases for *future research recommendations.* What role does a study's limitations have in future research recommendations?
9. Sketch out ideas for how to gather *constructive feedback* to a preliminary research report that has been drafted.
10. Identify three ways to distribute the final research report.

Exercises

1. Explore content and style differences that exist in our professional journals. Begin by selecting (if not assigned one) an article from a recent (published in the past three years) issue of the academic journal, *Journal of Leisure Research.* Compare it with an article from a more practitioner-oriented journal, such as *Journal of Park and Recreation Administration.*
   A. What language and writing style differences exist? List the main differences.
   B. Using Figure 2 in this chapter, how do the two reports differ in their adopted outlines? What (dis)similar topic and subtopic headings are used in the two reports?

2. Using one of the articles from Exercise 1 above:
   A. Analyze the *Discussion and Conclusions* section of the report by using the checklist found in this chapter (make sure you complete the comments column).
   B. Analyze *Recommendations* found in the report by using the checklist found in this chapter.

3. Read the report *Directions: Youth Development Outcomes of the Camp Experience.* This report was written for multiple audiences and is available by going to American Camp Association's Web site at www.acacamps.org (click on "Education" then "Research," then finally choose the report name, "Directions").
   A. How would you classify this report? Is it an example of an academic report, a business report, or a blend of the two?

B. What did you like and dislike about the organization of the report?

C. What did you like and dislike about the style of writing used in the report?

D. What conclusions were reached by the authors of the report? Do you agree with these conclusions; that is, were conclusions supported by the findings?

E. What recommendations for future practice were made?

F. What recommendations for future research were implied or stated?

4. Practice drafting conclusions and making recommendations. If not assigned an article, select a journal article or other research report that is in an area of interest to you. Try to use a study that used a fairly simple research design.

A. Before reading the report, tape a piece of paper over the report's *Discussion* section, the part where interpretations and conclusions are drawn.

B. Read the article carefully up to the covered discussion section.

C. Write your own discussion of the results. Interpret the results in terms of the research question(s) and hypotheses examined in the study and the literature reviewed. What do you conclude?

D. What implications do the results have for professional practice and/or policy?

E. Given the limitations of the study, what recommendations could be made for future research on the topic?

F. Remove the paper from the article, and compare your discussion with that of the original report. Did you hit the main points? Do not be so concerned at this time with the polish of your writing or differences in writing style.

G. Share your answers with those of your classmates.

5. Practice reading and thinking about recommendations associated with a research report. Go to the "Parks and Recreation Update" feature appearing in the *Parks and Recreation* magazine by accessing the following link, www.nrpa.org, in the "Search" box type "Research Update." If not assigned a particular reading, choose an *Research Update* column that has appeared in the past 12 months.

A. What is the research topic?

B. What recommendations for professional practice and/or policy do the research authors make?

C. What future research recommendations are proposed?

D. What recommendations were not made that you feel are warranted?

6. As a supplement to this chapter, go to the U.S. Department of Health and Human Services' Office of Planning, Research and Evaluation Web site at www.acf.hhs.gov/programs/opre and in the "Search" box type "Program Manager's Guide to Evaluation." Once in this document read, "Chapter 9: How Can You Report What You Have Learned." What three insights did you learn from reviewing the "Sample Outline for the Final Evaluation Report?"

A final research project report that is not communicated and distributed is like a flower that no one sees or smells. Peony, in Botanic Garden, Lacock, England. *Copyright © 2008 Carol Cutler Riddick*

STEP 17: Deliver an Oral Report

Identify the Audience

Plan the Presentation
Structure
Visual Aids
Handouts

Practice the Presentation

Develop Strategies for Handling Questions

**Good communication is as stimulating as black coffee
and just as hard to sleep after.**
Anne Morrow Lindbergh

In most instances, the culmination of a research endeavor includes an oral report. An oral presentation provides an opportunity to inform the study's users what was done and learned in the research endeavor. An example of an oral research presentation is a thesis or dissertation defense (Figure 1).

Figure 1. Anatomy of a Thesis or Dissertation Oral Defense.

- Once the faculty chair of the thesis or dissertation considers the written research report prepared by the student to be adequate, a final oral defense is scheduled. About two to three weeks prior to the scheduled defense, the written thesis or dissertation is distributed to the remaining committee members.
- Typically, the defense is limited to committee members. Yet, many universities require the defense to be announced to the entire campus community, and anyone in the university community is welcome to attend.
- At the beginning of the defense, the faculty chair asks the degree candidate to provide a brief (approximately 20 minutes) overview of his/her study.
- During the next two to three hours, committee members ask questions of the candidate. Other people in attendance may or may not be permitted to ask questions.
- Once the committee members have exhausted their questions, the candidate and any guests are asked to leave the room. The committee then discusses whether or not to pass the candidate's research thesis or dissertation. There are four vote outcomes: (1) The research is approved; (2) The research is approved but minor modifications are required; (3) Approval is withheld until major revisions are made; or (4) The research is failed. It has been our experience that if the student has followed the advice of the committee chair, "approved with minor modifications" is the most common vote.
- The candidate is then ushered back into the room and informed of the committee's vote and any imposed revision conditions.

Often an oral research report is presented informally. One informal mechanism, frequently used at professional meetings, is a poster session. A ***poster session*** involves researchers preparing and mounting information about their study on multiple-paneled storyboards, and then informally discussing the contents with session attendees as they walk around reading the posters. Figure 2 presents the layout commonly used for a poster session storyboard, and Figure 3 provides some tips related to preparing and presenting it.

These people are discussing thesis research conducted by a Gallaudet University student and reported at the 2004 National Therapeutic Recreation Society's poster session held in Reno, Nevada. *Copyright © 2008 Randi Baron-Leonard. Used with permission.*

Figure 2. Template for Poster Session.[1]

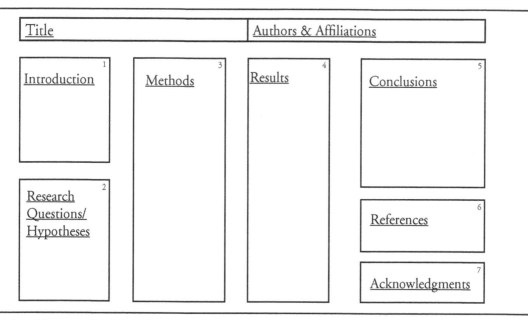

[1] Adapted from: Nicol and Pexman (2003); and Rosnow and Rosnow (2006).

Figure 3. Guidelines for Preparing a Poster.[2]

When preparing a multiple-panel poster, consider the following points:

1. **Know the space size allocated for the poster.** Typically, the assigned space is 4' high by 6' to 8' wide.
2. **Arrive on time.** Allow enough time to set up, especially if you have not been assigned a specific area to set your poster up in.
3. **Use black ink, print panels on white standard sized, 8½" by 11" paper set up in a landscape orientation.** Another option is to mount printed panels on stiffer, colored paper (such as red, blue, or yellow) that, in turn, is bonded to a white poster board.
4. **Use 48-point font for the title, and with two exceptions** (the *References* and *Acknowledgements* sections), **24-point type for the remaining sections in either Arial or Helvetica sans serif font**. If there is enough room to include the *References* and *Acknowledgements* sections, then smaller font can be used for these two sections.
5. **After the first two panels** (i.e., title and author identification) **number the panels.** This helps the reader follow the correct order.
6. **Limit each panel to 16 or fewer lines.**
7. **Use single-spaced text sparingly.**
8. **Whenever possible, in lieu of text, use bulleted or numbered lists and tables and figures.**
9. **Stick to the main point(s), present a few key findings and highlight conclusions supported by the data.**
10. **Bring push-pins, thumbtacks, or tape to mount your poster.**
11. **Have ready a 2-3 minute spiel about your poster.** As visitors approach, ask if they would like to be "walked through" the study.
12. **At the end of the session, promptly remove your poster board.** The room may be scheduled for another event.

---

[2]Adapted from: Nicol and Pexman (2003); and Rosnow and Rosnow (2006).

During the session, numerous posters are presented simultaneously. The author(s) stand by their respective poster boards, and the audience walks around reading posters that catch their interest. Sometimes people ask questions and/or make comments to the author about what has been presented in the poster.

Whether the oral presentation is as formal as a dissertation defense or as informal as a poster session, quite a bit of groundwork is needed to deliver it effectively and powerfully. In particular, you need to:

1. Identify the audience.
2. Plan the presentation.
3. Practice the presentation.
4. Develop strategies for handling questions.

Identify the Audience

Knowing beforehand who the audience will be is vital in planning and organizing an oral report. Generally, audiences for your research and evaluation studies fall into two broad categories: stakeholders and scientific/academic entities (Kielhofner, 2006). Recalling Step 1, stakeholders, for example, might include participants in the study, funding authorities, and agency staff members who will be expected to carry out the study's recommendations. Other stakeholders could be advocacy and lobby groups who represent the interests of people studied. For all these stakeholders the oral report should contain information about decisions and actions needed, based on the outcomes of the study.

The scientific/academic type of audience, on the other hand, is usually more intrigued by the study's methods and conclusions. Thus, oral presentations made to college classes, professional conferences, and thesis or dissertation defenses are focused on the accuracy of the research process used. This audience is also interested in what was learned from your study that could benefit future research.

In short, the audience for the oral report will not only define the content and coverage of the material but also the presentation style. In some situations another layer of audience applies to these choices as well. In most scientific/academic research dissemination situations, you must first submit your proposed oral report presentation (including posters) for *peer review*. This preliminary review process is used to ensure the quality of the information to be presented, and its suitability for the particular audience of the meeting or conference. Typically, a panel of experts on the subject and/or method of your study reads a short synopsis (*abstract*) of your intended report and collectively judges it acceptable for presentation. Sometimes the reviewers carry out what is labeled a *blind review*, meaning they do not know the names of the author(s) of the abstract.

Plan the Presentation

Once the audience has been identified, attention must be given to identifying objectives for the presentation. In particular, your talk should address what the audience members want to understand and need to know. Thorough preparation should be devoted to structuring the presentation, as well as developing visual aids and handouts for the presentation.

Structure

One way to organize a formal oral report is to think of it as a story you have to tell that has a beginning, middle, and end. The beginning consists of introductory remarks related to the study's background, the research purpose, hypotheses and/or research questions; the middle is the body of the report addressing main points related to methods, results, and discussion of results; and the ending focuses on recommendations and conclusions (Torres, Preskill, & Pionteck, 2005). Telling the beginning, middle, and end of the story well requires lots of planning because customarily you will have only 10 to 20 minutes to do it.

Something to Remember!

Try using this formula for structuring the content of a formal oral presentation:

• Start by telling the audience how the talk is organized.
• Then, provide an overview or introductory remarks.
• Review the methods used.
• Reveal and discuss major results.
• Make recommendations.
• State conclusions.
• Summarize what you told the audience.

Visual Aids

Visual aids are useful tools in oral communication. Examples of *visual aids* are PowerPoint slides, transparencies, flip charts, handouts, poster boards, and video presentations. Today, the most commonly used visual aid is PowerPoint slides followed by transparencies. Figures 4 and 5 outline points to consider.

Figure 4. PowerPoint Guidelines.[3]

When preparing a PowerPoint presentation, use the following guidelines:

1. **Choose a template design that supports your message and use the same design across all the slides.**
2. **Use the same font style for every slide and stick to font styles and font sizes that are readable.** Arial fonts are better than Times Roman fonts for PowerPoint presentations. Use a minimum font size of 24.
3. **Follow the "6 X 6" rule.** No more than six lines of text per slide and no more than six words per line. Use short sentences, phrases, or bulleted keywords.
4. **Number your slides.** This will help during the question-answer period.
5. **If using PowerPoint animation, drop slides down from above or from the left.** Once you choose, don't change the direction of entering text as this will cause confusion.
6. **Use upper and lowercase letters.**
7. **If using color, make sure the font and background colors are contrasting.** Use only black font and a light background color if the audience is large.
8. **Plan on one visual for each minute of your presentation.** Don't make the mistake of trying to cover too many slides in a short period of time.
9. **Arrive early to set up and make sure everything is working.** Find out if an extension cord or a cable between the computer and projection system is needed. If using your own laptop, have a backup copy to what has been stored on your hard drive. And, be prepared to provide printed handouts if all else fails!

---

[3] Adapted from: Gratton and Jones (2004); and Torres, Preskill and Piontek (2005).

Figure 5. Tips for Using Transparencies.[4]

In addition to the advice above for PowerPoint, when using transparencies also remember to:

• **Mount the transparencies into frames.** This prevents them from sliding off the projector.
• **Arrive early.** Make sure there is a second workable bulb on hand, in case the first bulb burns out. Also take the time to focus the projector beforehand.
• **Place the transparency as high on the projector's screen as possible.** This makes the transparency more readable to a greater number of audience members.

[4] Adapted from Torres, Preskill and Piontek (2005).

Using visual aids can increase audience understanding as well as sustain their interest during the presentation. Information on the various facets of the research can be presented through the use of visual aids. Nevertheless, care should be taken that the visual aids are relevant, readable, and have an uncluttered appearance. If not carefully planned, visual aids can actually distract from the oral report.

Visual aids can be spruced up with ***stock art*** or photographs, illustrations, clip art, and animations that are available online. Most stock art images must be purchased and there is tremendous variation in pricing, depending on the stock house itself, how the images are going to be used, and their quality.

Idea . . . Visual Images for Oral Reports of Evaluative Research.[5]

Consider using stock art such as these for reporting results and making recommendations:

On Target   **Making Progress**   **Needs Improvement**

[5] These clip art images can be downloaded free-of-charge from Microsoft Office's online web collections.

Stock art is available two ways: (1) Royalty-free art and (2) Licensed art. ***Royalty-free art*** is acquired either as a subscription or for an individual image fee, and can be manipulated and used as often as you desire. ***Licensed art*** is sold for one-time use and must be used as-is. Different conditions may apply for commercial use of stock art. Be very careful not to use online sources of photographs, animations, or illustrations unless given express permission by the copyright owner to do so. Sometimes such permission will require citing them as the source.

Handouts

Psychologists tell us that people forget about 90% of everything that is said to them within 24 hours of hearing it. So, the expectation is that at a formal oral presentation the speaker will provide a handout related to the presentation.

Handouts can vary from providing paper copies of an abstract or executive summary, PowerPoint presentation slides, or the full final report. Sometimes people take a shortcut and only distribute tables and figures or a list of references used for the research report.

There are three philosophies about when and how to distribute handouts to an audience. The debate is whether to distribute handouts prior to or immediately after the oral presentation, or mail them only to expressly interested people.

Some speakers like to distribute handouts prior to their presentation by either placing them on audience member seats or making them available to people as they enter the presentation room. The advantage of prior distribution is when complicated material is presented, such as in tables, the audience finds it easier to follow along with your remarks. The disadvantage is that handouts can be distracting because the audience tends to read the handout and not listen to the prepared talk.

Others don't make handouts available to the audience until after the formal oral report is concluded. The rationale is that the presenter does not want to distract the audience from listening.

A third strategy is to ask audience members to sign up to receive handouts later, such as via the mail. The reason often cited for this tactic is to minimize having to transport paper copies to the meeting or conference.

Practice the Presentation

The quality and effectiveness of an oral research report is determined by the study's content as well as the presenter's public speaking skills. Delivering a good oral report requires several rehearsals that focus on substance, delivery, and timing.

Try to enlist one or more friends or family members to listen to a dress rehearsal of your oral presentation. Then, use Figure 6 to solicit feedback from these practice listeners.

Figure 6. Judging a Dress Rehearsal of a Formal Research Presentation.

Does the Presenter:	Yes	NO
1. Stand erect?		
2. Avoid reading word for word from visual aids or a paper?		
3. Set the tone and expectations for the presentation?		

Does the Presenter:	Yes	No
4. Hold five to six second gazes at different audience members?		
5. Keep hands away from mouth?		
6. Keep hands from "playing with things" like paper clips, etc.?		
7. Speak clearly, enthusiastically, and at the right pace (not too fast and not too slow)?		
8. Change pitch and voice loudness as well as body language and position?		
9. Use subtle pauses between key points?		
10. Attend to the audience's body language and adjust content and/or delivery speed as necessary?		
11. Appropriately respond to the audience's questions and reactions?		
12. Act relaxed and appear natural?		
13. Use a laser pointer or pen, rather than fingers, when pointing to the visual?		
14. Dress professionally?		
15. Avoid chewing gum or sucking on candy?		

[6]Adapted from: Polonsky and Waller (2005); and Torres, Preskill and Piontek (2005).

It is important to stay within the allocated time limit otherwise you run the risk of not holding the audience's interest and being perceived as long-winded and boring. Furthermore, you could selfishly be taking time away from other presenters. Finally, knowing how to operate projection equipment beforehand will help in delivering a smooth and timely presentation.

Idea . . . For Experiencing a Successful Thesis/Dissertation Final Oral Defense.[7]

If you have worked closely with your committee chair and communicated along the way with other committee members, the final defense should come off without a major glitch.

The student's responsibilities for the final defense are to:

- **Be well prepared.** Be able to answer, in depth if necessary, questions about the research. It is the student's responsibility to convince the committee that he/she understood the research process.
- **Rehearse by setting up a simulation defense.** Consider asking fellow students to act the roles of committee members. Provide these "stand ins" with copies of the thesis/dissertation. Role-playing should hone in on learning to deliver clear responses.
- **Discuss concerns about the final defense with your advisor.** The student must feel confident to explain every aspect of his/her research.
- **Schedule the defense meeting and secure a room to hold the meeting.**
- **Be open and honest during the defense.** Admit limitations of the study. Be responsible for what

was done and not done in the study and what was written. Don't be defensive and don't be afraid to say "I don't know."
- **Be a note taker or ask someone else to assume this responsibility.** One option is to use a voice activated-tape recorder. Sometimes the committee chair may take on the note-taker role.

The chair's responsibilities for the final defense are to:

- **Inform the student, beforehand, what happens during the defense.** Expectations for the student should be clearly explained.
- **Advise the student on how to prepare for the final defense.**
- **Review limitations of the study.** The advisor's role is to help the student feel at ease in discussing and answering questions about his/her thesis/dissertation.
- **Ensure balanced participation of every person on the committee for asking questions and making comments.**
- **Ensure that observers are separated physically from the candidate and committee members.** As well, inform the observers they are not to talk (make comments, ask questions, etc.) during the defense unless expressly invited to.
- **Bring the session to a close.** Once every committee member has had a chance to ask questions and the student has had opportunities to respond, it is up to the chair to bring the defense to a close.
- **Guide the committee to a consensus.** If there is disagreement among committee members, the chair should encourage all members to weigh in on the matter and then help guide the group until a fair resolution occurs.
- **Clearly summarize, at the end of the meeting, the decision of the committee as well as any changes that are being required.**
- **Make sure the student executes any requested changes imposed by the committee.** If the committee votes to accept with revisions, then the chair should make sure these changes are made.

[7] Adapted from: Mauch and Park (2003).

Develop Strategies for Handling Questions

At some point(s) in the oral research presentation, the audience is encouraged to ask questions. Typically, at staff and board meetings, listeners often pose questions as the presentation progresses. At professional meetings, however, a 10-20-minute question-answer period is usually held after the conclusion of prepared remarks.

There are advantages and disadvantages to holding questions until the end. The advantage of waiting is that the speaker is ensured of having enough time to go through the prepared remarks. The disadvantage is that if an important point is not understood, the audience can become lost or preoccupied and not follow the remainder of the talk.

One challenge confronting research presenters is dealing with a difficult question. Our advice is definitely not to become defensive, answer a question that wasn't asked, or waffle. There is something endearing about admitting not knowing the answer to a question. If a typographic error is identified, then acknowledge it. If a more fundamental problem is pointed out, admit something is wrong rather than trying to rationalize or make an argument that attempts to defend the mistake. Answer questions concisely and clearly. You want to make the impression of being confident and competent.

Something to Remember![8]

Common questions asked at final defenses of theses and dissertations are the following:

- Why did you choose the topic?
- If you could do it all over again, what would you do differently in designing, implementing, or reporting the research?
- How has your research contributed to our professional practice? Our theoretical understanding?
- How should your line of research be continued?
- What have you personally learned from doing the research?

[8] Adapted from: Mauch and Park (2003).

Your Research

1. **Using the principles outlined in this chapter, draft a PowerPoint presentation of your research.**
2. **Rehearse your PowerPoint presentation in front of colleagues or classmates. Provide the assembled group a paper copy of your PowerPoint presentation.**
3. **Identify, with feedback from your rehearsal audience, the least successful aspects of your presentation in terms of preparation and/or delivery. Fix the problems and rehearse again. Did you improve?**

Review & Discussion Questions . . . What have you learned about delivering an oral report?

1. **Briefly describe what is involved with a *poster session*.**
2. **What are the four activities associated with creating an effective and powerful oral presentation?**
3. **Identify at least four behaviors to practice when *rehearsing* an oral research report.**
4. **Recall two things not to do when *responding to a difficult question* posed about the research presentation you make.**

Exercises

1. Read more about how to give a presentation by reading Kevin Boone's ideas at www.kevin-boone.com/PF_howto_presentation.html. Identify three additional points you learned from the web site about presenting.

2. Visit 3M's Presentation Center at www.mmm.com/meetingnetwork/presentations/index.html and review the various articles (the articles are short, generally two pages long) contained un-

der "Creating Presentations" and "Delivering Presentations." Identify three tips you learned, for each of the following topics:

  A. Deliver a masterful oral presentation.
  B. Improve visual aids.
  C. Improve handouts.

3. Unless another subject matter is identified by your instructor, locate two stock art visuals (photograph, clip art, illustration, etc.) related to recreation that are classified as royalty-free, from any of the following online resources:

  A. Adobe Image Library (studio.adobe.com) contains art, illustrations and photographic pictures.
  B. Getty Images (http://creative.gettyimages.com) offers animations, clip art, and photographs.
  C. ClipArt Connection (www.clipartconnection.com) supplies clip art images and animations.
  D. Super Stock (www.superstock.com), Comstock (www.comstock.com), Photo Spin (www.photospin.com), and Photos To Go (www.photostogo.com) provide photographic images.
  E. PhotoSphere (www.photosphere.com) and PictureQuest (www.pictureQuest.com) handles photographs and illustrations.

4. Attend an actual research presentation. Critique the presenter in terms of his/her:

  A. Structure or content.
  B. Use of visual aids.
  C. Distributed handouts.
  D. Dealing with posed questions.

An oral presentation provides the opportunity to inform the audience what was done and learned in the research project. Venice, Italy. *Copyright © 2008 Carol Cutler Riddick*

Part VI: Mise en Scène

Stemming from the theater, the French term ***mise en scène*** literally means putting into the scene. When applied to the cinema, *mise en scène* refers to the arrangement of everything that appears before the camera, namely the sets, props, lighting, as well as the positioning and movement of actors. By controlling the *mise en scène*, the film director guides the events for the camera (Bordwell & Thompson, 2004).

To conclude our presentation on evaluation and research on recreation, park, sport, and tourism topics, the *mise en scène* function serves as a useful analogy. Thus, for the book's finale, we'll pull together everything that appears in a research scene. We will do this in two ways. First, we'll review the notion that research is a process that when considered in its totality resembles an hourglass. Second, using this model as a guide, the checklist of steps involved in the discovery of knowledge will be reviewed.

As you should recall, conducting research can be thought of as a process that takes the shape of an hourglass (Figure 1). Simply put, you start broadly, narrow in on particulars then broaden out again. That is, the initial stage of determining your topic is a wide-open enterprise. After the topic is determined you narrow in by deciding on what information needs to be collected and how to collect this information. Data are then collected and analyzed. The final stage requires opening up your perspective again so that your conclusions and recommendations are useful to others. Taken together, this is the "scene" of the research process.

Figure 1. Hourglass Shape of Research.[1]

- Identify broad subject area

- Collect data

- Discuss and interpret results, state conclusions, and make recommendations

- Narrow topic and focus on concepts, instruments, and design

- Analyze data and present results

[1]Adapted from Trochim (2005).

The research process "scene" can be further examined up close. If you use a camera to zoom into what goes into the research process, a number of steps would be revealed (Figure 2).

Figure 2. Checklist for Starting, Designing, Developing, Implementing, and Reporting Research.

Getting Started

Step 1 – Decide on a Topic
[ ] Consider all sources for research topic ideas.
[ ] Determine whether your interest is in measuring program need, design, process, impact, economics, or basic research.
[ ] Sort through ideas to select the most interesting, plausible, ethical, manageable, and valuable one.

Step 2 – Review the Literature
[ ] Think about how a literature review helps to: select a topic, conceptual approach, rationale for a study, and methods for a study; as well as assist in understanding and interpreting results.
[ ] Conduct a search by using keywords to find secondary sources, general references, and primary sources of research literature.
[ ] Review and analyze primary sources.
[ ] Write up the literature review.

Step 3 – Identify Theoretical Underpinnings
[ ] Consider the appropriateness of a quantitative theoretical approach.
[ ] Consider the appropriateness of a qualitative theoretical approach.
[ ] Consider the appropriateness of a mixed-methods theoretical approach.

Step 4 – Develop a Scope of Study
[ ] Determine unit of analysis.
[ ] Determine variables.
[ ] Develop purpose statement.
[ ] Identify hypotheses, if appropriate.
[ ] Write research question(s).

Step 5 – Explain Study's Significance
[ ] Make the case for the study's significance to professional practice, social problems, and/or contributions to scientific knowledge.
[ ] Write a significance statement.

Developing a Plan

Step 6 – Select a Sample
[ ] Identify the population (if appropriate).
[ ] Choose a method of probability sampling, and/or
[ ] Choose a method of nonprobability sampling.

Step 7 – Choose a Design
[ ] Select a quantitative design.
[ ] Determine its validity, generalizability, and necessary sample size, or
[ ] Select a qualitative design and
[ ] Determine its rigor, or
[ ] Select a mixed-methods design.

Step 8 – Consider Measurement
[ ] Determine the kind of measurement to adopt.
[ ] Decide on multiple variable measures.
[ ] Choose between single- and multiple-item measures.
[ ] Take into account instrument validity.
[ ] Think about instrument reliability.
[ ] Consider using normative data measures.
[ ] Decide between developing your own instrument(s) and/or adopting those instruments previously used in research studies.

Step 9 – Specify Data-Collection Methods
[ ] Deliberate on the use of triangulation.
[ ] Select a quantitative data-collection method.
[ ] And/or select a qualitative data-collection method.

Step 10 – Address Ethical Responsibilities: Assure Your Responsibility to
[ ] Nonmaleficence.
[ ] Beneficence.
[ ] Respect.
[ ] Honesty.
[ ] Justice.
[ ] Competence.

Step 11 – Seek Proposal Approval
[ ] Write a study proposal.
[ ] Seek approval for the proposal from all relevant entities.

Implementing the Study

Step 12 – Conduct a Pilot Test
[ ] Determine the purposes for a pilot test.
[ ] Carry out the pilot test.

[ ] Revise the study procedures and/or data-collection tools according to the pilot test results.

Step 13 – Prepare for Data Collection
[ ] Inventory and gather all data-collection materials, supplies, and equipment.
[ ] Recruit, hire, and train data-collection and analysis staff, if necessary.
[ ] Manage the research team.

Step 14 – Analyze Data
[ ] Analyze quantitative data by calculating descriptions, relationships, and differences.
[ ] Analyze qualitative data by managing data, drawing tentative conclusions, and verifying conclusions.

Reporting the Research

Step 15 – Present Results Using Visual Aids
[ ] Prepare tables.
[ ] Prepare figures.

Step 16 – Prepare a Written Report
[ ] Write draft of research report.
[ ] Solicit constructive feedback on draft report.
[ ] Prepare final version of research report.
[ ] Disseminate research report.

Step 17 – Deliver an Oral Report
[ ] Identify the audience.
[ ] Plan the presentation.
[ ] Practice the presentation
[ ] Develop strategies for handling questions.

In closing, after reading and studying this text you should be ready to do two things. First, you now have the foundation to be able to read, with comprehension and understanding, about research. Second, you should possess some fundamental skills to design and implement a small-scale study. We believe you are ready . . . so lights, camera, action!

When pulled together, steps in the research process provide a pretty sight. North Lake Tahoe, California. *Copyright © 2008 Carol Cutler Riddick*

References

Allen, L., Stevens, B., & Harwell, R. (1996). Benefits-based management activity planning model for youth in at-risk environments. *Journal of Park and Recreation Administration, 14*, 10-19.

Alreck, P., & Settle, R. (2004). *The survey research handbook* (3rd ed.). NY: McGraw-Hill.

American Academy of Management. (2000). Code of ethical conduct. *Academy of Management Journal, 43*, 1296-1299.

American Association for Public Opinion Research. (2003). *Protection of human participants in survey research: A source document of Institutional Review Boards.* Retrieved November 9, 2005, from www.aapor.org.

American College of Sports Medicine. (2005). *ACSM's guidelines for exercise testing and prescription* (7th ed). Philadelphia: Lippincott, Williams & Wilkins.

American Psychological Association. (2001). *Publication manual* (5th ed.). Washington, D.C.: American Psychological Association.

Anderson, D., & Stone, C. (2005). Cultural competencies of park and recreation professionals: A case study of North Carolina. *Journal of Park and Recreation Administration, 23*, 53-74.

Anderson, L., & Heyne, L. (2000). A statewide needs assessment using focus groups: Perceived challenges and goals in providing inclusive recreation services in rural communities. *Journal of Park and Recreation Administration, 18*, 17-37.

Attarian, A., & Holden, G. (2001). *The literature and research on challenge courses: An annotated bibliography.* Raleigh, NC: NC State University and Alpine Towers International.

Babbie, E. (2004). *The practice of social research* (10th ed.). Belmont, CA: Sage Publications.

Bailey, K. (1994). *Methods of social research* (4th ed.). NY: The Free Press.

Baker, D., & Post, L. (2003). *Michigan after-school initiative: Survey implementation, data analysis, and report preparation.* Retrieved March 30, 2005, from http://www.prr.msu.edu/baker/fund.htm.

Baker, D., & Witt, P. (1996a). Evaluation of the impact of two after-school programs. *Journal of Park and Recreation Administration, 14*, 60-81.

Baker, D., & Witt, P. (1996b). Evaluation of two after-school recreation programs. *Journal of Park and Recreation Administration, 14*, 23-44.

Baker, D., & Witt, P. (2000). Multiple stakeholders' views of the goals and content of two after-school enrichment programs. *Journal of Park and Recreation Administration, 18*, 68-86.

Baldwin, C., Hutchinson, S., & Magnuson, D. (2004). Program theory: A framework for theory-driven programming and evaluation. *Therapeutic Recreation Journal, 38*, 16-31.

Barcelona, R., & Ross, C. (2004). An analysis of the perceived competencies of recreational sport administrators. *Journal of Park and Recreation Administration, 22*, 25-42.

Barker, T. (1988). *Doing social research*. NY: McGraw-Hill.

Baron-Leonard, R. (2004). *Effects of animal-assisted therapy on individuals who are deaf and mentally ill*. Unpublished master's thesis, Gallaudet University, Washington, D.C.

Barter, C., & Renold, E. (1999). The use of vignettes in qualitative research. Social Research Update, 25. Retrieved December 20, 2005, from www.soc.surrey.ac.uk/sru/SRU25.html.

Bedini, L., & Phoenix, T. (1999). Addressing leisure barriers for caregivers of older adults: A model leisure wellness program. *Therapeutic Recreation Journal, 33*, 222-240.

Bedini, L., & Wu, Y. (1994). A methodological review of research in *Therapeutic Recreation Journal* from 1986 to 1990. *Therapeutic Recreation Journal, 28*, 87-98.

Bengston, D., & Fan, D. (2001). Trends in attitudes toward the recreation fee demonstration program on the natural forests: A computer content analysis approach. *Journal of Park and Recreation Administration, 19*, 1-21.

Bennett, C. (1979). *Analyzing impacts of Extension programs*. Washington, D.C.: United States Department of Agriculture.

Berg, K., & Latin, R. (2003). *Essentials of modern research methods in health, physical education, and recreation* (2nd ed.). Philadelphia: Lippincott Williams & Wilkins.

Bickman, L. (Ed.). (1990). *Advances in program theory*. San Francisco: Jossey-Bass Inc.

Bizub, A., Joy, A., & Davidson, D. (2003). "It's like being in another world": Demonstrating the benefits of therapeutic horseback riding for individuals with psychiatric disability. *Psychiatric Rehabilitation Journal, 26*, 377-384.

Black, T. (1994). *Evaluating social science research: An introduction*. Thousand Oaks, CA: Sage Publications.

Bocarro, J., & Witt, P. (2003). Relationship-based programming: The key to successful youth development in recreation settings. *Journal of Park and Recreation Administration, 21*, 75-96.

Bogdan, R., & Biklin, S. (2006). *Qualitative research in education* (5th ed.). Boston: Allyn & Bacon.

Bordwell, D. & Thompson, K. (2004). *Film art: An introduction* (7th ed.). NY: McGraw-Hill.

Borich, G. (2006). *Effective teaching methods* (6th ed.). Englewood Cliffs, NJ: Prentice-Hall.

Borrie, W., Christensen, N., Watson, A., Miller, T., & McCollum, D. (2002). Public purpose recreation marketing: A focus on the relationships between the public and public lands. *Journal of Park and Recreation Administration, 20*, 49-68.

Bowker, J., Cordell, H., & Johnson, C. (1999). User fees for recreation services on public lands: A national assessment. *Journal of Park and Recreation Administration, 17*, 1-14.

Brannon, S., Fullerton, A., Arick, J., Robb, G., & Bender, M. (2003). *Including youth with disabilities in outdoor programs: Best practices, outcomes, and resources.* Champaign, IL: Sagamore Publishing.

Brown, R. (1996). *Key skills for writing and publishing research* (3rd ed). Brisbane, Australia: WriteWay Consulting.

Brown, T., Kaplan, R., & Quaderer, G. (1999). Beyond accessibility: Preference for natural areas. *Therapeutic Recreation Journal, 33,* 209-221.

Brownlee, S., & Dattilo, J. (2002). Therapeutic massage as a therapeutic recreation facilitation technique. *Therapeutic Recreation Journal, 36,* 369-381.

Bruyere, B. (2002). Appropriate benefits for outdoor programs targeting juvenile male offenders. *The Journal of Experiential Education, 25,* 207-213.

Burdge, R. (1985). The coming separation of leisure studies from parks and recreation education. *Journal of Leisure Research, 17,* 133-141.

Cacioppo, J., Tassinary, L., & Berntson, G. (2007). *Handbook of psychophysiology* (3rd ed.). Cambridge, England: Cambridge University Press.

Campbell, D., & Stanley, J. (1967). *Experimental and quasi-experimental designs for research.* Chicago: Rand McNally College Publishing.

Carruthers, C., & Busser, J. (2000). A qualitative outcome study of boys and girls club program leaders, club members, and parents. *Journal of Park and Recreation Administration, 18,* 50-67.

Carruthers, C., & Hood, C. (2002). Coping skills program for individuals with alcoholism. *Therapeutic Recreation Journal, 36,* 154-171.

Case, R., & Branch, J. (2003). A study to examine the job competencies of sport facility managers. *Sports Journal, 7,* 25-38.

Charmaz, K. (1999). Stories of suffering: Subjective tales and research narratives. *Qualitative Health Research, 9,* 362-382.

Clandinin, D., & Connelly, F. (2004). *Narrative inquiry: Experience and story in qualitative research* (2nd ed.). San Francisco: Jossey Bass.

Cook, T., & Campbell, D. (1979). *Quasi-experimentation: Design and analysis issues for field settings.* Boston: Houghton Mifflin Company College Division.

Cooper, H., & Hedges, L. (Eds.). (1994). *The handbook of research synthesis.* NY: Russell Sage Foundation.

Cooper, H., & Lindsay, J. (1997). Research synthesis in meta-analysis. In L. Bickman & D. Rog (Eds.), *The handbook of applied social research methods* (pp. 315-337). Thousand Oaks, CA: Sage Publications.

Coupal, R., Bastian, C., May, J., & Taylor, D. (2001). The economic benefits of snowmobiling to Wyoming residents: A travel cost approach with market segmentation. *Journal of Leisure Research, 33,* 492-510.

Couper, M. (2004). Web surveys: A review of issues and approaches. *Public Opinion Quarterly, 64,* 464-494.

Couper, M., Traugott, M., & Lamias, M. (2001). Web survey design and administration. *Public Opinion Quarterly, 65,* 230-253.

Coyle, C., Kinney, W., Riley, B., & Shank, J. (Eds.). (1991). *Benefits of therapeutic recreation: A consensus view.* Ravensdale, WA: Idyll Arbor, Inc.

Cozby, P. (2006). *Methods in behavioral research* (10th ed.). Boston: McGraw-Hill.

Creswell, J. (2003). *Research design: Qualitative & quantitative approaches* (2nd ed.). Thousand Oaks, CA: Sage Publications.

Creswell, J. (2005). *Educational research: Planning, conducting and evaluating quantitative and qualitative research* (2nd ed.). Upper Saddle Creek, NJ: Pearson/ Merrill Prentice Hall.

Crompton, J. (2001). Parks and open spaces: The highest and best use of public land? *Journal of Park and Recreation Administration, 19*, 133-154.

Crompton, J., & Kaczynski, A. (2003). Trends in local park and recreation department finances and staffing from 1964-65 to 1999-2000. *Journal of Park and Recreation Administration, 21*, 124-144.

Crompton, J., & Kim, S. (2001). Reactions to a larger increase in admission price to state parks. *Journal of Park and Recreation Administration, 19*, 42-59.

Crompton, J., & Lee, S. (2000). The economic impact of 30 sports tournaments, festivals, and spectator events in seven U.S. Cities. *Journal of Park and Recreation Administration, 18*, 107-126.

Cronbach, L. (1982). Designing evaluations of educational and social programs. San Francisco: Jossey-Bass.

Cunningham, J. (1993). *Action research and organizational development*. Westport, CT: Praeger.

Czaja, R., & Blair, J. (2005). *Designing surveys: A guide to decisions and procedures.* (2nd ed.). Thousand Oaks, CA: Pine Forge Press.

Danish, S. (2000). Youth and community development: How after-school programming can make a difference. In S. Daish, & T. Gullotta (Eds.), *Developing competent youth and strong communities through after-school programming* (pp. 275-302). Washington, D.C.: CWLA Press.

Datillo, J., Gast, D., Loy, D., Malley, S. (2000). Use of single-subject research designs in therapeutic recreation. *Therapeutic Recreation Journal, 34*, 253-270.

Datillo, J., Williams, R., Cory, L. (2003). Effects of computerized literature education on knowledge of social skills of youth with intellectual disabilities. *Therapeutic Recreation Journal, 37*, 142-155.

Derezotes, D. (1995). Evaluation of the late nite basketball program. *Child and Adolescent Social Work Journal, 12*, 33-49.

DeSchriver, M., & Riddick Cutler, C. (1990). Effects of watching aquariums on elders' stress. *Anthrozoos, 4*, 44-48.

Dieser, R. (2002). A cross cultural critique of newer therapeutic recreation models: The self-determination and enjoyment model, Aristotelian good life model, and optimizing lifelong health through therapeutic recreation model. *Therapeutic Recreation Journal, 36*, 352-368.

Dillman, D. (1978). *Mail and telephone surveys: The total design method.* NY: Wiley.

Dillman, D. (2007). *Mail and internet surveys: The tailored design method.* NY: Wiley.

Dixon, B., Bouma, G., & Atkinson, G. (1987). *A handbook of social science research: A comprehensive and practical guide for students.* NY: Oxford University Press.

Dunn, A. (1996). Getting started: A review of physical activity adoption strategies. *British Journal of Sports Medicine, 30*, 193-199.

Eichelberger, R. (1989). *Disciplined inquiry: Understanding and doing educational research*. United Kingdom: Longman.

Elias, N., & Dunning, E. (1986). *Quest for excitement: Sport and leisure in the civilizing process*. Oxford: Basil Blackwell.

Ellis, G. (1993). The status of recreation, leisure, and therapeutic recreation as a developing science. In M. Malkin, & C. Howe (Eds.), *Research in therapeutic recreation: Concepts and methods* (pp. 43-56). State College, PA: Venture Publishing.

Farrell, T., Hall, T., & White, D. (2001). Wilderness campers' perception and evaluation of campsite impacts. *Journal of Leisure Research, 33*, 229-250.

Fisher, C. (2005). *Impacts of discovery through nature course on deaf and hard of hearing students*. Unpublished master's thesis, Gallaudet University, Washington, D.C.

Fisher, J., & Corcoran, K. (2007). *Measures for clinical practice: A sourcebook Volume 1 couples, families and children* (4th ed.). NY: Oxford Press.

Fletcher, D., & Fletcher, H. (2003). Manageable predictors of park visitor satisfaction: Maintenance and personnel. *Journal of Park and Recreation Administration, 21*, 21-37.

Fletcher, J., Kaiser, R., & Groger, S. (1992). An assessment of the importance and performance of park impact fees in funding park and recreation infrastructure. *Journal of Park and Recreation Administration, 10*, 75-87.

Flick, U. (2006). *An introduction to qualitative research* (3rd ed.). London: Sage Publications.

Folkins, C., & Sime, W. (1981). Physical fitness training and mental health. *American Psychologist, 26*, 373-389.

Forsyth, K., & Kviz, F. (2006). Survey research design. In G. Kielhofner (Ed.), *Research in occupational therapy: Methods of inquiry for enhancing practice* (pp. 91-109). Philadelphia: F.A. Davis.

Fowler, F. (1998). Design and evaluation of survey questions. In L. Bickman, & D. Rog (Eds.), *Handbook of applied social research methods* (pp. 343-374). Thousand Oaks, CA: Sage Publications.

Fowler, F. (2002). *Survey research methods* (3rd ed.). Thousand Oaks, CA: Sage Publications.

Fraenkel, J., & Wallen, N. (2005). *How to design and evaluate research in education* (6th ed.). NY: McGraw-Hill.

Frauman, E., & Cunningham, P. (2001). Using a means-end approach to understand the factors that influence greenway use. *Journal of Park and Recreation Administration, 19*, 93-113.

Freeman, M. (1993). *Rewriting the self: History, memory, narrative*. London: Routledge.

Fullan, (2007). *The meaning of educational change* (4th ed). NY: Columbia University Press.

Gaines, P. (2004). *Effects of a hip-hop dance program on rhythm skills and bilateral coordination*. Unpublished master's thesis, Gallaudet University, Washington, D.C.

Glancy, M. (1987). Participant observation in the recreation setting. *Journal of Leisure Research, 18*, 59-80.

Glaser, B. (1978). *Theoretical sensitivity: Advances in methodology of grounded theory.* Mill Valley, CA: Sociology Press.

Glaser, B., & Strauss, A. (1967). *Discovery of grounded theory: Strategies for qualitative research.* Chicago: Aldine.

Gramann, J., Bonifeld, R., & Kim, Y. (1995). Effect of personality and situational factors on intentions to obey rules in outdoor recreation areas. *Journal of Leisure Research, 27,* 321-343.

Gratton, C., & Jones, I. (2004). *Research methods for sport studies.* NY: Routledge.

Green, J., & Thorogood, N. (2004). *Qualitative methods for health research.* Thousand Oaks: Sage Publications.

Green, L. (1976). *Research methods for evaluation of health education under adverse scientific conditions.* Paper presented at Extension Seminar in Health Education and Rural Health Care Research Forum, Phoenix, AZ.

Greene, J., Caracelli, V., & Graham, W. (1989). Toward a conceptual framework for mixed-method evaluation designs. *Educational Evaluation & Policy Analysis, 11,* 255-274.

Grosof, M., & Sardy, H. (1985). *A research primer for the social and behavioral sciences.* Orlando, FL: Academic Press, Inc.

Hagan, J. (1994). *Crime and disrepute.* Thousand Oaks, CA: Pine Forge.

Hara, K., Bunting, C., & Witt, P. (2005). Linking outcomes with ropes course program design and delivery. *Journal of Park and Recreation Administration, 23,* 36-63.

Harvard School of Public Health. (1998). *National college alcohol study finds college binge drinking largely uninhibited, four years later.* Retrieved April 16, 2007, from www.hsph.harvard.edu/news/press-releases/1998-releases/press09101998.html.

Hattie, J., Marsh, H., Neill, J., & Richards, G. (1997). Adventure education and Outward Bound: Out-of-class experiences that make a lasting difference. *Review of Education Research, 67,* 43-87.

Hedrick, T., Bickman, L., & Rog, D. (1993). *Applied research design: A practical guide.* Newbury Park, CA: Sage Publications.

Henderson, K. (1994). Theory application and development in recreation, park, and leisure research. *Journal of Park and Recreation Administration, 121,* 51-64.

Henderson, K., Hodges, S., & Kivel, B. (2002). Context and dialogue in research on women and leisure. *Journal of Leisure Research, 34,* 253-271.

Henderson, K., Presley, J., & Bialeschki, D. (2004). Theory in recreation and leisure research: Reflections from editors. *Leisure Sciences, 26,* 411-425.

Hendricks, W., Ramthum, R., & Chavez, D. (2001). The effects of persuasive message source and content on mountain bicyclists' adherence to trail etiquette guidelines. *Journal of Park and Recreation Administration, 19,* 38-61.

Hendricks, W., Schneider, I., & Budruk, M. (2004). Extending importance-performance analysis with benefit-based segmentation. *Journal of Park and Recreation Administration, 22,* 53-74.

Henry, G. (1990). *Practical sampling.* Newbury Park, CA: Sage Publications.

Herbert, J. (2000). Director and staff views on including persons with severe disabilities in therapeutic adventure. *Therapeutic Recreation Journal, 34,* 16-32.

Higgenbotham, J., & Cox, K. (Eds.). (1979). *Focus group interviews: A reader*. Chicago: American Marketing Association.

Hocking, C., & Wallen, M. (1999). *Australian occupational therapy journal manual for referees: Guidelines to assist referees and authors review manuscripts*. Melbourne, Australia: OT AUSTRALIA.

Hooyman, N., & Kiayk, A. (2004). *Social gerontology: A multidisciplinary perspective*. Boston: Allyn and Bacon.

Hudson, S., Thompson, D., & Olsen, H. (2004). How safe are our playgrounds? *Parks & Recreation, 39*, 53-59.

Hurd, A. (2004). Competency development for board members in public park and recreation agencies. *Journal of Park and Recreation Administration, 22*, 43-61.

Hurd, A. (2005). *Competency development for entry-level public park and recreation professionals*. Poster presented at the Annual Meeting of the National Recreation and Park Association's Leisure Research Symposium, San Antonio, Texas.

Hutchinson, S., & Dattilo, J. (2001). Processing: Possibilities for therapeutic recreation. *Therapeutic Recreation Journal, 35*, 43-56.

Institute of Medicine National Research Council. (2002). *Integrity in scientific research; Creating an environment that promotes responsible conduct*. Washington D.C.: National Academic Press.

Inventor of the Week: Roy Plunkett. (July 2000). Retrieved September 27, 2004, from http://web.mit.edu/invent/iow/plunkett.html.

Jackson, F. (2003). *Effects of a martial arts course on physical and psychological health of deaf collegians*. Unpublished master's thesis, Gallaudet University, Washington, D.C.

Janesick, V. (2003). *Stretching exercises for qualitative researchers* (2nd ed.). Thousand Oaks, CA: Sage Publications.

Jankowicz, A. (2004). *Business research projects* (4th ed.). London: Thomson.

Jasso, G. (2001). Formal theory. In J. Turner (Ed.), *Handbook of sociological theory* (pp. 37-68). NY: Plenum Publishing Company. Johnson, B. (1989). *DSTAT: Software for the meta-analytic review of research literatures*. Hillsdale, NJ: Lawrence Erlbaum.

Joiner, B. (1972). *How to read with a skeptical yet sympathetic eye*. Unpublished manuscript. State College, PA: Pennsylvania State University, Department of Statistics.

Jones, C., Hollenhorst, S., & Hammitt, W. (2004). Assessing the social construction of Visual-spatial preferences for wilderness impacts. *Journal of Park and Recreation Administration, 22*, 50-68.

Judd, C., Smith, E., & Kidder, L. (1991). *Research methods in social relations* (6th ed.). Fort Worth, TX: Harcourt Brace Jovanovich College Publishers.

Kanters, M., Carter, D., & Pearson, B. (2001). A community-based model for assessing the economic impact of sport and recreation services. *Journal of Park and Recreation Administration, 19*, 43-61.

Kellogg Company. (2003). *It works* (found on the back of Special K 18 oz. boxes)! Battle Creek, MI: Kellogg Company.

Kent, A., & Chelladurai, P. (2003). Multiple sources of leadership and employee reactions in a state parks and recreation department. *Journal of Park and Recreation Administration, 21*, 38-60.

Kerlinger, F., & Lee, H. (2000). *Foundations of behavioral research* (4th ed.). Fort Worth, TX: Harcourt College Publishers.

Kerstetter, D., Zinn, H., Graefe, A., & Chen, P. (2002). Perceived constraints to state park visitation: A comparison of former users and non-users. *Journal of Park and Recreation Administration, 20*, 61-75.

Kibler, A., & Smith, R. (2000). Leisure needs and leisure satisfaction of adult males with HIV and AIDS. *Therapeutic Recreation Journal, 34*, 120-131.

Kidder, L., & Judd, C. (1986). *Research methods in social relations*. NY: Holt, Rinehard, & Winston.

Kielhofner, G. (2006). Developing and evaluating quantitative data-collection instruments. In G. Kielhofner (Ed.), *Research in occupational therapy: Methods of inquiry for enhancing practice* (pp. 155-176). Philadelphia: F.A. Davis.

Kielhofner, G., & Fossey, E. (2006). The range of research. In G. Kielhofner (Ed.), *Research in occupational therapy: Methods of inquiry for enhancing practice* (pp. 20-35). Philadelphia, PA: F.A. Davis Company.

Kielhofner, G., Fossey, E., & Taylor, R. (2006). Writing a research report. In G. Kielhofner (Ed.), *Research in occupational therapy: Methods of inquiry for enhancing practice* (pp. 578-590). Philadelphia, PA: F.A. Davis Company.

Kim, S., & Crompton, J. (2001). The effects of different types of information messages on perceptions of price and stated willingness-to-pay. *Journal of Leisure Research, 33*, 299-318.

Kinlock, G. (1997). *Sociological theory: Its development and major paradigms*. NY: McGraw-Hill.

Kolcun, J. (2005). *Perceived constraints associated with participation in Gallaudet University's intramural sports program*. Unpublished thesis, Gallaudet University, Washington, D.C.

Kornblau, B., & Starling, S. (2000). *Ethics in rehabilitation: A clinical perspective*. Thorofare, NJ: Slack Incorporated.

Krejcie, R., & Morgan, D. (1970). Determining sample size for research activities. *Educational and Psychological Measurement, 30*, 607-610.

Kuhn, T. (1996). *The structure of scientific revolution* (3rd ed.). Chicago: University of Chicago Press.

Kyle, G., Absher, J., & Chancellor, C. (2005). Segmenting forest recreationist using their commitment profiles. *Journal of Park and Recreation Administration, 23*, 64-86.

Kyle, G., & Chick, G. (2002). The social nature of leisure involvement. *Journal of Leisure Research, 34*, 426-448.

Kyle, G., Kerstetter, D., & Guadagnolo, F. (1999). The influence of outcome messages and involvement on participant reference price. *Journal of Park and Recreation Administration, 17*, 53-75.

Lastrucci, C. (1963). *The scientific approach: Basic principles of the scientific method*. Cambridge, MA: Schenkman Publishing.

Leberman, S., & Holland, J. (2005). Visitor preferences in Kruger National Park, South Africa: The value of a mixed-method approach. *Journal of Park and Recreation Administration, 23,* 21-36.

LeCompte, M., & Schensul, J. (1999). *Designing and conducting ethnographic research.* Walnut Creek, CA: Alta Mira.

Lee, I., Floyd, M., & Shinew, K. (2002). The relationship between information use and park awareness: A study of urban park users. *Journal of Park and Recreation Administration, 220,* 22-41.

Leedy, P., & Ormrod, J. (2005). *Practical research: Planning and design* (8th ed.). Upper Saddle, NJ: Pearson Merrill Prentice Hall.

Lempert, R., & Sanders, J. (1986). *An invitation to law and social science: Desert, disputes, and distribution.* NY: Longman.

Lessler, J., Tourangeau, R., & Salter, W. (May 1989). Questionnaire design research in the cognitive research laboratory (DHHS Publication No. PHS-89-1076). *Vital and Health Statistics, Series 6, No. 1.* Washington, D.C.: U.S. Government Printing Office.

Lincoln, Y., & Guba, E. (2005). Paradigmatic controversies, contradictions, and emerging confluences. In N. Denzin, & Y. Lincoln (Eds.), *Handbook of qualitative research* (3rd ed.) (pp. 191-216). Thousand Oaks, CA: Sage Publications.

Lindsey, G., Man, J., Payton, S., & Dickson, K. (2004). Property values, recreation values, and urban greenways. *Journal of Park and Recreation Administration, 22,* 69-90.

Lipsey, M., & Wilson, D. (2001). *Practical meta-analysis.* Thousand Oaks, CA: Sage Publications.

Little, D., & Watkins, M. (2004). Exploring variation in recreation activity leaders' experiences of leading. *Journal of Park and Recreation Administration, 22,* 75-95.

Lofland, J., Snow, D., Anderson, L., & Lofland, L. (2006). *Analyzing social settings: A guide to qualitative observation and analysis* (4th ed.). Belmont, CA: Wadsworth/Thomson Learning.

Long, T., Ellis, G., Trunnell, E., Tatsugawa, K., & Freeman, P. (2001). Animating recreation experiences through face-to-face leadership: Efficacy of two models. *Journal of Park and Recreation Administration, 19,* 1-22.

Luborsky, M., & Lysack, C. (2006). Overview of qualitative research. In G. Kielhofner (Ed.), *Research in occupational therapy: Methods of inquiry for enhancing practice* (pp. 341-357). Philadelphia: F.A. Davis.

Lysack, C., Luborsky, M., & Dillaway, H. (2006). Gathering qualitative data. In G. Kielhofner (Ed.), *Research in occupational therapy: Methods of inquiry for enhancing practice* (pp. 341-357). Philadelphia: F.A. Davis.

Mactavish, J., & Schleien, S. (2000). Exploring family recreation activities in families that include children with developmental activities. *Therapeutic Recreation Journal, 34,* 132-153.

Maguire, J., & Young, K. (2002). *Theory, sport & society.* Oxford, UK: Elsevier Science & Technology Books.

Manning, R., Ballinger, N., Marion, J., & Roggenbuck, J. (1996). Recreation management in natural areas: Problems and practices, status and trends. *Natural Areas Journal, 16*, 142-146.

Marcus, B., Banspach, S., Lefebvre, R., Rossi, J., Carleton, R., & Abrams, D. (1992). Using the stages of change model to increase the adoption of physical activity among community participants. *American Journal of Health Promotion, 6*, 424-429.

Marcus, B., Emmons, K., Simkin-Silvermann, L., Linnan, L., Taylor, E., Bock, B., et al. (1998). Evaluation of motivationally tailored vs. standard self-help physical activity interventions at the workplace. *American Journal of Health Promotion, 12*, 246-253.

Martens, R., Vealey, R., & Burton, D. (1990). *Competitive anxiety in sport.* Champaign, IL: Human Kinetics Publishers.

Matchua, D. (1997). *The sociology of aging: A social problems perspective.* Needham Heights, MA: Allyn and Bacon.

Mauch, J., & Park, N. (2003). *Guide to the successful thesis and dissertation: A handbook for students and faculty* (5th ed.). NY: Marcel Dekker, Inc.

Maxwell, J. (1997). Designing a qualitative study. In L. Bickman, & D. Rog (Eds.), *Handbook of applied social research methods* (pp. 69-100). Thousand Oaks, CA: Sage Publications.

McClean, D., Havitz, M., Adkins, D. (2002). Demarketing leisure services: The case of municipal golf courses. *Journal of Park and Recreation Administration, 20*, 90-110.

McCrone, W. (2002). Law and ethics in mental health and deafness. In V. Guttman (Ed.), *Ethics in mental health and deafness* (pp. 38-51). Washington, D.C.: Gallaudet University Press.

McMillan, J., & Schumacher, S. (1993). *Research in education: A conceptual introduction.* NY: Harper Collins.

Melcher, S. (1999). *Introduction to writing goals and objectives: A manual for recreation therapy students and entry-level professionals.* State College, PA: Venture Publishing, Inc.

Merriam, S. (1997). *Qualitative research and case study applications in education: Revised and expanded from case study research in education.* San Francisco: Jossey-Bass.

Miles, M., & Huberman, A. (1994). *Qualitative data analysis: A sourcebook of new methods.* Beverly Hills, CA: Sage Publications.

Milkovich, G., & Boudreau, J. (1996). *Human resource management* (8th ed.). Chicago: Irwin.

Miller, J., & Glassner, B. (1997). The "inside" and the "outside": Finding realities in interviews. In D. Silverman (Ed.), *Qualitative research: Theory, method and practice* (pp. 99-112). London: Sage Publications.

Miller, K., Schleien, S., Brooke, P., Frisoli, A., & Brooks, W. (2005). Community for all: The therapeutic recreation practitioner's role in inclusive volunteering. *Therapeutic Recreation Journal, 39*, 18-31.

Milloy, S. (October 1, 2004). *Suburbs don't pose health risk.* Retrieved October 3, 2004, from http://www.foxnews.com/story/0,2993,134144,00.html.

Mills, C. (1959). *The sociological imagination*. NY: Oxford Press.

Monette, D., Sullivan, T., & DeJong, C. (2005). *Applied social research: Tool for human services* (6th ed.). Belmont, CA: Wadsworth.

More, T., & Stevens, T. (2000). Do user fees exclude low-income people from resource based recreation? *Journal of Leisure Research, 32*, 341-357.

Morse, J., & Richards, L. (2002). *Readme first: For a user's guide to qualitative methods*. Thousand Oaks, CA: Sage Publications.

Moustakas, C. (1994). *Phenomenological research methods*. Thousand Oaks, CA: Sage Publications.

Mowen, A., & Graefe, A. (2002). Public attitudes toward the corporate sponsorship of park agencies: The role of promotional activities and contractual conditions. *Journal of Park and Recreation Administration, 20*, 31-48.

Mullen, B., & Miller, N. (1991). Meta-analysis. In C. Judd, E. Smith, & L. Kidder (Eds.). *Research methods in social relations* (6th ed.) (pp. 283-295). Ft. Worth, TX: Harcourt Brace Jovanovich College Publishers.

Neuendorf, K. (2001). *The content analysis guidebook*. Thousand Oaks, CA: Sage Publications.

Neutens, J., & Rubinson, L. (2002). *Research techniques for the health sciences* (3rd ed). San Francisco: Benjamin Cummings.

Newman, P., Manning, R., Dennis, D., & McKonly, W. (2001). Informing carrying-capacity decision making in Yosemite National Park, USA using stated choice modeling. *Journal of Park and Recreation Administration, 23*, 75-89.

Nicol, A., & Pexman, P. (1999). *Presenting your findings: A practical guide for creating tables*. Washington, D.C.: American Psychological Association.

Nicol, A., & Pexman, P. (2003). *Displaying your findings: A practical guide for creating figures, posters, and presentations*. Washington, D.C.: American Psychological Association.

Nicholls, S., & Crompton, J. (2005). Impacts of regional parks on property values in Texas. *Journal of Park and Recreation Administration, 23*, 87-108.

Ostergren, D., Solop, F., & Hagen, K. (2005). National park service fees: Value for the money or a barrier to visitation? *Journal of Park and Recreation Administration, 23*, 18-36.

Padgett, D. (1998). *Qualitative methods in social work research*. Thousand Oaks, CA: Sage Publications.

Pallenik, M. (1976). A gunman in town! Children interpret a comic book. *Studies in the Anthropology of Visual Communication, 3*, 38-51.

Pan, M. (2004). *Preparing literature reviews: Qualitative and quantitative approaches* (2nd ed.). Glendale, CA: Pyrczak Publishing.

Patten, M. (2007). *Understanding research methods: An overview of the essentials* (6th ed.). Los Angeles: Pyrczak Publishing.

Patton, M. (1987). *Creative evaluation* (2nd ed.). Newbury Park, CA: Sage Publications.

Patton, M. (1997). *Utilization-focused evaluation*. Thousand Oaks, CA: Sage Publications.

Payne, L., Orsega-Smith, E., Roy, M., & Godbey, G. (2005). Local park use and personal health among older adults: An exploratory study. *Journal of Park and Recreation Administration, 23*, 1-20.

Payne, S. (1980). *The art of asking questions.* Princeton, NJ: Princeton University Press.

Peacock, N., & Paul-Ward, A. (2006). Contemporary tools for managing and analyzing qualitative data. In G. Kielhofner (Ed.), *Research in occupational therapy: Methods of inquiry for enhancing practice* (pp. 358-371). Philadelphia: F.A. Davis.

Peat, J., Mellis, C., Williams, K., & Xuan, W. (2002). *Health science research: A hand book of quantitative methods.* London: Sage Publications.

Pedlar, A., Hornibrook, T., & Haasen, B. (2001). Patient-focused care: theory and practice. *Therapeutic Recreation Journal, 35*, 15-30.

Pegg, S., & Patterson, I. (2002). The impact of a therapeutic recreation program on community-based consumers of a regional mental health service. *Journal of Park and Recreation Administration, 20*, 65-89.

Peterson, C., & Stumbo, N. (2003). *Therapeutic recreation program design: Principles and procedures* (4th ed.). Needham Heights, MA: Allyn and Bacon.

Polonsky, M., & Waller, D. (2005). *Designing and managing a research project: A business student's guide.* Thousand Oaks, CA: Sage Publications.

Powell, G., Bixler, R., & Switzer, D. (2003). Perceptions of learning among new and returning seasonal camp staff. *Journal of Park and Recreation Administration, 21*, 61-74.

Prescott, P., & Soeken, K. (1989). The potential uses of pilot work. *Nursing Research, 38*, 60-62.

Rappaport, J. (2000). Community narratives: Tales of terror and joy. *American Journal of Community Psychology, 28*, 1-24.

Rea, L., & Parker, R. (2005). *Designing and conducting survey research: A comprehensive guide* (3rd ed.). San Francisco: Jossey-Bass.

Reese, H., & Fremouw, W. (1984). Normal and normative ethics in behavioral science. *American Psychologist, 39*, 863-876.

Reichardt, C., & Mark, M. (1998). Quasi-experimentation. In Bickman, L., & Rog, D. (Eds.), *Handbook of applied social research methods* (pp. 193-228). Thousand Oaks, CA: Sage Publications.

Reissman, C. (1993). *Narrative analysis.* Newbury Park, CA: Sage Publications.

Richardson, L. (1990). Narrative and sociology. *Journal of Contemporary Ethnography, 19*, 116-135.

Riddick, C. (1985). Health, aquariums, and the non-institutionalized elderly. *Marriage and Family Review, 8*, 163-173.

Riddick, C., & Baron-Leonard, R. (2003). *Affiliate social behaviors scale for deaf adults.* Unpublished manuscript, Gallaudet University.

Riddick, C., DeSchriver, M., & Weissinger, E. (1991). *A methodological review of research in Journal of Leisure Research from 1983 through 1987.* Paper presented at the National Recreation & Park Association's Leisure Research Symposium, Baltimore, MD.

Riddick, C., Drogin, E., & Spector, S. (1987). The impact of videogame play on the emotional states of senior center participants. *The Gerontologist, 27,* 425-427.

Riddick, C., & Keller, J. (1991). The benefits of therapeutic recreation in gerontology. In C. Coyle, W.B. Kinney, B. Riley, & J. Shank (Eds.), *Benefits of therapeutic recreation: A consensus view* (pp. 151-204). Ravensdale, WA: Idyll Arbor, Inc.

Roberts, N. (2003). *Ethnic minority visitors and non-visitors: An examination of constraints regarding outdoor recreation participation in Rocky Mountain National Park.* Unpublished dissertation, Colorado State University, Fort Collins, CO.

Robson, C. (2002). *Real-world research: A resource for social scientists and practitioner-researchers* (2nd ed.). Oxford, UK: Blackwell.

Rojek, C. (1993). Disney culture. *Leisure Studies, 12,* 121-135.

Rojek, C. (1997). Leisure theory: Retrospect and prospect. *Loisir & Societe (Society and Leisure), 20,* 383-400.

Rosenberg, R., Sneh, Y., Phipps, T., & Gurvitch, R. (2005). A spatial analysis of linkages between health care expenditures, physical inactivity, obesity and recreation supply. *Journal of Leisure Research, 37,* 216-235.

Rosenthal, R., & Rosnow, R. (1991). *Essentials of behavioral research* (2nd ed.). NY: McGraw-Hill.

Rosnow, R., & Rosnow, M. (2006). *Writing papers in psychology* (7th ed.). Belmont, CA: Thompson Wadsworth.

Rossi, P., Lipsey, M., & Freeman, H. (2004). *Evaluation: A systematic approach* (7th ed.). Thousand Oaks, CA: Sage Publications.

Rubin, H., & Rubin, I. (2005). *Qualitative interviewing: The art of hearing data* (2nd ed.). Thousand Oaks, CA: Sage Publications.

Russell, R. (1991). [Observation of a hotel lobby]. Field Notes.

Ryan, G., & Bernard, H. (2005). Data management and analysis methods. In N. Denzin, & Y. Lincoln (Eds.), *Collecting and interpreting qualitative materials* (2nd ed.) (pp. 259-309). Thousand Oaks: Sage Publications.

Sale, J., Lofeld, L., & Brazil, K. (2002). Revisiting the quantitative-qualitative debate: Implications for mixed-methods research. *Quality & Quantity, 36,* 43-53.

Salkind, N. (2003). *Statistics for people who (think they) hate statistics* (2nd ed). Thousand Oaks, CA: Sage Publications.

Santiago, M., & Coyle, C. (2004). Leisure time physical activity among women with mobility impairments: Implications for health promotion and leisure education. *Therapeutic Recreation Journal, 38,* 188-205.

Schitovsky, T. (1976). *The joyless economy.* NY: Oxford Press.

Schneider, I., & Budruk, M. (1999). Displacement as a response to the federal recreation fee program. *Journal of Park and Recreation Administration, 17,* 76-84.

Schutt, R. (2006). *Investigating the social world: The process and practice of research* (5th ed.). Thousand Oaks, CA: Pine Forge Press.

Schwab, D. (2005). *Research methods for organizational studies* (2nd ed.). Mahwah, NJ: Lawrence Erlbaum.

Scriven, M. (1967). The methodology of evaluation. In R. Tyler, R. Gagne, & M. Scriven (Eds.), *Perspectives of curriculum evaluation* (AERA Monograph 1) (pp. 39-83). Chicago: Rand McNally.

Shank, J., & Coyle, C. (2002). *Therapeutic recreation in health promotion and rehabilitation*. State College, PA: Venture Publishing.

Shannon, D., & Davenport, M. (2001). *Using SPSS to solve statistical problems; a self-instructional guide*. Upper Saddle River, NJ: Prentice Hall, Inc.

Shinew, K., Hibbler, D., & Anderson, D. (2000). The academic cultural enrichment mentorship program: An innovative approach to serving African American youth. *Journal of Park and Recreation Administration, 18,* 103-121.

Slant, P., & Dillman, D. (1994). *How to conduct your own survey*. NY: Wiley.

Slavin, R. (2002). *Educational psychology: Theory and practice* (7th ed.). Boston: Allyn Bacon.

Solomon, D. (2001). Conducting web-based surveys. *Practical Assessment, Research & Evaluation, 7.* Retrieved March 6, 2005, from http://Pareonline.net.

Spengler, J., Connaughton, D., Zhang, J., & Gibson, H. (2002). An analysis of lightning safety policies and procedures in Florida's municipal recreation and park agencies. *Journal of Park and Recreation Administration, 20,* 38-50.

Spradley, J. (1980). *Participant observation*. Chicago: Holt, Rinehart and Winston.

Stake, R. (1995). *The art of case-study research*. Thousand Oaks, CA: Sage Publications.

Stangor, C. (2006). *Research methods for the behavioral sciences* (3rd ed.). Boston: Houghton Mifflin Company.

Stein, R. (September 27, 2004). Sprawl may harm health, study finds. *Washington Post*, A3.

Steward, D., Shamdasani, P., & Rook, D. (2007). *Focus groups: Theory and practice*. Thousand Oaks, CA: Sage Publications.

Stone, C. (2003). Exploring cultural competencies of Certified Therapeutic Recreation Specialists: Implications for education and training. *Therapeutic Recreation Journal, 37,* 156-174.

Strauss, A., & Corbin, J. (1998). *Basics of qualitative research: Grounded theory procedures and techniques* (2nd ed.). Thousand Oaks, CA: Sage Publications.

Strike, K., & Ternasky, P. (1993). Introduction: Ethics in educational settings. In K. Strike, & P. Ternasky (Eds.), *Ethics for professionals in education: Perspectives for preparation and practice* (pp. 1-9). NY: Teachers College Press.

Stumbo, N. (1985). Knowledge of professional and ethical behavior in therapeutic recreation services. *Therapeutic Recreation Journal, 19,* 59-67.

Swigonski, M. (1994). The logic of feminist standpoint theory for social work research. *Social Work, 39,* 93-101.

Sylvester, C. (2002). Ethics and the quest for professionalization. *Therapeutic Recreation Journal, 36,* 314-334.

Sylvester, C., Voelkl, J., & Ellis, G. (2001). *Therapeutic recreation programming: Theory and practice*. State College, PA: Venture Publishing.

Taylor, R., & Kielhofner, G. (2006). Collecting data. In G. Kielhofner (Ed.), *Research in occupational therapy: Methods of inquiry for enhancing practice* (pp. 530-547). Philadelphia: F.A. Davis.

Templin, D., & Vernacchia, R. (1995). The effect of highlight music videotapes upon the game performance of intercollegiate basketball players. *The Sport Psychologist, 9,* 41-50.

Tesch, R. (1990). *Qualitative research: Analysis types and software tools*. NY: Falmer.

Tew, C., & Havitz, M. (2002). Improving our communication: A comparison of four promotion techniques. *Journal of Park and Recreation Administration, 20*, 76-96.

Thapa, B., & Graefe, A. (2004). Recreation conflict and tolerance among skiers and snowboarders. *Journal of Park and Recreation Administration, 22*, 37-52.

Tharrett, S., McInnis, F., & Peterson, J. (2006). *ACSM's health/fitness facility standards and guidelines* (3rd ed.). Champaign, IL: Human Kinetics Publishers.

Thomas, A. (2004). *Research skills for management studies*. NY: Routledge.

Torres, R., Preskill, H., & Piontek, M. (2005). *Evaluation strategies for communicating and reporting* (2nd ed.). Thousand Oaks, CA: Sage Publications.

Trochim, W. (2005). Structure of research. Retrieved September 4, 2005, from www.socialresearchmethods.net/kb/strucres.htm.

Tyson, L. (2006). *Critical theory today: A user-friendly guide* (2nd ed.). London: Routledge.

United States Department of Health and Human Services. (2001). *OPRR Reports: Protection of human subjects, Title 45, Code of Federal Regulations Part 46, as amended December 13, 2001*. Washington, DC: Government Printing Office.

Van Dalen, D. (1979). *Understanding educational research* (4th ed.). NY: McGraw-Hill.

Van Raalte, J., & Brewer, B. (Eds.). (2002). *Exploring sport and exercise psychology* (2nd ed.). Washington, D.C.: American Psychological Association.

van Teijlingen, E., & Hundley, V. (Winter 2001). The importance of pilot studies. *Social Research Update, 35*, 1-11. Retrieved March 8, 2007, from http://sru.soc.surrey.ack.uk/SRU35html.

Vaske, J., Donnelly, M., & Williamson, B. (1991). Monitoring the quality control in state park management. *Journal of Park and Recreation Administration, 9*, 59-72.

Veal, A. (2006). *Research methods for leisure and tourism: A practical guide* (3rd ed). London: Pitman Publishing.

Vogt, C., & Andereck, K. (2002). Introduction to special issue on park marketing. *Journal of Park and Recreation Administration, 20*, 1-10.

Vogt, C., & Williams, D. (1999). Support for wilderness recreation fees: The influence of fee purpose and day versus overnight use. *Journal of Park and Recreation Administration, 17*, 85-99.

Walizer, M., & Wienir, P. (2000). *Research methods and analysis: Searching for relationships*. Boston: Addison-Wesley Educational Publishers, Inc.

Wann, D. (1997). *Sport psychology*. Upper Saddle River, NJ: Prentice-Hall.

Warnick, R. (2002). Rural recreation lifestyles: Trends in recreation activity patterns and self-reported quality of life and health—An explanatory study. *Journal of Park and Recreation Administration, 20*, 37-64.

Warzecha, C., & Lime, D. (2001). Place attachment in Canyonlands National Park: Visitors' assessment of setting attributes on the Colorado and Green Rivers. *Journal of Park and Recreation Administration, 19*, 59-78.

Webb, E., Campbell, D., Grove, J., Schwartz, R., & Sechrest, L. (1981). *Nonreactive measures in the social sciences* (2nd ed.). NY: Houghton Mifflin Company.

Webb, E., Campbell, D., Schwartz, R., & Sechrest, L. (2000). *Unobtrusive measures* (revised edition). Thousand Oaks, CA: Sage Publications.

Weber, R. (1990). *Basic content analysis* (2nd ed.). Newbury Park, CA: Sage Publications.

Weisberg, H., Krosnick, J., & Bowen, B. (1996). *An introduction to survey research, polling, and data analysis.* Thousand Oaks, CA: Sage Publications.

Weiss, C. (1972). *Evaluation research: Methods of assessing program effectiveness.* Englewood Cliffs, NJ: Prentice-Hall.

Wells, M., Ellis, G., Paisley, K., & Arthur-Banning, S. (2005). Development and evaluation of a program to promote sportsmanship in youth sports. *Journal of Park and Recreation Administration, 23*, 1-17.

Wheatley, K., & Flexner, W. (1988). Dimensions that make focus groups work. *Marketing News, 22*, 16-17.

Williams, R., Vogelsong, H., Green, G., & Cordell, K. (2004). Outdoor recreation participation of people with mobility disabilities: Selected results of the national survey of recreation and the environment. *Journal of Park and Recreation Administration, 22*, 85-101.

Winter, P., Jeong, W., & Godbey, G. (2004). Outdoor recreation among Asian Americans: A case study of San Francisco Bay area residents. *Journal of Park and Recreation Administration, 22*, 114-136.

Winter, P., Sagarin, B., Rhoads, K., Barrett, D., & Cialdini, R. (2000). Choosing to encourage or discourage: Perceived effectiveness of prescriptive versus proscriptive messages. *Environmental Management, 26*, 589-594.

Wirsching, A., Leung, Y., & Attarian, A. (2003). Swatting litter bugs. *Parks & Recreation, 38*, 16-22.

Witt, P., & Ellis, G. (1985). *Leisure diagnostic battery.* State College, PA: Venture Publishing.

Wolf, M., & Perron, B. (2003). *The videogame theory reader.* London: Routledge.

Wolfe, B., Dattilo, J., & Gast, D. (2003). Effects of a token economy system within the context of cooperative games on social behaviors of adolescents with emotional and behavioral disorders. *Therapeutic Recreation Journal, 37*, 124-141.

World Health Organization. (1947). *Constitution of the World Health Organization. Chronicle of W.H.O., 1.*

Yang, H. (2004). Establishing the reliability of the smiley face assessment scale: Test retest. *LARNet: The Cyber Journal of Applied Leisure and Recreation Research.* Retrieved September 8, 2006, from www.nccu.edu/larnet/2002-10html.

Yates, B. (1996). *Analyzing costs, procedures, processes, and outcomes in human services.* Thousand Oaks, CA: Sage Publications.

Young, S., & Ross, C. (2000). Web questionnaires: A glimpse of survey research in the future. *Parks and Recreation, 35*, 30-40.

Zabriskie, R. (2003). Measurement basics: A must for TR professionals today. *Therapeutic Recreation Journal, 37*, 330-338.

Zajonc, R. (1965). Social facilitation. *Science, 249*, 269-274.

Zuckerman, M. (1979). *Sensation seeking: Beyond the optimal level of arousal.* Hillsdale, NJ: Erlbaum.

Appendices

Appendix 1: Selected Refereed Journals

I. Related to Park, Recreation, Sports and Fitness

Assessment
Activities, Adaptation & Aging
Adapted Physical Activity Quarterly
American Journal of Sports Medicine Periodicals
Annals of Tourism Research
Athletic Insight: The Online Journal of Sport Psychology
Australian Journal of Outdoor Education
Australian Leisure Management
British Journal of Physical Education
Camping Magazine
Cyber Journal of Sports Marketing
Culture, Sport and Society
Current Therapeutic Research
Dance Research Journal
European Journal of Physical Education
European Sport Management Quarterly
European Physical Education Review
Event Tourism
Football Studies
Gaming Research & Review Journal
Health and Fitness
Human Dimensions of Wildlife
International Journal of Sport Psychology
International Journal of Sport Sociology
International Journal of Tourism Research
International Review for the Sociology of Sport
Journal of Adventure Education and Outdoor Learning
Journal of Applied Biomechanics
Journal of Applied Recreation Research
Journal of Applied Sport Psychology
Journal of Biomechanics

Journal of Canadian Association for Leisure Studies
Journal of Convention & Exhibition Management
Journal of Ecotourism
Journal of Experiential Education
Journal of Gambling Studies
Journal of Health, Physical Education, Recreation, and Dance
Journal of Hospitality and Leisure for the Elderly
Journal of Hospitality & Leisure Marketing
Journal of Hospitality, Leisure, Sport & Tourism
Journal of Hospitality & Tourism Education
Journal of Human Movement Studies
Journal of Interpretation
Journal of Leisurability
Journal of Leisure Property
Journal of Leisure Research
Journal of Leisure Sciences
Journal of Motor Behavior
Journal of the National Intramural-Recreational Sports Association
Journal of Park and Recreation Administration
Journal of the Philosophy of Sport
Journal of Sport Behavior
Journal of Sport Economics
Journal of Sport and Exercise Psychology
Journal of Sport History
Journal of Sport Management
Journal of Sport Psychology
Journal of Sport and Social Issues
Journal of Sport Tourism
Journal of Sports Medicine and Physical Fitness
Journal of Sports Science and Medicine: An On-Line Journal Alternative
Journal of Sports Sciences
Journal of Strength and Conditioning Research
Journal of Swimming Research
LARNet: The Cyber Journal of Applied Leisure and Recreation Research
    (www.nccu.edu/larnet/edlarnet.htm)
Journal of Teaching in Physical Education
Journal of Tourism and Cultural Change
Journal of Travel Research
Journal of Travel & Tourism Marketing
Journal of Travel & Tourism Research
Leisure/Loisir
Leisure Sciences
Leisure Studies
Loisir et Societe/Society and Leisure
Managing Leisure

Measurement in Physical Education and Exercise
Medicine and Science in Sports and Exercise
New Zealand Journal of Outdoor Education
Olympic Review/Revue Olympique
Parks and Recreation
Pediatric Exercise Science
Perceptual and Motor Skills
Physical Activity and Health
Play and Cultural Studies
Recreation Research Review
Recreation Sports Journal
Research Quarterly for Exercise and Sport
Scandinavian Journal of Hospitality and Tourism
Schole
Soccer and Society
Sociology of Sport Journal
Sociology of Sport Online (http://physed.otago.ac.nz/sosol/home.html)
Sport, Culture and Society
Sport History Review
Sport Marketing
Sport and Place
Sport Science Review
Sporting Traditions
Sports Law Bulletin
Sports Medicine
The Sport Psychologist
Therapeutic Recreation Journal
TOURISM: An International Interdisciplinary Journal
Tourism and Hospitality Research
Tourism Management
Tourism Recreation Research
Tourism Research Journal
Tourism Review International
Visions in Leisure and Business
World Leisure Journal
World Leisure & Recreation Association Journal

II. Other Professional Journals

American Educational Research Journal
American Journal of Sociology
American Sociological Review
Anthropology and Education Journal
Applied Behavioral Measurement
Basic and Applied Social Psychology

Behavior Assessment
Behavior Research and Therapy
Behavior Therapy
British Journal of Educational Studies
British Journal of Psychology
British Journal of Social and Clinical Psychology
British Journal of Sociology
Canadian Education and Research Digest
Canadian Journal of Behavioural Science
Canadian Journal of Experimental Psychology
Canadian Review of Sociology and Anthropology
Child and Adolescent Social Work Journal
Child Development
Clinical Sociology Review
Cross Cultural Research
Cultural Anthropology
Cultural Diversity and Ethnic Minority Psychology
Current Sociology
Educational Administration Quarterly
Educational and Psychological Measurement
Educational Gerontology
Educational and Psychological Measurement
Evaluation Family Practice
Experimental Aging Research
Gerontologist
Health Psychology
Hispanic Journal of Behavioral Sciences
International Journal of Aging and Human Development
International Journal of Behavioral Development
International Journal of Mental Health
International Journal of Rehabilitation Research
International Journal of Sociology and Social Policy
International Social Work
International Review of Education
Journal of Adolescence
Journal of Adolescent Research
Journal of Aging Studies
Journal of the American School Health Association
Journal of Applied Behavior Analysis
Journal of Applied Behavioral Science
Journal of Applied Gerontology
Journal of Applied Psychology
Journal of Applied Social Psychology: Asian
Journal of Applied Social Psychology: British
Journal of Applied Social Psychology: European

Journal of Asian and African Studies
Journal of Behavioral Assessment and Psychopathology
Journal of Black Psychology
Journal of Black Studies
Journal of Clinical Psychology
Journal of Comparative Psychology
Journal of Consulting and Clinical Psychology
Journal of Consumer Research
Journal of Contemporary Ethnography
Journal of Counseling and Development
Journal of Cross-Cultural Psychology
Journal of Educational Measurement
Journal of Educational Psychology
Journal of Educational Research
Journal of Environmental Psychology
Journal of Experimental Analysis of Behavior
Journal of Experimental Education
Journal of Experimental Psychology: General
Journal of Experimental Psychology: Applied
Journal of Experimental Social Psychology
Journal of Gender Studies
Journal of Gerontological Social Work
Journal of Gerontology: Series B Psychological Sciences and Social Sciences
Journal of Health Education
Journal of Health Promotion
Journal of Interdisciplinary Studies
Journal of Marketing Research
Journal of Marriage and the Family
Journal of Music Teacher Education
Journal of Nonverbal Behavior
Journal of Personal and Social Relations
Journal of Personality Assessment
Journal of Personality and Social Psychology
Journal of Psychology
Journal of Research and Development in Education
Journal of Research in Science Teaching
Journal of Research on Crime and Delinquency
Journal of Social and Clinical Psychology
Journal of Social Issues
Journal of Social Service Research
Journal of Social Psychology
Measurement and Evaluation in Counseling and Development
Media, Culture & Society
Psychological Assessment
Psychological Bulletin

Psychological Review
Psychology and Aging
Psychology of Women Quarterly
Qualitative Sociology
Research on Aging
Research Quarterly for Exercise and Sport
Social Forces
Social Problems
Social Psychology Quarterly
Sociological Quarterly
Sociology of Education
Theory and Research in Social Education
Women Studies Quarterly
Youth and Society

III. Journals Dealing with Program Evaluation

American Journal of Evaluation (formerly *Evaluation Practice*)
Canadian Journal of Program Evaluation
Evaluation: The International Journal of Theory, Research, and Practice
Evaluation and Program Planning
Evaluation Review: A Journal of Applied Social Research
Journal of Policy Analysis and Management
New Directions for Evaluation
Practical Assessment Research and Evaluation
The Qualitative Report (online serial at www.nova.edu/ssss/QR/index.html)

Appendix 2: Theory References for a Quantitative Approach to Research

I. Recreation/Park Theories

Davis-Berman, J., & Berman, D. (1994). *Wilderness therapy: Foundations, theory and research.* Dubuque, IA: Kendall/Hunt Publishing Company.

Devine, M., & Wilhite, B. (1999). Theory application in therapeutic recreation practice and research. *Therapeutic Recreation Journal, 33,* 29-45.

Ewert, A., McCormick, B., & Voight, A. (2001). Outdoor experiential therapies: Implications for TR practice. *Therapeutic Recreation Journal, 35,* 107-122.

Gari, N. (1997). *Outdoor education: Theory and practice.* London: Continuum International Publishing Group, Inc.

Heintzman, P. (2002). A conceptual model of leisure and spiritual well-being. *Journal of Park and Recreation Administration, 20,* 147-169.

Henderson, K., Presley, J., & Bialeschki, M. (2004). Theory in recreation and leisure research: Reflections from the editors. *Leisure Sciences, 26,* 411-425. NOTE: Reviews and identifies the theoretical bases of over 800 studies.

Heintzman, P. (2002). A conceptual model of leisure and spiritual well-being. *Journal of Park and Recreation Administration, 20,* 147-169.

Hood, C., & Carruthers, C. (2002). Coping skills theory as an underlying framework for therapeutic recreation services. *Therapeutic Recreation Journal, 36,* 137-153.

Leivadi, S., Yiannakis, A., & Aspostolopoulos, Y. (Eds.). (2001). *The sociology of tourism: Theoretical and empirical investigations.* London: Routledge.

Manfredo, M. (Ed.). (1992). *Influencing human behavior: Theory and applications in recreation, tourism, and natural resources management.* Champaign, IL: Sagamore Publishing Inc.

Mannell, R., & Kleiber, D. (1997). *Social psychology of leisure.* State College, PA: Venture Publishing.

Manning, R. (1999). *Studies in outdoor recreation: Search and research for satisfaction* (2nd ed.). Corvallis, OR: Oregon State University Press.

Mobily, K. (1999). New horizons in models of practice in therapeutic recreation. *Therapeutic Recreation Journal, 33,* 174-192.

Mobily, K., & MacNeil, R. (2002). *Therapeutic recreation and the nature of disabilities.* State College, PA: Venture Publishing. NOTE: Chapters 2 and 3 review intellectual and psychosocial theories.

Pedlar, A., Hornibrook, T., & Haasen, B. (2001). Patient-focused care: Theory and practice. *Therapeutic Recreation Journal, 35*, 15-30.

Phoenix, T. (2001). Who am I?: Identity formation, youth, and therapeutic recreation. *Therapeutic Recreation Journal, 35*, 348-356.

Prideaux, B., Moscardo, G., & Laws, E. (2006). Managing tourism and hospitality services: *Theory and international applications*. London: Oxford University Press.

Rojek, C. (2005). *Leisure theory: Principles and practice*. NY: Palgrave Macmillan.

Shank, J., & Coyle, C. (2002). *Therapeutic recreation in health promotion and rehabilitation*. State College, PA: Venture Publishing, Inc.

Wise, J. (2002). Social cognitive theory: A framework for therapeutic recreation practice. *Therapeutic Recreation Journal, 36*, 335-351.

II. Sport Theories

Anshel, M. (2002). *Sport psychology: From theory to practice* (4th ed.). San Francisco: Benjamin Cummings.

Begel, D., & Burton, R. (Eds.). (1999). *Sport psychiatry: Theory and practice*. NY: W.W. Norton & Company.

Biddle, S., & Mutrie, N. (2001). *Psychology of physical activity: Determinants, well-being, and interventions*. London: Routledge.

Caudwell, J. (2006). *Queer theory and sport*. London: Routledge.

Ferguson, D., & Jones, K. (2001). Cross-country skiing as a self-efficacy intervention with an adolescent female: An innovative application of Bandura's theory to therapeutic recreation. *Therapeutic Recreation Journal, 35*, 357-364.

Gibson, H. (Ed.). (2005). *Sport tourism: Concepts and theories*. London: Frank Cass & Co.

Gill, D. (2003). Psychology and study of sport. In J. Coakley, & E. Dunning (Eds.), *Handbook of sport studies* (pp. 228-240). Thousand Oaks: Sage Publications.

Henry, I., & Theodoraki, E. (2000). Management, organizations and theory in the governance of sport. In J. Coakley, & E. Dunning (Eds.), *Handbook of sport studies* (pp. 490-503). Thousand Oaks: Sage Publications.

Hinch, T., & Higham, J. (2001). Sport tourism: A framework for research. International *Journal of Research Tourism, 3*, 45-58.

Jones, R., & Armour, K. (Eds.). (2000). *Sociology of sport: Theory and practice*. Harlow, England: Longman Publishing Group.

Laker, A. (Ed.) (2002). *The sociology of sport and physical education: An introductory reader*. London: Falmer Press.

LeUnes, A., & Nation, J. (2001). *Sport psychology: An introduction* (3rd ed.). Pacific Grove, CA: Wadsworth Thomson Learning.

Maguire, J., Jarvie, G., Mansfield, L., & Bradley, J. (2002). *Sports worlds: A sociological perspective*. Champaign, IL: Human Kinetics Publishers.

Maguire, J., & Young, K. (Eds.). (2002). *Theory, sport, & society*. Oxford, UK: Elsevier Science & Technology Books.

Nest, M. (2005). *Existential psychology and sport: Theory and application*. London: Routledge.

Singer, R., Hausenblas, H., & Junelle, C. (Eds.). 2001. *Handbook of sport psychology* (2nd ed.). Hoboken, NJ: Wiley & Sons, Inc.

Sugden, J., & Tomlinson, A. (2003). Theorizing sport, social class and status. In J. Coakley, & E. Dunning (Eds.), *Handbook of sport studies* (pp. 490-503). Thousand Oaks: Sage Publications.

Van Raalte, J., & Brewer, B. (2002). *Exploring sport and exercise psychology* (2nd ed.). Washington, D.C.: American Psychological Association.

Waddington, I. (2000). Sport and health: A sociological perspective. In J. Coakley, & E. Dunning (Eds.), *Handbook of sport studies* (pp. 408-421). Thousand Oaks: Sage Publications.

Weinberg, R., & Gould, D. (2003). *Foundations of sport and exercise psychology* (3rd ed.). Champaign, IL: Human Kinetics Publishers.

Williams, A., & Hodges, N. (2004). *Skill acquisition in sport: Research, theory, and practice*. London: Routledge.

III. Other Theories (Education, Psychology, Sociology, Etc.)

Bratton, J., & Gold, T. (2003). *Human resource management: Theory and practice* (3rd ed.). NY: Palgrave Macmillan.

Calhoun, C. (Eds.). (2002). *Classical sociology theory*. Malden, MA: Blackwell Publishers.

Craib, I. (1997). *Classical social theory*. Oxford: Oxford University Press.

Gilbert, D., Fiske, S., & Lindzey, G. (1998). *Volumes I and II: The handbook of social psychology* (4th ed.). England: Oxford University Press.

Lemert, C. (Ed.). (2004). *Social theory: The multicultural and classic readings*. Boulder, CO: Westview Press.

Lengermann, P., & Niebrugge-Brantley, J. (Eds.). (1998). *The women founders: Sociology and social theory, 1830-1930*. Boston: McGraw-Hill.

Ritzer, G. (2002). *Contemporary sociological theory and its classical roots: The basics*. NY: McGraw-Hill.

Ritzer, G., & Goodman, D. (2003). *Classical sociological theory* (4th ed.). NY: McGraw-Hill.

Ritzer, G., & Goodman, D. (2003). *Sociological theory* (6th ed.). NY: McGraw-Hill.

Schilling, C., & Mellor, P. (2001). *The sociological ambition: The elementary forms of social life*. Thousand Oaks, CA: Sage.

Slavin, R. (2005). *Educational psychology: Theory and practice* (8th ed.). Boston: Allyn Bacon.

Thompson, N. (2000). *Theory and practice in human services* (2nd ed.). Maidenhead, England: Open University Press.

Turner, J. (Ed). (2001). *Handbook of sociological theory*. NY: Plenum Publishing Corporation.

Turner, J. (2002). *The structure of sociological theory* (7th ed.). Belmont, CA: Wadsworth Thomson Learning.

Turner, J., Beeghley, L., & Powers, C. (2001). *The emergence of sociological theory* (5th ed.). Belmont, CA: Wadsworth Thomson Learning.

Appendix 3: Qualitative Theory References

Birrell, S. (2003). Feminist theories for sport. In J. Coakley, & E. Dunning (Eds.), *Handbook of sport studies* (pp. 61-76). Thousand Oaks: Sage Publications.

Blanchard, K. (1995). *The anthropology of sport: An introduction*. Westport, CT: Bergin & Garvey.

Calhoun, C., et al. (Eds.). (2002). *Contemporary sociological theory*. Malden, MA: Blackwell Publishers.

Caroleo, O. (2002). Facing the self: The magic of qualitative methodology. *Therapeutic Recreation Journal, 36*, 382-390.

Creswell, J. (2006). *Qualitative research and research design: Choosing among five traditions* (2nd ed.). Thousand Oaks, CA: Sage Publications.

Creswell, J. (2006). *Research design: Qualitative, quantitative, and mixed-methods approaches* (2nd ed.). Thousand Oaks, CA: Sage Publications.

Denzin, N. (2000). Aesthetics and the practices of qualitative inquiry. *Qualitative Inquiry, 6*, 256-265.

Denzin, N., & Lincoln, Y. (Eds.). (2005). *The Sage handbook of qualitative research* (3rd ed.). Thousand Oaks, CA: Sage Publications. NOTE: Includes new chapters on critical theory, queer theory, performance ethnography, public ethnography, art-based inquiry, and narrative inquiry.

Donnelly, P. (2003). Interpretative approaches to the sociology of sport. In J. Coakley, & E. Dunning (Eds.), *Handbook of sport studies* (pp. 77-91). Thousand Oaks: Sage Publications.

Flick, U. (2002). *An introduction to qualitative research*. Thousand Oaks, CA: Sage Publications.

Flick, U. (2005). *The qualitative research handbook: How to plan and design qualitative research*. Thousand Oaks, CA: Sage Publications.

Gamson, J. (2000). Sexualities, queer theory, and qualitative research. In N. Denzin, & Y. Lincoln (Eds.), *Handbook of qualitative research* (2nd ed.) (pp. 347-365). Thousand Oaks, CA: Sage Publications.

Hall, A. (1996). *Feminism and sporting bodies: Essays on theory and practice*. Champaign, IL: Human Kinetics Publishers.

Josselson, R., Lieblich, A., & McAdams, D. (2003). *Up close and personal: The teaching and learning of narrative research*. Washington, D.C.: American Psychological Association.

Ladson-Billings, G. (2000). Radicalized discourses and ethnic epistemologies. In N. Denzin, & Y. Lincoln (Eds.), *Handbook of qualitative research* (2nd ed., pp. 257-277). Thousand Oaks, CA: Sage Publications.

LeCompte, M., & Schensul, J. (1999). *Designing and conducting ethnographic research*. Walnut Creek, CA: Alta Mira.

Marshall, B., & Witz, A. (Eds.). (2004). *Engendering the social: Feminist encounters with sociological theory.* Maidenhead, England: Open University Press.

Morse, J., & Richards, L. (2002). *Read me first for a user's guide to qualitative methods.* Thousand Oaks, CA: Sage Publications.

Moustakas, C. (1994). *Phenomenological research methods.* Thousand Oaks, CA: Sage Publications.

Olesen, V. (2000). Feminism and qualitative research at and into the millennium. In N. Denzin, & Y. Lincoln (Eds.), *Handbook of qualitative research* (2nd ed.) (pp. 215-255). Thousand Oaks, CA: Sage Publications.

Neuman, W. (2006). *Social research methods: Qualitative and quantitative approaches* (6th ed.). Boston: Allyn & Bacon.

Richardson, L. (2000). Special focus: Assessing alternative modes of qualitative and ethnographic research: How to judge? Who judges? *Qualitative Inquiry, 6,* 251-252.

Riessman, C. (1993). *Narrative analysis: Qualitative research methods Series 30.* Newbury Park, CA: Sage University Paper.

Stake, R. (1995). *The art of case study research.* Thousand Oaks, CA: Sage Publications.

Strauss, A., & Corbin, J. (1998). *Basics of qualitative research: Grounded theory and procedures* (2nd ed.). Thousand Oaks, CA: Sage Publications.

Theory bases for qualitative frameworks also can be found in a number of journals including: *International Journal of Qualitative Studies in Education, Qualitative Inquiry, Qualitative Sociology, American Education Research Journal, and Educational Researcher.*

Appendix 4: Secondary Sources for Instruments

Anastasi, K., & Urbaina, S. (1996). *Psychological testing* (7th ed.). Upper Saddle, NJ: Prentice Hall.

Beardon, W., & Netemeyer, R. (1999). *Handbook of marketing scales: Multi-item measures for marketing and consumer behavior research* (2nd ed.). Thousand Oaks, CA: Sage Publications.

Beere, C. (1990). *Sex and gender issues: A handbook of tests and measures.* Westport, CT: Greenwood Press.

Beere, C. (1990). *Gender roles: A handbook of tests and measures.* Westport, CT: Greenwood Press.

Birren, J., Lubben, J., Rowe, J., & Deuchman, D. (Eds.). (1999). *Concept and measurements of quality of life in the frail elderly.* San Diego: Academic Press.

Blaschko, T., & Burlingame, J. (2003). *Assessment tools for recreational therapy and related fields.* Ravensdale, WA: Idyll Arbor, Inc.

Bolton, B. (2004). *Handbook of measurement and evaluation in rehabilitation* (3rd ed.). Austin, TX: Pro-Ed.

Bonjean, C. Hill, R., & McLemore, S. (2000). *Sociological measurement: An inventory of scales and measurement.* San Francisco: Chandler.

Brannon, S., Fullerton, A., Arick, J., Robb, G., & Bender, M. (2003). *Including youth with disabilities in outdoor programs: Best practices, outcomes, and resources.* Champaign, IL: Sagamore Publishing. NOTE: Contains Outdoor Program Evaluation Battery.

Burlingame, J., & Blaschko, T. (2006). *Assessment tools for recreational therapy: Red book #1* (3rd ed.). Ravensdale, WA: Idyll Arbor, Inc.

Corcoran, K., & Fisher, J. (2000). *Measures for clinical practice: A sourcebook Volume 2 adults* (3rd ed.). NY: Free Press.

Coyle, C., Kinney, W., Riley, B., & Shank, J. (Eds.). *Benefits of therapeutic recreation: A consensus view.* Ravensdale, WA: Idyll Arbor, Inc.

DeVellis, R. (2003). *Scale development: Theory and applications* (2nd ed.). Thousand Oaks, CA: Sage Publications.

Fisher, J., & Corcoran, K. (2007). *Measures for clinical practice: A sourcebook Volume 1 couples, families and children* (2nd ed.). NY: Oxford Press.

Folkins, C., & Sime, W. (1981). Physical fitness training and mental health. *American Psychologist, 36,* 373-389.

Gitlin-Weiner, K., Sandgrund, A., & Schaefer, C. (Eds.). (2000). *Play diagnosis and assessment.* NY: Wiley.

Goldman, B., Mitchell, D., & Egelson, P. (2002). *Directory of unpublished experimental mental measures: Volume II.* Washington, D.C.: American Psychological Association.

Groth-Marnat, G. (2003). *Handbook of psychological assessment* (4th ed.). NY: Wiley.

Hersen, M., & Bellack, A. (Eds.). (2002). *Dictionary of behavioral assessment techniques*. NY: Eliot Werner Publications/Percherum Press.

Kane, R., & Kane, R. (2000). *Assessing older persons: Measures, meaning, and practical applications*. NY: Oxford University Press.

Mangen, D., & Peterson, W. (Eds.). (1982). *Clinical and social psychology: Volume 1 research instruments in social gerontology*. Minneapolis: University of Minnesota Press.

Maruish, M. (Ed.). (2004). *The use of psychological testing for treatment planning and outcomes assessment: Volume 3 Instruments for adults*. Mahwah, NJ: Lawrence Erlbaum Associates

McDowell, I., & Newell, C. (2006). *Measuring health: A guide to rating scales and questionnaires* (3rd ed.). NY: Oxford University Press.

Miller, C., & Salkind, N. (2002). *Handbook of research design and social measurement* (6th ed.). Thousand Oaks, CA: Sage Publications.

Morrow, J., Jackson, A., Disch, J., & Mood, D. (2005). *Measurement and evaluation in human performance* (3rd ed.). Champaign, IL: Human Kinetics Publishers.

Murphy, L., Plake, B., & Spies, R. (2006). *Tests in print VII*. Lincoln, NE: University of Nebraska Press.

Ostrow, A. (Ed.). (2002). *Directory of psychological tests in the sport and exercise sciences* (2nd ed.). Morgantown, WV: Fitness Information Technology.

Plake, B., & Spies, R. (2005). *The sixteenth mental measurements book*. Lincoln, NE: Buros Institute of Mental Measurements.

Robinson, J., & Wrightsman, L. (1990). *Measures of social psychological attitudes: Volume 1 Measures of psychological attitudes*. San Diego: Academic Press.

Safrit, M., & Wood, T. (Eds.). (2001). *Introduction to measurement concepts in physical education and exercise science* (3rd ed.). Boston: McGraw-Hill.

Scholl, G., & Schnur, R. (1976). *Measures of psychological, vocational and educational functioning in the blind and visually handicapped*. NY: American Foundation for the Blind.

Streiner, D., & Norman, G. (1995). *Health measurement scales: A practical guide to their development and use* (2nd ed.). Oxford, England: Oxford University Press.

Stumbo, N. (2002). *Client assessment in therapeutic recreation services*. State College, PA: Venture Publishing, Inc.

Stumbo, N. (2003). *Client outcomes in therapeutic recreation services*. State College, PA: Venture Publishing, Inc.

Stumbo, N., & Peterson, C. (2003). *Therapeutic recreation program design: Principles and procedures* (4th ed.). San Francisco, CA: Pearson Benjamin Cummings.

Thomas, J., & Nelson, J. (2005). Chapter 11: Measuring research variables. In J. Thomas, J. Nelson, & S. Silverman (Eds.), *Research methods in physical activity* (pp. 214-248). Champaign, IL: Human Kinetics.

Tritschler, K. (2000). *Barrow & McGee's practical measurement and assessment* (5th ed). Philadelphia: Lippincott Williams and Wilkins.

Tolman, A. (2005). *Depression in adults: The latest assessment and treatment strategies*. Kansas City, MO: Compact Clinicals.

Webb, E., Campbell, D., Schwartz, R., & Sechrest, L. (2000). *Unobtrusive measures* (revised edition). Thousand Oaks, CA: Sage Publications.

World Health Organization (2003). *International classification of functioning, disability and health. NY: World Health Organization*. Available at www3.who.int/icf/icftemplate.cfm.

Appendix 5: Supplemental Readings on Data-Collection Tools

Alreck, P., & Settle, R. (2004). *The survey research handbook* (3rd ed.). Boston: McGraw-Hill.

Altheide, D. (2002). *Qualitative media analysis.* Thousand Oaks, CA: Sage Publications.

DeWalt, K., & DeWalt, B. (2002). *Participant observation: A guide for fieldworkers.* Walnut Creek, CA: Altamira Press.

Emerson, R., Fretz, R., & Shaw, L. (1995). *Writing ethnographic fieldnotes.* Chicago: University of Chicago Press.

Fink, A., & Kosecoff, J. (2006). *How to conduct surveys: A step-by-step guide* (3rd ed.). Thousand Oaks: Sage Publications.

Hammersley, M., & Atkinson, P. (1995). *Ethnography: Principles in practice* (2nd ed.). London: Routledge.

Jorgensen, D. (2002). *Participant observation: A methodology for human studies.* Thousand Oaks, CA: Sage Publications.

Krueger, R., & Casey, M. (2000). *Focus groups: A practical guide for applied research* (3rd ed.). Thousand Oaks, CA: Sage Publications.

Neuendorf, K. (2001). *The content analysis guidebook.* Thousand Oaks, CA: Sage Publications.

Oster, G. (2004). *Using drawing assessment and therapy: A guide for mental health professionals* (2nd ed.). NY: Brunner-Routledge.

Riffe, D., Lacy, S., & Fico, F. (1998). *Analyzing media messages: Using quantitative content analysis in research.* Mahwah, NJ: Lawrence Erlbaum Associates.

Rubin, H., & Rubin, I. (2004). *Qualitative interviewing: The art of hearing data.* Thousand Oaks, CA: Sage Publications.

Shaffir, W., Stebbins, R., & Turowetz, A. (1980). *Fieldwork experience: Qualitative approaches to social research.* NY: St. Martin's Press.

Strauss, A. (2003). *Qualitative analysis for social scientists.* Cambridge: Cambridge University Press.

Weber, R. (1990). *Basic content analysis* (2nd ed.). Newbury Park, CA: Sage Publications.

Yin, R. (2002). *Case-study research: Design and methods* (3rd ed.). Thousand Oaks, CA: Sage Publications.

Index

(Test Stat)

T-test = has 2 variable continuous & categorical

☐ ☐ = category ⎫
↕ = continuous ⎬ Is diff btwn ☐☐ over ↕ ?

(Descriptive Stat)

split file

☐ ☐ ☐ ☐   Visual inspection

looking for mean satifisfaction
among ☐ ☐

When we have categories, NO CORRELATION!

Correlate only when 2 ↕ variables

- Instead of asking about "differences" we ask about
"relationships"

$$r \Rightarrow \alpha$$

cont ↕ ↕ cont

relationship

df = degrees of freedom

Crosstabs: when comparing 2 categories

Pearson r tells strength & correlation

To report things done on SPSS: look @ link from Gould

How to do a T-test:
- Analyze, compare means, independent sample T-test
    - Gender: grouping variable → define groups 1, 2
    - life sat: test variable

Split the file
- Data → split the file → compare groups → click ? then ↳
- Analyze → frequencies → mean
    - move what questions you want to compare by the split file

To make an Excel/PPT Graph
Self explanatory

Frequency Tables
Analyze → Descriptive → frequencies
1st through last ↳
Look for missing responses

What to do w/ Rank Questions

Include figure title when writing about it in results

4 Goals of Science Sept. 16

- Describe
- Predict
- Explain (can be lumped w/ describe sometimes)
- Control

9/18 <u>Probability</u>: Implise Chance

Cause & Effect

original
cause ≈
source

1993   Her +
        Now
         | | ▷
        2014

Evolution - the species is always
            evolving

All the probabilities that could ever
be were at the source (original cause)

10/30

| .05 cutoff | things related to 5% chance
              ↳ Sig. (2-tailed)

<u>Getting one mean score for ___ # of items</u>   11/4/14

- compute variable Analyze - descriptive - frequencies -
                    reset - stats - mean
  - Target variable ___
    - Numeric variable = mean(?, ?, ?, etc.)
- click OK
- Data view : at the very end.

<u>Relationship btwn previous ↑ and # of items</u>

- Analyze → correlate → Bivariate

* Diagonal splits table in ½, only focus on ½
* Pg 305 for interpretation

↵